Fodor's

FAMILY
ADVENTURES

by Christine Loomis

Fodor's Travel Publications

New York • Toronto • London • Sydney • Auckland

http://www.fodors.com/

Copyright © 1996 by Fodor's Travel Publications, Inc.

Fodor's Family Adventures

Editor: Linda Cabasin
Editorial Contributors: Chelsea Mauldin, Amy McConnell, Linda K. Schmidt, Nancy van Itallie
Creative Director: Fabrizio La Rocca
Cover Photographs: Family and rafting, Warren Morgan/Westlight; cyclist, Doug McSpadden/Backcountry; girl with horse, American Wilderness Experience; skiers, David Brownell at the Balsams Wilderness
Cover Design: Tigist Getachew

Special Sales

CONTENTS

Foreword

Everyone who has contributed to *Family Adventures* has worked hard to make the text accurate. All prices and opening times are based on information supplied to us at press time, and the publisher cannot accept responsibility for any errors that may have occurred. The passage of time will bring changes, so it's always a good idea to call ahead and confirm information.

Fodor's would love your feedback, positive and negative. If you have complaints, we'll look into them and revise our entries when the facts warrant it. If you've happened upon a special place that we haven't included, we'll pass the information along to the writer. So please send us a letter or postcard (we're at 201 East 50th Street, New York, New York 10022). We'll look forward to hearing from you. And in the meantime, have a wonderful trip!

Karen Cure

Karen Cure
Editorial Director

Author's Acknowledgments

I couldn't have completed this project without help. My thanks to Dorothy Jordon and Candyce Stapen and their families for being terrific and generous companions on and off the road; to Karin Lazarus for unpacking, filing, and assisting in the midst of total chaos; to everyone at Fodor's, especially Linda Cabasin for her thoughtful editing and Karen Cure for believing in the book; and to all of the outfitters, guides, and tour operators who shared their adventures, expertise, insights, and humor with me.

Dedication

To my own crew of family travel experts: Kira, Molly, and Hutch; and especially to Bill who, thankfully, loves to drive.

GETTING STARTED ON THE ROAD TO ADVENTURE

The first thing you should know about adventure travel is that it's for everybody. Honest—everybody. You don't have to be a diehard daredevil or world-class athlete, you don't have to be young (though you can be), and you don't have to rough it unless you want to—even in the middle of the wilderness. In recent years, travelers of every age—parents, children, and grandparents—have packed up comfortable clothing and headed into the great outdoors, where the possibilities for fun, learning, and excitement are as boundless and varied as the American landscape itself.

Outfitters, schools, and guide services have responded to the increased number of adventure-loving families by offering more family-oriented trips and activities, as well as departure dates just for families traveling with children. The choices for physical activities are many: Biking, boating, hiking, horseback riding, fishing, and snorkeling are only a few. Opportunities for learning and for expanding every family member's horizons abound as well. You and your children can work with scientists digging for dinosaur bones or aid an archaeologist uncovering ancient native ruins. You can meet, live with, and learn about present-day Native American peoples and their culture in this country and in Canada.

Whatever your family chooses to do, wherever you choose to go, all of the activities in this book provide opportunities to strengthen the bonds that connect family members to each other and to the greater world. I know this has been true for my family. With no TV or phone to draw us apart, we seem to talk more, laugh more, and take the time to discover each other and the world around us.

Even the concept of what constitutes family entertainment is expanded in the world of nature vacations. Sometimes it's the array of stars in a vast, dark sky, or the music of the river or stories told by guides around a campfire. On a rainy afternoon in the Adirondacks, our family—my husband, Bill, and our children Kira, Molly, and Hutch—played a spectacularly silly game of charades in a tent. On one ranch vacation we all paused from a fireside game of Uno to watch Hutch sleeping in his crib. He was about a year old then and hardly the focus of anyone else's good time. But for our family at that moment, he was the perfect entertainment to share and remember. It's not that such moments don't happen on other vacations or at home. It's simply that adventure vacations provide more time for such moments than any other type of travel I know.

I mention that Hutch was only a year old to make another point: There is no age at which you cannot enjoy adventure travel. To be sure, many trips and certain activities have age restrictions. Many don't, however, and today an increasing number of trips are available to younger children as outfitters and schools learn what families want and are capable of.

At the ripe old age of four, Molly accompanied me on a four-night, five-day float and camping trip in the Tetons. More than three years later, she remembers parts of that trip vividly: her terror during the thunder and lightning on the first two nights, her bravery during the storm on the third; her first fishing lesson; and the fact that she got to spend special time with me, alone, while her siblings spent time with their dad. She remembers the two guides who taught her about wild huckleberries and told her stories about Jackson Hole. Molly also learned about our national parks and developed a budding love of the great outdoors. These things she will carry with her for a lifetime.

Adventure travel does has an element of risk that other vacations do not. This doesn't mean families should stay home: It means they should be prepared. Talk to your kids about safety; if you give them the responsibility of listening to guides' safety talks and then ensuring that your family does what's right, you are likely to find that they will take this responsibility seriously. Parents need to listen to guides, too, and to be prepared in other ways, such as using appropriate safety equipment and carrying clothing for sudden changes in weather. When you book a vacation, don't exaggerate your family's abilities in order to be accepted on a particular trip. Not only will you put them at risk for injury, your family—and the other participants—won't enjoy the trip.

On adventure vacations, rules don't cut down on enjoyment; they increase it because they keep you safe even when risks are present. In addition, rules protect the environment and the wildlife you have paid to experience. Children who learn this at an early age have a world of exciting opportunities open to them.

All the outfitters, schools, and trip operators in this book are very good, but not every one is right for every family. The ranch that is perfect for a family with pre-teens may be less than ideal for a family with a two-year-old. To help you connect with the right group, here's a list of questions you should consider before signing up, as well as some general trip-planning questions. In addition, you will find adventure-specific questions at the beginning of each chapter. You can use these lists as a basic guide for asking questions of your own.

Questions to Ask

As you talk with each outfitter, you want to hear that your family will be whole-heartedly welcomed and that everything possible will be done to make this vacation work for all of you. By the same token, give the outfitter detailed information about the ages, abilities, and special needs of everyone in your family.

Will other children be on the same trip? If not, can you recommend an alternative date? Having peers on a trip can make a huge difference in how much fun your children have. It also lets you off the hook for entertaining them every minute. If your departure date is one for which only adults have signed up, consider traveling with another family you know or bringing along one of your child's friends. If you can be flexible about the date, you can probably find another trip on which families are already booked. Also, some adventure brokers and tour operators, as well as some outfitters, offer more than one kind of adventure, so even if there are no families on the July hiking trip, there might be kids on a canoe voyage around the same time.

Have the guides who will be on this trip worked with children before? If so, with what ages? Your guide should be comfortable with, and knowledgeable about, children the ages of yours. A guide who is used to working with children knows how to communicate information in an age-appropriate way, which both increases your kids' enjoyment and helps keep them safe.

Do you have child-size gear and clothing that will fit my child? Because technical and safety gear and clothing—whether it's bike helmets, coast guard–approved life vests, or extreme-weather clothing—are crucial for many activities, be sure to get accurate information ahead of time. Always check specific sizes of available gear and give outfitters your child's weight and height in addition to age, since the wet suit or cross-country ski boots that fit one 7-year-old may not fit another. Most outfitters send a pretrip list of required and suggested clothing and gear.

Do you include kid-favorite meals on your menus? Outfitters who work extensively with families know the kinds of food children like and make an effort to include some of those at all meals. However, if you have a picky eater, ask exactly what's going to be on the menu and then see if special requests can be accommodated.

Are there any special activities for children on your trips? For example, do the guides tell stories to the kids about the area you'll traveling in? Does the naturalist line up activities that will interest children? Such activities are most common on designated family departures, so if this is important to you, book those trips.

What if I want to participate in an activity that my child is too young for? Some activities, such as hikes or trail rides, may be appropriate only for older kids. If that's the case, you need to know if your younger child can stay back at camp or the ranch with a responsible adult. The younger your children are, the more likely it is that these situations will come up, so ask in advance to avoid disappointment.

How flexible is the trip itinerary? The hallmark of a good family guide is flexibility. When I took Molly on the Teton float, the itinerary included a long hike on the first day and a change of campsites each of the four nights. With a four- and five-year-old on the trip, the head guide quickly changed the hike to a fishing lesson and kept us at the same campsite for two nights. It made all the difference in the world to the families.

What will the group size be? While I believe group size is less important than the quality and attributes of an outfitter, it's still something to consider. Many outdoor enthusiasts think only in terms of small, intimate groups. Indeed, for some families that's optimal. Keep in mind, though, that larger groups are likely to have more companions for children as well as parents.

Will you supply references from others who have taken your trips? If possible, ask for the reference to be a parent with children who were also on the trip. Your child might enjoy hearing about the trip from a peer.

Where is the nearest medical facility? What emergency training and equipment does the guide have? When you're in the wilderness, the closest facility may be hundreds of miles away. Be prepared by bringing small amounts of normal childhood medications: acetaminophen (pain reliever); decongestant; cough medicine; and medication to prevent or cure upset stomach, diarrhea, and motion sickness. Ask your pediatrician for an antibiotic in powder form (you'll have to add water) or a type that doesn't require refrigeration—especially if you're traveling out of the country. Find out whether the guides know basic or wilderness first aid and CPR for adults and children or have wilderness training. If you'll be on the water, they should know water safety and rescue. Also ask what medical supplies will be on hand (carry your own first-aid kit in any case) and whether there will be a radio to call for help if necessary.

Are passports or other official documents needed? If passports are required for adults, your child needs one, too; start this process well in advance of your trip. All children must have a Social Security number in order to get a passport. For anyone under 18, you must apply in person at a passport office. If only a birth certificate is required, it must be the original or a notarized copy with a raised seal. Finally, some destinations require additional documentation. If you travel to Mexico with your child but without your child's other parent, you must bring a notarized letter from that parent stating that you have permission to travel to Mexico with your child. Health documents proving inoculations are also required in some cases.

Will insects be a problem? Lots of wilderness areas have them, so be prepared. However, the most common insect-repellent ingredient, DEET, should be used with caution on children. Most health experts recommend applying DEET only on children's clothing, not directly on skin. There are some non-DEET repellents, too. Ask your pediatrician's advice.

How far in advance should we book our vacation? Adventure travel has become extremely popular, and trips—especially those designated just for families—often fill up quickly. The rule is this: Book as far in advance as possible but don't hesitate to call at the last minute if free time suddenly comes your way.

How much of a deposit is required and when is the balance due? Most schools and outfitters require a deposit well in advance of a trip. You then pay the full amount just prior to departure.

What's the cancellation policy? You may or may not get a full or partial refund if you cancel your reservation early enough. Policies vary from full refunds up to 30 days before the trip to partial refunds up to 7 days before departure or no refunds at all. Ask if allowances are made for medical emergencies. If the outfitter offers cancellation insurance, take it. That way you'll receive a refund if for any reason your family can't take the trip.

Are taxes and tips included in the cost? Generally, taxes and tips aren't part of the price, and these can add substantially to a trip's cost. Be sure to ask who customarily gets tipped and how much. Guides who are exceptionally good with children are invaluable, so if you're happy with a guide, tip generously; it could encourage other guides and outfitters to work on family-friendliness, too. If you're traveling to Canada, the GST (goods and services tax) is sometimes included in the cost, and it is sometimes refundable to non-Canadians; ask in advance.

How to Use This Book

Each chapter covers one sport or activity and profiles outfitters, companies, and schools that have great family trips. In most chapters, the outfitters and schools are in alphabetical order; in a few, the outfitters are given alphabetically within a geographical region. Each profile has an age icon with the minimum age the outfitter or school accepts, but read the full description for specific requirements and occasional exceptions. The profiles have information about where the company operates and descriptions of the best trips for children of different ages. Each chapter ends with Resources, a section with organizations, periodicals, books, and products of interest to a family considering that adventure.

Families looking for adventure in a particular part of the country can use the section called Finding the Fun, which lists outfitters by the regions in which they operate. Here are the states in each region:

Northeast: Connecticut, Maine, Massachusetts, New Hampshire, New York, Rhode Island, Vermont

Mid-Atlantic: Delaware, Maryland, New Jersey, Pennsylvania, Virginia, Washington, D.C., West Virginia

South: Alabama, Arkansas, Florida, Georgia, Kentucky, Louisiana, Mississippi, North Carolina, South Carolina, Tennessee

Midwest: Illinois, Indiana, Iowa, Kansas, Michigan, Minnesota, Missouri, Nebraska, North Dakota, Ohio, Oklahoma, South Dakota, Wisconsin

Southwest: Arizona, Nevada, New Mexico, Texas, Utah

Rockies: Colorado, Idaho, Montana, Wyoming

West Coast: California, Oregon, Washington.

There are separate heads for trips in Alaska, Hawaii, and destinations farther afield. At the end of the book, an appendix tells you the sports, activities and outfitters in each state and country.

Descriptions of outfitters and schools include a range of trip prices, in most cases the lowest children's price to the highest adult price. Sometimes adventure pricing is complex: It can depend upon the number of people in your family, the ages of your children, the particular accommodations you choose, and the season. The price ranges have been simplified where possible; always ask specific questions about particular trips, children's discounts, and off-season rates.

Finally, most of the information here concerns guided trips and tours, as well as courses in various outdoor activities. Why guides and instructors? Because for the vast majority of families, that is the safest way to take children into the wilderness or onto the water, or to introduce them to these kinds of adventures. There are, of course, excellent outfitters who will provide you with all of the equipment and maps you need to find your own way. Some of those are given, too, since they can be a good option for parents who are experienced wilderness travelers.

Guided trips have appeal even for parents proficient in a sport. Leading a trip requires many skills: child CPR and lifesaving, basic and wilderness first aid, and water safety and rescue, for example. Moreover, a parent can be an excellent hiker, cyclist, or kayaker, but if he or she isn't thoroughly familiar with the area or the particular river, guiding is better left to those who are. Besides, with everything that outfitters are offering families these days—storytelling, special children's counselors, and lots of other kids—even the most resourceful parent is hard pressed to compete. Leaving the details to someone else has its rewards. You have more time to enjoy the area through which you're traveling, the insights of those who know it well, and, most important of all, the company of your children. Happy adventuring.

ARCHAEOLOGY ADVENTURES

Digging in dirt comes naturally to most children, so it's not surprising that archaeology lends itself to family adventure. But it's not just the digging: Children are often fascinated with ancient civilizations, with the ways people lived, worked, and played long ago. Add to that interest the opportunity to experience Native American cultures—such as those studied at archaeological sites throughout the American Southwest—and you have the stuff of an exciting family adventure vacation.

Uncovering ruins, pottery, and ancient artwork is a way for families to learn not only about ancient worlds but, by extension, about themselves. Archaeology is rewarding work; however, it is work. When you "vacation" by volunteering on a research site, you may not come home rested, and you probably won't have had time to read that novel you've been saving for months. On the other hand, you will return home with the satisfaction of knowing that by volunteering, your family has contributed to our understanding of the earth's past, present, and future.

Questions to Ask

What kinds of objects have been uncovered at this site? Although archaeology is painstaking work, the rewards of uncovering something no one else has seen for hundreds, or even thousands, of years are great. You want your family to have reasonable expectations about the possibility of rewards, so ask ahead of time what kinds of artifacts or other material might be found and how often volunteers like you find them.

How much time is spent digging? Generally, days are a mix of digging and other kinds of archaeological activities, but three to six hours of digging is typical. You might dig in the mornings and work in a lab in the afternoons, or you might dig eight hours straight one day and not at all on other days. Some programs give you a few choices; at other sites the itinerary is more rigid. Be assured, however, that in most cases much of your time will be devoted to digging. If you don't want to spend many hours on your knees involved in fairly painstaking work, these trips are probably not for you.

Are there other activities? In some cases, especially at sites in the United States, other activities are available. There may be recreation areas nearby or places of interest related to the project. Some programs include hikes and day trips; on other projects your opportunity to pursue recreational activities may come only at night. In extremely remote areas, options may be quite limited. If you feel your family will have a hard time focusing just on archaeology, choose a site with some alternatives.

Will I be with my children most of the time? Volunteers are often separated, working at different activities or in different areas of a site. If this concerns you, ask ahead of time.

What kind of housing is there? In research housing travelers must often share facilities (kitchen, bathrooms), and males and females usually sleep in separate quarters. Single parents traveling with a child of the opposite sex may be lodged in separate rooms. That's true for spouses, too. At the least you will probably share housing with part of the group. If this is a problem, see if other lodging arrangements can be made (utilizing tent sites instead of bunkhouses, for example). If there are no alternatives, you'll need to prepare your family for the possibility of separation or choose another project.

What are the field conditions? These are scientific research sites, not vacation destinations. Field conditions are typically primitive; sites are hot, dusty, and dirty; and work often requires walking over uneven or rocky terrain. There may or may not be tarps or other kinds of shelter to shield you from hot sun or rain. Get all the specifics about the project you're interested in so you and your family can be 100% prepared.

Are my trip costs tax deductible? When you volunteer your time and labor on bona fide research projects, a portion of your fee is probably tax deductible, as are some of your out-of-pocket expenses and transportation costs to project sites. The tax code is complex, however, so check with your accountant or tax expert.

Is it possible to get college credit for this volunteer work? In some cases, yes. Keep in mind, though, that if you pursue college credit your trip may no longer be tax deductible.

Will there be opportunities to meet local residents? Whether you're traveling in this country or abroad, a research project can be a great opportunity to get to know people from another background or culture. At foreign sites, local residents often work at project sites or provide housing. You can make cultural exchange part of your trip's focus by doing some reading on the area ahead of time. If another language is involved, you might try to use it as much as possible.

What's included in the cost? On multiday trips lodging and meals are included, unless noted otherwise. Transportation to and from the sites is not usually part of the cost. If you'll be camping or staying in dorms or bunkhouses, you may need to bring your own camping gear and bedding. Tents are provided at some sites, but ask.

Instruction

You don't need any special skills or knowledge to participate in these trips because discussions about the project, lectures, and hands-on instruction in excavation and lab work are part of the experience. The excavation sites contain valuable and fragile materials, so you and your children will be taught the proper way to dig and to handle any finds. Sometimes reading lists are part of your advance information packet. If so, everyone in the family can learn something before your adventure.

Finding the Fun

South: Earthwatch. **Southwest:** Denver Museum of Natural History, White Mountain Archaeological Center. **Rockies:** Crow Canyon Archaeological Center. **Alaska, Canada, Europe, the Middle East, Africa, Asia, Australia:** Earthwatch.

Favorite Digs

Crow Canyon Archaeological Center

👫 12+

For more than 10 years Crow Canyon archaeologists have been working on a puzzle: Why did the Anasazi people, who flourished in the Southwest until the late 13th century, suddenly abandon the area? Their mysterious disappearance is just one aspect of research at this facility in southwestern Colorado, where several ancient villages are being excavated. Researchers hope work here will not only provide answers about prehistoric Pueblo communities but will also produce information that will benefit contemporary society, especially Native American cultures. Like those in Mesa Verde National Park, 10 miles to the east, some of the Crow Canyon villages are in spectacular cliffside settings. The facility's work has been recognized by the National Science Foundation, National Geographic Society, National Endowment for the Humanities, and the President's Advisory Council on Historic Preservation. Despite its national renown, the center is a place where all are welcome to participate. "Crow Canyon specifically encourages the elimination of barriers between generations, cultures, and levels of learning," the information packet says right up front. And

that's just one reason it's a place for family adventure and learning.

FOR FAMILIES. Family Week, usually scheduled in August, is for parents, grandparents, and students in seventh grade or higher. Middle school students spend about 2½ days in the field and the rest of the time in the lab or in other activities and programs designed for this age group. High school students and adults alternate field work with time in the lab and experimental archaeology activities, such as learning how to use ancient tools or participating in an experiment on Anasazi farming. Everyone begins the week by examining artifacts and reconstructing the cultures and chronologies they represent. At the end of the week, the group joins a guided tour of Mesa Verde. There are evening lectures throughout the week.

Accommodations are in a main lodge, which sleeps 60 in nine rooms, or in modern Navajo-style hogans, which sleep up to four people in a room. Families bring their own bedding. Depending on the makeup of the participants, families may be housed together, or the whole camp may be divided into male and female groups. There are no private baths or showers. Meals are served cafeteria-style in the dining hall. 🏠 *Crow Canyon Archaeological Center, 23390 County Rd. K, Cortez, CO 81321, tel. 303/565–8975 or 800/422–8975. Aug.: 7 days, $475–$795. Basic membership, required for participation in workshops, costs $15–$40 per person, depending on age.*

Denver Museum of Natural History

 5+

The Denver Museum of Natural History, one of the finest facilities of its kind in the country, also offers families unusual and enlightening trips (see Cross-country Skiing and Rafting). One fascinating excursion is to Chaco Canyon, New Mexico. Although it's not a research-based dig in the same sense as other trips, this exploration of an ancient civilization is an archaeology learning vacation for those who love the subject but don't necessarily want to spend days on their knees digging. That also makes it perfect for families with children younger than those usually allowed on research sites.

FOR FAMILIES. Chaco Canyon for Families, generally scheduled every other year, combines astronomy, anthropology, and archaeoastronomy (a discipline that focuses on the importance of the sky to various ancient human cultures) in addition to archaeology. The trip and its itinerary have been designed by gifted high school students, who participate as trip leaders. The setting, Chaco Canyon, is striking. This "Anasazi Capital," in a desolate area of northwestern New Mexico, was a thriving center of civilization from AD 900 to AD 1150. The Anasazi left behind a vast and complex network of roads, masonry walls, and stairways carved into cliffs, all of which connected some 12 major pueblos and numerous smaller ones. Ruins of the road system and pueblos are now part of Chaco Culture National Historic Park, where the trip takes place.

After settling into reserved campsites (bring your own tents or RVs), the group tours the visitor center museum for background on Chaco Canyon. Over the weekend there are hikes—one on the Penasco Blanco trail includes a stop at a pictograph recording an ancient supernova—lectures, discussions, and activities for different age groups. The group works on a simulated dig and learns about the ruins, artifacts, and other aspects of archaeology. There's also a mythology and constellation workshop. A highlight is the chance to experience one of Chaco Canyon's greatest archaeoastronomical phenomena in the kiva Casa Rinconada. Researchers believe the kiva is part of an ancient astronomical observatory built so that light will enter a particular window only on the summer or winter solstice. This trip coincides with the summer solstice. The price does not include any meals; bring your own food and cook it at the campsite. **⌂** *Denver Museum of Natural History, 2001 Colorado Blvd., Denver, CO 80205, tel. 303/ 370–6304. June: 3 days, $75–$125. Museum membership, a requirement, is $50.*

Earthwatch

 16+

Earthwatch, a nonprofit organization, funds research projects of all types around the globe and brings lay participants together with researchers to work on those projects. The benefit to both groups is clear: Researchers have a pool of volunteers who provide not only labor but money to offset research costs, and volunteers can work beside some great scientists in a wide variety of fields. Earthwatch's archaeological digs are found in the Human Impacts section of its extensive catalog.

FOR FAMILIES. There are so many sites that families will probably make their choice based on location, historical period, and related activities. If medieval life interests you and your teenager, there's a castle in Wales, a city in Morocco, and several sites in Moscow. For those who like Roman history, there are excavations at a fort in northern England and a farm in Tuscany. A Bronze Age village in Spain, an 8th-century Islamic site in Portugal, and an Australian aboriginal cave with art estimated to be 37,000 years old—all have their own special appeal. You might also dig in Thailand, Alaska, the Bahamas, Canada, and in various parts of the United States. Families interested in the history of slavery in this country, for example, might join ongoing research at Andrew Jackson's Tennessee mansion.

In addition to excavating, volunteers are often called upon to photograph or sketch artifacts and sites and to assist in lab work. Moreover, related activities—architecture, anthropology, paleontology, history, literature, ecology, the study of wildlife, and linguistics—play a role for volunteers at the sites. Accommodations range from primitive campsites to modern hotels. Projects sometimes end and new ones begin, so that catalogs may not be up-to-date. Call once you've decided that an archaeological adventure is for you.

Earthwatch, 680 Mt. Auburn St., Box 403BO, Watertown, MA 02272, tel. 617/926–8200 or 800/776–0188. Year-round (all sites not available at all times): 12–22 days, $995–$1,995.

White Mountain Archaeological Center

9+

Raven Site Ruin, named for the many bird symbols found on ceramics and petroglyphs in the area, is in the White Mountains of Arizona, about 2½ hours southeast of Flagstaff. On the 5-acre site overlooking the Little Colorado River, a prehistoric pueblo contains two kivas and more than 800 rooms. Both Mogollon and Anasazi cultures are represented; people lived here from about AD 1000 to AD 1450. Raven Site was the scene of extensive vandalism in the 1920s and again in the 1980s, which is one reason White Mountain Archaeological Center came into existence. This nonprofit field school protects and preserves southwestern Native American sites. Since 1991, when the site opened to the public, archaeology buffs of all ages and from all backgrounds have participated in hands-on work under the center's direction.

FOR FAMILIES. You can sign up for a day, a few days, or a week at Raven Site. Along with field excavation, volunteers spend time working in the lab cleaning, conserving, bagging, and labeling pottery and other artifacts. There are also hikes to areas with petroglyphs. Most volunteers dig at least three to four hours each day; family members may work in different areas. If you want a break one day, Lyman State Park, about 6 miles away, has boating, fishing, waterskiing, and an excellent petroglyph trail. Also of interest is the center's ethnobotanical garden, an experiment using prehistoric seeds found in the area. You can study (but not eat) the kinds of foods native people grew more than 1,000 years ago.

Lodging is in a bunkhouse and rooms are usually divided for male and female volunteers, though a few private rooms can accommodate families for an extra charge. Tent and RV sites are also available. Day programs include lunch. In this mountain location, digging takes place at 6,500 feet, meaning hot days, cool nights, and changeable weather.

White Mountain Archaeological Center, HC 30, St. Johns, AZ 85936, tel. 520/333–5857. Mid-Apr.–mid-Oct.: 1–6 days, $37–$498.

Resources

Books

Children can get a general sense of archaeology and anthropology from *What Do We Know about Prehistoric People?* by Mike Corbishley (Peter Bedrick Books). Culturally oriented books for school-age children include *The Ancient Cliff Dwellers of Mesa Verde* by Caroline Arnold (Clarion), *The Anasazi* by David Petersen (Children's Press), and *Cities in the Sand* by Warren Scott (Chronicle Books), all of which focus on the ancient civilizations of the American Southwest. *Kidding Around the National Parks of the South-*

west by Sarah Lovett (John Muir Publications) is a travel guidebook for ages 8–12 with detailed information on Mesa Verde as well as 26 other national parks in the region.

For adults, Brian Fagan's *In the Beginning: An Introduction to Archaeology* (Harper) is a general guide to the subject. Those digging in the Southwest will want to read *Anasazi World* by Dewitt Jones and Linda Cordell (Graphic Arts Center Publishing), *Ancient Land, Ancestral Places* by Paul Logsdon (Museum of New Mexico Press), *Chaco Canyon: A Center and Its World* by S. H. Lekson, J. R. Stein, and S. J. Ortiz (Museum of New Mexico Press), and *The People: Indians of the American Southwest* by Stephen Trimble (School of American Research).

Also See

If digging vacations are for your family, check out Digging for Dinosaur Bones and Other Fossils. If present-day native cultures are of particular interest, see Native American Experiences.

BIKING

Have child, will cycle" could well be the motto of today's bike-loving parents. Child-friendly inventions such as carts and tandems have made multiday cycling tours a feasible option for toddlers and preschoolers across the country. For families with older children, mountain biking is a popular vacation alternative. With all these choices, many families have begun choosing two-wheel road trips over four-wheel vacations.

The best option for families with very young children is actually an old concept. The handy cart, which attaches to the back of a bicycle, is now being made in deluxe versions by Burley and other manufacturers. Though carts work best on easy to moderate road tours, the range within these categories is vast. Among the trips that allow carts are road tours through Michigan's Amish country; nature-oriented treks in Washington's San Juan Islands; and scenic trips through Vermont. A more family-friendly mode of travel would be hard to find.

A more recent invention, the Trail-A-Bike, is a child-size bike (without the front wheel portion) that attaches to an adult's bicycle, turning the whole thing into a tandem. It's made especially for children aged 1–10. Some outfitters are starting to stock these neat bikes; if they don't you can bring your own. There are even real tandem models that allow two children to bike with you, as well as models with baby seats or support for special-needs children. The tandem device allows children to share the physical labor, and also offers a safer, lighter, and more stable alternative to on-bike child seats and a less wind-resistant alternative to carts.

For families with preteens and teens, mountain biking can be a welcome physical challenge. However, since riding day in and day out strikes many in this age group as a monotonous proposition, outfitters have found great success with combination trips: biking and rafting, biking and horseback riding, biking and climbing. These trips are also good for families who enjoy bike rides but are not necessarily dedicated cyclists.

Whether you're road biking or mountain biking, it's best to search out those trips designated specifically for families. Cycling, like hiking, has high appeal among empty-nesters and hard-core outdoor adventurers who challenge themselves by racking up the daily miles; some may feel hampered by a family's slower pace and need for more frequent stops. Moreover, some adults have little tolerance for even the best-behaved children. If your heart is set on a romantic New England inn-to-inn tour, do it when you and your spouse can get away as a couple. The good news, though, is that there's no need to insist on a less than appropriate trip. Every year there are more wonderful biking trips for families and more outfitters eager to cycle with you in the mountains, near the shore, or anywhere in between.

Questions to Ask

What ages are your trips best for? Cycling outfitters are very specific about the ages of children allowed on their trips. Most have an excellent understanding of how well a child of a given age can meet the physical and mental requirements of the trip. Listen to the outfitter and go with the recommendations given.

How experienced or physically fit should my family be for this trip? This is an important question to ask right up front. The outfitter will be able to recommend the best trips for families of all different levels, from those who cycle once or twice a year to those who cycle regularly. Moreover, outfitters can also give you information about exercises and routines to do in the weeks before the trip to get in shape.

Will there be other children on the trip I'm considering? The presence of other children can make the difference between a good trip and a great one both for you and your children. Not only do other kids mean playmates for your children; other families mean fellow parents who understand the ins and outs of traveling with kids.

How many miles a day do the trips average? Bike trips can cover as few as 8 miles a day or as many as 50. Many children can handle 25 miles a day, and those with some experience might ride as many as 35 miles. Ask very specific questions about the miles, the type of terrain, and whether or not there are options for shorter routes or van pickup. Make sure you choose a beginner trip if that's what you are. If hiking is included on a combination adventure, ask how many miles a day will be covered on foot. Three to 8 miles is well within the range of most children (depending on age and experience), with the exception of toddlers or preschoolers who can be carried in a backpack, provided you can handle the extra weight.

Do you have children's rates? Many bicycle tour operators have discounts for children under a certain age, and for children sharing a room with parents. In addition, various inns used by bike touring companies may offer children's discounts. Rates may vary according to how many children you bring on the trip; your discount may be smaller if there is only one parent on the trip. Sometimes special family departures give parents an even bigger break off the regular cost of the trip. Read the fine print and ask plenty of questions.

Do you rent children's bikes and helmets? Some outfitters allow children but do not provide bikes or other equipment for them. Others have rental equipment but only for children of a certain age or height. If you aren't planning to bring your own bikes and helmets, this is important. If you bring your own helmets, keep in mind that they should be of high quality and not the flimsy ones available at some toy stores. When in doubt about your equipment, ask the outfitter.

Do you allow Burleys or other pull-carts? Some outfitters may rent them; others may not even permit them on tours.

Is there van support on the trip? Van support allows beginners to go on tours that have some intermediate terrain, and it gives a break to any cyclist who gets tired during the day. It's a crucial option for families with young cyclists since most routes aren't chosen with only the eight-year-old in mind. If there are stretches your child can't handle, the van is there to provide a lift while you continue on the tour.

Are guides qualified to fix bikes in case of a breakdown? Unless you know how to fix your bike, you'll want someone along who knows what to do and who has the proper tools to do it.

What kind of food can we expect on our trip? Many bike trips these days include overnights at fine inns and resorts where exceptional food is part of the package. If your child is a particular eater, talk to outfitters in advance to find out whether they accommodate special requests. You may want to bring some of your child's favorite foods with you—but consider that you may have to carry the load.

What's included in the cost of the trip? Generally, all accommodations and meals are included, but van transfers and travel to and from the start of the trip are not. Guides, maps, and energy-producing snacks are part of the package. Bike rentals may be included in some cases, although that's more the exception than the rule. Helmets are often but not always provided; they are usually available for rent. Rates quoted in brochures are generally per person and based on double occupancy.

Instruction

In general, road touring companies don't offer much in the way of instruction, though some give minimal information about bike care and easy repair. Some companies have day or weekend courses devoted entirely to repair; these are especially useful for families who are considering becoming serious road cyclists (you might also find such courses at your local community college or Y). Mountain biking tour operators are more likely to provide instruction on techniques that are helpful in off-road cycling. This information is not just for adults; kids too might enhance their enjoyment by learning the techniques. Of course, most tour operators will happily answer questions if you ask them.

Finding the Fun

Northeast: Backroads, Bike Vermont, Brooks Country Cycling & Hiking Tours, Northern Outdoors, Vermont Bicycle Touring. **Mid-Atlantic:** Brooks Country Cycling & Hiking Tours, Vermont Bicycle Touring. **South:** Nantahala Outdoor Center. **Midwest:** Michigan Bicycle Touring; Sun, Sky, Wind. **Southwest:** Backcountry, Escape the City Streets. **Rockies:** Backroads, Wilderness River Outfitters. **West Coast:** Backcountry, Backroads. **Hawaii:** Backcountry. **Canada:** Backcountry, Backroads. **Europe:** Backroads, Nantahala Outdoor Center, Brooks Country Cycling & Hiking Tours. **New Zealand:** Backcountry.

Favorite Outfitters

Backcountry

👨‍👦 6+

This Montana-based company knows the West. In fact, every guide is either a native or long-time resident of the area, so you're always with someone who can share insights, local history, and interesting knowledge about the land. Backcountry is also a small outfitter; personalized service and excellent support for its clients are guaranteed, and owners Doug and Carmen McSpadden, who have young children of their own, are dedicated champions of family travel.

FOR FAMILIES. Backcountry's adventure trips come in two categories. Most are for families with kids ages 10 and up who have some biking and outdoors experience, but there are several departure dates for families with children as young as 6. Backcountry has found that children respond well to trips that combine biking with one or several other activities, such as hiking, sea kayaking, rafting, and horseback riding. Much of the biking is on paved roads, and van support is available for anyone who needs it. Participants stay in the area's best inns, resorts, mountain lodges, and hotels, and eat regional and international fare that will appeal to the pickiest palates. You can choose the trip that best suits your family by activity preference or location.

Puget Sound Adventure takes place in and around Washington's wildlife-rich San Juan Islands and combines biking, hiking, and sea kayaking. Arizona Adventure is centered in Sedona and includes riding, tennis, and Jeep touring in addition to biking. Canyonlands Adventure brings cyclists to Arches and Canyonlands national parks, whose dramatic landscape of monoliths and red rock arches creates the perfect backdrop for hiking, riding, and rafting. Grand Teton, Yellowstone, and Glacier adventures take guests to three

other spectacular national parks: You can hike, ride, raft, and boat in Grand Teton and Glacier, or ride and raft in Yellowstone. Montana Adventure, one of the easiest trips, is based in southwestern Montana's backcountry, with biking, hiking, riding, and rafting through the Gallatin Range, the Spanish Peaks, and the beautiful blue-green pools of Ouzel Falls. Yellowstone and Montana adventures are the designated trips for ages six and up.

Four adventure trips take families beyond the continental United States. Hawaii Adventure starts and ends on the Garden Isle of Kauai, where you can explore by sea kayak and snorkel as well as bike. Canadian Rockies Adventure shows families the breathtaking regions in and around Banff and Lake Louise, where hiking and canoeing offer spectacular scenery and unparalleled views. Another choice is Alaska Adventure, a trip in the Kenai Peninsula. Finally, if you're looking for adventure far from home, consider New Zealand Adventure, where travel through South Island (home of Mount Cook and the Tasman Glacier) includes hikes and bike rides as well as ferry and boat trips.
🏠 *Backcountry, Box 4029, Bozeman, MT 59772, tel. 406/586–3556 or 800/575–1540. Year-round (not all trips available at all times): 5 ½–8 ½ days, $1,198–$1,698.*

Backroads

👨‍👦 2+

Founded in 1979, this company is known for its ability to handle the details of a family trip with finesse and humor. Though most of its trips focus on cycling, they often include other family-oriented activities, such as wildlife viewing, fishing, riding, and hiking. Itineraries are relatively slow-paced, giving kids time to explore tidal pools or wildflower fields. Family departures are scheduled spring through fall, with a choice of destinations from California to Maine and beyond. Participants either stay at inns or camp out; some destinations offer both options. The organization rents Burley carts for those under five.

FOR FAMILIES. The rolling hills and black-and-white killer whales of the San Juan Islands in Washington make them a favorite destination for families. Farther south, there are family trips in three parts of California—Napa Valley, Alexander Valley, and Point Reyes National Seashore, a peninsula just north of San Francisco (this trip combines road and off-road cycling). For those who want adventure in the rugged West, try the Sawtooth Mountains trek, a mountain biking trip on which families camp out in view of the jagged granite peaks of the Sawtooth Mountains in central Idaho. There's also a Canadian Rockies itinerary, both inn and camping variations, which takes cyclists through Banff and Jasper national parks. On the other side of Canada, Nova Scotia offers rocky headlands and fertile valleys along the Atlantic seaboard. In the eastern United States, biking families can explore Penobscot Bay along Maine's rocky coast, or the southeast corner of Vermont, which includes a stop at a re-created farm museum.

One of the newest family departures is a six-day trip through the Czech Republic, with visits to Prague and southern Bohemia; it's especially good for families with older children. More traditional cycling terrain can be found on the two family trips to France, one through the Loire Valley, with its medieval villages and opulent chateaux, the other through the Dordogne River valley east of Bordeaux, where 20,000 year-old cave paintings are among the highlights.
 Backroads, 1516 5th St., Berkeley, CA 94710, tel. 510/527–1555 or 800/462–2848. May–Oct.: 3–6 days, $199–$1,798, van transfers and rentals extra.

Bike Vermont

 10+

Bike Vermont has been in business for 20 years and is the only touring company oper-

ating exclusively in Vermont and the Connecticut River valley. Guides are knowledgeable about the area and its accommodations. Most Bike Vermont trips include overnight stays in New England inns and B&Bs, some with antiques and interesting histories, some with upscale, gourmet menus. Many of these inns are family-friendly even though they aren't geared for very young children.

FOR FAMILIES. The best trips for families are the weekend Manchester Highlands Inn tour, the three-day Strong House Inn tour, and the five-day trip to Proctorsville. All are fairly easy rides, though the Strong House Inn tour, near Burlington in the northwestern part of the state, is a bit more challenging than the other two. Proctorsville, in southeastern Vermont not far from Woodstock, has lakes, rivers, and one inn—the Golden Stage, which has a constantly replenished cookie jar to keep kids happy. The Manchester Highlands Inn has a pool and a spectacular view of Mt. Equinox; that tour includes a visit to Norman Rockwell's house and a dip in the swimming hole under the covered bridge near Rockwell's home. All three tours are good for beginner, intermediate, and advanced riders. Rental bikes are available for ages 10 and up.
 Bike Vermont, Box 207, Woodstock, VT 05091, tel. 800/257–2226. May–Oct.: 3–5 days, $255–$720

Brooks Country Cycling & Hiking Tours

 ALL

Brooks has no age guidelines, and they've had kids of all ages on their tours (no seats or carts are available for rental, however). The company is based in New York City; if that's your area, you can take day trips with Brooks in addition to the multiday tours recommended here.

FOR FAMILIES. Children are welcome on any tours; however, the best for families are the Berkshire Camping Weekend and the Pedal & Paddle Weekend. The Berkshire trip through western Massachusetts includes cycling in and around West Stockbridge and optional tickets to a performance at the superb Tanglewood Music Festival. Accommodations are spacious tents set up on platforms, complete with electricity; food is gourmet vegetarian. If you enjoy rafting, try the pedal and paddle along the Delaware in New York and Pennsylvania. You'll stay at a great old inn with a huge porch, family-style meals, and activities such as swimming or rafting in a private lake.

If you feel like venturing farther afield, consider the Barging and Biking Holland trip, one week of blue canals, flower-filled fields, and picturesque windmills. Barges have a sun deck, spacious cabins with showers, and easy access to Holland's extraordinary network of bicycle paths. Three-speed bike rental is included in the Holland trip.

Brooks Country Cycling & Hiking Tours, 140 W. 83rd St., New York, NY 10024, tel. 212/874–5151. June–Oct.: 3–7 days, $225–$869; children receive discounts of 5%–50% , depending on age and number of children traveling.

Escape the City Streets

7+

The brochure of this mountain-biking outfitter tells you immediately that this company has a sense of adventure—and humor to match. "Hey, teenagers," it says, "we love your eclectic energy." That enthusiastic attitude works well with parents and younger kids, too. Escape the City Streets believes in playing hard in the great outdoors, but they also understand limits, Support vehicles—4x4 trucks and vans—accompany every trip, and meals will satisfy even a demanding gourmet. Most of the trips are in Utah and the surrounding states.

FOR FAMILIES. There are four multiday family tours in July and September, in addi-

tion to day hikes for families every day of the year. Children must know how to mountain-bike, and everyone should be in good physical condition. The 80-mile Brian Head–to–Bryce minitour, three days of riding and camping, starts at Brian Head Ski Resort in south central Utah and winds through aspen groves and lava beds on the way to Bryce Canyon National Park. There's a 2,000-foot ascent, but support vehicles are always nearby. On the Grand Canyon Family Tour, a four-day camping trip, you cycle 120 miles—many of them through Arizona's Kaibab National Forest, on a trail used by early explorers. The destination is the canyon's still uncommercialized North Rim, a thrilling discovery for anyone who's seen only the developed South Rim. The five-day, 170-mile tour of Zion and Bryce national parks departs in July (camping) and September (inn and lodge stays). Utah's "Color Country" has it all: mountains, lakes, rivers, multihued canyons, and the region's natural rock sculptures. You look out from the highest plateau in North America and splash through creeks 44 times—the guides counted. If your family has only a day to spare, you can sign up at any time of year for the Redrock Canyon Family Bike Tour, near Las Vegas.

Ages 12 and up can join all other tours. Combination trips pair biking with hiking, riding, rafting, canoeing, rock climbing, cross-country skiing, or snowshoeing, among other sports. If someone in your family uses a wheelchair, try a wheelchair backcountry tour. Cyclists can come along, too.

Family tours meet in St. George, Utah; shuttles to the trailhead are free. There's also shuttle service from Las Vegas for an extra fee (free on Redrock Canyon tours). All trips include meals and lodging, and you can rent bikes (kids' and adult) and camping gear.

Escape the City Streets, Box 50262, Henderson, NV 89106, tel. 702/596–2953 or 800/596–2953. Year-round: 1–5 days (family tours), $45–$819.

Michigan Bicycle Touring

👫 1 – 4, 9+

A small, family-run business, Michigan Bicycle has been guiding families through the valleys and hills of its home state since 1978. Michigan is geographically and culturally diverse: Dunes and islands, orchards, farmland, meandering rivers, quaint towns, an Amish community, and an international center for performing arts are among its attractions.

FOR FAMILIES. A special family departure on the Platte River Pedal & Paddle trip combines canoeing on the easygoing Platte with biking through gently rolling farmland in the northwestern part of the state, near the shores of Lake Michigan. Several other trips are also ideal for families: The Mendon Amble takes cyclists through Amish country and to Colon, "Magic Capital of the World." Here magician Harry Blackstone perfected his craft and helped form Abbott's Magic Manufacturing, the world's largest producer of magic paraphernalia. Magic shows are performed here throughout the summer. For those who enjoy the performing arts, the Interlochen Sightseer includes a chance to attend rehearsals and performances of music, theater, and dance productions. Children aged 9 and up may participate fully on any of these trips, while parents can tow children under age 5 in a cart, available for rent from MBT.
🏠 *Michigan Bicycle Touring, 3512 Red School Rd., Kingsley, MI 49649, tel. 616/263–5885. May–Oct.: 2–5 days, $259–$675 per adult, children receive a 10%–25% discount.*

Nantahala Outdoor Center

👫 13+

Western North Carolina has some of the best mountain-biking terrain in the country, and Nantahala Outdoor Center is as adept at teaching fat-tire cycling skills as it is at teaching paddling (see *Canoeing and Kayaking*).

FOR FAMILIES. Families with teens can opt for a one-day sampler course that begins with a morning of instruction and ends with an afternoon trail ride at the popular Tsali Recreation Area near the school. The course includes a guide, bikes, helmets, and even a water bottle. This is ideal for families who have been leery of purchasing mountain bikes. With Nantahala's sampler, you invest a minimum of money and time to find out if the sport is up your alley. If it is, check out Nantahala's overseas cycling tours by calling the Adventure Travel department.
🏠 *Nantahala Outdoor Center, 13077 U.S. 19 W, Bryson City, NC 28713, tel. 704/488–6737. Mar.–Oct.: 1 day, $70*

Northern Outdoors

👫 12+

Northern Outdoors' resort center, The Forks, is set on more than 100 acres of forest along the Kennebec River in central Maine. It has its own secluded lake, as well as a sauna, hot tub, and pool. This may not sound like adventure, but it's certainly a nice place to return to after a hard day of mountain biking in Maine's challenging backcountry. If you're up for it, you can indulge in volleyball, platform tennis, canoeing, or kayaking before spending the night in accommodations that range from campsites to luxury lodge units.

FOR FAMILIES. A day of backcountry bike touring is a great introduction to the area. You'll cycle in the Kennebec Gorge, watch rafters tackle Magic Falls, picnic in the woods, and end the day at 90-foot-high Moxie Falls, where you can take a dip in one of the scenic pools. Guide, bike, helmet, lunch, and transportation are all included; lodging at The Forks is an extra charge. If you want to combine two days of adventure, Northern Outdoors makes it easy. You can bike one day, overnight at The Forks, and raft Maine's rushing rivers in the morning.
🏠 *Northern Outdoors, Box 100, Rte. 201, The Forks, ME 04985, tel. 207/663–4466.*

July–Sept.: 1 day biking, $45. Lodging (extra) is $8–$50; one child half-price per full-paying adult.

Sun, Sky, Wind

🕴️ 2½+

This Michigan resort is devoted almost exclusively to mountain bikers and their families. Near the top of the Michigan "mitten," just east of Grand Traverse Bay, Sun, Sky, Wind is in the heart of Michigan's ski country. Although it may not compare to the Rockies for downhillers, it's the perfect environment for mountain bikers of all ages and abilities. Guests at the resort can try all kinds of activities, including swimming, boating, and fishing on the lake; accommodations are in comfortable cottages, complete with kitchens. Before or after your stay you may want to visit some of Michigan's other terrific family vacation destinations, such as Sleeping Bear Dunes National Lakeshore, Traverse City, and Mackinac Island—all within an easy drive of Sun, Sky, Wind.

FOR FAMILIES. Sun, Sky, Wind schedules daily bike tours for all abilities, and guides will happily modify tours so that six- or seven-year-olds can participate. Rides for children of that age might include some paved-road riding as well as off-pavement excursions on flat, gentle terrain. Each day there are challenging rides, easy rides, and long and short rides throughout the area. If you have nonbiking children or toddlers in your family, the resort also has a supervised children's activity program for those ages 2½ to 12. If your kids want to try out a NORBA (National Off-Road Bicycle Association) children's race course, you'll find one that's open to Sun, Sky, Wind guests, just a few miles from the resort.
🏠 *Sun, Sky, Wind, 8275 W. Old State Rd., Central Lake, MI 49622, tel. 616/544–2069 or 800/424–5297. Open year-round, biking May–Nov.: 2–7 days, $300–$975 per family.*

Vermont Bicycle Touring

🕴️ 10+

In 1972 this company began offering inn-to-inn bicycle tours in Vermont, its home state. Today it has trips throughout the country and the world for cyclists to choose from. There are weekend getaways and 17-day expeditions. Vermont Bicycle Touring (VBT) does not have any family-only departure dates; however, children 10 and up can join all domestic tours, while ages 13 and up are allowed on international trips. Most trips are better for families with some biking experience. Keep in mind that VBT has no rental bikes for children less than 4 feet, 10 inches tall.

FOR FAMILIES. VBT's Colonial Williamsburg weekend tour is the ultimate trip for families, thanks to its flat, easy riding and the hands-on history at Williamsburg. Eighteenth-century homes and shops with costumed interpreters bring the past to life. On the first day you cycle along the York River and through the Yorktown battlefields. Day two takes you to Jamestown Island, site of the first permanent English colony. There's ample time for exploring Colonial Williamsburg, because the group stays at an inn just a mile from the historic district.

The Pennsylvania Dutch Weekend, which includes visits to a farm museum and a chocolate factory, and the Plymouth, Vermont weekend, where the inn has a pool and hot tub, are two others that families with some biking experience are bound to enjoy.
🏠 *Vermont Bicycle Touring, Box 711, Bristol, VT 05443, tel. 802/453–4811 or 800/245–3868. Mid-Apr.–Oct.: 2–3 days, $269–$489; children's discounts vary with accommodations.*

Wilderness River Outfitters

🕴️ 11+

As its name implies, Wilderness River began as a rafting outfitter, but it has expanded its trip list with some of the most interesting biking and hiking trips around. Owners Joe and Fran Tonsmeire have been guiding wilderness trips since their college days back in the '60s, and their knowledge and love of nature are evident.

FOR FAMILIES. Those older than 10 can follow the trail the Nez Percé Indians used to get to their buffalo-hunting grounds east of the Bitterroot Mountains. The Nez Percé Trail trip starts and ends in Missoula, Montana; travel is on a combination of paved and dirt roads through such exotic-sounding backcountry as the River of No Return Wilderness. You'll camp under the stars in forested meadows along the way. If you have time, this trip can also be combined with a Salmon River rafting expedition (see Rafting).

The Glacier Park Lodge Tour, a slightly easier trip in Montana, is perfect for those who like roughing it during the day and settling into comfortable inns at night. Among the accommodations is historic Glacier Park Lodge, built in 1913. Morning and evening meals are not included in the price of this trip, but lunch is.

Both tours are suitable for beginners with a little experience as well as for more advanced riders. If you have a child under 11 who has biking experience, talk to Fran or Joe; they make exceptions to the age limit on an individual basis.

🏨 *Wilderness River Outfitters, Box 871, Salmon, ID 83467, tel. 208/756–3959 or 800/252–6581. July–Aug., 5–8 days, $750–$900.*

Resources

Products

Trail-A-Bike (Norman Rogers Airport, Kingston K7M 4M1, Ont., Canada, tel. 800/265–9815) customer service can send you a brochure on this product or tell you where to find it. If there is no dealer near you, you can buy direct from the company.

The following companies make helmets for children, as well as for adults: **Bell** (Rte. 136 E, Rantoul, IL 61866, tel. 217/893–9300 or 800/456–2355) will send consumers a pamphlet on helmet use and safety, a catalog, and dealer information. **Giro Sport Design** (380 Encinal St., Santa Cruz, CA 95060, tel. 408/457–4476 or 800/294–6098) will send a catalog or give you the name of the nearest dealer, as will **Specialized Bicycle Components** (15130 Concord Circle, Morgan Hill, CA 95037, tel. 408/779–6229). All these companies have a crash replacement policy, so if someone in your family damages a helmet in an accident, you can purchase a new one for a nominal fee.

Also See

If you want to mix biking and cross-country road travel, check out RV Adventures. Many of the parks and RV resorts have mountain bike trails and rentals. Cyclists can also load their bikes onto houseboats on the New York State Canal System and in Florida, too, so take a look at Houseboating for more combination adventures.

CANOEING

Serenity, although elusive in everyday life, is the very essence of a flatwater canoe trip, especially one that takes your family gliding through the still backwaters and meandering rivers of North America's great wilderness areas. Sounds are few—the rhythmic dip of your paddle, rustling leaves, the occasional cry of a bird startled into flight—so even normally boisterous children often quiet down to watch and listen intently to nature's life signs.

There's a feeling of historical continuity in canoeing, too. Many of America's early European explorers—and the natives who came before them—traveled by canoe, using the pathways nature provided. Today canoeing is an excellent way to explore protected areas without impacting negatively on fragile environments.

All this said, parents should know that kids from the age of about 6 to 10 can have a hard time sitting for long stretches of quiet paddling. Savvy outfitters frequently suggest combination trips that pair canoeing with hiking, snorkeling, nature studies, swimming, and fishing. Base-camp trips, where you're taking day voyages from one camp, are an alternative to long days of paddling from camp to camp. Some multiday trips are better than others because outfitters make frequent stops en route and set up camp early enough in the day for kids to have time to run around. Before committing to an adventure, carefully assess your family's abilities, personality, and needs.

Canoeing isn't just about quiet forays on mellow streams, however. White-water canoeing is fast-paced and exhilarating, and you can discover its challenges on some of the great rivers. There are schools throughout the country with courses for all kinds of families. Teens, especially, may welcome a family vacation if it entails exciting work with skilled instructors on rushing rivers. And parents may come away from such an experience seeing themselves and their teens in a whole new light. The bottom line is this: Canoeing is for everyone from utter beginner to skillful paddler, quiet nature lover to wild white-water enthusiast, rambunctious toddler to adventure-addicted teen.

Questions to Ask

Are child-size life vests provided? Anytime you're in a boat, you need a coast guard–approved safety vest that fits properly. If the company you choose doesn't have the sizes you need, purchase them before your trip.

Are helmets needed? On a lake or pond you probably won't need a helmet, but on any river with even a minimum of white water, a helmet is a good idea. Ask about a white-water helmet for yourself and for your children. If the right sizes aren't available from the outfitter, check at an outdoor store that sells equipment for white-water enthusiasts.

Is the guide/instructor trained in CPR, lifesaving, and first aid? What type of emergency equipment is carried? When it comes to water and wilderness, accidents can happen—especially with children along. If you are going into the wilderness or will be a long way from a hospital or medical help, someone should be familiar with procedures for reviving and rescuing children and adults. Many parents take child CPR and first aid themselves these days, but you should also ask about an outfitter's training and emergency supplies. Is there, for example, a radio for emergency contact with a home base or local medical personnel?

Are instructors certified by a reputable organization, such as the American Canoe Association or the British Canoe Union? Certification can help you compare schools and instructors. Word of mouth is also an indicator of whether a school is good and whether instructors work well with children and families. When you're dealing with a guide, most are not certified. Many, however, are members of state guiding associations, another indicator of commitment to safety and certain standards of quality. Always ask about experience and the number of years a guide has worked, too.

Will other families be on this trip or in this class? Although many paddling courses and trips are available to older children, they aren't necessarily the best choice for your family. Being the only child in a class of adults can be difficult. Having one child in a group of older adults who want to focus on bird-watching, for example, can be taxing for everyone. If the outfitter does not designate specific family trips, try for a date on which other families have signed up.

What kind of canoes are provided? Different canoes provide different experiences. Some outfitters, too, charge based on the number of canoes your family needs. A family of five might all fit in some types of canoes or might require two canoes if only smaller varieties are available. Do you want to learn solo paddling? Do you want to put children in the middle or give them a chance to paddle, too? Do you have lots of gear? There are many options, so ask questions to avoid surprises.

How many miles or hours does the group paddle each day? Multiday trips average anywhere from 5 to 12 miles a day, with participants spending two to six hours each day on the water. Courses generally require five or six hours a day of paddling, but some have longer days. Base-camp trips are usually more flexible, with options for families to stay closer to camp and do less paddling if they wish.

How many portages/carries are there and how long are they? Portages (or carries, in the Adirondacks) are those places where you must cross land to get from one body of water to another, or go around an obstacle, such as a waterfall, on a river. When you portage, you carry the canoes and equipment by hand. While portages are sometimes a necessity, many can be avoided by changing routes. Talk to guides about your family's abilities. Although small children can manage some portages and even help carry equipment, big people take on most of the burden. With portages ranging from a few yards to more than a mile, the route is an important consideration when you're choosing a trip.

What's the group size likely to be? Your family will be by itself on custom trips. Scheduled trips may take only 6 to 12 people, especially in wilderness areas where permits are limited. Base-camp trips in state parks often allow for 25 or even 30 in a group. In courses, students are usually divided into small groups, averaging three to six per instructor.

What is done with diapers in the wilderness? Some outfitters accept infants on canoe voyages, but there is often no place to dispose of soiled diapers during a trip. Parents must store and carry out all diapers. Families who use cloth diapers must do the same thing, because washing soiled diapers in, or even near, lakes and streams can contaminate the water.

What's included in the course or trip? Course prices listed here cover instruction, equipment, and lunch, unless otherwise noted. For a few, your fee pays for lodging, too. Trips include canoes, camping gear, meals, guides, and some instruction, unless otherwise noted. Participants usually have to bring their own sleeping bags and often pads, too. Transportation to or from the put-in or take-out site may be part of the price or may be an extra fee.

Instruction

All outfitters in this chapter provide instruction in basic canoeing and general water and wilderness safety. Some teach paddling and maneuvering techniques as a matter of course, others only if asked. Schools are geared for instruction at all levels. Canoeing is appealing because you can begin to do it with almost no instruction, yet there are many skills to master if you want to enjoy the sport to the fullest. For families this means no waiting to start, and a lifetime of learning and exploring opportunities—a near perfect adventure.

Finding the Fun

Northeast: Adventure Quest, Bear Cub Adventure Tours, L.L. Bean, Sunrise County Canoe Expeditions. **South:** Nantahala Outdoor Center, Outward Bound, Wilderness Southeast, Wolf River Canoes. **Midwest:** Boundary Country Trekking, Gunflint Northwoods Outfitter/Gunflint Lodge, Kayak & Canoe Institute, Outward Bound, Wilderness Inquiry. **Southwest:** Laughing Heart Adventures, Outward Bound. **Rockies:** Boulder Outdoor Center. **West Coast:** Laughing Heart Adventures. **Canada:** Kayak & Canoe Institute, Outward Bound, Sunrise County Canoe Expeditions, Wells Gray Park Backcountry Chalets.

Favorite Schools and Guides

Adventure Quest

 7+

A little more than 8 miles south of Woodstock in east central Vermont, a 40-acre preserve of green woodlands and rolling hills makes an ideal classroom setting for students at Adventure Quest, one of the country's top paddling and outdoor schools. Although Adventure Quest focuses on teaching children and teens—and excels at doing just that in summer camp programs for kids 7 to 17—its family workshops are every bit as good. Because the workshops are customized, you can schedule them at your family's convenience.

FOR FAMILIES. If you want to learn whitewater paddling, sign up for Adventure Quest's open canoeing workshop. An open canoe has special equipment for whitewater use; like a kayak, the craft can be rolled, a maneuver in which the boat turns from right side up to upside down and back with the paddler sitting in it. Either one or two people can paddle, using single-blade paddles, but the canoers kneel for stability and better visibility. Like all of Adventure Quest's family workshops, this one gives parents and children the knowledge and skills they need for safe outings on their own, and it's geared to the group's abilities and interests. On average, a group with some canoeing skills but no white-water experience starts on flatwater and moves to white water in one to two days. Participants spend about six hours each day on one of several local rivers—the White, the Ottauquechee, or the Connecticut.

You can book a family workshop for one day, but multiday sessions provide a continuity that will get you out on your own faster. The Woodstock area has plenty of lodging (ask Adventure Quest for suggestions), or, if space is available, you can stay at the school's campground for a small additional charge.

🏠 *Adventure Quest, Box 184, Woodstock, VT 05091, tel. 802/484–3939. Apr.–Oct.: 1 or more days, $200 per day for up to 4 people; $50 more for each additional family member.*

Bear Cub Adventure Tours

 4+

In the 6 million acres of northern New York's Adirondack Park, you'll find outstanding canoeing opportunities and a wilderness of surprisingly rugged terrain. More than 30,000 miles of brooks and streams meander through these ancient mountains, feeding into 1,000 miles of rivers. If that's not enough, there are 2,300 ponds and lakes. Besides being enthusiastic about taking families into the wilderness, Bear Cub owner Gary Marchuk is certified in canoe instruction, water safety and outdoor emergency care, and CPR. He has studied environmental conservation and also happily shares historical anecdotes—all of which makes him a terrific choice for families.

FOR FAMILIES. Bear Cub, based in the two-time Olympic village of Lake Placid, schedules two family canoe trips each summer in July and August. Because space is limited to two or three families (10 people), sign up early if you're interested. These three-day trips mix canoeing with Adirondack history, nature studies, geology, swimming, hiking, exploring, and camping. They're usually base-camp experiences (unless participants want otherwise), a plus for families with younger children. If you can't make the scheduled dates, your family can arrange a private trip of three to five days at any time. There are one-day wilderness trips, too.

Adirondack Park abounds in terrific canoe routes, but Gary favors three areas for family trips. The St. Regis Canoe Area, the state's only designated canoe area, has no motorboats or crowds—just beautiful lakes and ponds in an 18,000-acre wilderness area. Remote but easy to access—and requiring only one short carry—the trip from Bog River Flow to Low's Lake makes another great family route. The 14-mile-long Low's provides exceptional lake paddling. Those who prefer rivers can opt for the Raquette, with rushing falls, otters, and ospreys. Gary has some colorful stories about people who guided and visited here more than 150 years ago.

Canoe clinics for all levels run primarily in spring and early summer; the minimum age is 12. A two-day clinic on calm and scenic waters teaches beginners paddling skills, canoe maneuvers, self-rescue techniques, and all about safety, equipment, and outfitting. A two-day white-water training program for canoers with basic skills takes students from moving water to rapids. Paddling strokes, eddy turns, upstream ferries, wave surfing, river reading, and rescue skills will all be covered. The number of white-water canoes for rent is limited, so book this one well in advance. One note of caution: Black flies are ferocious from mid-May to mid-June. If you go into this wilderness area during those weeks, take repellent and netting.

 Bear Cub Adventure Tours, 30 Bear Cub Rd., Lake Placid, NY 12946, tel. 518/523–4339. May–Oct.: 1–5 days, $70–$125 per person per day (trips); $150 per day for 2 people, $35 for each additional person (clinics).

Boulder Outdoor Center

👫 10+

The Boulder Outdoor Center has a variety of classes in Colorado. Among other choices, families can spend a summer week paddling the legendary Colorado River during the day and returning to a mountain inn for good food and the company of other nature-loving families at night. This resort-based course takes place just outside Glenwood Springs, Colorado, where the hot springs and vapor caves have been drawing

visitors for more than a century. Boulder Outdoor Center hasn't been around quite that long, but the company does have more than 15 years of experience teaching river skills to both adults and kids.

FOR FAMILIES. All classes and clinics welcome ages 10 and up; parents must take the same class with children under 17. The center's canoe classes are almost identical to its kayaking classes (see Kayaking) in format. At weeklong resort-based courses for beginning, intermediate, and advanced canoers, students spend four to five days (depending on level) paddling various sections of the Colorado—generally somewhat gentler stretches than those favored by the kayakers. The price includes lodging at the Sunlight Inn in Glenwood Springs. Other options are one-day lake and river clinics in Boulder and Denver; you pay extra for lodging.

 Boulder Outdoor Center, 2510 N. 47th St., Boulder, CO 80301, tel. 303/444–8420 or 800/364–9376. May–Sept.: 1–7 days, $25–$754. Children's discounts are available on 1-day clinics.

Boundary Country Trekking

👫 ALL

Minnesota's Boundary Waters Canoe Area (BWCA) is the premier canoeing destination in the United States. Thousands of clear blue lakes mirror the towering pines and granite cliffs of this northern wilderness that stretches across the Canadian border. Linking the lakes are well-worn trails first walked by Native Americans, then by French fur traders and other European explorers. Today families follow these same paths, carrying canoes from one pristine lake to the next on backcountry paddling adventures. Ted Young, Boundary Country Trekking's owner, has guided groups through the BWCA for more than 40 years.

FOR FAMILIES. The Introductory BWCA Canoe Adventure, designed for both novice canoers and families, is a three-day guided trip with two nights of camping in the BWCA. Ted shares his knowledge of local history and lore, and he's ready and willing to teach canoeing and camping skills. Although Ted goes out on the water throughout the summer, May and September are his favorite months. Routes for this adventure vary but generally require five or six portages, the longest of which is about ¼ mile. You paddle 6 to 8 miles each day and stand a good chance of seeing moose, loons, ospreys, eagles, or even the ferocious fisher, a relative of the mink. The trip fee covers lodging the nights before and after the trip, either at the company's cabin or in a local inn along the Gunflint Trail.

Ted and his company also run longer canoe adventures for those with boating and wilderness experience, as well as one-day paddles to several lakes.

 Boundary Country Trekking, 590 Gunflint Trail, Grand Marais, MN 55604, tel. 218/ 388–9972 or 800/322–8327. May–Sept.: 1–4 days, $80–$540. Children's discounts vary for each trip.

Gunflint Northwoods Outfitters/Gunflint Lodge

👫 ALL

The Kerfoots excel at introducing families to the joys of the wilderness. They've been in the business for almost 70 years—guiding, outfitting, and running Gunflint Lodge in Minnesota's Boundary Waters Canoe Area. If your family already has some experience with wilderness canoeing and camping, the Kerfoots will custom design and outfit a self-guided paddling adventure for you.

FOR FAMILIES. In July and August, scheduled guided canoe trips for families begin and end with an overnight at Gunflint Lodge. For the four nights and five days in between, families explore the waterways of the BWCA, watch beavers feeding, listen to stories and the sounds of the forest, and help set up camp at three different sites. You paddle a comfortable three to five hours

per day. One of the best family routes in the BWCA takes in Ham, Long Island, Winchell, and Horsehoe lakes. There's lots of wildlife (moose, otters, eagles), which is why the Kerfoots subtitle this trip Mystical Moments with Kids and Critters. The route does have about nine portages, most about a block long, though one is nearly ½ mile. The trip price includes dinner and breakfast on the lodge nights.

Families with even a little experience can head out without guides if they wish—after Bruce Kerfoot has given them all the orientation they need to paddle and camp on their own. There's a choice of routes especially for families.

Gunflint Northwoods Outfitters/Gunflint Lodge, 750 Gunflint Trail, Grand Marais, MN 55604, tel. 218/388–2296 or 800/362–5251. June–Sept.: 5–8 days, $425–$625 for scheduled trips, $295–$500 for self-guided trips. Children under 4 are free.

Kayak & Canoe Institute

👫👶 7+

The Kayak & Canoe Institute, part of the Outdoor Program at the University of Minnesota at Duluth, sponsors some trips but really focuses on instruction. Classes range from the most basic clinic for beginners to certification courses for canoe instructors.

FOR FAMILIES. One-, two-, and three-day fundamentals courses cover white-water and flatwater canoeing, both solo and tandem. These classes, for ages 15 and up, utilize fairly large open canoes that provide room for stretching out a bit and carrying equipment. Most are based near Duluth, but a Fundamentals II course takes place on the Vermilion River, near the Canadian border, and includes camping and meals. The Multi-day Canoe Trip Planning & Paddling Course also teaches canoeing basics—equipment design, stroke technique, rescue, river reading, and safety. Its main function, though, is to prepare you to outfit your own trip, so there's information on trip planning, route finding, and packing. Families with younger children of about 7 or so can sign up for private classes in both flatwater and white-water canoeing.

As for trips, join the 13-day expedition to the Bloodvein River in Canada. Named for the veins of red granite in its bed, the Blood-vein passes through Woodland Caribou and Atikaki provincial parks in Ontario and Manitoba, respectively. You'll get to know your fellow paddlers on the 12-hour van ride from Duluth, which is just one reason this adventure is best for those 15 and up. Quiet lakes, wild-rice marshes, and pulse-pounding rapids provide a variety of canoeing experiences. Look for woodland caribou along the way.
🏕 *Kayak & Canoe Institute, Outdoor Program, University of Minnesota at Duluth, 121 Sports & Health Center, 10 University Dr., Duluth, MN 55812, tel. 218/726-6533. May–Aug.: 1–13 days, $55–$243 for courses, $685 for trip.*

Laughing Heart Adventures

🚻 14+

The name really conveys what this northern California outfitter is all about. Trips "are conducted in the spirit of adventure, fun, and discovery," the owners note in their brochure, and that's exactly what many teens and parents want. In return, Laughing Heart requests those who sign up to arrive "with an open mind, flexible attitude, and a smiling face." This isn't too much to ask for, especially when you're providing terrific canoe trips on some of California's best rivers. Laughing Heart will consider younger children on some trips, but call and discuss specifics.

FOR FAMILIES. Laughing Heart has expeditions on various rivers in and outside California, but two rivers that suit families particularly well are the Eel and the Trinity, both in the northernmost part of California. The Eel, a designated Wild and Scenic River in

Humboldt County, flows through old-growth redwoods, rolling hills, and canyons; it's good for all levels of canoers. There are challenges, but instruction is provided throughout each trip. Large sand beaches make excellent campsites, and the warm water will entice swimmers. The Eel area has abundant wildlife: ospreys, coyotes, deer, and bears. The Trinity, another Wild and Scenic River, gets its green color from the serpentine rocks in its riverbed. Otters play in the Trinity and bald eagles nest in the ancient fir forests through which it rolls. The most famous sightings in the area, however, are those of Bigfoot. Although Laughing Heart does not guarantee an appearance, keep your eyes open. Fishing is good on the Trinity, so bring your poles.

If you want to mix canoeing, a visit to a hot springs, and hiking, Laughing Heart suggests its Black Canyon run on the Lower Colorado River in Arizona. There's even a hot waterfall to "massage" your sore shoulders. Utah's Green is another river for all levels. Paddle through Stillwater and Labyrinth canyons with their 1,000-foot walls, past Anasazi ruins, bighorn sheep, and the mesmerizing geological formations that make up Canyonlands National Park. Hiking is part of this adventure, too.
🏕 *Laughing Heart Adventures, Box 669, Willow Creek, CA 95573, tel. 916/629-3516 or 800/541-1256. May–Nov.: 3–5 days, $295–$530.*

L.L. Bean

🚻 14+

L.L. Bean, the outdoor store and catalog company based in Freeport, Maine, has conducted canoeing workshops for more than 15 years. Bean sells canoes and gear and, not surprisingly, the classes have a special emphasis on learning about equipment; there's no suggestion that students buy anything, however. Introducing families to canoeing is what the classes are all about.

FOR FAMILIES. Designed for the beginning paddler, the Introduction to Canoeing workshop generally takes place over a June weekend at Camp Winona on the shores of Moose Pond in Bridgton, Maine. Participants learn not only on-water techniques but also the skills necessary for transporting and caring for a canoe once they own it. Most class time is spent on the water, with breaks for lunch. You may have the option of evening paddling, too.

More advanced paddlers can choose another Camp Winona workshop offered in June—freestyle solo canoeing. Participants focus on developing a fluid paddling style. The goal is to help paddlers improve boat handling skills and increase their "sensitivity" to the canoe, resulting in tighter turns, better steering under varied conditions, and better overall control.

Both Camp Winona workshops include lodging and meals. For those looking for a quick course sometime from May through September, Bean offers two-hour classes near Freeport in solo and tandem canoeing. **fi** *L.L. Bean, Freeport, ME 04033, tel. 207/865–4761 or 800/341–4341. May–Sept.: 2 hrs.–2 days, $25–$250.*

Nantahala Outdoor Center

(👫 5+)

In addition to lakes, rivers, and mountain scenery that entice canoers of every level, western North Carolina can also claim a superb paddling school. If your family is serious about learning paddling or improving its skills, Nantahala Outdoor Center (NOC) stands second to none in terms of the quality and variety of its courses; you can hone your skills on a number of area rivers. Before or after your canoeing adventure, you might visit the nearby Great Smoky Mountains, which draw families from all over the country to hike, trek with llamas, or explore Great Smoky Mountain National Park, among many outdoor pursuits.

FOR FAMILIES. Participants in regular courses—including two- to five-day sessions for beginning, intermediate, and advanced paddlers—must be 16. Despite some differences based on group dynamics and the instructor's style, all classes emphasize a mix of effective paddling techniques, safety, and fun. NOC's catalog gives detailed information on assessing your skills; look at it before deciding on a class. Six-day River Intensive courses take you camping and paddling white-water rivers in the Chattahoochee National Forest of northern Georgia and the free-flowing Chattooga River on the border of South Carolina and Georgia. Those who want to check out the white-water river used in the 1996 Olympic games can sign up for the intensive course on the Ocoee in eastern Tennessee. Some paddling experience is a prerequisite for these courses. If you don't want to commit to longer courses, try one of NOC's samplers; the minimum age for these one-day clinics is 13. Meals and lodging, either at NOC in shared facilities or in local motels, are included in multiday course prices.

Another alternative for families is private instruction. Kids 5 and up can take private canoeing classes with parents; a family with a child that young would probably stick to the lakes in the area. Many of the rivers have minimum weight or age requirements set by the state. The Nantahala, for example, allows children only if they weigh at least 60 pounds, and to paddle the French Broad you must be 8 years old. Families opting for private instruction pay extra for staying right at NOC (about $50 per room per night, if it's available) or at nearby lodging arranged by NOC. **fi** *Nantahala Outdoor Center, 13077 U.S. 19 W, Bryson City, NC 28713, tel. 704/488–6737. Mar.–Oct.: 1–5 days, $70–$725.*

Outward Bound

(👫 14+)

Parents and children can choose among three locations and a number of seasons to challenge themselves and one another on the water. Florida's Everglades, the Boundary Waters Canoe Area in Minnesota, and the Rio Grande in Texas each give participants a different spin on canoeing in the wilderness. Like all Outward Bound programs, these are not just about learning sports skills; they're about life skills, too.

FOR FAMILIES. Weeklong parent/child canoe courses are scheduled in the Everglades during spring and winter; in the Boundary Waters Canoe Area in summer; and on the Rio Grande just after the Christmas holidays. These courses often involve eight-hour days on the water. The Everglades course takes families backpacking on the Florida Trail as well as paddling through the Wilderness Waterway and the Ten Thousand Islands of the Gulf Coast. In Minnesota students learn portaging techniques in addition to on-water skills, and the course includes rock climbing and rappelling. The Rio Grande course focuses on white-water canoeing on a river that changes from gentle currents to churning rapids. The land along the Rio Grande—especially the spectacular multicolored rock canyons—brings its own challenges. Families learn the basics of canyon exploration, as well as rock climbing and rappelling.

Families with kids older than 15 can also consider two courses not specifically aimed at families: canoeing in Atikaki Provincial Wilderness Park and white-water canoeing on the Bloodvein River, both in Manitoba, Canada.
🏠 *Outward Bound, Route 9D, R2 Box 280, Garrison, NY 10524, tel. 914/424–4000 or 800/243–8520. Dec.–July (all courses not all months): 7–8 days, $645–$795.*

Sunrise County Canoe Expeditions

(👫 **3+**)

Sunrise County is the nickname for Maine's Washington County in the easternmost sec-

tion of the state, along the Canadian border. This company is headquartered there and runs many of its trips in the area. Sunrise owners Martin Brown, David Watson, and Kendra Flint are knowledgeable outfitters and guides who have personal as well as professional experience with family travel; they've taken their own school-age kids canoeing with them since they were babies. Sunrise has many years of experience in guiding and outfitting, and quality technical instruction is integral to every trip.

FOR FAMILIES. Kendra recommends two very different rivers as terrific for families. The St. Croix, close to Sunrise County's headquarters, is the company's "home" river. Four-or six-day trips start out at a base camp on Cathance Lake. A river of easy to moderate white water, the St. Croix flows from a chain of lakes through woodlands and meadows in an area known as one of the principal nesting sites for bald eagles. The fishing is excellent (bring your own rod if you're serious about fishing), and there's just one short portage on the six-day trip.

Families might also choose a mellow six-day float through Québec's Gaspé Peninsula on the Cascapedia River. Black spruce forests mix with hardwoods; moose, deer, and maybe even bears can be seen along stretches of very easy white water. The trip has no portages, and the last night's lodging at an inn in Bonaventure, Québec, is included in the price.

Sunrise doesn't offer family-only departure dates, but it does try to group families together. Custom trips are always another option. Minimum ages are usually determined on a case-by-case basis. If your 3-year-old has been canoeing and camping, that's great; if your family has little or no experience, the minimum age may be higher.
🏠 *Sunrise County Canoe Expeditions, Cathance Lake, Grove Post Office, ME 04638, tel. 207/454–7708. May–Oct.: 4–6 days, $309–$839. Custom prices average $100–$120 per person per day; ask about family discounts.*

Wells Gray Park Backcountry Chalets

 ALL

Based just outside British Columbia's Wells Gray Park, this outfitter specializes in trips to the park's rugged interior. In more than a million acres of backcountry, multihued flower meadows ring still lakes, and snow remains almost perpetually on the surrounding peaks. Lava canyons and ash cones—created by the long-ago volcanic activity that formed much of the area—add geologic texture and contrast. Wells Gray is a destination of extraordinary beauty that draws canoers because of the exceptional lake paddling.

FOR FAMILIES. You can choose between a six-day wilderness canoe trip paddling two magnificent lakes—Clearwater and Azure— or an adventure that combines three days of hiking and three days of canoeing, with one night at the Wells Gray Guest Ranch in between. Clearwater and Azure lakes are each 17 miles long, with numerous inviting campsites. None, however, is more beautiful than Azure's Rainbow Falls, a wide white crescent-shaped beach where Angus Horn Creek tumbles into the lake. Guides try to schedule a two-night layover here, to give families a respite from the normal four to five hours of paddling each day. This trip has one short portage.

On the combination trip, hikers stay at either Fight or Trophy chalet (owned by the company), heading out for three- to six-hour hikes each day. There's no need to pack much in; the chalets have kitchens, baths, bedding, books, games, and even sandals to wear around. For the canoeing portion, the group goes out paddling several hours each day from a lakeside base camp.

Best of all, because of increased family bookings, Wells Gray owners Ian Eakins and Tay Briggs now schedule family-only departures, including one in July for the wilderness canoe trip. It's a wonderful opportunity to introduce your children not only to Canada

but to Canadian and European families, who are the majority of trip participants.

 Wells Gray Park Backcountry Chalets, Box 188, Clearwater V0E 1N0, British Columbia, Canada, tel. 604/587–6444. June–Sept.: 6 days, $440–$535; 30% discount for children under 14.

Wilderness Inquiry

2+

This nonprofit organization strives to bring all kinds of people, including those with disabilities, into the wilderness. "Our trips are shared cooperative adventures that combine the strength and positive energy of all the members in the group," executive director Greg Lais says. Whether or not disabilities are involved, this goal is exactly what many parents hope to achieve in traveling with their children. Based in Minnesota, Wilderness Inquiry offers canoeing adventures all over the country.

FOR FAMILIES. Of primary interest to parents and kids are the specially designated family canoeing and camping trips. Two trips in Minnesota state parks should appeal to the very youngest canoers. Both are base-camp trips with structured activities for kids and families throughout each day and evening, including interpretive talks by park rangers; guides provide canoeing and low-impact camping instruction.

Bear Head Lake State Park, in the heart of Superior National Forest at the gateway to the Boundary Waters Canoe Area, has towering pines and excellent fishing (bring your own gear). The park has primitive campsites, and you'll probably see deer, black bears, or even moose. Aside from canoeing, swimming, and hiking, the group might also tour local sights, such as the International Wolf Center.

At 32,000-acre Itasca State Park, the state's biggest, you can explore prehistoric archaeological sites and native burial areas. The highlight of any visit, though, may be a small stream just 15 steps across—the headwaters of the mighty Mississippi. When you're not jumping back and forth across America's most famous river, you can paddle on beautiful Lake Itasca.

Families with children 5 and up can join the three-day St. Croix River family canoe trip, just a two-hour drive from Minneapolis. Designated a National Scenic Riverway, the St. Croix flows through remarkably pristine wilderness areas; a portion of the trip takes place in St. Croix State Park. Wilderness Inquiry uses 24-foot-long cedar-strip voyageur canoes on this trip. Each of these exceptionally stable boats holds 7 to 10 people and has enough space for a kind of play area for kids in the middle. Sandstone cliffs and stands of pine and balsam line a river that was once a logger's highway and an important gateway for adventurers of the last century, who settled new towns like Stillwater, Taylors Falls, and Lindstrom. There are numerous small islands and sandy beaches to stop at and creek mouths to explore—but no portages. Guides teach basic canoeing techniques throughout the trip.

🏠 *Wilderness Inquiry, 1313 5th St. SE, Box 84, Minneapolis, MN 55414, tel. 612/379–3858 or 800/728–0719. June–Aug.: 3–4 days, $73–$195.*

Wilderness Southeast

👫🏻 12+

Wilderness Southeast, a nonprofit organization, dedicates its programs "to all who find nature not an adversary to conquer, but a storehouse of infinite knowledge and experience linking people to all things past and present." If the description is appealing and if you want to combine canoeing with an indepth understanding of the wilderness areas through which you're traveling, this is the company for you.

FOR FAMILIES. Two canoeing trips in Georgia and Florida are perfect for families. Those with kids at least 14 can join the

Okefenokee wilderness canoe trip, with about six possible routes through the peat prairies and towering cypress forests of the swamp. Time is spent hiking the periphery and exploring the east side of Okefenokee; there's a stroll on a boardwalk, and a 50-foot tower offers panoramic views of this unique area. Naturalists help participants identify swamp vegetation and wildlife. Although canoeing experience isn't necessary, participants should be in condition to paddle as much as 12 miles in a day. The last night is spent at an historic fish camp on the banks of the Suwanee River—where hot showers are welcomed by all.

The Florida Springs canoe trip for ages 12 and up combines canoeing with two other favorite family activities: snorkeling (bring your own equipment or rent it from the organization) and close encounters with wildlife. From a base camp in the vast Ocala National Forest, near Silver Springs, Florida, participants venture out each day on and into turquoise waters filled with schools of iridescent fish. The area's springheads pump an estimated 6 billion gallons of water into Florida's extensive waterways each day; this fascinating geological feature provides the basis for many group discussions. Canoes share the waters with otters and turtles, among other creatures; overhead, a variety of raptors rise and circle on swirling thermal currents. If weather and nature allow, the group may visit Crystal River National Wildlife Sanctuary and swim with the endangered West Indian manatee.

🏠 *Wilderness Southeast, 711 Sandtown Rd., Savannah, GA 31410, tel. 912/897–5108. Feb.–May, Oct.–Nov.: 4–5 days, $445.*

Wolf River Canoes

👫🏻 5+

In 1980, Joe and Jennifer Feil opened Wolf River Canoes on what they consider to be one of the world's greatest canoeing rivers. What makes the Wolf so great? World-class beaches of powdery white sand—and lots of them. If this sounds intriguing, head into Mississippi, about halfway between Mobile and New Orleans.

FOR FAMILIES. Clean and uncrowded, the Wolf winds peacefully past magnolias and cypresses, wild azaleas and cottonwoods. It is truly a river a family, even beginners, can handle without a guide. Just tell Joe how far you want to go in how many days (15 to 23 miles in two days is typical), and he'll transport you and the boats upriver to the appropriate put-in spot. His canoes can easily fit two adults and two children, with gear. You can paddle a lot, or relax and play on a beach as you watch great blue herons, ducks, wild turkeys, and otters. There are alligators down toward the Gulf of Mexico, but they're not a problem upriver.

This trip allows your family to do everything at your own pace. Just set up your own camping equipment wherever you wish (Joe will give you tips on what to bring), and you probably won't see anyone else while you're traveling. At the end of the trip you'll return to Wolf River Canoes and your car. If you decide you want a guide after all, Joe will be happy to tag along and provide insights into both paddling and the local area, but you and the kids have to help with the camp chores and cooking.

🏕 *Wolf River Canoes, 21652 Tucker Rd., Long Beach, MS, tel. 601/452-7666. Year-round: 2–4 days, $45–$75 per canoe; $120 per day extra for a guide.*

Resources

Organizations

Several organizations set standards and guidelines for outfitters and guides. **America Outdoors** (Box 1348, Knoxville, TN 37901,

tel. 615/524–4814) is the national association for river guides. Ask for its magazine listing outfitters and guides, although the group cannot recommend one member over another. The **American Canoe Association** (7432 Alban Station Blvd., Suite B226, Springfield, VA 22150, tel. 703/451–0141) publishes a newsletter, *The American Canoeist*, and is one of the main certifying organizations for instructors. The **National Association of Canoe Liveries and Outfitters** (Box 248, Butler, KY 41006, tel. 606/472–2202) will send consumers information on guides and outfitters across the country; it also has lists of relevant books and periodicals.

Periodicals

Canoe & Kayak Magazine (Box 3146, Kirkland, WA 98033, tel. 800/692–2663) runs an extensive list of schools and outfitters in the back of the magazine and has several stories each year about family paddling. *Paddler Magazine* (Box 1341, Eagle, ID 83616, tel. 208/939–4600) lists guides and outfitters across the nation and also has family paddling articles.

Books

Paddle America by Nick Shears (Starfish Press, tel. 202/244–7827) represents one man's effort to provide a central place for paddlers to get all the information they need about waterways and outfitters in various regions of the country.

Also See

If your family loves paddling rivers, lakes, and coastal waterways, check out additional courses and adventures in Kayaking and Rafting. If boating and animal watching appeal to you, there are trips in Wildlife Encounters that combine these activities.

CATTLE DRIVES

My friend David, an attorney in Washington, D.C., has traveled throughout this country and much of the world. Of all his adventures, the cattle drive he went on tops his list of great vacations. Why? Because, he says, his abilities and endurance were tested and he was able to meet the challenges head on. He discovered, in fact, that he was capable of more than he ever thought possible—and it was fun.

That, in a nutshell, is what a cattle drive is about for modern-day families. You work hard, play hard, and fall into your sleeping bag exhausted at night—but you feel great about yourself and your day. What better gift to give children than positive reinforcement of their abilities and accomplishments? And that's not the end of it, for this self-esteem is nurtured in places of awesome beauty. You also have the opportunity to learn about American history, modern-day ranching, and wilderness ecology.

There's another important aspect to cattle drives, too. Many third-, fourth-, and fifth-generation ranchers have entered the tourism business because they believe it's a way to preserve their ranches and a unique way of life in today's changing economic times. The truth is, once traditional ranching is gone, it will be gone forever. When your family goes on a cattle drive with an honest-to-goodness rancher, you will hear, from the heart, about a way of life that shaped America's history and economy for years. *City Slickers* notwithstanding, cattle drives are an excellent mix of adventure, education, hard work, and old-fashioned fun.

Questions to Ask

How experienced do we have to be? In most cases, not very. Some drives take folks who have never ridden horses; others require riding experience. Generally it depends on the terrain or sometimes on the livestock. Always ask so that you choose the right drive for your family.

Is the drive walking only? Can experienced riders go faster? Ranchers tend to put inexperienced riders in the back or on the sides of the drive. If you want to work hard, stay up at the front. There's usually a place for riders of any ability, but some drives are better than others for very good riders.

How many hours a day are spent in the saddle? Six or 7 hours is the average for the drives listed here, with some as few as 4 and some as many as 10. The most direct answer is, plenty long enough to make you sore if you aren't used to it. Bring acetaminophen or another pain reliever for aches, and adhesive bandages and antibiotic cream for saddle sores. A little adversity is part of the adventure.

If someone gets tired of riding, are there options? On ranch-based drives or on those with a base camp, you may be able to quit early. On drives accompanied by a wagon, you can probably trade your horse for a wagon seat. On trail drives, though, there are few options. Anyone considering a cattle drive should think carefully about whether the family can handle a single-activity vacation for four to seven long, hard days in a row. Kids, in particular, may get bored on drives that offer no breaks and no other activities.

Is this a real drive to move cattle for a purpose, or is it simulated? There are outfitters that move cattle solely to entertain tourists, but they are not among those listed here. A ranch with real needs will provide you with a real experience.

How many guests go on the drive? Ten to 20 is average, plus wranglers plus a whole lot of cattle.

Are cowboy boots necessary? What about gloves? Most drovers recommend boots—and not brand-new ones. Get everyone in the family a pair and break them in well before the drive. Why? Cowboy boots are designed to keep your foot from slipping through the stirrup. If that happened and you fell, you'd be dragged by the horse. As for gloves, a pair of decent leather ones will protect your hands from sores and allow you to handle a rope better. Everyone should have a pair.

Do you have helmets? When we asked this question, the answers ranged from "Yep, but no one wears them" to utter amusement. No one will require you or your child to wear a riding helmet, so you have to decide on your own. The bottom line: A helmet is the safe way to go. You can purchase riding helmets at a store that sells riding apparel and equipment.

Where will we sleep? On ranch-based drives guests generally stay in cabins or lodge rooms. Drives that use a permanent or semipermanent cow camp might have wall tents or cowboy tepees. On trail drives a campsite is set up each night and guests sleep in tents or cowboy-style under the stars.

Are there showers? Some drives do offer this amenity. I wouldn't pick a cattle drive based on the presence or absence of showers, but if you care about this, ask.

What kind of food is served? Hearty and delicious chow is typical. Besides all the steaks and barbecue and Dutch oven desserts, most drives also have salads and fruit. Some outfitters can even accommodate vegetarians if asked ahead of time.

Will there be women and girls? Every rancher in this chapter said at least half the participants are female. In some cases, there are many more women than men. One outfitter speculated that this is because women are often better riders. Whatever the reason, cattle drives are not just a man's world, although men still outnumber women among the wranglers and drovers.

What's included in the cost? Drives include everything from the first day of the adventure to the last, meaning tents or cabins, meals, a horse, some instruction, and stock to move, unless otherwise noted. Some also include lodging the night before the drive starts and transportation to and from the nearest airport. You have to bring your own sleeping bag on some drives but not on others. Airfare to the ranch or meeting site is not included.

Instruction

All ranchers provide riding instruction to anyone who wants or needs it. Kids as well as adults have their riding ability checked before the drive starts, and there's discussion of basic safety issues and how to handle life on the trail. If you're a good rider, you'll be taught more advanced techniques of herding, trailing, and rounding up cows. On some ranches you learn to brand, provide health care for livestock, check fence lines, or even help castrate calves. Roping is part of every drive. Beyond that, most ranchers want to teach participants about the complexities of modern-day ranching and about the cultural and natural history of the land.

Finding the Fun

Southwest: American Wilderness Experience, Cottonwood Ranch, Hunewill Circle H Guest Ranch, Off the Beaten Path, Rockin' R Ranch. **Rockies:** American Wilderness Experience, Broken Skull Cattle Company, Cheyenne River Ranch, Cow Camp, Hargrave Cattle & Guest Ranch, High Island Ranch, Laredo Enterprises, Montana High Country Cattle Drive, Off the Beaten Path. **West Coast:** Hunewill Circle H Guest Ranch.

Favorite Cattle Drives

American Wilderness Experience

 8+

American Wilderness Experience, a company that represents many ranchers and other outfitters, has several choices for cowpokes hoping to fulfill their western dreams. The two best for families are along the Colorado/Wyoming border and in central Arizona.

FOR FAMILIES. Lone Tree Land & Cattle Company and the historic Terry Bison Ranch have joined up to offer two types of stock drives along the Colorado/Wyoming border. Families with wranglers 12 and up can help move powerful Texas longhorns to greener pastures; those with teens 16 and up can test their skills and stamina against a thundering herd of American bison. There's 50 square miles of rangeland—small, perhaps, in comparison to the open spaces of yesteryear, but plenty to excite and exhaust a novice cowhand. Trips start at the ranch, where you spend one night in a cabin before moving to various camps. Don't plan on roughing it too much; a specially equipped wagon provides hot showers and a pretty civilized toilet at every site. Evening entertainment includes cowboy troubadours, roping demonstrations, a night of dancing to a cowboy band, and a trip to a local rodeo.

The Ellinwood Ranch in central Arizona spreads over 33,000 acres of wilderness. The terrain ranges from ponderosa pine and aspen high country along the Mogollon Rim to the Hellsgate wilderness area, where cacti vie with grasslands to dominate the landscape and streams are marked by stands of cottonwood. Two springs and three natural swimming holes provide much-needed water and recreation. Ages 8 and up with some riding experience can help cut, brand, or round up the stock, depending on the season and the rancher's needs. If you still have energy when work's done, you can hike, fish, practice roping, or swim. You sleep in tents on the trail and listen to tall tales and western tunes around the campfire. Fly into Phoenix to join up; you'll then be driven three to four hours north to the ranch. The price includes pre- and post-trip lodging.

🏠 *American Wilderness Experience, Box 1486, Boulder, CO 80306, tel. 303/444–2622 or 800/444–0099. Mar.–Nov.: 6–8 days, $1,005–$1,500.*

Broken Skull Cattle Company

(👨‍👧 9+)

Jerry Garcia owns the Broken Skull Cattle Company in Colorado; despite his name, about which he does occasionally get kidded, he's alive and well and running one of the great cattle drives in the West. Jerry notes that he often gets more women and girls than men and boys on his drives. Affable and charming but serious about his cattle business, Jerry is willing to accommodate just about anyone, as long as you're willing to put in some long days.

FOR FAMILIES. There are horses for all ages and abilities. Jerry will take greenhorns or experienced riders and give them nine days of real cowhand experience. Novices can stay where the going's slower; good riders can challenge themselves with hard riding at the front of the herd. The group of about 10 meets in Steamboat Springs at the Ptarmigan Inn, where Jerry's wife is assistant manager. You can leave your car here, and if you choose to overnight in Steamboat, she can help with good rates.

In July you'll probably be moving the herd of up to 100 longhorns from the ranch outside of Steamboat, over Buffalo Pass, and down into North Park Basin, 50 miles away. The group spends one night camped near Steamboat's famous Strawberry Park Hot Springs and one day up on the Continental Divide, where there's time for swimming, fishing, hiking, or just looking at the awesome views. In September a van transports the group to the North Park area, and the drive takes place in reverse. Evenings are spent learning to rope, listening to a singer/cowboy poet, or playing a little poker. On the last day you help with the branding and other chores.

Jerry is also an artist, and he gives each participant one of his cattle drive prints, along with a buckskin "poke"—a pouch—containing nine silver dollars: a dollar a day for cowboy wages. There are discounts for families and returnees; Jerry decides these on a case-by-case basis.

🏠 *Broken Skull Cattle Company, Box 774054, Steamboat Springs, CO 80477, tel. 303/879–0090. July, Sept.: 9 days, $1,300; ask about family rates.*

Cheyenne River Ranch

(👨‍👧 8+)

Fifty miles north of Douglas, in eastern Wyoming, the Cheyenne River Ranch spreads over 8,000 acres in the Thunder Basin National Grassland. It's grassland by Wyoming standards—rolling hills covered in sagebrush, cactus, and, yes, some grass. The Pellatz family, low-key and friendly, runs both sheep and cattle on the ranch. They also drive the cattle of a niece and brother-in-law, which is why they can have five authentic drives a year.

FOR FAMILIES. Betty Pellatz says 8-year-olds are welcome on the spring and summer drives if they have some riding experience and are completely comfortable around horses; with no experience at all, children should be at least 11. These drives are primarily walking, so really good riders should opt for the faster, harder, and steeper fall roundup. Guests help drive 75–250 head of cattle (depending on the month) from the rolling prairie through the Rochelle Hills and Cow Creek Buttes.

The land is arid—even the Cheyenne River and Antelope Creek, both of which you camp beside, are dry except during flash floods. Up in the hills, stands of pine offer shade and shelter for camping. At each site there's a big tent for men and one for the women; married couples can have a smaller tent to themselves. Kids generally like to stay in the big tents, but the other option would be a second small tent next to their parents. The "prairie loo" is a trailer affair with a hot shower on one side and a potty on the other. At night, everyone practices roping and eats well, but most guests, Betty says, really want to visit and get to know one another and the wranglers.

🏠 *Cheyenne River Ranch, 1031 Steinle Rd., Douglas, WY 82633, tel. 307/358–2380. May–Oct.: 5–6 days, $900–$995; discounts for families of 5 or more.*

Cottonwood Ranch

For five generations, the Smith family has raised cattle in Elko County, Nevada, on a ranch 6,200 feet up in the high desert. Twelve hundred head of cattle and 100 horses roam over 2,000 acres of ranch property and thousands of additional leased acres. Although many guests come just for the ranch experience, one of Cottonwood's biggest draws is its famous four-day horse drive in May, as well as cattle work throughout the summer.

FOR FAMILIES. If you've never experienced the staggering beauty of a herd of horses on the run over wild and rugged land, sign up for Cottonwood's spring drive. After meeting at the ranch, the group of no more than 16 travels by van to the Jackpot

area, where 100 horses are corralled and ready to move. It takes three nights and four days on the trail to drive the horses along rimrock canyons, over the North Fork of the Little Salmon River, and on to the ranch, 50 miles away. Horses move a lot faster than cattle, so the drive requires riding experience and a minimum age of 12.

In order for your family to try cattle work—gathering, rounding up, and moving the herd to new pastures—your children only have to be 8 years old, and you don't need a lot of experience. You work mostly at the ranch (on some summer days, cattle work is based at a high camp), though you can be out all day working hard if you choose. Accommodations are in a seven-bedroom lodge, with both private and shared baths.
🏠 *Cottonwood Ranch, HC 62, Box 1300, O'Neil Rte., Wells, NV 89835, tel. 702/752–3604. May: 4 days (horse drive), $995. May–Sept. (ranch stay only): $95 per day. Ask about family discounts.*

Cow Camp

Just the name sounds like family fun—and Cow Camp is, although it's work, too. The Rivera and Hewitt family ranches cover a combined 45,000 acres on the Wyoming/ Montana state line in the Powder River canyons area. These working ranchers and their neighbors use the help of novice cowhands several times each year. Rural would be a good description of Recluse, Wyoming, where the Riveras' ranch is located. "There's a dance hall and post office," says Kate Rivera. The Hewitts' ranch is near Biddle, Montana, about 100 miles south of Miles City. Cow Camp is in between, an easy drive to Devil's Tower National Monument, the Custer Battlefield National Monument, and the Black Hills of South Dakota, so plan on spending some time in the area before or after camp.

FOR FAMILIES. One thing that makes Cow Camp a great summer activity for families with younger children is that you set up one camp for the whole time. Everyone spends the first night in the bunkhouse of one of the ranches, depending on where the cattle are. On the trail, cowboy tepee tents accommodate two adults and one or two children. If you want, your family can sleep out under the stars, too.

During the day, you help move parts of the herd from one grazing area to another, brand, or do other chores. Saddle time each day is six or more hours; you cover anywhere from 7 to 30 miles. You can also help in the morning and stay around camp in the afternoon, or even opt to spend one whole day at camp, hiking or swimming in Buffalo Creek (if there's been enough rain). Evening highlights are singing, horseshoes, and card games, all against a backdrop of fiery sunsets. You'll see ancient Native American carvings on some of the cliffs you pass, as well as old homesteads and cabins. Local history, range management, and ranch life are popular topics, so you leave Cow Camp with a real understanding of life in the '90s for American ranchers.

Families with teens 16 and up can also join spring and fall roundups, which are based on the ranches but require gathering, branding, and finding the cattle in rugged timberland. The dates vary each year because of the weather and other factors.

🏠 *Cow Camp, 931 Beason Rd., Recluse, WY 82725, tel. 307/687–1210 or 406/427–5056. May–Oct.: 6 days, $800–$1,200.*

Hargrave Cattle & Guest Ranch

🚹🚼 10+

Forty miles west of Kalispell, Montana, the Thompson River creates a valley of broad green meadows and cool pine forests. Native Americans trapped and fished in the area, and homesteaders made a living growing hay. The Hargrave Cattle & Guest Ranch, with its main buildings tucked at the head of

the valley, spreads out over 88,000 acres of mostly leased land. There are only 10 to 14 guests at a time even in the busy summer season, and Ellen Hargrave makes every one of them feel at home. Take time to visit nearby Glacier National Park while you're here; if you don't have a car, the Hargraves will lend you one.

FOR FAMILIES. This adventure is not a cattle drive or roundup in the traditional sense; you won't be on the trail camping out. The Hargraves offer an honest-to-goodness cattle experience during the day, and hot showers and a cozy comforter on your bed at night. If you want to "test drive" being a cowhand, this is an excellent place.

In calving season (April and May), guests help with a variety of chores. Mothers-to-be need to be checked every three hours throughout the day and night before they give birth, and you can get up with the wranglers to do it. There's also branding, ear tagging, riding herd, or even giving the calves their first vitamin shot.

May through June means cattle drives to pastureland 10 or so miles from the main ranch. In September and October the pastured cattle are rounded up and brought back. During those drives guests are on the trail at least eight hours a day—breakfast is at 5 AM. Sometimes you stop for lunch, but you may eat in the saddle. Sometimes you're moving moms and calves; other times it's bulls. The opportunities for experiencing real ranch life are endless here; the more you do, the more you'll learn.

🏠 *Hargrave Cattle & Guest Ranch, 300 Thompson River Rd., Marion, MT 59925, tel. 406/858–2284 or 800/933–0696. Year-round (Apr.–Oct. for most cattle work): 7 days, $980.*

High Island Ranch and Cattle Company

🚹🚼 12+

High Island in Wyoming is not anywhere near water. But when you stand and look around at the high peaks, you feel almost as if you're on an island, which is how the ranch got its name. Your family can come here to help brand and care for cattle, or you can join a trail drive—one that's '90s-style or one that re-creates the drives of the 1800s.

FOR FAMILIES. The 45,000-acre ranch has several drives and one spring branding week. Ages 12 and up can participate in branding week at the ranch, where accommodations are in rustic cabins. The drives, which cover about 15 miles per day over rough sage and prairie high country, are for ages 16 and up only. Fly into Cody and someone from the ranch will pick you up.

On drives, plan on 8 to 10 hours a day in the saddle—a long time for greenhorns—chasing and trailing cattle through the Washakie Wilderness in northern Wyoming. Depending on the season, the drive moves cattle from a lower lodge at about 6,000 feet to an upper lodge at 9,000 feet, or the reverse. The group camps on a different part of the trail each night; although tents are available, almost everyone sleeps in the open unless the weather is really bad. You stay in rooms in the very simple lodges on both ends of the drive. There is sometimes entertainment—a cowboy poet and singer or someone to teach you clog dancing—but most wranglers on this trip are too beat to do much except eat and sleep. If you want to learn roping, buy a rope from the ranch and one of the wranglers will be glad to teach you.

Once each summer High Island re-creates a real 1800s drive, where period clothing is worn and all the cooking and sleeping arrangements are as they would have been before the turn of the century. The ranch provides shirts, armbands, dusters, and silk "wild rags" (a bandanna). Don't wear watches or newfangled gear—everyone tries to be as authentic as possible. The biscuits are legendary and the traditional sweet-and-sour cider vinegar drink is popular. They do use coolers to keep the food

safe but they're covered in canvas, and, yes, the outhouses are still available. This is an experience of a lifetime for history buffs; 16 is the minimum age.

🏠 *High Island Ranch and Cattle Company, Box 71G, Hamilton Dome, WY 82427, tel. 307/867–2374. June–Sept.: 7 days, $1,195, $1,495 for 1800s drive.*

Hunewill Circle H Guest Ranch

One of California's top guest and cattle ranches, the Hunewill Circle H is in the eastern Sierra, near the northeastern border of Yosemite National Park. It's often booked far in advance for the popular summer months, but one of the great experiences here is working the cattle in the fall.

FOR FAMILIES. The big drive takes place the second week of November, when the herd travels from the Hunewills' summer ranch to the winter ranch 50 miles away in Nevada's Great Basin area. It's a good choice for families who don't want to sleep out every night. You move the herd over five days, spending anywhere from five to nine hours a day in the saddle. Your route goes through sage and piñon desert, up into the Sweetwater Mountains, and down into the wide, high desert of Nevada; ask about the Paiute cemetery you pass on the way. Each night vehicles drive you back to the ranch and your comfortable cabin. A maximum of 25 participants, who must be at least 12 years old and intermediate to advanced riders, go along. This adventure includes lodging at the ranch the days before and after the drive, plus a meal out at a restaurant the last night—nope, no one showers first.

In September, regular ranch guests can help round up the herd of about 2,000 and move it from high pastures down to the ranch. You'll be out one full day, returning to the ranch that night. Beginner riders and kids as young as 9 can go on this one. It's an opportunity to try out a cattle drive and experience the Hunewill Circle H Ranch, which is family heaven. Kids 6 and up can ride the trails at the ranch. Most guests fly into Reno, 120 miles away, and drive a rental car to the ranch.

 Hunewill Circle H Guest Ranch, Box 368, Bridgeport, CA 93517, tel. 619/932–7710 (summer); 200 Hunewill La., Wellington, NV 89444, tel. 702/465–2201 (winter). Sept. (ranch stay, including roundup): 5–7 days, $655–$915, depending on cabin. Nov. (drive): 7 days, $690. Children under 13 receive a 25%–50% discount, depending on age.

Laredo Enterprises

👫👤 4+

Lifelong ranchers Bob and Judy Sivertsen own and operate Laredo Enterprises. Although their own Montana ranch isn't conducive to an authentic drive because of farming and development in the area, the Sivertsens wanted to give families an understanding of today's cattle business. To do this, they teamed up with ranchers in both the eastern and western parts of the state to offer seven cattle drives each year.

FOR FAMILIES. Families with young children should consider the X Hanging H, in the eastern part of Montana, near Glendive. Any child 6 or older who can ride (9 is the minimum for kids who have never ridden a horse) is welcome on the trail; those under 6 or nonriders can still go along in one of the covered wagons. On the June drive, 300–500 cattle are moved from the ranch to summer pastures, over rolling hills and through parts of the Yellowstone River Valley. You ride 8 to 12 miles a day and set up new campsites most, but not all, evenings. This drive finishes with fun back at the ranch: barrel racing and tests of other cowhand skills. In August the group "trails" about 500 yearlings from the ranch to market. The trip includes transportation between the ranch and the airport in Billings.

Over in western Montana, at the Rumney Ranch, all children must be experienced riders, and adults should have some experience, too. This land is a little steeper—50,000 acres of ranch right up against the Rockies. Fly in and out of Great Falls for these five drives in May, June, and September. Rumney runs more than 4,000 head of cattle, and you participate in all forms of ranch work. Guests stay in the bunkhouse or, depending on the weather, in tents. Plan on covering 10 to 25 miles a day; in spite of long hours moving cattle to different pastures, you do return to the ranch each night. You'll probably hear tall tales around the campfire, but the most spectacular evening entertainment at Rumney is the abundance of stars up above you.

 Laredo Enterprises, Box 2226, Havre, MT 59501, tel. 800/535–3802. May–Sept.: 7 days, $999–$1,329; wagon seat and no riding, $777–$999. Parents with 2 or more children get a 12% discount off the adult rate; also ask about day rates.

Montana High Country Cattle Drive

👫👤 12+

This organization of 10 Montana ranchers and outfitters is trying to diversify in order to keep their ranches as they've been for generations. John Flynn, whose family came into the area in the 1860s as miners and horse traders, is the group's point man. Soft-spoken but passionate about ranching and what that life has to offer, he believes participants in a working cattle drive go home with a new perspective on life. John's into perspective—he's also a novelist (see Resources, *below*).

FOR FAMILIES. You spend the first and last nights of the week at a ranch in Townsend and four days out on the trail about halfway between Bozeman and Helena, 30 miles from the source of the Missouri River. Each of the 35 participants is assigned to a wrangler. Whether you're a beginner or experienced, there's a place for you—five or six can even just ride in the wagon.

Depending on the drive, cattle travel from a 4,000-foot valley up to 7,000 feet, through sagebrush, juniper, yucca, and alpine meadows to lodgepole pine and spruce forests, or back down to the ranch. Views of Old Baldy rising nearly 10,000 feet in the Big Belt range remind you that this is Rocky Mountain country. Plan on four to six hours a day on the trail to move between 400 and 1,200 head of cattle 8 or so miles. This is a big drive; the herd is 1½ to 2 miles long. If you've never seen real cow dogs (usually Border collies and Australian shepherds) hard at work, here's your chance. They're remarkable animals.

In addition to a regular cook, the procession usually includes an authentic restored chuck wagon from which desserts—cobblers, cinnamon rolls, and homemade ice cream—are served. The outfitter can accommodate vegetarians; otherwise there's lots of barbecue. Entertainment might be a singer/poet or the "rattlesnake guy" who brings his snakes out for everyone to see and touch. John Flynn's brother, who has a master's degree in range management, shares his knowledge and demonstrates which desert plants are edible. *Montana High Country Cattle Drive, 669 Flynn La., Townsend, MT 59644, tel. 406/266–3534 or 800/345–9423. June–July: 7 days, $1,350.*

Off the Beaten Path

(🕻🕻 **ALL**)

Off the Beaten Path's Bill and Pam Bryan work with many of the West's best outfitters. Because their company specializes in custom vacations, they've had the opportunity to find out from both guests and outfitters exactly what makes a successful western vacation. They recommend two cattle outfits as terrific for families.

FOR FAMILIES. The rangeland of the All 'Round Ranch in Jensen, Utah, flanks the Blue Mountains and Dinosaur National Monument. All 'Round offers several cattle drives from March to September, but the July Family Course remains the best bet for parents and children. Al and Wann Brown, former Outward Bound leaders who run the program, say this adventure is the outgrowth of an OB course—"but geared more for fun." The minimum age is 12, and while the emphasis is on horsemanship, participants work with cattle, too, doing whatever needs to be done: moving cattle to new pastures, branding, and "doctoring" sick animals.

On this educationally oriented week, participants split their time between two campsites; there's a pond at one and a creek at the other. Both setups have tepees. You don't need to bring a thing—even sleeping bags and foul-weather gear are provided. Ask about other courses and drives; the minimum age for those is 16.

The Bassetts own three ranches; depending on the season and the work, your family will be at one or more of these. Spring drives start out at the Lovell Ranch in Wyoming, where the cattle winter. Summer ranch weeks and fall drives are based about 50 miles away in Montana at the Schively or Dryhead ranches. The Bassetts enjoy having kids around and don't have rigid age restrictions.

Ranch weeks, available throughout the summer, are especially appealing because even babies are welcome as long as parents take turns riding with the cattle. If you bring young children and are willing to watch them closely, the Bassetts can find something on the ranch for them to do. Ranch week guests help with chores such as pregnancy testing on cows, branding, rounding up strays, taking care of sick animals, moving the herd, and weaning calves. Your family stays in cabins or a bunkhouse with shared showers.

On the big drives, which move 250 to 300 cow/calf pairs over six days, kids as young as

5 or 6 can join the action if they are good riders. Wranglers stay in a cow camp with tepee tents and a chuck wagon.

🏠 *Off the Beaten Path, 109 E. Main St., Bozeman, MT 59714, tel. 406/586–1311 or 800/445–2995. Mar.–Oct.: 4–7 days, $700–$1,095.*

Rockin' R Ranch

👫 12+·

Thirty-seven miles north of Bryce Canyon National Park, the 1,000-acre Rockin' R is in a stunning area of Utah where redrock canyons open onto wide green valleys. Although the ranch has a guest capacity of more than 200, visitors still experience the land in a very personal way. People tend to be in different areas doing different things, and the cattle drives take only 20 guests at a time.

FOR FAMILIES. The ranch leases 5,000 acres from the forest service; drives take place within the borders of Dixie National Forest. The group stays at one of the ranch's two permanent cow camps. Sweetwater, at 7,000 feet, is set in the foothills of the Boulder Range among the pines, close to a natural spring. Griffin Springs camp edges a meadow at 10,000 feet; there's a lake and spring nearby. The camps have wall tents and mattresses, and food is plentiful. In October, when snow in the mountains is common, drives are based at the ranch.

Cowhands stay in the saddle about seven hours a day moving the cattle, helping doctor any sick stock, and checking miles of fence. Even when the 1,000 head of cattle split into two drives, the herd can still be as much as 2 miles long. Everyone is pretty tired at night, but there's singing around the campfire and entertainment by a cowboy poet at least one night. Deer, antelope, and elk are often seen on the trail. The Rockin' R

also offers horse pack trips (*see* Horse Packing).

🏠 *Rockin' R Ranch, Reservation Office, 1021 N. University Ave., Suite 205, Provo, UT 84601, tel. 801/344–8588. June–Oct.: 4–6 days, $695–$1,115 (includes 1 night at ranch before drive begins.)*

Resources

Organizations

The **Dude Ranchers' Association** (Box 471, LaPorte, CO 80535, tel. 970/223–8440) has information on 109 guest ranches in 13 western states. Not all of the ranches are working cattle ranches, but the association can identify these and help your family choose an appropriate one.

Besides the booking agents mentioned in this chapter you can can use **Pat Dickerman's adventure travel advisory service** (7550 E. McDonald Dr., Scottsdale, AZ 85250, tel. 602/596–0226 or 800/252–7899) to set up a cattle drive vacation. Pat has been in the adventure travel business for several decades.

Books

Montana Pursuit by J. T. Flynn (Aegina Press, tel. 304/429–7204) is Montana cattleman John Flynn's novel. He calls it "an adventure hunting mystery" with lots of local geography and color. If you're driving cattle with him, pick up a copy first.

Also See

If you want a western riding experience that is generally a bit slower and more relaxed than a cattle drive, turn to the Horse Packing chapter. The chapter on Ranches lists ranches where you may work with cattle.

COVERED WAGON ADVENTURES

Few experiences give families a feel for the Old West and pioneer life in the way a wagon train can. Some "modernization" to wagons (such as rubber tires and padded seats) means you'll be more comfortable than pioneers were, yet wagon masters today take great care to preserve the authenticity of the experience by following wagon train traditions and, in many cases, historic routes. Education is mixed with fun as guides spin stories about the men, women, and children who persevered in the face of tremendous difficulties to reach the West, and about the mountain men, Native Americans, and Pony Express riders who sometimes appeared on the trail.

Because wagon trains are easygoing adventures, they can accommodate a variety of ages in a way many western experiences cannot. Your family can, in most cases, ride saddle horses in addition to traveling in the wagons, but you certainly don't have to, so you don't need any special skills. All you need is a willingness to suspend disbelief and, for a few days, imagine you are traveling across the United States 150 years ago.

Questions to Ask

Can we help? Guests are often encouraged to help with camp chores and to learn traditional skills such as cooking over an open fire and driving the wagons. In some cases you are responsible for taking care of the horses and helping set up camp each night. Find out what's expected of your family and especially what the kids can do. Pitching in helps you re-create the real experience.

Are there horses to ride, too? Typically guests take turns riding a few saddle horses brought along for that purpose. On one wagon train all guests have the option to ride half of each day, but you don't have to ride. Some guests choose to walk part of the way, too, which is in keeping with what pioneer wagon trains were really like. The minimum age for riding horses may be higher than that for riding in the wagons.

What are the sleeping arrangements? Guests on most wagon train adventures sleep in tents provided by the outfitter, though on some trips you may sleep in the wagons. On still others, guests opt to sleep out under the stars, the way cowboys and pioneers did. If your children have never slept in sleeping bags or tents before, borrow equipment to try it out or let them test sleeping bags and tents at an outdoor store.

What kind of food is served? Hearty meals are the norm on these trips, with most offering standard chuckwagon fare—beef, beans, and biscuits are typical.

Some outfitters go further, with near-gourmet meals, including fresh salads and fruit as well as fresh-baked desserts.

What kinds of bathroom facilities are there? Several wagon trains pull a separate wagon with a chemical toilet or other toilet facility. Those that camp on forest service land have access to regular toilets or outhouses. Young children going into the wilderness for the first time may be reluctant to use unfamiliar kinds of toilets. Ask ahead of time so you can prepare your kids if necessary.

How many miles are covered each day? Traveling between 6 and 12 miles is typical. Wagons are not a speedy means of transportation; instead, they let you settle into a slower mode and take in the country and history in a relaxed way.

Will there be other recreational activities on the trip? Some trips do allow for hiking, swimming, or other activities at the campsites. On many trips, though, it takes an hour or two to set up camp once you arrive; then it's time for dinner and evening activities such as campfire programs and other western-style entertainment. This is why some outfitters think a child should be at least 6 for this experience. If you don't ride horses and if you get bored sitting, this may not be the trip for your family.

Are the guides knowledgeable about wagon train history and local lore, and about the area's wildlife and plant life? History—both human and natural—is a big part of a wagon train experience, so make sure guides are going to provide that.

Will there be surprise "attacks" during the trip? Although this is fun entertainment for most, young children may be scared by these re-creations of wagon train experiences. Even though outfitters don't like to ruin the surprise, explain that you need to prepare your child ahead of time.

What's included in the cost? Wagons, food, tents, and use of horses for at least part of the time are included on the trips, unless otherwise noted. In some cases you must bring your own sleeping bags. Some outfitters will pick up guests at a local airport or other location; others require you to get to the trailhead on your own. Because wagon trains generally start first thing in the morning and return in the afternoon, you'll probably have to arrange local lodging the night before the trip starts, and possibly at the end of the trip, too.

Instruction

A covered wagon adventure requires no prior experience or ability: If you don't know how to set up a tent, the crew will teach you and help you. If you or your kids don't know how to ride, you'll get some pointers. You'll only be traveling at a walk on the horses, so even the inexperienced should be just fine. On some wagon trains young children may not ride or may have to be led by parents. Take the opportunity to learn a new skill out on the trail, whether it's cooking over a fire or taking care of the horses: The majority of wagon masters and guides really want to share their knowledge with you.

Finding the Fun

Midwest: Grandtravel, Oregon Trail Wagon Train. **Rockies:** American Wilderness Experience, Carter County Wagon Train, Grandtravel, Myers Ranch Wagon Trains, Teton Country Wagon Train.

Favorite Wagon Trains

American Wilderness Experience

 5+

Old logging roads through Bridger-Teton National Forest, just outside the town of Jackson, Wyoming, provide ideal trails on which to relive a piece of American history. The Grand Tetons and the Gros Ventre and Wind River ranges form an authentic and inspiring backdrop. Wagons West, the outfitter with whom American Wilderness Experience contracts for this trip, will meet your family in Jackson and drive you to the trailhead, which is north of town toward Grand Teton and Yellowstone national parks.

FOR FAMILIES. Pioneers never had it quite so good. These wagons are cushioned with rubber tires and foam-padded seats that convert into deluxe bunks at night. You can expect four or five wagons on this train and a maximum of 25 people. One nice experience with this group is that they're happy to let guests help drive the wagons. Each guest also rides horseback for half of each day. Children as young as 7 or 8 can do this but must have riding experience; those 10 and up don't need previous experience. Most days there's time for fishing and hiking, and guests visit a historic homestead, too. At night, plan on cowboy singing around the campfire.

American Wilderness Experience, Box 1486, Boulder, CO 80306, tel. 303/444–2622 or 800/444–0099. June–Aug.: 4–6 days, $415–$700.

Carter County Wagon Train

 6+

The southeast corner of Montana, near the borders of South and North Dakota, is a land of steep hills and grasslands. This area, where Custer National Forest meets the Badlands, is typical of the terrain that wagon trains and pioneers struggled over on their journey west. Most of the trail for this wagon train runs through forested areas in Custer. There are no big tourist sites or tacky shops. "What you get here," says Eileen Larson, who with her husband, Keith, has been taking folks out on the wagon train for 13 years now, "is a real experience with real working cowboys and down-to-earth people."

FOR FAMILIES. The Larsons generally run one wagon train a summer but will schedule a second if there's enough interest. They can accommodate 50 to 75 people in five wagons and on horseback. Children as young as 3 can come along, but Eileen doesn't believe those younger than about 6 will really have a good time. Two-person tents are provided, and there are two big tents—one for girls, one for boys. Most of the kids, however, seem to prefer sleeping out under the stars. Each night around the campfire there's time for meeting fellow travelers, singing cowboy songs, listening to stories, and maybe even hearing real cowboy poetry.

The night before the wagon train starts, you can join the crew camping out at the trailhead (all gear provided by the Larsons will be there), or you might be able to stay overnight at the Larsons' large house. There's no extra charge for either.

🏠 *Carter County Wagon Train, Box 275, Ekalaka, MT 59324, tel. 406/775–6273. July: 3 days, $350–$700.*

Grandtravel

 7 – 17

Grandtravel's Western Parks, Western Space trip attempts to bring the romance and adventure of the West alive for grandparents and grandchildren. This itinerary, like all of Grandtravel's trips, is specifically designed to meet the needs of both senior citizens and young children; travel is primarily by motor coach. But that doesn't mean coddling: Grandtravel is for active people who love travel and new experiences. There's a lot to take in on this journey from Rapid City, South Dakota to Jackson, Wyoming—including a ride in a covered wagon.

FOR FAMILIES. Two trips—one for grandparents with grandkids 7 to 11, one for grandparents with grandchildren 12 to 17—are available each summer. The groups visit important landmarks, natural wonders, and national monuments and parks, and have a chance to meet Native Americans and cowboys who share their perspective on the West, past and present.

In Rapid City, members of the Lakota tribe give a presentation. In Cody, Wyoming, the groups visit the impressive Buffalo Bill Historical Center, which is four museums in one: the Buffalo Bill Museum, the Whitney Museum of Western Art, the Museum of the American Indian, and the Winchester Arms Museum. Here much of the history of

the West is captured in historical documents and art. You also stop at Mt. Rushmore in South Dakota and Devil's Tower in eastern Wyoming. There's lunch at Old Faithful in Yellowstone, and, in Sheridan, Wyoming, a visit to a historic ranch to see what life was really like in the early 1900s. One day, after a float trip on the Snake River, the group climbs into covered wagons, accompanied by cowboys and mountain men, for a trip to dinner in Cache Canyon outside of Jackson.

There is no camping on this adventure (lodging is in hotels with private baths), but still, the rugged beauty of the West and the strength and courage of its people are at the heart of this experience.

🏠 *Grandtravel, 6900 Wisconsin Ave., Suite 706, Chevy Chase, MD 20815, tel. 301/986–0790 or 800/247–7651. July–Aug.: 10 days, $2,815–$2,995. Per-person price depends on number of family members sharing accommodations.*

Myers Ranch Wagon Trains

6+

Sharon and Wayne Myers have a unique piece of property in southeastern Montana. It includes a portion of General Custer's last route from North Dakota to Miles City, Montana, and a section of the old Deadwood Stage route. Hills, pine forests, prairie, and badlands give families a taste of the varied terrain pioneers and wagon trains encountered. One highlight is the climb up a 3,000-foot hill for a view of four states: Montana, Wyoming, North Dakota, and South Dakota.

FOR FAMILIES. The Myerses will consider children younger than 6 but talk to them first to decide if this is something your child will handle well. To keep the trip small and personal, there are generally five or six wagons for up to 25 people. You can ride in the wagons (some are more comfortable than others, so guests are encouraged to exchange places) or spend some time riding a saddle horse. Although you don't need to be an advanced rider, you should have some experience—and you must have riding boots.

Along the way you see an old stagecoach stop with a barn and other buildings, and you visit a cave in which pioneers from the 1800s scratched their names and the date on the walls. At night, there's cowboy poetry, music, and a chance to dance around the campfire under a billion stars. This country is intriguing and beautiful at all times, but Sharon Myers believes June, when the grass is green and the deer and antelope—along with coyotes and wild turkeys—are out and about playing, is the best.

🏠 *Myers Ranch Wagon Trains, HC 80, Box 70, Ismay, MT 59336, tel. 406/772–5675. June–Aug.: 3–5 days, $660–$1,100.*

Oregon Trail Wagon Train

👫🏻 **5+**

The 2,000-mile-long Oregon Trail was the pioneer wagon route from Independence, Missouri, on the Missouri River, to the Columbia River region of the Pacific Northwest. In the 1840s alone, at least 10,000 pioneers made the arduous trek through northeastern Kansas, up along Nebraska's Platte River, and on to Ft. Laramie in Wyoming. From there, they crossed the Rockies at South Pass, journeyed through Snake River country, and, if they made it all the way, stopped finally in the Willamette Valley in Oregon. Today, as people rush across I-80 in minivans and RVs, it's hard to imagine what this journey was really like. If your family wants to know, though, you can find out with the Oregon Trail Wagon Train.

FOR FAMILIES. Starting from a base camp in Bayard, just north of the Platte River in western Nebraska, the wagon train makes a circle tour through rolling hills and prairie

along portions of the original Oregon Trail. Five wagons for 40 people is typical. Some wagons hold 16 passengers; some hold just 4. All of the guides—current or former cowboys or retired farmers—are well versed in the history of the Oregon Trail and the area.

Participants can ride in a different wagon each day to get a different perspective, and many choose to walk much of the route, as the original pioneers did. The group takes turns riding the saddle horses, too. At night, before turning into your tent and sleeping bag (both supplied), you might be surprised by a Pony Express delivery or an "Indian attack," after which the visitors will share stories and historical information. Guests are encouraged to participate in camp chores and to lend a hand with open-fire cooking.

Before or after your adventure, visit nearby Chimney Rock National Historic Site, the famous landmark on the Oregon Trail that marked the end of the prairie.

🏠 *Oregon Trail Wagon Train, Rte. 2, Box 502, Bayard, NE 69334, tel. 308/586–1850. June–Sept.: 4–6 days, $399–$579.*

Teton Country Wagon Train

👫🏻 **4+**

When the wagon master shouts "Roll the wagons!" the train rumbles onto the back roads of Targhee National Forest, between Grand Teton and Yellowstone national parks in Wyoming. These modern-day prairie schooners, originally named because they looked like "sails on a sea of grass," have rubber tires and padded seats but are authentic in every other detail. Teton Country Wagon Train is run by Billy Thomas, whose family history in the area dates back to 1854, when Billy's great-great-grandfather, Nick Wilson, passed through Jackson as the adopted son of a Shoshone chief. In 1889, Nick drove the first covered wagons over Teton Pass into Jackson Hole and a settlement that was eventually named Wilson—a name the town still bears.

FOR FAMILIES. Three wagons and up to 40 guests travel to a different area each day, forming a circle once camp has been reached. Two camps are on the shores of alpine lakes, where loons, trumpeter swans, moose, elk, and deer are likely to be seen. The wagon train arrives early enough that guests have time to hike, swim, canoe, or just relax. They take turns riding the saddle horses during the day and can ride them in camp, too. This range of recreational activities makes the trip perfect for younger children, who may need a change of pace to keep their interest up.

Meals are cooked in Dutch ovens over an open fire, and evenings are spent around the campfire, singing and listening to cowboy yarns. Mountain men, "Indians," and Pony Express riders will probably pay surprise visits during the trip. There are forest-service outdoor toilets at all campsites.

Guides will pick you up and drop you off at the Jackson airport for no extra charge. This is high country: You need lots of sunscreen during the day and warm clothes at night. **♠** *Teton Country Wagon Train, Box 2140, Jackson, WY 83001, tel. 307/733–3534 or 800/772–5386. July–Aug.: 4 days, $445– $595.*

Resources

Organizations

You can get information about the history of the Oregon Trail, as well as a reading list and other materials for families, from two groups: the **Oregon-California Trails Association** (Box 1019, Independence, MO 64051, tel. 816/252–2276) and **Jefferson National Expansion Memorial** (11 N. 4th St., St. Louis, MO 63102, tel. 314/425–6010).

Software

Your kids may have played **Oregon Trail** (Mecc) on the computer at home or school. You'll want to join them before heading out on a wagon adventure. It gives insights into life on the trail as well as good background information.

Also See

For more adventures that can take your family back to the days of the Old West, see Cattle Drives, Horse Packing, and Ranches.

CROSS-COUNTRY SKIING

ross-country, or Nordic, skiing has gained popularity in this country in recent years, and for good reason. The sport gives families a wonderful workout in the wintery outdoors, often at a lower cost than a downhill-skiing vacation. Although it may not hold the thrill of downhill skiing, neither does it suffer from the noise or the often crowded slopes. There's also less chance for injuries with this slower, more easygoing sport. Cross-country skiers stride and glide through silent, snowy forests; their skis can carry them into the heart of nature, to backcountry wilderness areas where they are more likely to encounter deer and all kinds of wildlife than to see other humans.

Although most cross-country ski lodges and day-use areas do not yet have the extensive children's programs found at downhill resorts, many do carry some child-size equipment. Some even have special sleds that parents can use to tow their youngest kids behind them as they ski. Lessons and other children's activities are most available during holidays, though some family activities may be offered year-round. Besides ski lodges, multiday tours with outfitters and even single-day ski classes are opportunities for cross-country ski adventures. Most lodges and outfitters have both groomed and ungroomed terrain, which is nice if your family has skiers of different ability.

The listings in this chapter are an eclectic mix of backcountry wilderness possibilities, courses, ranches, and those inns or lodges that have either new or innovative programs for families. This selection is by no means exhaustive: There are also hundreds of day-use lodges and ski centers throughout North America where cross-country skiing is available, as well as countless trail systems in national forests and parks that are used primarily by families who feel comfortable skiing without a guide. Also not here are some very well-known lodges that have been offering cross-country skiing for years; the listings focus on less-publicized establishments. Once your family gets into the sport, you will find thousands of miles of trails on which to hone your skills and enjoy serenity and winter beauty far from the madding crowds.

Questions to Ask

What kinds of skiing do you teach? Instruction in the traditional "diagonal" cross-country stride is commonly available and is most appropriate for families, because even fairly young children can master it. Skating, a style used by more experienced skiers, and telemark, a sort of cross between downhill and cross-country technique, may also be taught.

Are instructors certified by the Professional Ski Instructors Association? Some terrific skiers may not necessarily be great teachers of skiing. PSIA-certified instructors not only know how to ski, they've been taught how to teach. This can be especially important when it comes to children. Ask the lodge, school, or outfitter if instructors are certified and particularly if they are trained to work with kids; you want an instructor who will use age-appropriate language and have expectations that are on par with young students' skill and stamina levels.

What kind of clothing and equipment are needed? You work hard and get warm when you cross-country ski, so wearing layers of clothing is important. It's not generally necessary to invest in the expensive outerwear downhill skiers require. Fleece and wool garments and wind-resistant shells are good choices; all clothing should be breathable. Beyond this, the weather will dictate specific clothing needs. For equipment, skis, cross-country boots and poles are pretty much it. Many down-hill skiers like to take backpacks with them to carry extra clothing, water, and snacks. One tip for parents: If you ski with your children and they're slower than you are, wear extra clothes; you'll get cold going at their pace.

Is equipment available for rent? For children, too? Lodges and ranches usually rent skis, poles, and cross-country boots, but outfitters may not. If gear isn't available, ask for the name of a reputable rental shop in the area. In either case, be sure that the children's equipment will fit a child the size of yours—ask specific questions about what you need. Supplies of child-size items are often limited, so try to make reservations for equipment when you make your trip arrangements.

Are trails groomed or ungroomed? Groomed trails—those on which machines have packed down the snow and sometimes even preset tracks—are easier to ski. Families with beginner or intermediate skiers should look for a high ratio of groomed to ungroomed trails. In most cases you'll find a mix of trails, a plus if your family has skiers of different skill levels.

Is there terrain for all abilities? Look for ski territory with a combination of flat, open land, such as meadows, and steeper, more challenging terrain. It's typical for areas to cover a variety of landscapes.

How long are your trails? Do they connect to other systems? Most trail systems have a number of shorter loops and longer routes, so you can get away from the main area without committing to an all-day venture. Lodges and ranches often border national or state forests or recreation areas, and their trails may connect to a larger network of trails, usually ungroomed, where you can ski for long distances and have the wilderness practically to yourself.

What other activities are available? You will sometimes find sledding, hiking, wildlife viewing, riding, sleigh rides, and other outdoor winter activities in cross-country ski areas. Families who don't want to spend all of their time skiing will probably do best at a ranch or lodge.

What's included in the cost? Accommodations, meals, trail passes (if required), and activities are included in the fee for ranches and lodges, unless otherwise noted.

Equipment is occasionally part of a package, as is instruction, but more often costs extra. There may or may not be an extra charge for tours. Outfitters usually include lodging and meals on multiday trips, guide service, and permits (if necessary); equipment is generally extra. The price for schools covers instruction only, unless otherwise noted.

Instruction

Most guides and tour leaders will teach the basics of cross-country skiing, but if your goal is to develop more than a passing knowledge of the sport, choose a lodge, ranch, or school where instruction is the focus. That doesn't mean you have to spend a lot of time in classes before you can explore the great outdoors. Unlike beginning downhill skiers, who usually require a considerable amount of instruction before they can venture to most of the mountain, cross-country novices can ski many trails while they're still learning. Know your limits, though. Don't tackle long routes unless you're sure you have the stamina to finish—there may be no shortcuts back.

Finding the Fun

Northeast: Appalachian Mountain Club, Backroads, L.L. Bean, Telemark Inn. **Midwest:** Gunflint Northwoods Outfitters/Gunflint Lodge. **Rockies:** Adventures to the Edge, C Lazy U, Izaak Walton Inn, Lone Mountain Ranch, Off the Beaten Path. **West Coast:** Backroads. **Canada:** Wells Gray Park Backcountry Chalets.

Favorite Outfitters and Lodges

Adventures to the Edge

 ALL

Jean Pavillard, the former director of the Crested Butte Ski School, is well qualified to guide families into the Colorado backcountry. As a native of Switzerland, where alpine activities are part of daily life, Jean brings a perspective not often found among American-born guides: that skiing and mountaineering can be shared by all ages. As the father of two young skiers, he is well versed in finding innovative ways to take kids into wilderness areas. Jean and his partners will custom design a backcountry experience on which your family will both learn and push the limits of your imaginations and abilities.

Customized trips are the company's specialty but by no means its only offering. One unusual activity, common in Europe, is alpine ski touring, with gear that resembles a cross between downhill and cross-country skis. The heels of touring bindings can be freed for ascending slopes (like those on cross-country skis) and snapped down for downhill terrain (like those on downhill skis).

FOR FAMILIES. The fondue-dinner ski tour is a popular option for families. You ski a 2-mile route out to a wilderness hut and eat dinner next to a roaring fire; if you have children too young to ski, Jean or his guides will pull them in a cozy sled. The evening can end with dinner, or you can stay overnight at the hut. If your family wants a longer adventure, the company uses several huts and yurts in the mountains around Crested Butte, and guided hut-to-hut adventures can be arranged for all abilities and for any length from a day to a week.

Instruction is part of every adventure, but some tours and routes are still best for families with older children or for those who have considerable ski experience. Beginners should take a lesson and go on a half-day outing before heading out on longer excursions.

🏠 *Adventures to the Edge, Box 91, Crested Butte, CO 81224, tel. 303/349–5219 or 800/349–5219. Nov.–May: ½–7 days; $15–$55 for tour and dinner, $135–$195 for ski tour and lessons, $280–$300 per day for private guide on custom trip, depending on group size and destination.*

Appalachian Mountain Club

👫 6+

The Appalachian Mountain Club (AMC) is perhaps best known for its hiking programs and other summer activities (*see* Fishing, Hiking and Backpacking, *and* Trekking with Llamas, Goats, and Burros), but it does offer a few winter courses. AMC's Catskill campus—near Phoenicia, New York, in the heart of the Catskill Mountains—is just 8 miles from an excellent cross-country area, Frost Valley Ski Center. You can bring your own skis or rent equipment at Frost Valley; lodging and meals for families are in the Valley View Lodge, AMC's Catskill center.

FOR FAMILIES. The Frost Valley Ski Center generally holds Cross-country Skiing for Families courses each February; the AMC group has its own instructors, usually two for a class of about 20 students. Whether your family includes accomplished skiers or "never-evers," this course is for you. Families are taught together; learning games keep children interested, but the instruction meets the needs of all ages. Instructors cover tech-

niques for negotiating both uphill and downhill terrain, as well as how to ski flat terrain using the traditional diagonal stride.

🏠 *Appalachian Mountain Club, Box 298, Gorham, NH 03581, tel. 603/466–2727 (catalog) or 518/624–2056 (Catskill campus). Feb.: 2 days, $175; 50% discount for ages 6–12, 10% discount for AMC members. Price does not include nominal day-use fee for Frost Valley.*

Backroads

👫 14+

Like its stellar biking and hiking tours, Backroads' cross-country ski vacations are a mix of adventure and pampering, with rugged workouts on skis during the day and relaxing stays in elegant country inns at night. Food served on the trips is of gourmet quality. Beyond the luxurious touches, the best thing about Backroads' ski programs is their flexibility. Trips are geared toward beginners, but itineraries accommodate advanced skiers, too. Formal and informal instruction is offered daily, and there's a choice of groomed or ungroomed trails and easy or challenging terrain. Some participants ski only 3 or 4 miles a day, while others cover 10 or more—a range that allows families to ski together or apart as they choose. Rental equipment is available. The best trips for families are tours in California's Sierra Nevada range and in northeastern Vermont.

FOR FAMILIES. While Backroads does not run family-only ski trips, teens are always welcome to accompany parents. Groups generally consist of 18 to 20 guests accompanied by two leaders certified in cross-country instruction. The Sierras trip begins in Soda Springs, near the largest cross-country ski resort in the country, Royal Gorge; lodging for two nights is in the resort's Rainbow Lodge, built in the 1920s. The group takes lessons from Royal Gorge's excellent instructors before exploring the varied terrain of Tahoe National Forest. The next stop is

Truckee, site of the first California ski club and the historic Truckee Hotel. Trails at Tahoe Donner Cross-Country Ski Resort pass through pine and aspen forests, and beginners will find ski heaven in the broad meadows of Euer Valley. There's also a visit to the Resort at Squaw Creek, where you can continue the cross-country life or go vertical at one of the country's great downhill areas. Because both Royal Gorge and the Resort at Squaw Creek are large, first-class resorts, teens will probably find plenty to do and may even find skiing buddies.

The Vermont tour, which centers around New England inns and quiet, pastoral ski settings, may be less exciting for teens, but it does visit Stowe, where participants have a choice of downhill or cross-country skiing. Between stays at the gracious Inn on the Common in Craftsbury Common and the Georgian-style Edson Hill Manor in Stowe, the group takes lessons at the Craftsbury Nordic Ski Center and explores the scenic trails of the Stowe Recreation Path and Mount Mansfield Nordic Center.

Backroads, 1516 5th St., Suite L102, Berkeley, CA 94710, tel. 510/527–1555 or 800/462–2848. Jan.–Mar.: 5–6 days, $1,300–$1,400; 10% discount for ages 14–16.

C Lazy U

3+

This ranch, tucked high in the Colorado Rockies in a valley carved by Willow Creek, has been hosting guests since 1925. Its summer family programs are excellent, but C Lazy U is also a winter wonderland, a paradise for cross-country skiers looking for backcountry adventure in the daytime and serious pampering at night. You can wander over 15 miles of groomed trails and 5,000 acres of unspoiled wilderness (the ranch owns 2,000 of them). Instructors and guides will help you make the most of your skiing, whether you prefer diagonal style, skating, or telemark. Downhill skiers are not forgot-

ten—the ranch provides shuttle service to nearby Winter Park and SilverCreek.

FOR FAMILIES. The ranch's comprehensive children's program is divided into three age groups (3–5, 6–12, and teens) and runs for the two weeks around Christmas and New Year's and over the Presidents' Day weekend. Group sizes vary widely, depending on the number of guests with kids. While adults are on the trails, children receive daily ski instruction and participate in other winter activities. Ski games, tubing on the hill, sledding, broomball hockey, and being pulled on an inner tube behind a snowmobile are favorite snow sports, and indoor crafts are offered, too. A skating pond is lighted at night, and there are skates in all sizes.

Families can also head out together to ski the groomed trails or the backcountry. At the ranch's Nordic center, cross-country ski gear (part of the price) comes in many sizes—there are even strap-on skis for very small children.

For horse lovers, C Lazy U has a winter riding program. You can use the 10,000-square-foot indoor arena or wander through the valley and mountains on silent, snowy trails for a riding experience that's unique to the season. Levi and Strauss, the ranch's Belgian draft horses, can take you for a whirl in an old-fashioned sleigh.

C Lazy U, Box 379, Granby, CO 80446, tel. 303/887–3344. Dec.–Jan. and Feb.: 5–7 days, $900–$1,250; for children under 18, 20%–40% discount during Christmas season, 40% in February.

Denver Museum of Natural History

14+

In February Yellowstone National Park is a profoundly different and more peaceful place than it is in warmer months. Frost, wind, ice, and snow sculpt fantastic shapes on the uncrowded landscape. Steam and vapor rise in eerie clouds around geysers that are all but unvisited in winter. This is the time to take in the true natural beauty of the park—and what better way than on cross-country skis?

Every year the Denver Museum of Natural History schedules a ski trip though the park. Besides phenomenal skiing, an added bonus is that two professors from area universities come along to provide an enlightening educational component. Highlights are classes on Yellowstone's winter wildlife, animal tracking, and the famous geysers and hot springs, and a slide show on the reintroduction of wolves to the park. Accommodations include the historic Mammoth Hot Springs Lodge and Old Faithful Lodge; ski rentals are available at both.

FOR FAMILIES. This trip is not specifically geared to families, but parents and teens with an interest in skiing and a desire to unravel winter's mysteries are welcome. You don't need to be an expert skier. Each day participants can choose between two ski outings, one of 5 to 7 miles and one of 7 to 12 miles. You should be in good physical condition, but the pace is a pretty relaxed 2 to 3 mph. The group of 16 to 20 participants is led not only by the professors but also by two guides from the Four Corners School of Outdoor Education, which cosponsors the trip. Guides give ski instruction each day to all participants who want it.

🏠 *Denver Museum of Natural History, 2001 Colorado Blvd., Denver, CO 80205, tel. 303/370–6304. Feb.: 8 days, $1,725.*

Gunflint Northwoods Outfitters/Gunflint Lodge

 ALL

At this four-season resort in northern Minnesota, families can take guided and self-guided ski adventures along more than 60 miles of groomed and tracked trails through Superior National Forest, which borders the

Boundary Waters Canoe Area. Trails range from a flat, easy, 3-mile loop to longer routes over more challenging terrain.

FOR FAMILIES. Families booking the Skiing Adventure Week package get two half-day guided treks. The lodge doesn't have formal lessons, but if you need instruction, a staff member will fill you in on the basics; then it's up to you. The Kerfoots, owners of the Gunflint lodge, recommend 8 as a good minimum age for children to accompany parents on the trails, though good skiers often carry babies in backpacks. One convenient feature of this area is that four resorts on Gunflint Lake work together; families are welcome to stop at any of these to call for a pickup if the kids—or their parents—get too tired to make it back on skis. Out on the trails, three warming huts with radiant propane heaters make convenient rest stops; the heaters are on timers, so you don't even have to remember to turn them off when you leave.

Although the wilderness skiing is superb, not everyone in your family has to be a cross-country skier to enjoy the lodge. You can relax in a sauna or hot tub or accompany your children on a stroll to search for wildlife. Be sure to head to the main lodge every day at 3:30, when the Kerfoots put 50 pounds of corn out in the yard and dozens of wild deer arrive for an afternoon snack. At night, you can bundle the family up and walk out on the lake for some amazing star-gazing.

🏠 *Gunflint Northwoods Outfitters/Gunflint Lodge, 750 Gunflint Trail, Grand Marais, MN 55604, tel. 800/362–5251. Dec.–Mar.: 7 days, $695; 50% discount for ages 4–12, children under 4 free.*

Izaak Walton Inn

 3+

One of the great cross-country ski inns, Izaak Walton is about 60 miles from Kalispell, just outside Glacier National Park in Montana. Now listed in the National Register of Historic Places, the inn was built in 1939 by the Great Northern Railroad to house snow-removal crews. Memorabilia and authentic furnishings carry you back to the romantic era of train travel, and four renovated cabooses have been converted into guest quarters. Amtrak still stops practically at the door.

FOR FAMILIES. The inn has always had superb lessons and tours for adults and experienced skiers, but the same could not be said of its classes for young guests. Happily, this has changed. Jay Richards, the cross-country director, has introduced playful, innovative programs for kids. Games and fun activities help build skills and get children used to the winter outdoors. Depending on how many children are present, lessons may be on an individual or group basis. The inn has trails and areas appropriate for young children just learning to ski and rents equipment for ages 3 or 4 and up (depending on size); snowshoes are also available, but the smallest rental size is an adult four.

Packages are the best way to go here. Families staying on the inn's five- or seven-day plan are entitled to a guided ski tour of Glacier National Park. The all-day tour is best for teens and adults, but Richards can lead groups with younger children on half-day tours over Glacier's easier trails. Another activity for families is kick sledding. These fun Scandinavian sleds work something like those used for mushing—but with no dogs. You balance on the runner with one foot and push with the other; since the action is similar to skiing, it's an easy way to get a feel for the sport while having a great time.

🏨 *Izaak Walton Inn, Box 653, Essex, MT 59916, tel. 406/888–5700. Nov.–Mar.: 3–7 days, $265–$755 per person for family of 3; children's rates on 5- and 7-day packages only.*

L.L. Bean

 5+

L.L. Bean, the famous outdoor and catalog store in Freeport, Maine, has long stocked winter gear and clothing for families, so it's not surprising that its education department—well known for canoeing and fly-fishing courses—also provides instruction in cross-country skiing.

FOR FAMILIES. The primary family-oriented course is the L.L. Bean Cross-Country Ski Festival, which generally takes place in early February at the Gould Academy in Bethel, Maine. This workshop runs over a weekend (9–3:30 both days) and teaches families how to ski and how to have fun on the trails. The entire course is conducted on skis over groomed terrain with a mix of easy, moderate, and challenging trails. Instructors stress learning how to get your balance, sliding, and feeling confident on skis; they also discuss proper clothing and how to stay warm while skiing. You must arrange your own lodging, but the school will supply a list of local accommodations. Although it's best to bring your own equipment, you can rent gear in a variety of sizes; manufacturers display demo equipment at the festival, too.

In addition to ski lessons, there are dogsled rides and snowshoe demonstrations. Kids over 7 years old can try the biathlon, a sport that combines cross-country skiing and target shooting; members of the U.S. Biathlon team are on hand to give demonstrations and tips.

Adult-oriented courses, which kids 14 and up can take with their parents, are scheduled most Saturdays throughout the ski season. These courses are taught on a golf course in Freeport that has groomed tracks; you'll get information on both diagonal skiing and skating, and the focus is on finding your own comfort level on cross-country skis. These courses are just 1½ hours long, but instructors may take an additional 15 minutes at the end of class to answer students' questions about specific problems. Although equipment isn't provided, you can rent it at the L.L. Bean store.

 L.L. Bean, Freeport, ME 04033, tel. 207/865–4761. Jan.–Feb.: $15–$35; kids under 15 are free in the family course.

Lone Mountain Ranch

 3+

Lone Mountain is a year-round family guest ranch in Montana's Gallatin Canyon, down the road from Big Sky and a short drive from the northernmost border of Yellowstone National Park. The ranch's renowned naturalists don't stop working in winter; instead, they lead cross-country ski tours, including treks into the Spanish Peaks region and Yellowstone's backcountry, that meld excellent skiing with education about the winter environment and the area's natural history. Even lunch on the trail is impressive—a buffet is set out on huge blocks of snow. The 23 roomy, one- and two-bedroom log cabins at the ranch have rock fireplaces or Franklin stoves in addition to electric heat; the outdoor hot tub is popular with all ages; and no one misses gourmet meals in the tremendous log-and-stone dining room.

FOR FAMILIES. There's no formal children's program at Lone Mountain during the winter, but children are always welcome. Group lessons are an option if enough kids are at the ranch; otherwise, individual instruction can be arranged. Rental equipment fits ages 3 and up. Lone Mountain has nearly 50 miles of tracked and groomed trails that wind through meadows, up along ridges, down into mountain valleys, and through portions of the Gallatin National Forest. Miles of ungroomed trails give guests access to exceptional backcountry skiing.

A particular favorite with families is the groomed Ranch Loop, a 3½-mile trail across rolling terrain through aspen groves and open meadows. Ermines, moose, coyotes,

or a variety of winter birds may be seen along the trail. Because the trail passes near ranch buildings but also goes into wilderness areas, you feel close to home and miles away simultaneously, which can be comforting for kids and beginners.

Among the backcountry tours with naturalists (all extra charge), Spanish Peaks is appropriate for teens and adults with skiing experience. Yellowstone is less technical, and skiers who are over 7 are welcome on the shorter (four- to five-hour) tour over moderate terrain. Before joining a tour, every guest must take one lesson or be otherwise evaluated by the staff.

Families also have the option to snowshoe, skate, go sledding, or head for the downhill slopes at Big Sky, 7 miles away. Horse-drawn sleighs can carry guests to a lantern-lighted log cabin for dinner cooked on a century-old wood stove.

Lone Mountain Ranch, Box 160069, Big Sky, Montana 59716, tel. 406/995–4644. Dec.–Apr.: 7 days, $560–$1,250. Price does not include rentals and lessons.

Off the Beaten Path

12+

Although Pam and Bill Bryan of Off the Beaten Path are known primarily for their custom Rocky Mountain summer vacations, their organization also offers a variety of winter escapes, including cross-country ski adventures. Yellowstone on Skis, Tetons/Absarokas Adventure, and Glacier to Oneself are three of the company's popular ski excursions. Typical of the accommodations you can choose from are the historic Mammoth Hot Springs Hotel in Yellowstone and the Izaak Walton Inn (*see above*), just outside Glacier National Park.

FOR FAMILIES. Although the scheduled cross-country ski trips are not geared toward children, the company works with many families on a custom basis, meaning you can adapt one of the trips with regard to timing, destination, and the amount and level of activity. Custom trips are definitely pricey, but every detail—accommodations, food, guide services, and daily skiing—is taken care of. Your guide can take you on a variety of trails, from groomed to pure untracked backcountry powder, and instruct you on skiing techniques; you'll also learn about the diverse ecosystems through which you venture.

Access to Yellowstone is limited, so you must book a custom trip there at least nine months in advance. The other destinations are more flexible—even last-minute arrangements may be possible. The company can also arrange all travel and ski rentals (extra charge) if you wish.

 Off the Beaten Path, 109 E. Main St., Bozeman, MT 59715, tel. 406/586–1311 or 800/445–2995. Dec.–Mar.: 5–6 days, $1,500–$2,000; custom nonguided trips available for less.

Telemark Inn

👫 ALL

The turn-of-the-century Telemark Inn, 10 miles from Bethel in southwestern Maine, has its pick of adjectives: Rustic, elegant, intimate, remote, and historic all accurately describe the wood-paneled retreat, which has hand-built cabinetry and a huge stone fireplace. Well-known for its family-friendly llama treks in summer (see Trekking with Llamas, Goats, and Burros), the inn becomes a winter mecca for families who like to cross-country ski. Six rooms sleep two to four guests each, and everybody likes the wood-fired hot tub and sauna. Many different lodging packages are available, some with breakfast only, some with three meals. You can also get hearty home-cooked meals packed for the trail.

FOR FAMILIES. Twenty-two kilometers (14 miles) of groomed trails, most of them wide and tracked for both traditional diagonal skiing and the more difficult skating style,

surround the inn. Families with ski experience may want to head into the maintained trails beyond the inn, which are part of the backcountry system of the White Mountain National Forest. At night there's skating on a pond lighted by kerosene lanterns, and parents can choose a romantic ride in a horse-drawn sleigh built for two or a family outing in the six-seater.

Instruction in both traditional skiing and telemark is available for an extra charge. Families have the option to rent equipment even for very young children; you should request it when you make your reservation. Parents can strap on a pulk—a ski sled that can be used to pull toddlers—if their stamina and skiing ability allow. Small children learn to ski by holding on to a nylon rope with a handle (like those used for waterskiing) and being pulled by parents or instructors to get the feel of ski movements. *Telemark Inn, RFD 2, Box 800, Bethel, ME 04217, tel. 207/836–2703. Dec.–Mar.: 2–5 days, $125–$375.*

Wells Gray Park Backcountry Chalets

👫 12+

Of the three chalets owned and operated by this group, only Fight Meadow Chalet is really suitable for family cross-country skiing. If you're up to the challenge of a helicopter flight in and several days of skiing in wilderness areas inaccessible to the less adventurous, this Canadian company, based eight hours from Seattle, Edmonton, and Calgary, will provide a memorable guided experience for your family. Once you have plenty of experience and knowledge of backcountry safety and survival skills, you can book the chalets on your own, including the two that require heavy ski-touring and ski-mountaineering equipment.

FOR FAMILIES. The guides don't give lessons in cross-country skiing, but they do educate families on wilderness travel, ski mountaineering, and avalanche safety. Fight Meadow Chalet is surrounded by a large alpine meadow system that is ideal for novice skiers in spite of its remoteness. More advanced slopes are also easily accessible, so there's something for everyone. Families take a helicopter in; the inbound flight is part of the trip cost. Unless they're up for a four- to eight-hour trek (depending on skiing ability), most are also flown out. The road out is the only marked trail; the rest of your skiing is on unmarked, ungroomed, untracked backcountry snow. Scheduled trips to the chalet are limited, but groups of 6 to 12 can arrange their own trip on the dates of their choice.

🏠 *Wells Gray Park Backcountry Chalets, Box 188, Clearwater V0E 1N0, British Columbia, Canada, tel. 604/587–6444. Dec.–Apr.: 5 days, $500; 30% discount for children under 15. Helicopter flight out is $80 per person.*

Resources

Organizations

The **Cross Country Ski Area Association** (259 Bolton Rd., Winchester, NH 03470, tel. 603/239–4341) has information on how to get started in the sport and great places to do it. Beginners should ask for the sheet explaining why lessons are important and how to dress properly.

Periodicals

The Best of Cross Country Skiing is a directory of more than 200 member areas, primarily in North America, published by the Cross Country Ski Area Association (see *above*). Listings have general and technical information, as well as notes on things of special interest to families, such as whether or not the area has equipment rentals for children, day care, programs for kids, and specially tracked trails for children or other child-oriented trails. You must mail in for the directory; the cost is $3.00.

Products

Nordlig Imports (10962 W. Hampden Pl., Denver, CO 80227, tel. 303/692–4815) imports a Norwegian kick sled called a Spark (the word for "kick" in Norwegian) in four sizes appropriate for toddlers through tall adults. Infant seat carriers are also available for the sleds, as are special floats for powder snow. If the lodge you want to go to doesn't already have these terrific sleds, consider buying your own.

Also See

For more winter adventures, check out Dogsledding. Many of the adventures also include some cross-country skiing.

DIGGING FOR DINOSAUR BONES AND OTHER FOSSILS

Dinosaurs may be extinct in the real world, but they're alive and well in the hearts and minds of children everywhere. Long before that purple phenomenon Barney, dinosaurs were a formidable presence in children's books, games, TV shows, movies, and imaginations. Ask your average 5-year-old how to pronounce *hadrosaur* and she'll tell you without stumbling over a syllable. When my own daughter, Kira, was 5, she would quiz her father and me about dinosaurs endlessly, but we never reached her level of expertise. If Dinamation International Society's Family Dino Camp had existed back then, I would have taken her in a flash.

Today families can choose among places all over the world where they can dig for bones and help in paleontological labs. Most of these digs are dinosaur related; however, whale fossils, mammoth and saber-toothed tiger bones, and plant fossils are found at working digs, and you or someone in your family might be the first to uncover them for all the world to see.

Paleontology is mostly painstaking, slow, hot, and tedious work. Consider in advance whether your child has a real interest and the personality to enjoy this type of vacation. Even Dino Camp, which offers a variety of child-friendly activities, is best for kids who already appreciate the subject. Some children do, of course, discover a love of paleontology once they get into it, but it could just as easily turn out the other way around. Teens and parents, too, should fully discuss the itinerary, accommodations, hours, and location of a particular trip before committing. These experiences are definitely work. They're also great fun—if you're into it—and always an incredible learning experience. The best news is that at the end of a few days at a bona fide dig, parents just might be able to match their offsprings' knowledge, if not their all-embracing love, of these prehistoric wonders.

Questions to Ask

Is it possible to talk directly to the expedition coordinator or leader? In many cases, this is a prerequisite. The trip leader wants to make sure that you are right for the trip and that you're aware of what the expedition entails. For parents, it's especially important to discuss a child's ability, experience, and interest with someone who's been out in the field.

What are the typical conditions? Some work sites are extremely primitive; others are in towns with modern conveniences and amenities. You might be in the desert or by the ocean. Knowing the conditions can help you find the expedition that meets your family's needs.

What are the accommodations? Tents, dorms, hotel rooms, condos, government or university housing—all these are possibilities. What can your family handle? How well will you fit into community housing? This is an important consideration for any trip.

Has an expedition uncovered an important fossil lately? Dreams of a big find are part of the draw for this kind of vacation. Ask in advance how many bones or fossils have been uncovered at that particular site, and how many have been uncovered by trip participants like you. Neither you nor your children should have unreasonable expectations, but dreams are definitely in order.

Is there lab work or other work related to digging? You might have a chance to assist in a real paleontological lab; you might be asked to record, sketch, or keep notes out in the field. Analyzing soil samples or amber could be part of your duties. Paleontology encompasses a variety of skills.

What kind of clothing is needed? Much digging work is hot and dirty. You may also hike long distances, and digs may or may not provide shade or shelter from the sun. Even in the desert, the best clothing may be long-sleeved cotton shirts and long pants. Boots are probably preferable to sandals on many sites, and hats can be an important accessory. Review clothing lists carefully, paying particular attention to sun protection.

Will my child and I spend all of our time together? Usually this is the case, but at places such as Dinamation International Society's Dino Camp, you don't.

What else is there to do? Is there anywhere to swim? Time to hike or bike or eat out or shop? Are there museums or other local points of interest to visit? Some trips provide opportunities for such activities; other digs, particularly those in remote areas, are strictly geared toward accomplishing work. If this matters to you, choose accordingly.

What does the expedition cost include? Accommodations, food during the trip (participants often help with cooking), and local transportation are included, unless otherwise noted. Transportation to and/or from the expedition site is usually extra. Expeditioners who will be camping out will probably need to bring their own sleeping bags and perhaps their tents. Because accommodations vary greatly, be sure to find out what you're paying for.

Instruction

It's assumed that most people do not know a great deal about the intricacies of digging for fossils, so lectures, talks, and hands-on lessons are very much part of the fun on this type of adventure. Reading lists of books and other materials about paleontology are often part of the pretrip information for expeditions. Any advance reading you do will definitely enhance your family's experience.

Finding the Fun

Midwest: Earthwatch. **Southwest:** Dinamation International Society. **Rockies:** Dinamation International Society, Earthwatch. **Mexico:** Dinamation International Society. **Great Britain, Australia:** Earthwatch.

Favorite Expeditions

Dinamation International Society

👥 6+

Dinamation International Society (DIS) is a nonprofit organization that promotes education, research, and preservation in the biological, earth, and physical sciences, with a special emphasis on dinosaur paleontology. If the name Dinamation sounds familiar, that's because another branch of the outfit manufactures the robotic dinosaurs that DIS has toured at various museums. DIS works with universities, museums, and public land management agencies on projects including the identification and protection of important fossil sites. One of the society's main contributions to research and education, however, is the Dinosaur Discovery Expeditions program, which helps fund research work and creates ongoing public awareness of important paleontological work.

FOR FAMILIES. Family Dino Camp, for ages 6 and up, is probably the most well known of DIS's expeditions. The camp, based in Fruita and Grand Junction, Colorado, mixes learning fun and games, serious digging, lab work, hikes, and time at DIS's stellar facility, Devil's Canyon Science and Learning Center. Kids don't actually dig at the Mygatt-Moore Quarry where loads of fossils have been found, but parents do. Young Dino Campers excavate fossil replicas, do simulated lab work, and hike the Trail through Time to see fossils embedded in area rocks. They join parents for a variety of dino-related activities, from studying plant fossils to solving a dinosaur murder mystery. The camp runs in the summer only, and accommodations are at local motels. A few, but not all, meals are included.

One recent major discovery at the Mygatt-Moore Quarry was an egg—the only egg of an armored dinosaur (a nodosaur, to be exact) ever found. It was uncovered not by a renowned paleontologist but by a 14-year-old girl on a DIS expedition. She was participating in the five-day Colorado Canyons Expedition, which runs spring through fall and is open to ages 13 and up. You or someone in your family might be lucky enough to discover another fossil that will make its way into paleontological history.

Ages 16 and up can choose among expeditions with digs in Colorado, Utah, Wyoming, and Arizona. A trip in Mexico, once open only to those over 17, is now available for families with younger children on a case-by-case basis. Jonathan Cooley, DIS's director of expeditions, has an excellent sense of how children and teens will do on a particular trip. Talk to DIS if you have a dino-maniac. They'll find you a dig that will satisfy those prehistoric obsessions and open the door to the world of scientific research. Accommodations for these adventures range from camping to first-class hotels.

🏔 *Dinosaur Discovery Expeditions, Dinamation International Society, 550 Crossroads Ct., Fruita, CO 81521, tel. 800/344–3466. Year-round (all trips not available at all times): 5–8 days, $575–$1,325.*

Earthwatch

 16+

Earthwatch helps fund five different fossil-finding programs, in addition to dozens of other types of scientific projects around the world. As part of that funding, Earthwatch arranges for adventurous participants to join scientists on site and work as assistants. Your fee partially defrays the cost of running the project. As scientists find it increasingly difficult to get funding from more traditional sources such as the government and universities, organizations like Earthwatch become even more valuable.

FOR FAMILIES. Scholars have been in Oxford, England, only a short time compared to the mammoths who stomped around the region some 200,000 years ago. Today the mammoths' fossils, along with those of many other animals, insects, and plants, make up one of the richest sites in Europe—and it's only about 15 minutes from Oxford University. You stay in bed-and-breakfasts and work closely with the University Museum of Oxford. For a different experience, Earthwatch offers a trip to the Australian outback to uncover and catalog fossil fruits. Once a rain forest, the area is desert now, remote and fascinating. Families can also assist researchers at a new dig in Triassic Park, in San Juan, Argentina.

Closer to home, at a dig in central Montana, Dr. Keith Rigby is working to prove his theory that dinosaurs died out because of changing climatic conditions to which they were unable to adapt. Another Earthwatch dig is in Hot Springs, South Dakota, a famous mammoth site. Here, in the southwest corner of the state, locals are justifiably proud of their mammoths. They've raised money to fund continued research and helped build a complex over the site that shades workers from the sun and allows tourists to watch the digging. Expedition

participants stay in local homes and can expect a warm welcome from Hot Springs residents. Accommodations on other trips include tents, inns, and private houses.

Scientists ask Earthwatch for funding throughout the year, so sites do change. Ask for the latest information when you call. ⌂ *Earthwatch, 680 Mt. Auburn St., Box 403BO, Watertown, MA 02272, tel. 617/926–8200 or 800/776–0188. June–Sept.: 10–15 days, $1,395–$1,895.*

Resources

Books

Many children's book publishers have dinosaur books, but Dorling Kindersley offers one-stop shopping for dinosaur lovers. Titles for younger children include *The Big Book of Dinosaurs, Incredible Dinosaurs,* and the *Ultimate Dinosaur Sticker Book.* Older kids and adults can check out *Dinosaurs and How They Lived, Prehistoric Life, The Ultimate Dinosaur Book, The Visual Dictionary of Dinosaurs,* and *The Visual Dictionary of Prehistoric Life.* If you want a reference to fit in your pocket, there's *Pocket Dinosaurs.*

Dinosaur Safari Guide by Vincenzo Costa (Voyageur Press, tel. 612/430–2210 or 800/888–9653) lists more than 160 dinosaur quarries, museums, parks, or trails throughout the United States and Canada. Costa also provides an excellent pronunciation guide and solid introductory material about dinosaurs, as well as a discussion of current extinction theories.

Also See

If digging is what you love to do, look into family camps at ancient Native American ruins and other types of digs listed in Archaeology Adventures.

DOGSLEDDING

Dogsledding may well be on the farthest edge of "soft" adventure. This is not a sport for timid spirits; it's not for the adventurer who wants excitement but who doesn't want to push his or her limits. Working with the dogs is physically demanding and involves spending a lot of time in the cold—bone-chilling cold. Temperatures as low as 40° below zero are common, and if you are miles out in the wilderness, you can't suddenly change your mind about the trip. You must be prepared, and you must really want to go. That goes for your children, too. They need to be ready for cold, hard work, including caring for the dogs, and real wilderness.

But if the thrill and romance of dogsledding appeals to your family, you'll find it to be one of the all-time great adventures. Dogs run at a fairly fast pace—it's not uncommon to travel 30 or 40 miles in a day—so you can cover a fair amount of wintry territory. By the end of your trip you'll feel a closeness to your dogs, to your guides (some of whom are natives whose people have traveled this way for generations), and to the raw and wild land through which you'll dash. Ask anyone who's ever done it. They'll tell you the experience changed them, and that they are the better for it.

Questions to Ask

Will we mush our own sled and dogs? Some trips give every participant a sled to work; on other trips you share sleds and spend time snowshoeing and cross-country skiing in addition to mushing (as traveling by dogsled is called). Decide what activity your family wants most and go with the outfitter that provides it.

How many miles are covered each day? Typically, anywhere from 15 to 35 miles traveled over a four- to eight-hour period make up a day of mushing, though there are variations. Ask before you sign up, and consider the strenuousness of an itinerary and your family's abilities before making a final decision.

What kind of accommodations and meals are there? Cabins, tents, igloos, and even hotel rooms are possibilities. Winter camping can be surprisingly cozy and comfortable, but if it's not for you, or if you have younger children who might not be up to this challenge, choose an outfitter with more permanent lodging. As for meals, some outfitters offer a selection, and much of the food is incredibly good. Even if it isn't, it tastes great in the frozen wilderness. Food is fuel out in the cold, so most meals are the real stick-to-your-ribs type: stews, chili, spaghetti, and lasagna, and snacks like gorp and brownies. Alcohol is generally not part of the menu. If you have any concerns about your child eating what's available, talk to the outfitter well ahead of time.

What is the temperature going to be on the trip? Canada's Northwest Territories will likely be well below zero in March, but a balmy 15°F or 20°F in May. If you have a 12-year-old, you might choose the warmer May trip. A cold child is definitely a miserable child, and if your children are unhappy, the truth is that you will be, too.

What outerwear or gear is provided? Some outfitters supply nothing; others offer traditional caribou clothing, parkas, special boots, and gloves, in addition to sleeping bags and tents. Check and recheck the clothing lists outfitters send you and ask questions about gear. If you're depending on the outfitter to provide severe-weather outer clothing, make sure it's available in your child's size as well as yours. If you bring your own, do not skimp and do not deviate from the outfitter's suggestions. The winter wilderness is a deadly place without proper clothing and equipment.

How much camp and dog work are expected? On some trips clients and guides work equally, setting up camp, harnessing and unharnessing the dogs, feeding and caring for the dogs, and helping prepare meals. Other outfitters offer a more catered experience. If you are real doers, go with an outfitter that will depend on you to be a working member of the expedition.

What is the minimum age for the trip and why? Trust your outfitter. He or she knows the conditions, the itinerary, the physical demands of a particular trip. If you're told your 14-year-old is just too young or inexperienced to handle the trip, believe it.

How long have you been running dogs in this area? Knowledgeable guides are especially important when you're dealing with severe conditions and extreme temperatures. You want a company with several years' experience not only in the area but also with the particular itinerary. Before you plunk down a considerable chunk of change, you want to be sure that all possible kinks have been worked out. You're also looking for a crew that will know how to deal with emergencies small and large quickly and in a professional way.

What's included in the cost of the trip? Most dogsledding adventures start and end in remote wilderness areas, so you'll probably pay extra for transportation there. In addition, because of the location and limited transportation, you may have to overnight at your own expense before and/or after a trip. The per-person prices for all trips listed here include lodging or camping, meals, guides, instruction, sleds, and dogs, unless otherwise noted. Adventurers may also be lent some expedition clothing and supplies; however, you will definitely have to buy, borrow, or rent quality cold-weather gear of your own, including, in some cases, sleeping bags. Local transportation or pickup at airports might be available at no cost or for a nominal fee, so ask.

Instruction

No matter how many times you watched *Sergeant Preston of the Yukon* as a kid, your family will need instruction in driving a sled. Good dog teams are valuable, and no musher will turn his team over to someone who can't drive a sled properly. Moreover, dogsledding can be dangerous; by listening to your guide and learning the proper commands, safety procedures, and techniques, you ensure your family's safety as well as that of the dogs and anyone else on the trail. The time spent on instruction depends in part on how involved guests are in driving and caring for the dogs; much of it will take place during the trip.

Finding the Fun

Northeast: Adventure Guides of Vermont/Konari Outfitters. **Midwest:** Boundary Country Trekking, Gunflint Northwoods Outfitters/Gunflint Lodge, Outward Bound, Trek & Trail, Wilderness Inquiry. **Rockies:** Telluride Outside. **Alaska:** American Wilderness Experience, National Outdoor Leadership School. **Canada:** Arctic Odysseys, Boundary Country Trekking, Kanata Wilderness Adventures/Wells Gray Ranch.

Favorite Outfitters

Adventure Guides of Vermont/Konari Outfitters

⛄👥 8+

Adventure Guides represents some 30 outfitters in Vermont that specialize in a variety of sports and activities. Although the state has no guidelines or standards for outfitters, Adventure Guides requires that its members meet any existing national standards for each specialty and that all guides be certified in CPR, first aid, and wilderness first aid. Ed Blechner, who owns and operates Konari Outfitters, is the perfect dogsledding outfitter for families for another reason as well: He's a former teacher who still visits schools in the Northeast and educates children about winter outdoor skills and about dogs and dogsledding. He loves to work with families and knows just how to present the necessary information.

Most of Ed's trips are either in central Vermont—in and around Goshen and the Green Mountain National Forest—or around Lake Champlain. Goshen, once called Moosalamoo (meaning "Moose here") by the native population, doesn't have all that many moose these days, but it has rolling hills, forests, and historic Native American sites and trails. Snowmobiles like the area, too, and they pack down the trails perfectly for folks out in the wilderness with dogs. You may run into some snowmobilers and you'll certainly see cross-country skiers. Still, winter travel in Vermont forests is still light in comparison to summer months. Lake Champlain stretches 120 miles and touches Vermont, New York, and Canada. Two-thirds of it lies in northwestern Vermont, and Ed will take you around these shores, if the snow is right.

FOR FAMILIES. Ed takes kids as young as eight only if they can ski moderately well. There's no riding on these trips, which range from single-day to five-day outings. You either mush (all members of the group take turns) or cross-country ski. Occasionally there's snowshoeing, too. That doesn't mean you have to be an expert, however. Ed takes one family out at a time, and the trip is organized at the pace you can handle. February offers the best conditions for dogsledding in either area, though there are trips in January, too. And don't forget to ask Ed about "skijoring," which amounts to being pulled on skis by a single dog. You might fall a lot, you'll probably laugh a lot, and the kids will love it.

 Adventure Guides of Vermont/Konari Outfitters, Box 3, North Ferrisburgh, VT 05473, tel. 802/425–6211 or 800/425–8747. Jan.–Feb.: 1–5 days, $150–$565 (these are family rates for 3 or more). Konari supplies tents on overnights; bring your own sleeping bags or rent through Adventure Guides.

American Wilderness Experience

👫 12+

Experience the power and majesty of the Brooks Range as generations of Alaskan natives have—on a traditional mushing sled, with only the sounds of your dog team racing and the swoosh of the runners over pure North Country snow. Alaska's vast, inhospitable landscape remains unconquerable by most standards, which is exactly why it offers an adventure beyond even the dreams of most people. Yet dogsledding through the Arctic wilderness requires no previous experience; you need only a sense of adventure and good physical condition, because you'll be traveling between 15 and 30 miles in four to eight hours each day. Communal cabins and tents are used throughout the trip, and everyone helps with chores.

American Wilderness Experience, which contracts with top outfitters throughout the world, puts you in the capable hands of the Mackey family, owners of Sourdough Outfitters and professional mushers all. Becky has been running dogs since the age of five. In 1978, her father, Dick, won the Iditarod, the 1,049-mile race from Anchorage to Nome in which exhaustion and rampaging moose are just two of the difficulties racers encounter. Rick, one of her brothers, won in 1983.

FOR FAMILIES. Everyone works together on the six- and eight-day trips available February through March or April. Late spring trips offer warmer temperatures (lows below zero at night but in the teens and twenties during the day) and as much as 15 hours of daylight, which is an exciting experience in itself. On clear nights you will have a chance to experience nature's pyrotechnics—the aurora borealis.

Six-day trips leave from Bettles, in north central Alaska, and take you along the Koyukuk River and through the boreal forests. Wolves, caribou, and high, rugged peaks share this wilderness area. Eight-day trips from Bettles travel to Gates of the Arctic National Park. You'll camp at places with names like Deadman's Creek and Red Star Mountain, and view spectacular peaks such as Frigid Crags and Boreal Mountain. You may have a chance to fish through the ice for arctic grayling or northern pike. Otherwise, you'll dine on hearty stews and pasta dishes. No one, though, eats until the dogs have been fed. Mushers are clear on their priorities. Trip prices include special arctic gear, such as parkas, boots, mittens, and sleeping bags and pads, as well as snowshoes. Additional lodging necessary before or after a trip is not included, but is available.

 American Wilderness Experience, Box 1486, Boulder, CO 80306, tel. 303/444–2622 or 800/444–0099. Feb.–Apr.: $1,660–$1,980. Price includes airfare from Fairbanks to Bettles and transportation to and from the airport in Bettles.

Arctic Odysseys

👫 12+

Arctic Odysseys pioneered consumer-oriented group travel in the High Arctic almost 20 years ago. Although the company changed ownership a couple of years ago, there isn't a better outfitter with which to explore the almost unimaginable treasures of the seemingly infinite Arctic wilderness. Customized trips and small groups (one to three people per guide) are the trademark of the company.

FOR FAMILIES. You and your Inuit guide will plan your family's personal odyssey; the five-day and nine-day itineraries start and end in Ottawa. Children as well as adults must be in excellent health and good physical condition. Although trips are available mid-March through May, owner Robin Duberow recommends late May, when the temperature warms up to 15°F or 20°F, for families with children. On this trip through Canada's Northwest Territories, you spend the first and last nights in a hotel in the Inuit community of Cape Dorset on Baffin Island. Tents or traditional snow houses (igloos) provide shelter on the other nights of your journey. You may encounter polar bears, seals, or ptarmigans; you'll ice fish for arctic char. The most rewarding part of the experience, however, may well be the chance to experience a world unknown to most through the eyes of a people whose ties to the land remain strong and deep. If three or six nights out in the Arctic seem too much for your family, you can opt to add extra nights in the hotel ($50 per person per night) and travel by dogsled on day trips only.

During the very cold season you are lent traditional Inuit caribou clothing; children's sizes are available. The outfitter will send you a list of appropriate clothing and gear and give you the names of catalogs and regional chains from which you can purchase it at reasonable cost.

 Arctic Odysseys, 2000 McGilvra Blvd. E, Seattle, WA 98112, tel. 206/325–1977. Mid-Mar.–May: 5–9 days, $2,975–$3,450. Price includes 2 nights in hotel and flights between Ottawa and the Northwest Territories.

Boundary Country Trekking

👨👧 9+

These folks started offering dogsled trips in 1978, and they've been providing ordinary adventurers with extraordinary thrills ever since. Most trips take place in northern Minnesota's winter wonderlands—the Boundary Waters Canoe Area, the wild and scenic Brule River valley, and Superior National Forest. The company headquarters is in Grand Marais, about 110 miles north of Duluth on the rugged coast of Lake Superior, and that's the starting point for many of the sledding trips. Trips are limited to no more than six participants. Accommodations vary with the particular trip but may include yurts (dome-shaped tents or huts) along the trail, rustic cabins, a homey lodge, or Arctic Oven tents that can hold a heater.

FOR FAMILIES. Children aged 9 and up are welcome on trips, but only those 12 and older can mush their own sled. Younger kids share a sled with a parent. You can plan on mushing about 20 to 25 miles per day; on some of the longer trips you may travel farther—but you won't do it on an empty stomach. Meals include such treats as grilled rainbow trout and a Mongolian firepot dinner for those overnighting in a yurt. There are two- to five-day scheduled trips in Minnesota; you can also set up your own custom camping trip for any dates between November and March, as long as dogs are available. This company also offers 8- to 15-day treks through the Canadian Arctic.

 Boundary Country Trekking, Gunflint Trail HC 64, Box 590, Grand Marais, MN 55604, tel. 218/388–4487 or 800/322–8327. Nov.–Apr.: 2–15 days, $350–$3,700.

Gunflint Northwoods Outfitters/Gunflint Lodge

👨👧 6+

The Boundary Waters Canoe Area wilderness (BWCA) encompasses more than a million pristine acres of forests and lakes in northeastern Minnesota. Ideal for dogsledding, the area receives an average snowfall of more than 10 feet each winter. Here you can find the kind of solitude that few modern-day families ever experience. Gunflint Lodge, on the famous Gunflint Trail (Route 12), serves as your base camp. Fifteen of the lodge's 25 cabins are used in winter, as is the main lodge, which houses the reception area and dining hall. The lodge sits on the shores of Gunflint Lake, a body of water divided almost in half by the border between Minnesota and Canada. In winter, as in every season, families are warmly welcomed.

FOR FAMILIES. Mushing Week, the formal course of instruction and sledding, is for ages 16 and up. It gives you three full days working with a team of dogs, learning how to feed, care for, and harness them. You will average 20 to 25 miles a day on your sled, rarely taking the same trail twice. You'll also get three days to explore the BWCA on cross-country skis. And if the days rev you up and give you a feeling of accomplishment, the nights, spent in a first-class cabin with fireplace, hot tub, and sauna, are all about winter warmth and cozy togetherness. Children six and older may also have a chance to ride on a sled if there's room or if one parent opts to stay back at the lodge one day. Those under six will probably get too cold for a full-day adventure and will enjoy being at the lodge with a parent. If you're uncertain about committing to a week of dogsledding, you can opt for a one-hour, half-day, or full-day dogsled ride during your Ski Adventure Week (see Gunflint Northwoods Outfitters/Gunflint Lodge in Cross-country Skiing). You must bring appropriate winter wear; a limited number of mukluks and anoraks are available for rent.

🏠 Gunflint Northwoods Outfitters/Gunflint Lodge, 750 Gunflint Trail, Grand Marais, MN 55604, tel. 800/362–5251. Jan.–Mar.: 1 hr–7 days, $45–$895.

Kanata Wilderness Adventures/Wells Gray Ranch

🚹🚺 6+

Western Canada remains a rugged land of wild, untamed beauty, with mountain ranges that rise from deep blue lakes to piercing blue skies. Kanata Wilderness Adventures is the outfitter that does all of the bookings for Wells Gray Ranch. Popular with Europeans and Canadians but less well known to Americans, this year-round guest ranch sits at the entrance to Wells Gray Park, one of British Columbia's largest provincial parks. Riding is the main summer activity, but in winter, the Kanata dogs and guides are busy giving ranch guests and independent families the thrill of sledding.

FOR FAMILIES. Sign up to mush or ride (a sled can hold one musher and one child riding) on three- or seven-day adventures. For the most part adults will do the mushing; however, a strong preteen or teen with an interest in learning can probably do so. Owner Mike Mueller says parents should talk to him about their child before deciding on a trip. If Mike thinks it will work out, he'll bring a lighter sled and run it with fewer dogs for a young musher.

The three-day Musher Package takes you from the ranch to Grizzly Mountain Plateau, where you'll spend two nights in a rustic log cabin at a base camp. Each day you'll mush over abandoned logging roads, along lakeshores, and over mountain ridges. Those who choose the seven-day trip spend the first few nights at the ranch. After a training day, you head out for day trips and then follow the itinerary of the three-day adventure. Meals are included, but you have to bring your own cold-weather clothing and sleeping bag, or you can rent both from Kanata.

🏠 Kanata Wilderness Adventures/Wells Gray Ranch, R.R. 1, Clearwater V0E 1N0, British Columbia, Canada, tel. 604/674–2774. Dec.–Mar.: 3–7 days, $590–$1,490 per musher, $290–$790 per passenger.

National Outdoor Leadership School

🚹🚺 17+

If you and your older teen want to immerse yourselves in an experience that pushes you to test your physical, emotional, and mental limits in the vast Alaskan landscape, National Outdoor Leadership School has the course. The school offers learning situations designed to increase skills and self-esteem and to teach students how to enter the wilderness with minimum impact on the environment. Courses average 8 to 17 participants, with 2 to 4 leaders. The group travels through either Denali National Park or the Alaska Range, facing blue skies and violent winter storms, as well as temperatures that reach above freezing during the day and plummet to 40° below zero at night. Above it all, nature's dazzling theatrics, the northern lights, will dance.

FOR FAMILIES. The primary mode of travel for this two-week course is cross-country skiing, but everyone in the group takes on mushing duties and dog care. After two days at base camp you head into the wilderness accompanied by two dog teams, ready to learn winter wilderness skills, cooking, map reading, and route selection. You'll also find out how to set up tents even when it's so cold the shock cords in the tent poles freeze. What may surprise you is how snugly and well you can sleep in the intense cold. The group travels about 5 to 10 miles per day and spends about eight hours on the trail before camping. The course starts and ends at the school's headquarters in Palmer, just north of Anchorage. Some cold-weather clothing is available for rent.
🏠 *National Outdoor Leadership School, 288 Main St., Lander, WY 82520, tel. 307/332–6973. Mar.: 14 days, $1,850.*

Outward Bound

👫 14+

Dogsledding and cross-country skiing, held in Minnesota, are among the most challenging of all Outward Bound courses. That doesn't mean your family must already be expert in—or even familiar with—winter skills, but you must all be physically and mentally prepared for the challenges you will face. Your reward for such hard work is the self-empowering knowledge that you can succeed in ways you never believed possible.

FOR FAMILIES. In December and March, parents and children can take the combination dogsledding and cross-country skiing course together. You'll spend eight days in the Boundary Waters Canoe Area, traveling the silent, snowy forests and lakes by ski and by dog team. Up to six participants mush and ski four to six hours, 2 to 10 miles a day. You don't need to be an expert skier— beginner level is fine. In addition, you'll learn how to care for the dogs and run them, how to construct a winter shelter, and how to remain safe and comfortable during winter camping. There's a chance to try snowshoeing, too. As with all Outward Bound courses, everyone helps set up camp and prepare food each evening.
🏠 *Outward Bound, Rte. 9D, R2 Box 280, Garrison, NY 10524, tel. 914/424–4000 or 800/243–8520. Dec. and Mar.: 8 days, $795 each parent/child pair.*

Telluride Outside

👫 9+

The wide-open mesas above the increasingly popular Colorado town of Telluride are perfect for mushing: a mix of flat and steep terrain, drifted snow, and trails that wind through patches of forest. When you're not mushing, take to Telluride's slopes for a day of superb skiing. Telluride Outside specializes in very small groups, for a personalized experience.

FOR FAMILIES. Here's your chance to ride with a guide—you can stand on the runners and help mush or sit in the basket, where you must shift your weight to maneuver the sled around turns. There's a limit of 350 pounds per sled, with typically two guests on a sled; four guests is the average number for each outing. Half-day trips are offered, but overnights provide additional time for instruction and a more customized tour. You sleep in a cabin on the mesa, and there's a winter moonlight ride in addition to a hearty dinner and breakfast, cooked by the guides. Hands-on instruction is part of the tour; your active involvement is both required and encouraged. Several considerations determine the speed and distance you travel: your sense of adventure, ability, and fitness; the weather; and the well-being of the party, including the dogs. Telluride Outside provides uninsulated anoraks to help cut wind chill, but warm clothing and boots are a must. If you want your children (aged 9 or older) to receive instruction, let the company know when you book.

 Telluride Outside, Box 685, Telluride, CO 81435, tel. 970/728–3895 or 800/831–6230. Dec.–Mar.: ½ day–2 days, $125–$295.

Trek & Trail

 10+

The winter woods and icy beauty of northwestern Wisconsin and Lake Superior prove a dramatic backdrop for adventuring. Trek & Trail has been running dogsled trips in this area for six years. The instructors are well qualified to pass on their winter survival skills and mushing expertise, and their enthusiasm for the majesty and solitude of the wilderness in winter is contagious.

FOR FAMILIES. There are one-, two-, three-, and five-day trips available. Best for families is the two-day dogsledding and wilderness cabin adventure on Bayfield Peninsula, within the Red Cliff Indian Reservation and the Apostle Islands National Lakeshore. This is the only overnight sledding trip on which children under the age of 16 are allowed; the cabin you stay in is rustic but cozy and sleeps up to eight. For longer trips you stay in tents, tepees, and snow shelters.

After a three-hour winter safety course, including information about ice rescue,

nutrition, hypothermia, and winter camping, you'll be ready to use the cabin as a base from which to take day-long trail runs. The traditional sugaring cabin was built by the Newago family, members of the Red Cliff tribe, who use it at maple-sugar time when the family is harvesting and cooking down the syrup. They come out to spend the evening with you on Friday night, telling stories of present-day and historical "sugar bushing" and other facets of Native American life. Saturday and Sunday you'll learn a variety of winter skills and graduate from running teams of 4 or 5 dogs to 10-dog teams, if you wish. You can even try a night run. If your children are enthusiastic and comfortable with the dog teams, they can learn to mush, too. No winter adventuring experience is necessary but you must be in good physical condition, and you must bring appropriate clothing.

 Trek & Trail, Box 906, Bayfield, WI 54814, tel. 800/354–8735. Jan.–Mar.: 1–5 days, $125–$650.

Wilderness Inquiry

 6+

Since 1978 this nonprofit organization has been bringing people with and without disabilities, and from diverse backgrounds, together in the wilderness—in this case, in Minnesota. Teaching, learning, and sharing are the foundations on which every course is built.

FOR FAMILIES. Ages 6 and up can choose a five-day ski and dogsled trip into the Boundary Waters Canoe Area, where you'll follow ancient Native American trails across the many frozen lakes and through deep snow and pine forests. The outfitter will consider younger children on an individual basis, but call and discuss it; 2-year-olds have taken this trip.

You will pick your routes, ski, snowshoe, dogsled, and take on the challenge of winter wilderness survival. If you or your child has a disability, ask Wilderness Inquiry about their facilities for accommodating your needs. Most daily outings cover 3 to 8 miles, though you can also choose to relax with a cup of hot chocolate in the remote but comfortable YMCA Camp Menogyn lodge (with sauna), where you spend your nights. There's an optional overnight camp-out with tents, snow shelters, or maybe even just double sleeping bags under the dark, starry skies. One of the mushers who regularly works this trip taught his own kids to run dogs at age 4, so a child's ability isn't prejudged. If your 6-year-old is ready and willing, he or she can stand on the runners with a musher and get the feel of driving a sled.

Families with teens 16 and up can head into Minnesota's rugged north country for six days of sledding over the frozen lakes and wooded hills of Superior National Forest. This more intense trek begins at a base camp and includes two nights out on the trail in wall tents, which have vertical sides and can hold heaters. You'll sled 15 to 30 miles per day.

🏕 *Wilderness Inquiry, 1313 5th St. SE, Box 84, Minneapolis, MN 55414-1546, tel. and TTY 612/379-3858 or 800/728-0719. Dec.–Mar.: 5–6 days, $545–$845. Round-trip van transportation from Minneapolis (6 hrs each way) is available for $60.*

Resources

Organizations

The **International Sled Dog Racing Association** (Box 446, Nordman, ID 83848, tel. 208/443-3153; membership $25) will send information on the sport and a sample copy of its magazine, *Info*, which is published 10 times each year. The magazine features families throughout the year, and four issues have pieces about junior mushers.

Books

Nearly every preteen and teen is familiar with Gary Paulsen, whose acclaimed novels about wilderness survival and adventure speak to adults, too. Paulsen, whose passion for years was dogsledding in the Minnesota wilderness, writes in *Woodsong* (Orchard Books, ages 8 and up) about his dogs, his home, and participating in the 1,049-mile Iditarod dogsled race. *Dogteam* (Dell), also by Paulsen, is a picture book for younger readers about the beauty of a nighttime dogsled run.

Also See

For more winter adventures, look at the trips in Cross-Country Skiing. For more adventures with animal companions, see Horse Packing and Trekking with Llamas, Goats, and Burros.

FISHING

City kids, country kids, small- and big-town kids—they all love to fish. Whether it's the connection with water or the lazy, Huckleberry Finn feel of floating along with no place in particular to go, I don't know. Maybe it's the challenge, or maybe it's the simplicity of the endeavor. In a high-tech, high-speed world, fishing takes you back to a simpler era when families made their own fun. Fishing requires almost nothing except patience and a little time.

Of course there is an art to it. In particular, fly-fishing, which involves almost continuous casting with an artificial fly, is a learned skill. It has complexities (avoiding parents, trees, and reeds while casting, for example) and intricacies (knowing where fish lurk and what they eat) beyond what most of us associate with fishing. There is a right and wrong way to cast—and you can bet the wily trout in streams across the country know that by now.

Today families can discover, or rediscover, the joys of fishing in a number of ways. There are schools and clinics that teach specialized skills, usually fly-fishing, and outfitters who will take you out and teach you while you vacation. You can find lodges that focus on fishing and provide instruction as well as good old-fashioned fishing fun. Children of almost any age can fish, though most outfitters agree that fly-fishing takes a level of coordination and understanding that most children under 12 don't possess. For this reason, lodge-based fishing and lake fishing are often best for families with young children. But the bottom line is really this: Fishing, in one form or another, is for everyone.

Questions to Ask

What method is taught? Most schools concentrate on fly-fishing, but instruction in spin casting (casting a line with a worm or lure or other bait and slowly reeling it in), trolling (dragging a line behind a moving boat), and other techniques is also available. Fly-fishing is harder for young children than trolling, so consider your kids' ages and ability, as well as their level of tolerance for sitting or standing for long periods, before booking.

Do you have equipment for kids? Experts disagree on whether a shorter rod is necessarily better for children, but be sure there's a rod your child can use comfortably. Kids older than 12 and those large for their age don't usually have a problem with the adult equipment generally available either as part of the package or for rent. Children who are younger and smaller may have problems with available rods, so buy or borrow your child's equipment before you leave home. Get detailed information from the guide or school about what kind is best, though. *Fly-Fishing with Children* by Philip Brunquell (see Resources, *below*) has an excellent section on buying rods for kids.

What kind of fish will we be catching? Trout is the primary focus at most schools and on many wilderness trips, but there are other possibilities. Bluefish, bonitos, salmon, walleyes, and northern pike also provide a challenge for anglers of all ages. Even within species there can be differences in ease of catch. Because children may have less patience than adults, picking a fish or an area that is likely to bring success is a good idea.

Where does casting instruction take place? You'll be taught how to throw a line out so a fish will take whatever lure or bait you're offering. Most schools have casting ponds stocked with trout; in some cases instruction takes place on a river or even in the surf. On a guided trip, you put skills to work in real situations rather than the artificial environs of a stocked pond. However, kids actually like the ponds, and guided trips can be expensive. Schools also give families a chance to try the sport to see if they like it and to test equipment before investing in it. Before booking either alternative, make sure the scenario is what you want.

How much time is spent in the classroom? Many schools use about half the course time to give lectures on equipment and environmental concerns, present slide shows, lead fly-tying demonstrations, and discuss pretty much anything that's not directly related to casting. Be certain your children understand that the entire class will not take place near water. In some cases, no time is spent by the water, so read descriptions carefully.

Are licenses needed? In most states adults need a fishing license but children under a certain age do not. Sixteen is a common cutoff, but in some states 12-year-olds must have one. Check with the school or guide. Find out if you can purchase your license from them or if you have to stop somewhere before your class or trip begins. The cost may be anywhere from $4 to $40 or so. In a very few courses, a temporary license is part of the course fee.

Can we keep our fish? In most cases, no. The sport lies in outsmarting the fish, and the primary goal of most schools and guided trips is to teach you to catch fish, not keep them. Catch-and-release is the phrase you'll hear; it means once you catch your fish, you must quickly unhook it and place it back in the water. Many places recommend nonbarbed hooks for that reason. Ask if you need to bring them.

Are there things for nonfishing family members to do? You'll probably find more additional activities at lodges than at schools or with wilderness guides. Some guided trips, however, are perfect for photographers or wildlife artists, or for anyone who simply likes relaxing in a boat. There are schools in towns or areas that are popular family destinations, too. Even if one of you isn't fishing, you can still have a family experience.

How far in advance should we book? When it comes to parent/child courses, which are very limited in number, booking several months in advance is a good idea. On the other hand, last-minute cancellations are always possible, so don't hesitate to call.

What's included in the cost? Guided trips include boats, guides, all meals, most camping equipment (you usually have to bring or rent a sleeping bag), life vests, instruction, and transportation to and from the river, unless noted otherwise. Fishing equipment is occasionally available, but check. The cost of lodge-based trips generally covers lodging, meals, and the use of a boat; private guiding is extra. School prices include equipment but reflect course costs only, without lodging or meals, unless otherwise noted. Transportation to and from schools or guided trips is never part of the price given.

Instruction

Instruction is the focus of a school course, but a good guide on a trip will always provide instruction, too. If you have specific interests—fly tying, casting techniques, learning about equipment—let your guide know ahead of time so he or she can prepare materials and equipment as necessary. Ask in advance whether there are charts of local fish or written materials or directions on fly tying or using equipment. Some children—and some adults, for that matter—learn better by visual clues.

Finding the Fun

Northeast: Appalachian Mountain Club, L.L. Bean, Orvis Fly Fishing School. **Midwest:** Gunflint Northwoods Outfitters/Gunflint Lodge. **Southwest:** Derringer Outfitters and Guides. **Rockies:** L.L. Bean, Montana River Outfitters, Orvis Fly Fishing School, Telluride Outside. **West Coast:** Fly-Fishing Outfitters Clinics, Trinity Canyon Lodge. **Canada:** Babine Norlakes Lodge.

Favorite Schools and Outfitters

Appalachian Mountain Club

 13+

The Catskills campus of this venerable organization sponsors a fly-fishing clinic based at Valley View Lodge, not far from Phoenicia, New York. Although the course is strictly a landlubber affair—you don't actually go out on the water or even near a stream—your family does get to enjoy spring in the Catskills while learning the techniques and skills to fish for trout on your own.

FOR FAMILIES. Instructors, all members of the Upper Susquehanna Chapter of Trout Unlimited, have plenty of fishing experience; some are New York State–certified guides. This group focuses on enjoying fishing themselves and promoting fly-fishing across the country. The class is limited to 20 people, and like other Appalachian Mountain Club courses held in the Catskills, it includes lodging Friday and Saturday nights, as well as all meals from Saturday breakfast to Sunday lunch.

Participants spend some time in a classroom setting, learning how to select tackle, tie flies, and read the waters (recognize the kinds of places fish like to lurk and feed); instructors also teach a bit about entomology as it relates to fly-fishing. Saturday's class runs from about 9 to 5, while Sunday's ends around noon. Casting instruction takes place in a big field, with no hooks on the rods. Equipment is available for free if you don't yet have your own.

🏠 *Appalachian Mountain Club, Box 298, Gorham, NH 03581, tel. 603/466–2727 (for catalog), 518/624–2056 (for Catskills campus). Apr.: 2 days, $175; family membership is $65, and members receive a 10% discount on classes.*

Babine Norlakes Lodge

(👫 **ALL**)

Pierce and Anita Clegg, owners and managers of the Babine Norlakes Lodge, have four children of their own. They love having families as guests, and their guides enjoy teaching kids about fishing. There aren't many activities if you don't want to fish—maybe a little volleyball or badminton. And of course, the Cleggs' children are around for play companions.

The lodge itself, in a remote area of northern British Columbia, is accessible only by boat or floatplane. Eight hand-hewn cabins sleep two to four, and generators supply electricity; two of the cabins are larger and have kitchens, if you prefer to cook. This woodsy, isolated living does not lack nice touches: In the morning Pierce personally visits each cabin, serving coffee, tea, or hot chocolate to guests and starting up each cabin's woodstove or stove oil heating. Guests gather for a big breakfast in the main lodge and make their lunch from a buffet; then most head out onto Nilkitkwa Lake and the Babine River for some of the best trout fishing in North America.

FOR FAMILIES. Accommodations include a boat, with no limit on fuel, so you are free to fish as much as you like. The lodge encourages catch-and-release only (and requires all steelhead to be released), in order to preserve the population. The fish here are all wild; there's no stocking, no hatchery. Most guests bring their own equipment, though a few rods are available for guests' use, and the Clegg children generously loan their life jackets.

First-time guests receive one day of complimentary guiding; you can hire guides other days for an additional charge. With enough notice, Anita can arrange to have a mother's helper on the property (extra charge) so you and your spouse can spend some time fishing on your own.

In keeping with the informal atmosphere, minimum ages and pricing structures are flexible. Anita says "preschoolers and youngsters are free until they really start fishing." At that point they receive a 50% discount. Large families, she adds, "can usually make a deal."

🏠 *Babine Norlakes Lodge, Box 1060, Smithers V0J 2N0, British Columbia, Canada, tel. 604/846–5259. May–Aug.: 1–7 days, $120–$1,575; guides are $50 per day.*

Derringer Outfitters and Guides

(👫 **10+**)

Only 10 guests at a time stay with David and Susan Derringer at their 40-acre ranch in New Mexico's Gila National Forest. Families mix and match their five-day package as they wish. They can hang out at the ranch or take multiday trips river or lake fishing, goat packing, canoeing, rafting, horse packing, or backpacking; they can also combine any of these activities. Fishing works with almost any trek, so if your family wants variety, call the Derringers. On the other hand, if you want strictly fishing, you can have that, too. Families with younger children are welcomed on a case-by-case basis.

FOR FAMILIES. When you're with the Derringers, your family stays together for all wilderness experiences. That goes for fishing, too, which includes instruction as well as guiding. The San Francisco and Gila rivers are 30 to 45 miles away, and there are three lakes between 8 and 60 miles from the ranch. Young children will probably find lake fishing—casting and trolling—easier, but good fly-fishing is available on the rivers. You can keep what you catch in this area, unless you happen to hook the endangered Gila trout.

David Derringer thinks families do well with a combination of activities, and he notes that the fishing is excellent on two canoe trips—the San Francisco Canoe/Horse Packing trip and the Wilderness Run on the Gila. Just let him know in advance that you want to fish and he'll pack in the gear; it's best if you have your own, but he has some extra adult and child-size rods. David or Susan leads every trip, so personalized service is guaranteed, along with the benefit of their tremendous combined experience.
🏠 *Derringer Outfitters and Guides, Box 157, Quemado, NM 87829, tel. 505/773–4860. Feb.–Nov. (river fishing is best May–Oct.): 5 days, $400–$600.*

Fly-Fishing Outfitters Clinics

👫 10+

This group has run clinics since 1985, both in San Francisco and on streams and rivers in various parts of northern California. Because Fly-Fishing Outfitters also owns well-regarded equipment shops, they'll provide rods and reels for clinics, but you'll have to bring or rent tackle.

FOR FAMILIES. A two-day parent/child clinic in July usually takes place on the North Fork of the Yuba River in the Sierra, near Downieville. Because kids—even those with a real interest in angling—have shorter attention spans, the weekend focuses as much on having fun in the outdoors as on mastering fly-fishing skills. Even so, you'll learn a lot, especially if you opt to camp by the river rather than stay in one of the many local motels or bed-and-breakfasts. The

guides usually camp, and they'll happily talk fishing, and fish stories, even after clinic hours. Bring your own camping gear. You'll fish for rainbow and brown trout, but it's strictly catch-and-release.

The organization's other workshops (which families can also join) have a very structured itinerary, so make certain your kids are up for a fairly adult-oriented experience if you opt for these.
 Fly-Fishing Outfitters Clinics, 3533 Mt. Diablo Blvd., Lafayette, CA 94549, tel. 510/ 284–3474. July: 2 days, $230 per parent/child pair.

Gunflint Northwoods Outfitters/Gunflint Lodge

👫 ALL

Members of the Kerfoot family, who own the outfitting/guide service and the lodge, have been welcoming adventurers of all ages to this wilderness retreat since 1928. The lodge itself, about 150 miles north of Duluth, sits on the shore of 9-mile-long Gunflint Lake. Many families visit the lodge for a week, taking canoeing and fishing trips into the vast Boundary Waters Canoe Area (BWCA). Others stay at the lodge only before or after a guided or self-guided adventure. Both the lodge and the guiding service will take children of any age, though different activities will have specific age requirements. Whatever your choice, one talk with Bruce Kerfoot will convince you that Gunflint and families are made for each other.

FOR FAMILIES. All children 6 and up staying at the lodge at least seven days will be taken out on a kids-only half-day guided fishing trip twice during the week. They'll learn spin casting with some live bait and some artificial lures as they try their luck on walleyes and smallmouth bass. A family with children of any age also has the option of hiring one of Gunflint's excellent guides for a full-day trip (extra charge) on one of the many lakes in the vast BWCA. Lodge-based guests can use Gunflint's canoes and kayaks free of charge; there are kid-size kayaks, too. Families on the all-inclusive package also have use of a motorboat; other guests pay extra for this. The Gunflint nature program runs from June to September, with about 30 free activities a week, such as hikes, bird-watching, moose searches, and boating to interesting sites—even evening beaver watches.

The 41 cabins at Gunflint Lodge give families various options. Sixteen rustic "canoer" cabins sleep four to six in one big room; a bathhouse with hot showers, toilets, sinks and a sauna is nearby. The more luxurious cabins have one to four bedrooms, bathrooms, and carpeting, and each has a sauna; the most deluxe have outside hot tubs. Among the family package options are a housekeeping plan, for those who wish to cook their own meals, and a modified plan that includes dinner every day.

You can also book camping trips of two or more days with Gunflint's regular guiding service. Smallmouth bass are easier to catch than other local fish, so they're a good choice for children to go after on these adventures. An ideal family trip takes you to Rose Lake, in the eastern portion of the BWCA along the Canadian border. It requires about a five-hour paddle the first day, and there are two portages on the trip. Families camp amid stands of white pines with a soft carpeting of pine needles. There's no minimum age, but the trip is a lot easier once children are out of diapers. Bruce recommends a four-night trip. "The kids come back wishing it had been a little longer, not complaining that it was a couple of days too long," he says, and that gives them the best possible introduction to the wilderness.

Gunflint Northwoods Outfitters/Gunflint Lodge, 750 Gunflint Trail, Grand Marais, MN 55604, tel. 218/388–2294 or 800/362–5251. May–Sept.: 7 days: $295–$2,500 for a family of 4, depending on cabin choice and *meal package; less if kids are under 4, more if you have more than 4 in your family. Guiding costs $125 per person per day, with 50% discount for ages 4–12.*

L.L. Bean

 12+

The stated mission of this renowned outdoor store and catalog company is to help people enjoy the outdoors through its products, services, and education. L.L. Bean opened a fly-fishing school nearly 15 years ago and inaugurated a parent/child introductory school at the company's Freeport, Maine, headquarters in 1993. It's been going strong ever since.

FOR FAMILIES. In late June and again in July, Bean schedules a two-day parent/child school that runs from 8 to 5 both days and includes lunch. Instruction takes place outside Freeport at Fogg Farm, which has both a natural and a stocked pond. Participants remove their shoes and wade in, picking up rocks and studying reeds in order to get to know a fish's environment—and what it eats. Once you know what the fish like to eat, you try to match it in your lure box. The 12 parent/child pairs in the course also learn fly-casting and fly-tying techniques, how to read the water, and how weather can affect fishing conditions. Twelve is the minimum age but call the school if a younger child is really interested; they're flexible. Lodging isn't part of the deal, but participants receive a list of area accommodations ranging from campgrounds to a luxury hotel. Be sure to check out Bean's store, which has quality outdoor clothing and gear for all ages, while you're in the area.

Families with fishing aficionados 14 and up can join any of Bean's other fishing schools. There's an introductory and an intermediate school, as well as more specialized courses, including saltwater, Atlantic salmon, and western trout fly-fishing schools. Introductory courses are held in Freeport and include equipment; lodging is extra. The cost for other courses, in popular fishing areas in Maine and Montana, covers lodging.

All graduates receive a copy of the *L.L. Bean Fly Fishing Handbook*, in addition to a diploma and pin.

 L.L. Bean, Freeport, ME 04033, tel. 207/ 865–4761. June–July (parent/child school): 2 days, $495 for parent and child. May–Sept. (all other courses): 3–6 days, $395–$2,500 per person.

Montana River Outfitters

10+

Dan Kelly of Montana River Outfitters believes that the best class in the world puts you out on a river catching wild fish with guides who love what they're doing. That's just what this organization offers. Guides take only two anglers in a boat (four–eight guests in all on a trip) in order to personalize instruction and service. The "classrooms" are the Missouri, Smith, and Flathead rivers. Most people bring their own rods and sleeping bags, but you can rent them if you wish.

FOR FAMILIES. There are one-day trips on the Missouri, but Dan recommends a five- to seven-day trip on the South Fork of the Flathead for families. Getting there adds to the adventure—it's two days in by horse, with all equipment and food packed along. The resident cutthroat trout make the river particularly family-friendly. Cutthroat are easy to catch, which can be very satisfying to kids (and adults). The South Fork of the Flathead flows through the remote Bob Marshall Wilderness in northwest Montana, and in the unlikely event the fishing is less than perfect, the beauty and drama of the wilderness landscape will more than make up for it.

Another good five- to seven-day family trip is on the Smith—along 61 miles of river with no public access. Limestone canyons, cliffs, and meadows cradle a river so narrow here that you can cast to either side. The rainbow and brown trout are apparently smarter than the greedy cutthroat, so you need more patience on the Smith. Still, the fishing is excellent. Catch-and-release is, for the most part, what you're doing, but if you have an unstoppable craving for trout one night, your guides will let you cook one.

To join up with Montana River Outfitters, you fly into and out of Great Falls for most trips. They'll pick you up at the airport and take you to your pre-trip lodging (not included in the price, but they can arrange it), then transport you to the start of the trip. After your adventure they'll drop you off at the airport. At the end of the Flathead trip you fly out of Kalispell; to avoid the drive to the airport, which includes 80 miles of dirt road, you can have a small plane pick your family up not too far from the river (extra charge) and fly you to Kalispell.

 Montana River Outfitters, 1401 5th Ave. S, Great Falls, MT 59405, tel. 406/761–1677 or 406/235–4350. Mar.–Oct.: 1–7 days, $290–$2,700.

Orvis Fly Fishing School

12+

Orvis, the long-established fishing-tackle manufacturer, opened the first fly-fishing school in the country; it began offering courses back in 1967 at its Manchester, Vermont, corporate headquarters. Several years ago an Evergreen, Colorado, campus was added, followed by one near Chatham, Massachusetts, on Cape Cod. Hundreds of Orvis retail outlets (where you can buy fishing gear and outdoor clothing) also run courses, but the individual stores choose their offerings. The clinics at the three corporate centers—Vermont, Colorado, and Massachusetts—generally remain the same from year to year, and you'll find the parent/child schools there.

FOR FAMILIES. Parent/child school is a two-day event, usually scheduled twice a year in April at the Vermont campus and once in June in both Colorado and Cape Cod. The course accommodates up to 10 pairs, which split into smaller groups (parent and child stay together). You spend half the time in the classroom, the other half at the casting ponds or, on Cape Cod, in the surf. In Vermont and Colorado, students visit a local stream or river to learn proper wading and other techniques.

The course meets from about 9 to 4:30 both days and emphasizes basics: rigging a fly rod, tying essential knots, trying various fly-casting techniques, and learning what fish eat and what lures to use. You learn, too, how to "mend" your line by adjusting its placement in the water based on currents. Not surprisingly, Orvis schools also emphasize proper equipment and clothing, and the gear provided is strictly Orvis. This is a catch-and-release program, with an exception sometimes made for kids. In Vermont, children have kept one fish, and the school has arranged for the Equinox Hotel (where most students stay) to cook and serve it to the young angler.

The school recommends that you sign up for parent/child courses several months in advance—November is not too early for the April school. Kids 12 and up can also participate in Orvis's regular courses, but parents should note that the parent/child course has less structure and more emphasis on fun.

The popular women-only schools in Vermont, Massachusetts, and Colorado are another option for mother-daughter pairs. These are run like regular courses: The class of 36 or so divides up, and lecture time is lengthier and more detailed than in parent/child courses. As with all Orvis courses, the price does not cover lodging, but reservationists give detailed information on local accommodations.

🏠 *Orvis Fly Fishing School, Rte. 7A, Manchester, VT 05254, tel. 800/235–9763. Apr.–Aug. (all courses not all months): 2–3 days, $340–$395.*

Telluride Outside

 11+

The rivers of southwestern Colorado teem with trout, and the mountain town of Telluride, with the Uncompahgre National Forest to the north and the San Juan National Forest to the south, makes an enviable base from which to pursue them. Telluride Outside has been guiding and teaching fly-fishing for more than 12 years, and the outfitter welcomes parents and children who want to fish and learn together. The company is somewhat flexible on ages; call and consult with the staff before booking any family course or trip.

FOR FAMILIES. Telluride Outside lets you choose between "walk and wades" (where you fish standing on the bank or in the water) and "floats" (fishing by boat). There are schools and guided trips for both approaches; however, walk and wades are better for older teens and adults with fly-fishing experience.

Of the three rivers the outfitter regularly visits—the San Miguel, the Gunnison, and the Dolores—the San Miguel probably suits families best. Although its fish aren't as big, there are lots of them, so you don't have to be as exact on your cast or your drift as you do on a river with just a few big fish spread out between pools. A one-day school covers such topics as approach (trout behavior and reading the water), presentation (equipment and fly casting), and fly selection. You spend half the day in Telluride in a classroom and the rest on the San Miguel. Another option, a three-day school, divides the days the same way. You're on your own for lodging each night in Telluride.

Those looking for a multiday camping and fly-fishing school should consider the awesome Black Canyon of the Gunnison class, about a two-hour drive from town. Fly fishermen come from all over the world to test their skills on the Gunnison River, which is best for ages 14 and up. The fishing is harder, but the scenery, the striking Precambrian rock of the canyon, and wildlife (bighorn sheep, otters, eagles, deer, and more) make the trip well worthwhile. The course includes an instructional video for you to keep, handouts, and lots of hands-on instruction and practice. Students stay one night in a rustic cabin (no in-cabin baths or showers) at the Gunnison River Pleasure Park, where huge old cottonwoods line the river, and camp out the other two nights. On the last night, there's a big barbecue for the group. You should have your own equipment and sleeping bag, but rentals are available if necessary.

If you take a float trip rather than one of the schools, you'll still get instruction from the guides but it will be less formalized. Consider taking Telluride Outside's half-day casting clinic before a trip to get in shape. Guides review various casts in detail, and the outfitter provides all equipment.

🏠 *Telluride Outside, Box 685, Telluride, CO 81435, tel. 970/728–3895. June–Sept.: ½–4 days, $50–$900 per person for schools, $225–$2,100 per boat (2 people) for float trips.*

Trinity Canyon Lodge

👫 10+

Trinity Canyon Lodge, in northwestern California near Weaverville, lies between two major trailheads that lead into the Trinity Alps Wilderness Area. It makes a great family base for hiking, rafting, kayaking, and tubing the Trinity River (tubes are available); fishing, however, holds center stage. Joe and Diane Mercier run Trinity Canyon, which accommodates about 25 people in seven housekeeping cottages and three motel units; Joe teaches the fly-fishing clinics.

FOR FAMILIES. Joe Mercier is an avid angler and committed environmentalist. Each half- or full-day clinic includes a classroom portion focusing on the environment within the context of fly-fishing. Even members of the family not taking the clinics can—and do—come to this part of the program. The rest of the clinic is spent on the Trinity River, which runs through the lodge property. Only two people at a time can take Joe's clinic, which is purely instruction, not guiding. Salmon, trout, and steelhead call the Trinity home, but this is catch-and-release only. What you'll take home is a great deal of valuable information. Joe also specializes in instructing people about gear and letting them try different equipment before they make a major buying decision; he provides all gear for the clinics.

🏠 *Trinity Canyon Lodge, Box 51, Helena, CA 96048, tel. 916/623–3306 (for workshops), 916/623–6318 (for lodge reservations). Year-round: ½–1 day, $160–$250 for 2 people; the full-day course includes lunch. Accommodations are $28–$118 per night.*

Resources

Books

Michael J. Rosen's *The Kids' Book of Fishing and Tackle Box* (Workman) is the perfect beginners' guide to the sport for anglers 8 and up. It emphasizes freshwater catch-and-release fishing.

Fly-Fishing with Children, by Philip Brunquell, M.D. (The Countryman Press) is an excellent guide to teaching children, with sections on buying equipment and diagrams on casting and fly tying.

Also See

For more river and lake adventures in which fishing is possible, see Canoeing, Kayaking, and Rafting. The Horse Packing chapter also lists trips on which families can fish at lake and river campsites.

HIKING AND BACKPACKING

Hiking is one of the most popular adventure vacations, in part because of accessibility. A family can hike just about anywhere, anytime. There are treks for all ages and all abilities, and for campers and noncampers alike. Some families enjoy carrying major backpacks into remote wilderness areas; others prefer the comfort of a cozy inn or lodge each evening. Hiking itself doesn't require lots of expensive equipment (although campers need gear), nor does it involve a large investment of time. Even day hikes with young children can be fun—and educational—family adventures.

So why sign up with a group or outfitter when hiking is something you can so easily do on your own? One reason is that outfitters work in the same areas year after year and really know the country. In terms of planning, safety, and interest, this benefits your family. Whether you're heading into the wilderness or hiking inn to inn, there are myriad details to take care of: mapping a great route, arranging for backcountry permits, finding a campsite, booking accommodations. Guides do all of this in advance. They also provide memorable facts and stories about an area, as well as a level of safety individuals usually can't match. Moreover, they can get you into some areas that might be inaccessible on your own—unless you have backcountry experience and are well equipped with appropriate safety and camping gear.

Outfitters also contribute to the educational aspect of your family's experience. The naturalists and outdoor educators who accompany you on many trips can share the wonders of nature with your children—and answer their many questions—in a way you probably can't. In addition, if your family has hikers of different abilities, you may need to compromise on the route when you're on your own. Guided trips generally have two to three hiking options each day. Experienced hikers can be challenged by steep trails and long distances while beginners take shorter routes at a slower pace as they build their stamina and skills.

Traveling with an outfitter can make financial sense, too. They have up-to-date gear, which means you don't have to go out and buy it. Tents, pads, tarps, cooking equipment, fire starters, topographical maps, backcountry first-aid kits, compasses, and radios are necessary in the wilderness. Unless you're certain that camping and hiking is a long-term family interest, why invest in so much equipment?

Finally, when you travel with a hiking company, especially on a trip geared for families, you're guaranteed companions, not just for yourself but for your children. You'll meet families from all over the world who share your love of the outdoors. Most important, perhaps, kids help motivate each other. This can make a big difference when you're still 2 miles from camp and your 5-year-old doesn't want to walk any farther.

Of course you can hike on your own; there are city and state parks and recreation areas, with marked and maintained trails, within a short drive of most communities—even large cities. These are good trails on which to introduce children to hiking and build skills. But for that multiday exploration of backcountry or unfamiliar locales, or a special adventure that integrates hiking with history, ecology, botany, marine biology, or sociology, try a guided trip. You'll be amazed at what you see and what you can learn.

Questions to Ask

How far will we hike each day? The trips listed here average 3 to 8 miles per day for the easy options; some hikes are as short as 1.8 miles and others as long as 12. Challenging options generally range between 6 and 12 miles per day. Although size and experience are factors, in general you can expect a preschooler to walk 1 to 3 miles a day, and 5- to 8-year-olds to handle between 5 and 8 miles, depending on the terrain and their experience.

How difficult is the trip? Most hiking companies designate trips easy, moderate, strenuous, or difficult. All of the trips in this chapter are easy or moderate, unless otherwise noted. Difficulty is determined by the distance you hike, the ascent or descent, and the trail surface. One company, Hiking Holidays, puts it this way: An easy trip is the equivalent of a half hour of walking three times per week. Moderate and challenging routes are the equivalent of a half hour of aerobic exercise two or three times per week. These guidelines may help you decide your family's ability level, but you should also ask lots of questions and be candid about the fitness and normal activity level of everyone in your family.

How often can we rest? Outdoor experts know that children need to stop more often than adults, but everyone needs to rest on the trail. Taking a couple of breaks in the morning and afternoon, besides stopping for lunch, is good for the group. Along the trail you'll pause frequently to look at everything you're out there to see: views, bugs, interesting plants, wildlife. To rush down the trail is to miss the point. If your guide tries to hurry you or your children, ask him or her to slow down.

Who carries the gear? Sometimes you do; sometimes support vehicles lug the heavy stuff while you hike. In general, if the trip is a backcountry trek with a different campsite each night, everyone in the group will probably be expected to carry a backpack of at least 30 pounds. If this isn't for you, check out inn-to-inn hiking; support vehicles usually take all but what you need in your day pack. On lodge-based treks, you leave almost everything in your room while you hike each day. Without food, tents, bedding, and camping equipment to carry, hiking is a lighter activity.

Are there any special safety precautions for kids on the trail? Although you're with a group and guides, there's a remote chance that someone might get separated from the group for a while . Carrying a whistle is a good idea. If your children can read, write safety instructions and place them in their day pack or backpack. Kids should know when to blow the whistle, how to use three sticks or stones to mark the direction they've gone, and to stay in one place if it gets dark.

What if my child is too tired to finish a hike? A good trail strategy is to encourage children along the way, whether they are tired or not. Praise all their accomplishments—making it up hills, making it until break time, making it to the next bend in the trail. You and they will be surprised at their natural abilities. For those times children really can't go on, you should know your options. Some trips include van support; others have shorter loops you can take. Once you've committed to a trail in the wilderness, though, your choices may be limited.

Will an experienced hiker be bored on easy or moderate hikes? On family trips, the key is to look at the experience in a new way. You won't cover the same distances you're used to, and you won't be on terrain that's as challenging. On the other hand, you will have opportunities to see the world through your children's eyes, to slow down, and to share your knowledge of the trail with them. If you feel the need for a challenge or two, take a trip that offers several hiking options every day. You and your spouse can take turns walking with the kids and going on more difficult hikes.

How many people will be in the group? Camping trips usually accommodate 10–20 people, inn-to-inn trips typically have 15–25, and lodge-based trips as many as 30–40. Individual listings for outfitters note any exceptions to these averages. Remember, however, that the group is divided every day into two or three smaller hiking groups, based on ability and preference. You will rarely hike with more than 10 or 11 people at one time.

Do my kids need hiking boots? In some cases, on some terrain, boots may be better than sneakers because they provide more support. There are good national outlets for children's outdoor wear (see Resources, *below*), and hiking boots come in a range of prices. After the trip, boots are useful at summer camp and around town.

Are day packs needed? Most outfitters ask each hiker to carry his or her own day pack; that goes for kids, too. Even preschoolers can carry a small pack with the essentials: safety instructions, water, trail snacks, and rain gear.

Are snacks available? Outfitters usually provide trail snacks each day, but they may not hand them out as often as your children need them. They also may not have what your kids like, so pack easy-to-carry, energy-producing trail snacks in your family's day packs. Good choices include dried fruit, nuts, hard salami, and trail mix. If you have hard cheese or bagels at breakfast, take leftovers on the trail. A word of caution: In wilderness areas, especially bear country, it's not safe to keep food in your tent. At night, give snacks to your guides to put in safe containers.

What's included in the cost? On a camping trip, the outfitter supplies guides, meals, tents, and sleeping pads, unless otherwise noted. Inn-to-inn trips or expeditions that use lodges and hotels typically include guides, lodging, and most, but not necessarily all, meals. Participants must sometimes get to the trailhead on their own or meet at a designated spot for group transfer to the trailhead. The cost may cover airport pickup and delivery. Airfare and lodging before or after the trip dates are not part of the price, although most outfitters can help you book these.

Instruction

Those companies or organizations that sponsor courses, such as the Appalachian Mountain Club, provide instruction as well as fun. Efficient hiking techniques, orienteering, nature studies, and how to pack a backpack and set up reliable camps are typical of what your family can learn from a course. Although vacation-oriented trips aren't geared to teaching, you learn a tremendous amount anyway. Good guides and naturalists are fonts of wilderness wisdom who will share their knowledge of everything from animal prints to edible berries.

Finding the Fun

Northeast: Appalachian Mountain Club, Hiking Holidays, Sierra Club. **Mid-Atlantic:** Sierra Club. **Southwest:** Hiking Holidays, Sierra Club. **Rockies:** REI Adventures, Sierra Club. **West Coast:** All Adventure Travel, Backroads, REI Adventures, Sierra Club. **Alaska:** Alaska Wildland Adventures, All Adventure Travel, Camp Denali, REI Adventures. **Hawaii:** All Adventure Travel, American Wilderness Experience, Backroads, REI Adventures, Sierra Club. **Canada:** All Adventure Travel, American Wilderness Experience, Backroads, Canadian Mountain Holidays, REI Adventures, Sila Sojourns, Wells Gray Park Backcountry Chalets, Western Expedition Company. **Central America:** Butterfield & Robinson. **Europe:** Butterfield & Robinson, Hiking Holidays. **Africa:** Butterfield & Robinson.

Favorite Outfitters

Alaska Wildland Adventures

 12+

At the request of its clients, Alaska Wildland Adventures made a commitment to provide a guided backcountry adventure that costs less than many of its other trips. The company came up with an expedition that focuses on hiking and camping in two national parks and in other areas of stunning beauty in Alaska.

FOR FAMILIES. The Alaska Campout Adventure begins and ends in Anchorage. Besides hiking and camping, there's also a bit of rafting, a lot of wildlife viewing, boating, and several scenic drives. Walking on a glacier and a chance to see whales are only two trip highlights. The group spends two of the nine nights at lodges, but your tent is the real room with a view. You set up camp in Kenai Fjords National Park, Kenai National Wildlife Refuge, and Wrangell–St. Elias National Park, the largest in the U.S. park system. Those who wish to can opt for a rustic cabin rather than a tent on two of the camping nights. Everyone helps with cooking and camp chores. Drop-off at the Anchor-

age airport is included in the trip cost.
 Alaska Wildland Adventures, Box 389, Girdwood AK 99587, tel. 907/783–2928 or 800/334–8730; in AK, 800/478–4100. June–Sept.: 10 days, $1,995–$2,095.

All Adventure Travel

 ALL

Susie Smyle of All Adventure Travel is a longtime adventure broker. As of press time she is no longer on her own but is working with American Wilderness Experience (*see below*) to provide the same top-notch service All Adventure offered—and the same terrific trips. Five family walking/hiking tours explore parts of the West Coast, Alaska, Canada, and Hawaii. The Canadian tours are best for families with wilderness experience. Washington and Hawaii are moderate trips, and Alaska is easy to moderate.

FOR FAMILIES. Because it's ideal for family hiking, Washington's Olympic Peninsula appears on several outfitters' family trip lists. This trek begins in Seattle, then takes adventurers to Lake Quinault and the peninsula's rain forests. There are tidal pools to study and forests and waterfalls to inspect, but you also have time to swim and boat at Lake Crescent. The group stays in hotels and lodges, and at the end of the trip you ferry back to Seattle.

The Alaska Family Safari mixes walking, driving, boating, and wildlife viewing with overnights at inns and lodges from Anchorage to the wildlands of Denali National Park's backcountry. Moose graze, eagles soar, and salmon run in this land that humans can neither tame nor dominate. This is the only hiking trip with an age restriction(6 to 11) for the kids. Older children can probably come along (ask the outfitter), but activities are geared for younger kids and there may not be older kids in the group.

In Canada, one tour visits Jasper National Park's magnificent wilderness areas, including Athabasca Glacier, the Columbia Icefield,

and Maligne Lake—the largest glacier-fed lake in the Canadian Rockies. A second tour ventures into both Alberta and British Columbia, homes of Banff and Yoho national parks, respectively. On the itinerary is one of Canada's most-photographed sites, Lake Louise, with its brilliant turquoise waters set against wildflower-filled meadows and the snow-laden, glaciated peaks of the Canadian Rockies.

Your family can also trek around the Big Island of Hawaii, a place of spectacular contrasts: eerie landscapes of black lava and cool, verdant valleys. On the coast the blue-green Pacific rolls into wide crescent beaches; Hawaii's interior hides seething craters and smoking summits where Pele, goddess of volcanoes, waits to reemerge.
 All Adventure Travel, c/o American Wilderness Experience, Box 1486, Boulder, CO 80306, tel. 303/444–2622 or 800/444–0099 (ask for Susie). July–Aug., Nov.: 6–8 days, $745–$2,560; children's discounts may be available on some trips.

American Wilderness Experience

 6+

As an adventure broker, American Wilderness Experience (AWE) works with a variety of outfitters, primarily in the American West but also around the world. Although there aren't many hiking vacations in AWE's catalog, two in Hawaii and Canada stand out as excellent family trips.

FOR FAMILIES. The 10-day, three-island Hawaiian adventure for ages 6 and up takes in Kauai, Maui, and the Big Island, combining hiking with kayaking and snorkeling in Hawaii's alluring waters. The group stays in inns and bed-and-breakfasts along the way. You hike the dramatic sea cliffs of Kauai's Na Pali Coast, visit a wildlife refuge, and swim in both the sea and the island's serene lagoons. On Maui you trek into the jungle and swim beneath the 420-foot Waimoku

Falls. No trip here is complete without a sunrise stop at Haleakala, a dormant volcano with a spectacularly massive crater at its center. This is the longest hike of the trip—9 miles down into the crater. The Big Island of Hawaii, the youngest island of the chain, is the most rugged. You explore Kilauea and the rest of Volcanoes National Park—with its still-active volcanoes—as well as snorkel along the Kona coast and participate in a traditional luau before heading to the Kona Airport.

For heli-hiking in the Canadian Rockies, join the lodge-based trips that include helicopter transport to the remote wilderness areas where you hike each day. This adventure for ages 8 and up lets you choose from a number of trip lengths and itineraries. Depending on the lodge you select, the trip begins in either Banff, in Alberta, or in Kelowna, in southern British Columbia. Relaxing in whirlpools and saunas at the lodges makes a perfect end to perfect days—as long as you consider trekking high wilderness trails, with not another soul around, perfection. Up to 48 guests can stay at the lodges, but hiking groups aren't bigger than 10 or 11.

American Wilderness Experience, Box 1486, Boulder, CO 80306, tel. 303/444– 2622 or 800/444–0099. Apr.–Dec. (all trips not available all months): 4–10 days, $960– $2,315; children's discounts available on some trips.

Appalachian Mountain Club

 ALL

The Appalachian Mountain Club (AMC) sponsors too many hiking, backpacking, and camping courses to list them all here. Four campuses in four mountain ranges—New Hampshire's White Mountains, the Berkshires in Massachusetts, New York's Catskills, and the Poconos in eastern Pennsylvania—allow AMC to develop classes that are not only extensive but varied. The club's family workshops, available at all campuses except the Poconos, are particularly worthwhile. In AMC, parents and children find a support network of teachers and outdoor professionals who give them the knowledge and skills to go out and enjoy the wilderness on their own.

FOR FAMILIES. In the White Mountains, families have several choices. Leaders of the Family Discovery Weekend (for all ages) teach forest ecology, map and compass reading, low-impact camping, and nature crafts, among other activities. Curious Explorers in Zeland centers around a 2½-mile hike to AMC's Zealand Falls hut, where preschoolers (ages 3 to 5) spend the night with their parents and guides. Curious Explorers is for ages 4 to 8 and their parents; overnight on that trip is at AMC's main lodge at Pinkham Notch Visitor Center. Family Overnight at Greenleaf Hut is for parents with kids 7–12. The whole family can join trips to Lonesome Lake and Crawford Notch; children under 13 are free at the Crawford Notch workshop. Lonesome Lake students overnight in a hut, and the Crawford Notch group sets up a woodland base camp from which to explore the surrounding area.

Berkshires workshops center around Bascom Lodge in the middle of Mt. Greylock State Reservation. A weekend Curious Explorers program here introduces kids 4 to 8 and their parents to the outdoors.

In the Catskills, a Grandparent-Grandchild Nature Weekend for ages 5 and up brings different generations together for a night hike and hands-on discovery of the natural environment. The group stays at Valley View Lodge in the High Peaks region of the Catskills. A workshop for all ages, Introduction to Family Backpacking and Camping, incorporates moderate hikes and overnight camping. At this campus, tents and backpacks are available for rent if you don't have your own.

Appalachian Mountain Club, Box 298, Gorham, NH 03581, tel. 603/466–2727 (White Mountains and AMC headquarters), 413/443–0011 (Berkshires), or 518/624–

2056 (Catskills). Apr.–Oct. (all courses not available all months): 2–3 days, $35–$175. AMC family membership is $65; members receive a 10% discount on all workshops.

Backroads

 ALL

Backroads, with one of the largest selections of family trips of any adventure travel company, seems to add more family departures every year. By the time you try all the hiking Backroads currently offers, new destinations will be beckoning families to the trails of North America and beyond.

FOR FAMILIES. Eight family departures to four locations accommodate those wishing to explore parts of Washington, Canada, and Hawaii. On the Olympic Peninsula in Washington, families follow trails, park service roads, and beaches, staying in Victorian inns and rustic lodges throughout the trip. The other adventures are for those who prefer to hike and camp out under the stars.

The Canadian Rockies tour takes you through Banff and Yoho national parks; high peaks, lodgepole pine forests, glaciers, and clear, deep lakes form great backdrops for the trails and campsites. On the last night, the group unwinds at Emerald Lake Lodge, where an enormous hot tub helps soothe sore muscles.

Jasper, largest of the Canadian Rockies parks, makes another appealing trip. Trails lead hikers from fragile alpine meadows to massive ice fields. A Sunwapta River rafting adventure and a final night at Sunwapta Falls Resort are special treats; your family may see moose and bighorn sheep, too.

During the Big Island adventure, the group explores Hawaii from the remote Waipio Valley to the historic town of Hilo. You visit a taro farmer as well as Hawaii Volcanoes National Park, where a volcanologist explains the mysteries of Kilauea Caldera and Kilauea Iki Crater. One night is spent

indoors at the Hilo Hawaiian on Hilo Bay. *Backroads, 1516 5th St., Suite L102, Berkeley, CA 94710, tel. 510/527–1555 or 800/462–2848. July–Aug., Nov.: 5–6 days, $735–$1,253; 10%–75% discount for children, depending on age and accommodations.*

Butterfield & Robinson

13+

Butterfield & Robinson (B&R) believes a walking trip "should move along at a leisurely pace, like a well-told story." That analogy works well for family hikes, too. B&R hiking trips designated specifically for families may be few in number, but the destinations are exceptional. This is a luxury operation, and prices reflect the exceptionally high quality of the tours, staffing, and accommodations.

FOR FAMILIES. B&R typically schedules family departures on three walking expeditions, with some variations in the destinations from year to year. The walking tour of the Swiss Alps combines the shop-lined streets of Zermatt, world-class-resort towns such as Crans-Montana, and flowering alpine meadows in the shadow of the Matterhorn. Accommodations are in hotels and traditional Swiss chalets.

In Central America, ancient Mayan temples and 1,000-foot waterfalls hide in the lush rain forests of Belize. Caracol, Xunantunich, and the magnificent city of Tikal (over the border in Guatemala) are among the Mayan ruins you visit. Popular family activities on the itinerary include snorkeling inside Belize's 185-mile-long barrier reef and canoeing on a jungle river, as well as traveling by four-wheel-drive vehicle from Belize City to the interior. Lodgings vary from beachfront hotels to thatched jungle cottages.

B&R's Kenya walking tour is unique in a land where crowded bus safaris have become more the rule than the exception. In partnership with two guides who have led luxury safaris for more than 20 years—one a former warden in the national park system, the other an expert in Kenya's bird, plant, and animal life—B&R takes hikers through the Samburu National Reserve and portions of the Masai Mara plain. Four-passenger Range Rovers supplement walking for an experience that allows close-up wildlife viewing and contact with native cultures; the group stays off the routes and out of the areas used by other safari guides. Service is incomparable; expect every need to be catered to, including daily laundry service. Maximum group size is 6 to 12 on this journey.

 Butterfield & Robinson, 70 Bond St., Toronto M5B 1X3, Ontario, Canada, tel. 416/864–1354 or 800/678–1147. July–Aug., Dec.: 8–10 days, $2,940–$6,850.

Camp Denali

🚹🚺 6+

Camp Denali isn't for everyone. Its location in the geographic center of the 5.7 million acres of Denali National Park in Alaska puts it seven hours from the nearest town, and the lodge, which has no television or bar, accommodates just 35–40 guests at a time. Camp Denali's commitment to the preservation of the park's unique ecosystem guides all the activities it offers. Active families who love learning will appreciate the lodge's remote but dynamic wilderness setting—it's one of only two park lodges with views of Mt. McKinley. You don't have to rough it entirely, however. Fresh baked goods, jams and syrups made from the tundra's bountiful supply of wild berries, and fresh greens from the lodge's innovative greenhouse (heat is made from recycled waste) mean excellent food.

FOR FAMILIES. There are no separate activities for children; walking and hiking take center stage for everyone. Although there's no hard-and-fast rule about the minimum age, the feeling is that kids 6 and older have the capability to explore the area and take

in the information shared by staff members. You can hike the few maintained trails or head for unspoiled backcountry. Naturalists guide guests on hikes of varying lengths; your family can also map out a route with the help of lodge employees. Hikes can take you to see beavers at work, grizzlies digging for food, or moose and caribou silhouetted against Denali (the native name for Mt. McKinley) itself. For a change of pace, try canoeing in the deep blue waters of Wonder Lake or biking the park roads.

Families have a number of other ways to learn more about Denali. Evening activities—slides and naturalist talks—attract all ages. Camp Denali's Natural History Resource Center has interactive exhibits in addition to a herbarium and extensive resource library. Throughout the season, too, experts lead multiday special-interest sessions on topics from the aurora borealis to nature photography. There are no additional charges for these or any of the lodge's instructional programs.

 Camp Denali, Box 67, Denali National Park, AK 99755, tel. 907/683–2290 (mid-May–mid-Sept.); Box 216, Cornish, NH 03746, tel. 603/675–2248 (mid-Sept.–mid-May). May–Sept.: 4–8 days, $540–$1,680. Price includes round-trip transportation from Denali Park Rail Station.

Canadian Mountain Holidays

🚹🚺 ALL

The Cariboo, Purcell, Bugaboo, and Selkirk wilderness areas of southern British Columbia may be too challenging for many families to hike into on their own. With a helicopter lift from one of its lodges each day and treks for every ability, Canadian Mountain Holidays helps hikers of all ages discover mountain landscapes that are as breathtaking as they are remote.

FOR FAMILIES. At the company's four lodges, groups of about 11 are divided by ability and taste, so you can hike with your family or go your separate ways and meet back at the lodge. Hikes from Cariboo Lodge, about 80 miles southwest of Jasper in the Cariboo Mountains, lead to massive glaciers and heather-filled alpine valleys. The Bobbie Burns Lodge is about 195 miles west of Calgary, deep in the Purcell Range. Trails high on Grizzly Ridge have unparalleled views of the vast Conrad Icefield and the Bugaboo and Vowell peaks. Bugaboo Lodge, across Grizzly Ridge from the Bobbie Burns, sits at the base of the Bugaboo Glacier. The terrain here encompasses sunny meadows and blue alpine lakes, forests, glaciers, waterfalls, and rushing mountain streams. The company's newest lodge, the Adamant, is in the Selkirk mountains, some 75 miles north of Revelstoke. Here, open meadows and gentle ridges make it possible to hike in an area dominated by imposing granite peaks and spires.

The lodges have just 22 to 28 rooms each, almost all of which have private baths. The lack of a strict rule about the age of children allows families with young children to enjoy these remote areas. The company requests, however, that parents with children under 8 call and discuss details before booking a stay. Transportation is included in the price but differs for each lodge. For Bugaboo and Bobbie Burns lodges, transportation from Banff is included; for Adamant, transportation is from Kelowna or Revelstoke; guests at the Cariboo meet in Jasper.

 Canadian Mountain Holidays, Box 1660, Banff T0I 0C0, Alberta, Canada, tel. 403/762–7100 or 800/661–0252. July–Sept.: 1–8 days, $125–$2,300.

Hiking Holidays

10+

Although Hiking Holidays, the sister company to Vermont Bicycle Touring (see Biking), doesn't designate specific family trips, children 10 and up can join parents on domestic tours. Kids over 12 can sign up for international expeditions. Not surprisingly,

the Vermont-based company has many New England trips, but if your heart is set on hiking in Virginia, North Carolina, Arizona, or New Mexico, you can do that, too, or head for trails in Canada and throughout Europe. On all trips, accommodations are in inns and small lodges.

FOR FAMILIES. The company recommends several trips for families. Vermont Villages, an easy tour, focuses on history rather than wilderness as you visit Plymouth, Woodstock, Grafton, and Windsor. Calvin Coolidge's birthplace and summer White House can be seen in Plymouth, along with several state-owned historic buildings and a working cheese factory. Windsor has a large museum of machine tools. The Maine Coast trip meanders through small fishing villages, where you can sit on the wharf and watch the boats come in, and parts of Acadia National Park. An Arizona trek presents more challenging options, with hikes on trails along the Mexican border and through Chiracahua National Monument with its eerie rock formations. Ridges high above Coronado National Memorial on the Mexican border and the saguaro cactus forest, with its stands of 50-foot-high cacti, highlight the diversity of the fragile desert landscape.

Hiking Holidays doesn't get many children on its international tours, but the trips through England's gentle Cotswolds and along Ireland's rugged, romantic coast deserve consideration. If you're looking for companions for your teens, though, try to book these adventures with another family.

 Hiking Holidays, Box 750, Bristol, VT 05443, tel. 802/453–4816. Mar.–Nov.: 5–8 days, $895–$1,695.

REI Adventures

11+

REI, the nationwide outdoor gear store that has always been outfitting adventurers since 1938, has always allowed children on its trips, but only on a case-by-case basis. Now, because so many people have requested it, a number of hiking-only and hiking combination tours have departure dates designated for families. REI takes 6 to 12 adventurers on most trips.

FOR FAMILIES. You can choose a family departure on three hiking-only trips. One in California is excellent for families just beginning to venture into the wilderness. REI supplies all camping equipment for this adventure in the High Sierra, including sleeping bags, so just bring a day pack and camera. The first and last nights are spent at Bass Lake Resort; on the remaining days you explore the Ansel Adams and John Muir wilderness areas on Yosemite National Park's southern border from your base camp. Participants on the Olympic Peninsula outing hike Olympic National Park and Washington's coastal area by day and overnight in historic lodges and hotels. The Hidden Treasures Camping Adventure in Alaska takes in Denali, Wrangell–St. Elias, and Kenai Fjords national parks. Get ready to experience one of nature's most impressive auditory endeavors when you cross Prince William Sound: the earthshaking roar of a glacier as huge chunks of it calve into the water.

Combination trips take the adventurous to Hawaii, Canada, and Colorado for a variety of activities in addition to hiking. A two-week combination pairs trips to the Big Island of Hawaii and Kauai. You can sign up for either adventure separately, but linking the two lets you explore vastly different islands. On the Big Island, hikers experience the otherworldly terrain of lava flows and camp on a black sand beach. In the warm, clear waters off the Kona coast there's snorkeling among the humuhumunuku-nukuapuaa, Hawaii's beautiful state fish. Kauai's Na Pali Coast, accessible only by trail or boat, is a favorite area for kayakers and hikers. Those who visit Kauai with REI will kayak the waters off Na Pali as well as jungle rivers. The group also visits parts of the spectacular wet and mountainous interior that few tourists see. You hike portions of

the ancient Kalalau trail into Kalalau Valley and end the trip in the Kokee highlands around Waimea Canyon, often called the Grand Canyon of the Pacific. Among the trails of Kokee are those in Waimea Canyon, the Na Pali-Kona Forest Reserve, and Alaka'i Swamp, the highest swamp in North America and the largest alpine swamp in the world.

The Canadian combination trip takes you hiking, biking, and rafting through the Canadian Rockies and the country's most famous national parks—Banff, Jasper, and Yoho. You also have a chance to tour Calgary.

Durango, in southwestern Colorado, is another setting for hiking, biking, and rafting; this trip includes a visit to the Mesa Verde cliff dwellings of the Anasazi. Mountain biking along an old stagecoach road melds the history and views that draw adventurers. 🏠 *REI Adventures, Box 1938, Sumner, WA 98390, tel. 206/395–8111 or 800/622–2236. Mar.–Dec. (family departures June–Aug.): 7–14 days, $885–$2,090.*

Sierra Club

👫 ALL

Of the Sierra Club's 25 family trips, 17 focus primarily on hiking. The majority of these explore western states, but you'll find several eastern destinations each year, too. Sierra Club leaders are highly experienced in guiding families. All trips, family and otherwise, emphasize respect for, and preservation of, America's wilderness areas. This is one of the few organizations of its kind to welcome children on some service trips as well—expeditions that involve clearing and maintaining trails.

FOR FAMILIES. There are family trips for all ages, but not all trips are suitable for every age. Families with toddlers (aged 2 and up) have a choice of the A–Z Toddler Tromp in Virginia's Prince William Forest Park or the Acadia Toddler Tromp in Acadia National Park, Maine. Both trips highlight age-appropriate activities such as bug collecting, tidal pool explorations, easy hikes, and nature education by trip leaders and park rangers.

The club's outings for all ages—including babies in backpacks—explore colonial Maryland, the island of Kauai, and Arches and Canyonlands national parks in Utah. In Maryland families take day hikes and visit a farm museum, a cypress swamp, and tidal marshes rich in wildlife. You stay at local campgrounds and do some traveling by car. The trip cost does not cover most dinners. On the Kauai itinerary are all the island's intriguing natural sites: the Na Pali Coast, Waimea Canyon, Alaka'i Swamp with its dwarf trees and wild pigs, and glorious beaches sloping down to a blue-green sea. In addition to hiking, families can snorkel and sightsee. Rustic beachside lodging provides a base for these adventures. The Utah trip includes Canyonlands and the less well-known Arches, whose natural red rock spans make it one of the most dramatically beautiful parks in the system. There are evening ranger presentations for all ages and a layover day on which families can explore on their own.

Children as young as 5 are welcome on a separate Arches and Canyonlands adventure with the same basic itinerary as the trip for all ages. A Grandparents and Grandchildren outing in Tahoe National Forest in the Sierra, also for those 5 and up, gives different generations a chance to learn and play together. Using the club's Clair Tappaan Lodge as a base, children and adults can hike, swim, and do some exploring away from the group, too.

Another group of trips targets kids 6–12 and their parents. Families can join the base-camp trip to Coconino National Forest in Arizona. This outing uses four-wheel-drive vehicles to get to day-hike destinations, where guides explain the area's geology and the importance of ancient native cultures. Everyone needs to be in good shape for a strenuous climb of about 3,800 feet. In

Washington, families travel 50 miles by ferry to a base camp of rustic cabins on Lake Chelan in the northern Cascades. Hikes on Stehekin Valley's glaciated terrain vary from easy to strenuous. Finally, of two California trips for this age group, one visits the John Muir Wilderness in the Sierra; the other combines the Santa Cruz mountains and coast. In the Sierra, reaching camp requires a moderate 6-mile hike. Once you've done that, you can fish, hike, or just relax and gaze at the peaks around you. The Santa Cruz expedition to California's redwood forests and rugged coast includes a lighthouse stay.

Families with children 8 and up have a number of choices. They can trek around the Ansel Adams Wilderness, fish in Emily Lake, and even tackle a Sierra peak or two on the Minarets and Emily Lake excursion in California. Those interested in native cultures should consider the Grand Canyon Adventure, most of which takes place deep in the canyon on the Havasupai Reservation. Families on this trip will hike down four geologic strata of the Grand Canyon to a base camp on Havasu Creek. Turquoise pools and dramatic waterfalls cool swimmers and challenge photographers. A visit to the native village of Supai is part of the trip.

For families who want to combine their vacation with outdoor work, two trail service trips give children a firsthand understanding of what it means to volunteer. Pick your destination: Coconino National Forest in Arizona or Tahoe National Forest in the Sierra. The first is a camping experience with a minimum age of 5; the second is a lodge-based trip for volunteers 4 and older. These are great ways for children to learn about stewardship of the land.

🏨 *Sierra Club, 730 Polk St., San Francisco, CA 94109, tel. 415/923–5522. Apr.–Sept.: 4–8 days, $130–$785. Price does not include Sierra Club membership, required for all participants over 11.*

Sila Sojourns

(👫 10+)

Sila is an Inuit word for nature and free-spiritedness. To the people of the Arctic, it signifies a mysterious power in the universe. A walk through Canada's Yukon wilderness will help you understand why Joyce Majiski and Jill Pangman gave their company this name. Nature's scale here is immense, giving a sense of an undefinable force. Joyce and Jill, longtime Yukon residents, have considerable wilderness experience as guides. They bring another dimension to their company as well: Both are biologists, naturalists, and fine artists. Their trips challenge adventurers to stretch their physical and creative limits. Families with older children may find in Sila Sojourns an experience that is as good for the soul as it is for the body.

FOR FAMILIES. Although Sila has some scheduled expeditions for up to 10 hikers, the company specializes in personalized trips. All journeys start and end in Whitehorse; any wilderness flights are included in the trip cost. Joyce recommends two areas for custom family treks. In either, a hiking trip can be combined with a four-day rafting adventure down the Alsek River to Lowell Lake, where the calving Lowell Glacier provides a visual and auditory feast. For ages 10 and up, Primrose Lake, a half-hour flight from Whitehorse in the southern section of the Yukon, offers moderate hikes that follow game trails across rolling hills and past clear lakes and streams. The land changes from alpine meadows to northern boreal forests of spruce, poplar, and lodgepole pine. Because much of the hiking is above tree-line, there are uninterrupted views of the landscape and opportunities to see Dall sheep, grizzlies, black bears, and moose. You spend two nights of the trip in a wilderness lodge; on the rest you camp out.

Bordering Alaska in the southwest corner of the Yukon, Kluane National Park encompasses 8,500 square miles, with glaciers, marshes, and mountains that are dramatic and untamed. Challenging hiking terrain makes this trip best for ages 16 and up; the park contains both Mt. Logan and Mt. St. Elias, the second- and third-highest peaks in North America. An astonishing variety of wildlife inhabits the park: moose, wolves, foxes, lynx, wolverines, otters, and black bears, as well as a large grizzly population. You camp in alpine areas or by rivers and glaciers.

Some multi-activity trips for women focus on the creative process. Mothers and teenage daughters who want to experience the wilderness and explore perspectives on creative writing, journal keeping, and other means of artistic expression should ask about these camping or lodge-based trips. Depending on the location, participants hike from a lodge, kayak on Atlin Lake in northern British Columbia, or even canoe or raft. 🏠 *Sila Sojourns, Box 5095, Whitehorse Y1A 4Z2, Yukon, Canada, tel. 403/633–8453. June–Sept.: 7–12 days, $925–$1,300; the raft add-on is $615.*

Wells Gray Park Backcountry Chalets

(👫 8+)

The Cariboo Mountains reign over the 1.3 million acres of Wells Gray Provincial Park in southeastern British Columbia, a pristine land of alpine meadows and mountain lakes. Wells Gray Park Backcountry Chalets, a family business, operates two high wilderness chalets and a secluded valley cabin here; a separate guest ranch (not owned by this company) is near the entrance to the park. The chalets can be rented individually without guides or used as part of a guided hiking trek. Although there's no stated age limit, the hut-to-hut hike is very challenging—perfect for families with teens. Families with children under age 8 should talk to staff members before booking a vacation. Because of increased interest, the company now designates a hiking trip in August just for families.

FOR FAMILIES. If you have preteens and younger, or just can't decide whether you prefer land or water, check out the Canoe and Trek Combo. Families camp along the shore of Clearwater Lake for three days of canoeing, then spend a night at Wells Gray Guest Ranch before beginning three days of trekking based at a secluded mountain hut.

Parents with teens or with solid backcountry experience might opt for the company's premier trip, the six-day hut-to-hut trek. Although it's just a little more than 1½ miles in to Trophy Mountain chalet, the ascent is about 1,300 feet. This area presents the most rugged terrain of the trip; you can reward yourself with a swim and glorious views. Table Mountain Cabin, the next stop, is reached by crossing the Trophy Mountains and descending into the isolated Moul Valley. Fight Meadow Chalet, the third and last hut, is 6,500 feet up at the head of an expansive alpine meadow. There are no trails between huts; this is true wilderness hiking for those who want to challenge themselves and each other. Parents should be sure of their own and their children's abilities before undertaking this trek.

 Wells Gray Park Backcountry Chalets, Box 188, Clearwater V0E 1N0, British Columbia, Canada, tel 604/587–6444. June–Sept.: 6 days, $405–$470.

Western Expedition Company

👫 13+

Harold Esau and his partners in Western Expedition Company have a firm belief: The family that camps together, stays together. Given this conviction, it's not surprising that the company welcomes families and seeks to give them challenging experiences and lasting memories. Besides being excellent trail leaders, Western Expedition guides will teach your family all you want to know, from backcountry hiking techniques to the history and ecology of an area. The company is headquartered in southwestern British Columbia, about 45 miles east of Vancouver, with access to one of the greatest hiking areas in the world.

FOR FAMILIES. Two-, three-, and five-day expeditions meet the needs of a variety of families. Tour One (the company uses these numbers) is a five-day trek to the Cathedral Lakes region in southern British Columbia, close to the U.S. border. The most challenging of the three tours, this is best for ages 16 and up. To get to base camp, hikers must carry 25- to 30-pound packs over 10 miles, with an ascent of more than 3,000 feet. From camp, the group takes day hikes to such awesome formations and natural landmarks as Stone City (a quartz and monzonite formation), Devil's Woodpile, Smokey the Bear, and the Giant Cleft. The Cathedrals themselves are a series of alpine lakes. You may see a few of the shy mountain goats and bighorn sheep that share the area with hiking humans.

Tour Two, a three-day outing, takes you to Manning Provincial Park and the subalpine meadows surrounding Nicomen Lake and Grainger Creek, in the shadow of the Four Brothers peaks. From mid-July to mid-August, the valley floor is 15 miles of wildflowers in bloom. Also in Manning, which is three hours east of Vancouver, is Tour Three, the two-day expedition. Those who don't want to commit to a longer trip will find this a perfect introduction to the world of nature, hiking, and camping. Both Manning trips are good for children aged 13 and up; the company will make exceptions for younger kids with solid experience—but call first. Even on these shorter adventures, children must be able to carry fairly heavy gear. Bring warm clothes; this area is typically 40° in the evening—and occasionally in the daytime, too.

 Western Expedition Company, 35704 Sunridge Pl., Abbotsford V3G 1E5, British Columbia, Canada, tel. 604/855–0840. June–Oct.: 2–5 days, $200–$425.

Resources

Books

For solid information on taking children into the wilderness, check out the newly revised *The Sierra Club Family Outdoors Guide,* by Marlyn Doan (Sierra Club Books) and *Kids in the Wild,* by Cindy Ross and Todd Gladfelter (Mountaineers Books, tel. 800/553–4453). Michael Elsohn Ross's *The Happy Camper Handbook* (Yosemite Association, tel. 209/379–2648) comes with a flashlight and rescue whistle and is full of essential camping information for school-age kids; it's perfect for parents to read aloud and discuss with younger kids, too.

Products

The following companies sell clothing or footwear for wilderness-loving families. **Patagonia** (Box 150, Ventura, CA 93002, tel. 805/643–8616 or 800/638–6464) is an excellent mail-order source for clothing and outerwear. You can also buy the company's products in most stores that sell outdoor and camping clothing and accessories. **REI outdoor stores** (Box 1938, Sumner, WA 98390, tel. 800/426–4840) are found nationwide; items can be ordered from their catalog, too. You'll find the greatest selection of children's clothing and gear in the stores,

but the catalog has a fair representation. REI's own brand is excellent. **Nike** (1 Bowerman Dr., Beavertown, OR 97005, tel. 503/671–6453 or 800/344–6453) has hiking boots, water sandals, and aqua socks for all ages, as well as some children's sport clothing and outwear. **Hi-Tec Sports USA** (4801 Stoddard Rd., Modesto, CA 95356, tel. 209/545–1111 or 800/521–1698) makes hiking boots and "adventure racing shoes" for kids and adults.

The following companies make camping gear for children and adults. **Tough Traveler** (1012 State St., Schenectady, NY 12307, tel. 518/377–5434), a parent-owned and -operated company, produces quality outdoor gear and luggage for kids. Of special interest are the internal-frame backpacks and a sleeping bag that adjusts for growing kids, as well as backpack-style baby and child carriers for parents. Call or write for a catalog. **Mountainsmith, Inc.** (18301 W. Colfax Ave., Golden, CO 80401, tel. 303/279–5930 or 800/426–4075) manufactures daypacks suitable for most ages and inner-frame backpacks for older children and adults. **Crazy Creek Chairs** (Box 1050, Red Lodge, MT 59068, tel. 406/446–3446 or 800/331–0304) makes camping comfortable with 12 models of take-anywhere, fold-up soft chairs that provide back support and insulation from cold, wet ground.

HORSE PACKING

Like hiking adventures, horse pack trips take your family into some of the world's most incredible backcountry wilderness areas. With these trips on horseback, though, you don't have to walk on your own two feet to get there, and you don't have to carry a heavy backpack. Often it's not even necessary to be an expert rider. Adults and teens need no riding experience on many pack trips, although for everyone's safety and enjoyment outfitters often require that children who are under the age of 11 or 12 ride moderately well and be comfortable around horses. For this reason, horse packing (with a couple of exceptions) is not usually appropriate for families with very young children. Anyone else who wants to experience glorious land and a mode of travel that has been around for centuries should give it a try.

There's another nice benefit to horse pack trips, too. Because horses and mules are capable of carrying a lot more than a human, you can escape the spartan atmosphere of long backpacking adventures: Food and supplies are first-rate and plentiful.

Questions to Ask

How much time is spent riding each day? On average, outfitters keep you in the saddle four to six hours per day, but on some trips you may ride as long as eight hours. Depending on the group's size and whether there is a specific or flexible destination for camp, riding time can also change from day to day. Keep in mind that layover days are usually scheduled into multiday trips, too.

Will we be uncomfortable? Riding requires the use of leg muscles you probably don't use that often. A day in the saddle can leave you aching and with saddle sores if you're not a rider. The discomfort doesn't usually last that long, but do bring acetaminophen or another pain reliever, antibiotic cream, and a bunch of adhesive bandages.

Can the horses travel faster than a walk? Most horse pack trips are primarily walking because they often take place in hilly or otherwise challenging terrain. Although horses are very surefooted, walking is the safest way to negotiate these trails—both for horse and rider. Sometimes wranglers allow good riders to go a bit faster under controlled circumstances. If your family cares about this, speak up when you're booking. If you can't work something out, consider a cattle drive (see Cattle Drives), which often allows a faster pace.

Are there other activities? Packers generally head for camp early enough in the afternoon to give your family time for hiking, swimming and maybe even fishing. You usually need to bring your own fishing gear, however.

Is there a weight limit to what we can bring? Often, yes. A 30-pound limit per person is typical, and you should pack in duffel bags, not hard-sided suitcases.

Are riding boots necessary? Some packers require boots; even if they don't, everyone in the family should have them for safety and comfort. Shoes without adequate heels may allow your foot to slip through the stirrup. If that happened, and if by chance you fell off, you'd be dragged. Be sure to break new boots in well before the trip.

Is a cowboy hat or a riding helmet needed? A cowboy hat will keep the sun off your face and your hair out of your eyes, and that can be important. It won't, however, protect your head if you fall. Some outfitters provide helmets; most don't require them. To keep yourself and your kids safe, you should wear them. You can buy helmets at stores that sell riding apparel and equipment.

Should we bring our camera? You bet. Keep it in a case for protection against dust and dirt, and talk to packers about stopping occasionally for a good shot (most, actually, will tell you when a great photo op is coming up). Don't leave the group to get a good picture without telling someone first; you could get lost. If you're not comfortable carrying a camera when you ride, it can usually go in a saddle bag with your stuff.

What kind of food is served? If your family likes outdoor cooking—hearty egg and pancake breakfasts, Dutch oven meals, barbecue, steaks, salads, fruit, and desserts—you'll like the meals just fine. Special requests can usually be accommodated, so ask.

What kind of lodging is provided? These are backcountry trips. Sleeping is almost always in tents—or cowboy-style under the stars, if you prefer. A few packers use cabins or lodges.

What facilities are there for bathing and showering? Do you like the smell of horses? You should, because it will be the predominant odor on a pack trip. At the end of the day, though, some outfitters do provide portable showers or shower trailers. If you're staying in lodges or cabins, you may have access to showers.

What's the typical group size? The average is 8 to 12, though some outfitters take as few as 4 and others as many as 20. Two to four or five wranglers and/or packers accompany the group. A large group isn't necessarily bad, because it provides lots of companionship, and a small group isn't necessarily good if you don't want to be the only ones in the group.

What's included in the cost? Prices for the trips listed here include wranglers and/or packers, a horse, sleeping quarters, all meals from start to end of the actual pack trip, and local transportation to and from the trailhead, unless otherwise noted.

Instruction

Horsemanship is part and parcel of every horse pack trip; the wranglers will give you pointers and informal instruction on the trail. Your family can also learn about feeding and caring for horses—and even how to saddle bags. While you're out in the wilderness, guides will teach you about the cultural and natural history of the land, as well as wildlife identification.

Finding the Fun

Northeast: American Wilderness Experience. **Midwest:** Dakota Badlands Outfitters. **Southwest:** American Wilderness Experience, Cottonwood Ranch, Rockin' R Ranch. **Rockies:** Adventure Specialists, American Wilderness Experience, Fantasy Ranch, Great Divide Guiding & Outfitters, Skinner Brothers, Vista Verde Ranch, White Tail Ranch. **West Coast:** Mammoth Lakes Pack Outfit. **Alaska:** American Wilderness Experience. **Canada:** Spatsizi Wilderness Vacations.

Favorite Packers

Adventure Specialists

Horse pack trips are just one adventure offered by this somewhat unique outfitter. Based on a 5,000-acre ranch in southern Colorado, Adventure Specialists uses what it possesses—the ranch itself and 70 Appaloosa and Paso Fino horses—and all that's in its backyard, too: the rugged Sangre de Cristo Mountains, the gentler Wet Mountains, and the Arkansas River. You can hike, bike, climb, and raft, as well as ride, on some of the trips.

Owners Gary Ziegler and Amy Finger emphasize natural history and environmental awareness. Gary earned a doctorate in archaeology, discovered the ruins of an ancient city in Peru, and has made first ascents of several 20,000-foot South American peaks. Amy, a geologist, has studied languages, flora, and ecology extensively. She's worked with horses most of her life.

FOR FAMILIES. Three adventures are especially appropriate for families. The three-day pack trip into the Sangre de Cristo Mountains is best for spirited kids 10 and up who are ready for a challenge. They should have some riding experience and be comfortable around horses. There's one base camp, and rides go through dense forests and up to shimmery alpine lakes. The Surf and Turf trip combines the three-day pack trip with two days of rafting on the Arkansas; because the Arkansas is Class III and IV white water, the minimum age is 13. Accommodations during the rafting portion are at the Westcliffe Inn, with cozy rooms and a hot tub.

For a completely different experience, Mountain Sports Week has rock climbing, two days of riding the open range, two days of mountain biking including a day on the famous Rainbow Trail in the Sangre de Cristo (or you can opt for a hike), and a day of rafting. Participants are based at the ranch in a camp that has individual tents for sleeping, showers, and a large dining and kitchen tent. Kids under the age of 10 might be considered on an individual basis, but this is a physically challenging week. You can also customize your own course, choosing any of the activities.

Transportation to and from Colorado Springs, 1½ hours away, is included in all packages. Ask about the hiking and pack trips to Mexico and Peru, and unique adventure trips in Spain.

 Adventure Specialists, Bear Basin Ranch, Westcliffe, CO 81252, tel. 719/783–2519 (ranch, year-round) or 719/630–7687 (Colorado Springs office, Dec.–Apr.). May–Oct. (all trips not at all times): 3–6 days, $395–$825; customized courses, $125–$150 per person per day.

American Wilderness Experience

👫 6+

If you haven't picked the area you want to ride in or if you want an overview of your options, take a look at the American Wilderness Experience (AWE) catalog. It lists more than 10 pages of horse pack adventures. Some of the outfitters AWE uses are in this chapter, and you can book directly with them. But if research isn't your thing, AWE is an excellent choice. The company has already evaluated the outfitters, knows which ones work best with families, and can make recommendations based on experience and solid knowledge.

If the scheduled trips don't work for you, AWE will also customize a family trip for ages 6 and up. Your willingness to meet adventure head on and your imagination are the only limits to the horse pack vacation of a lifetime.

FOR FAMILIES. One trip takes riders deep into the Alaska Range, over passes and down into valleys on the edge of Denali National Park, where colorful wildflowers stand out against the icy blue of the north country's rivers, peaks, and sky. Children ages 8 or 9 with riding experience, age 10 without it, can go along to experience a part of Alaska few tourists will ever see.

In the lower forty-eight, kids 8 and up can explore Wyoming's Gros Ventre wilderness area on trails deep in the Bridger-Teton backcountry. The land is unspoiled but the guests aren't: A seasonal camp in the forest has a heated mess tent, log furniture, spacious wall tents, and a shower. Farther south, families with children 8 and up can ride through the mesas, meadows, canyons, and rugged landscape of the Gila Wilderness, part of New Mexico's 3.3 million-acre Gila National Forest. The Gila area is home to eagles, antelope, mountain lions, and elk, among other wildlife. Motel lodging before and after this trip is included.

Families interested in the Southwest might choose instead to explore Monument Valley, a wild western landscape straddling the Arizona-Utah border. Towering mesas and sand- and wind-sculpted monoliths define the valley, which is within the Navajo Nation. Guides share with the group the legends, lore, and remarkable natural wonders of Monument. At the base camp near Thunderbird Mesa, expect spacious wall tents, sleeping cots, bedrolls, pads, sheets, pillows, a hot-shower trailer, and fine food to welcome you each afternoon after your ride.

In the East, 80 miles of forest trails give riders aged six and up access to the gentler beauty of Vermont's Green Mountains; the Mountain Top Inn and Resort in Chittenden, near Killington, serves as your base. Guests ride English or western style through a quintessential New England landscape of rolling hills, forests, covered bridges, and lush valleys. At night, there are candlelit dinners and evening entertainment (chess or checkers, slide shows, talks by historians and naturalists) at the cozy lodge. If you have nonriders in your group, the inn also has boating, hiking trails, mountain bikes, and a pool.

American Wilderness Experience, Box 1486, Boulder, CO 80306, tel. 303/444–2622 or 800/444–0099. Apr.–Nov.: 3–8 days, $405–$1,405; custom trips average $150 per person per day.

Cottonwood Ranch

(👫 7+)

A horse pack trip with the Smiths is a gem of an adventure, far off the beaten path in Nevada. Their family ranch, 75 miles north of Wells in the northeast corner of the state, is near nothing—except clean, quiet high desert and the exquisite landscape of the Jarbridge Wilderness. Horace Smith will share with you his love of a land that few have a chance to experience.

FOR FAMILIES. Guests spend the first night at Cottonwood Ranch, then take off for five days in the wilderness. Deep canyons and high peaks make this terrain appropriate for riding at a walk only. You hit the trail from about 9 to 4 each day; camps with wall tents and cook tents are set up by the wranglers before you arrive. Photo stops are numerous, and you visit abandoned mining cabins that Horace says "look like the old miner just went into town for a day and forgot to come back." There's plenty of wildlife on the trail and good fishing at Emerald Lake (some gear is available); also you can swim in the lake if you can stand the cold water. On the last night you reach the old mining town of Jarbridge and stay in a remodeled barn-turned-hotel.
🏠 *Cottonwood Ranch, HC 63, Box 1300, O'Neil Rte., Wells, NV 89835, tel. 702/752–3604. July–Sept.: 6 days, $995; ask about family discounts.*

Dakota Badland Outfitters

(👫 5+)

John Husted, a fifth-generation South Dakota rancher, comes from a family that homesteaded in the Dakota badlands. He and his wife, Jane, enjoy showing the state they love to visitors. Their ranch in the state's other famous territory—the Black Hills—is the starting point for many of their pack trips, but they'll take you to the badlands, too.

FOR FAMILIES. Although children must be at least 5 to ride a horse with this outfitter, younger kids and nonriders can go along on a wagon on some trips. You cover 15 or more miles a day and spend five or six hours in the saddle, but the rides are strictly walking. All trips have base camp setups, with tepee tents that hold a family of three comfortably, maybe four if you squeeze. The group rides out in a different direction each day. If you're not too tired, you can hike around camp after your ride. Evenings are "nothing rehearsed," Jane says—just people sitting around a campfire getting to know one another.

The best trips for families with young children are in the Black Hills, in part because these are accompanied by a wagon. Trips in this area wind through portions of national forest land that surrounds the Husted ranch. Peaks and stands of pine hide abandoned mines and lots of wildlife—deer and elk primarily. A great four-day outing is in the Hell's Canyon area on the western edge of the Black Hills, not far from Wyoming. The family bonus: no bugs in the Black Hills.

Parents with kids 10 and up may choose the lunarlike badlands—a harshly beautiful place of eroded canyons and wide-open vistas, with sunrises and sunsets that are not soon forgotten. Trails take riders through part of the Lakota Pine Ridge Reservation. Trees are few and far between, but you might get a look at a rattlesnake or a fossil. If you're really lucky, you'll catch a glimpse of the horses that run wild here.
🏠 *Dakota Badland Outfitters, Box 85, Custer, SD 57730, tel. 206/659–2255 or 605/673–5363. May–Oct. (all trips not all months): 2–4 days, $100–$600.*

Fantasy Ranch

(👫 6+)

You won't meet a harder-working outfitter than Jim Talbot of Colorado. He'll clear snow from the trails by hand if Mother

Nature hasn't cooperated by the time the season's first pack trip is scheduled. Jim has a personality children can relate to, which makes learning from him easy, and he's enthusiastic and knowledgeable about the magnificent wilderness area that is his backyard. He's also flexible: Jim won't bend safety rules but he's willing to work with families to make their pack-trip fantasies a reality.

Fantasy Ranch has just started taking overnight guests in a small six-room lodge; a bigger lodge is in the works, as is an equestrian center. Ask Jim about staying over, and about hiking, fishing, and biking adventures. In winter, there are sleigh rides, riding, and cross-country skiing.

FOR FAMILIES. Ages 6 and up can try an overnight in the Oh-Be-Joyful Wilderness northwest of Crested Butte, Fantasy Ranch's hometown. These trails are gentle, but the views and scenery—rushing waterfalls and massive rock formations—are classic Colorado. Kids 8 and up can take a two- to five-day pack trip into the West Elk Wilderness area, where Castle Peak rises 14,265 feet above the meadows and mountain lakes that make this superb riding country. You can camp or stay in a rustic cabin on the boundary of the wilderness area. Kids 6 to 8 who have never ridden will be led by one of the wranglers.

One of the all-time great pack trips is Jim's Crested Butte to Aspen adventure, for experienced riders 13 and up. The three-day ride between the two mountain towns starts at 9,000 feet, just east of Crested Butte, on trails through Gunnison National Forest. You camp in the mountains, then ride four or so hours the following day before descending into alpine meadows and the trailhead outside Aspen. A van takes you into town for an overnight in this world-class resort. Lodging in Aspen is included, but meals are on your own. The next morning you begin one of the most spectacular rides anywhere—up and over 11,800-foot East Maroon Pass, then back into Crested Butte.

On some of these trips, you need to bring your own sleeping bag and pad; add fishing gear if you want to fish.

⚑ *Fantasy Ranch, Box 236, Crested Butte, CO 81224, tel. 970/349–5425. July–Oct. (for pack trips): 2–5 days, $145–$570.*

Great Divide Guiding & Outfitters

 8+

Richard Jackson, who has more than 16 years of guiding and outfitting experience, leads every group, with his teenage son along as a wrangler. All his trips take place in Montana's Lewis and Clark National Forest, which is surrounded by Glacier National Park, the Blackfeet Indian Reservation, the Bob Marshall Wilderness, and the Great Bear Wilderness. The combination of the Jacksons' expertise and the countryside means that Great Divide's adventure and wilderness credentials are impeccable.

FOR FAMILIES. A mixture of activities on two layover days makes one five-day trip a particularly good choice for families. On Monday morning the group is picked up in East Glacier Park for a 45-minute drive to the Jacksons' ranch, where gear is packed and guests meet their equine companions. A four-hour ride brings you to a broad mountain meadow and a clear stream, your "home" for two nights. The next day your family can opt to spend time riding, fishing, hiking, or working with cattle pastured in the area. After breakfast Wednesday, the group rides on to Two Medicine River and a campsite with views of Glacier National Park. There are the same choices of activities here.

Everyone helps set up and break down camp on this trip, and evenings center around cowboy cooking, cowboy coffee, and cowboy stories around the campfire. Bring your own fishing gear if you can, or rent from Richard. Sleeping bags are available for rent, too.

🏨 *Great Divide Guiding & Outfitters, Box 315, East Glacier Park, MT 59434, tel. 406/ 226–4487 or 800/421–9687. June–Sept.: 5 days, $795.*

Mammoth Lakes Pack Outfit

👫 7+

The old pioneer trails of the eastern Sierra and the John Muir Wilderness lead riders over high mountain passes and into hidden valleys where brilliant wildflowers dazzle the eyes and animals peer at you curiously from shaded glens and rocky outcrops. This is Mammoth Lakes Pack Outfit's third decade: Families can book scheduled and custom guided trips with confidence, knowing they're getting experience and knowledge that can be counted on. The many choices allow Mammoth Lakes to accommodate riders of all ages and abilities.

FOR FAMILIES. Mammoth Lakes sends out a brochure describing the various camping areas and how long it takes to get to each of them. Families with children 7 or 8 must book a custom guided trip; scheduled trips are for ages 9 up. People who want to spend less than three hours on the trail— such as families with young children—might choose Skelton and Woods Lakes, which are available on custom trips only. You don't lose out on views by staying close to the trailhead, because this area is at an elevation of about 10,000 feet.

Families with kids nine and up can ride three to four hours over 10,700-foot Duck Pass, camping along the timberline, near Duck and Pika lakes. The outfitter will even pack rubber rafts for fishing on this scheduled trip. Also for ages nine and up is Purple Lake, 4½ hours away. It makes an excellent base camp for rides and hikes into surrounding country.

🏨 *Mammoth Lakes Pack Outfit, Box 61, Mammoth Lakes, CA 93546, tel. 619/934–2434. June–Sept.: 4–5 days, $600–$750; custom trips (3–9 days) cost $180 per person per day.*

Rockin' R Ranch

👫 8+

The southern half of Utah contains country so magnificent that there are five national parks here. Rockin' R Ranch, in Antimony, is 37 miles north of Bryce Canyon National Park and not far from Zion, Capitol Reef, Canyonlands, and Arches. Adventurers could easily spend many days exploring the area any number of ways, but no one will be disappointed by a pack trip into the backcountry adjacent to the Rockin' R.

FOR FAMILIES. On a six-day trip, the trail leads from the ranch up into canyons, over creeks, under quaking aspens, and onto the Aquarius Plateau, with views across the valley and down into Bryce Canyon National Park. Each night the wranglers set up camp and have dinner waiting when you come off the trail. There's time for fishing as well as a free afternoon for hiking, photography, or just plain loafing. One day you take a break from trail riding to try your hand at real cowboy skills, rounding up some of the ranch's stray cattle or learning to rope.

On the last day out, you can check your aim in skeet, pistol, or rifle shooting. Then you leave your horse on the plateau and head by van to Bryce Canyon National Park for an afternoon hike. Later, just outside the park, the group rides in a covered wagon and faces a staged attack on the wagons. After dinner and a local rodeo, you overnight in the ranch's comfortable quarters.

If your family doesn't have six days, go for the four-day version, which doesn't include Bryce or some other activities. You can also join a cattle drive here (see Cattle Drives).

🏨 *Rockin' R Ranch, Reservation Office, 1021 N. University Ave., Suite 205, Provo, UT 84601, tel. 801/344–8588. June–Oct.: 4–6 days, $695–$1,115.*

Skinner Brothers

 ALL

The Skinner brothers—Robert, Monte, and Courtney—like nothing better than to share their beloved Wind River Range with families. These Wyoming mountains are not as well known as their neighbors the Grand Tetons, but they are impressive in their own right. The brothers' tremendous experience with children comes from running summer wilderness camps for kids 10 and up. When they're not doing that, they customize pack trips for groups as small as two. The Skinners have a few scheduled trips as well, if your family wants to ride with other families.

FOR FAMILIES. Customize your own trip, and the Skinners will provide everything except personal gear and a sleeping bag. You can spend as many days as you want on guided rides into the Bridger Wilderness and Wind River Range. Choose a base camp experience (the Skinners refer to this as a stationary pack trip) or move camp each night (a moving pack trip).

The Participants Wilderness trip is a one-week scheduled adventure on which you join others. The age range for this has been 6 months to 92 (though I don't advocate taking infants on horses). Guides help children take part in all activities and make it a terrific experience. You can spend time hiking, riding, and fishing, so these pack trips can meet almost anyone's needs; bring your own fishing gear if you want to fish.

Families with kids 13 and up can also join the Peak Rangers Holiday, a one-week combination pack and mountain-climbing trip. You don't need experience in either riding or mountaineering, but you should be in good shape. Experienced climbers can ascend Gannett Peak, Wyoming's highest. *Skinner Brothers, Box 859, Pinedale, WY 82941, tel. 307/367–2270. July–Sept.: 2–7 days, $125–$225 per person per day for scheduled and custom trips.*

Spatsizi Wilderness Vacations

 5+

The Collingwood family runs the only guide and outfitting service permitted to operate in Spatsizi Plateau Wilderness Park, one of Canada's truly untouched wilderness areas. Spatsizi comes from the Tahltan word meaning "red goat," a name given to the mountain goats that roll in the iron oxide–rich soil of the park. Goats aren't the only animals at home among the peaks, plateaus, and glaciers of Spatsizi. There are sheep, caribou and moose, black bears and grizzlies, wolves, and hundreds of species of birds. About 200 miles north of Smithers, this remote park in northern British Columbia has only about 200 human visitors each year.

FOR FAMILIES. The Collingwoods will help families choose among three pack trips into the Spatsizi wilderness. The shortest is two to four days in the Eaglenest Mountains, where you stay at a campsite with rustic cabins and a shower house. Photographers can shoot most varieties of the park's wildlife here. There's an excellent network of trails to ride as well as alpine basins and game trails to hike.

On the eight-day trip into the Eaglenest, you travel through the Gladys Lake Ecological Reserve and have a chance to test your fishing skills in some of the great trout streams of the north. The group stays at multiple-tented campsites. This trip mixes hiking and riding; there's one seven-hour day in the saddle.

Those who want to travel deep into the most isolated regions of the park should sign up for the expedition to Buckinghorse Lake and the Fireflats, the headwaters of the Spatsizi River. This trip is probably best for kids with some riding and wilderness experience. In July the area is the nursing grounds of mountain caribou and home to a large moose population. Rainbow trout on Buckinghorse Lake can weigh in at 6 pounds. Facilities here are restricted to very rustic tent sites.

 Spatsizi Wilderness Vacations, Box 3070, Smithers V0J 2N0, British Columbia, Canada, tel. 604/847–2909. July–Aug.: 2–8 days, $1,120–$1,630. Price includes bush plane flights between Smithers and the park.

Vista Verde Ranch

13+

Vista Verde is about 25 miles north of Steamboat Springs, Colorado, near Wyoming. The ranch's eight log cabins and three lodge rooms can accommodate about 35 guests. Vista Verde's four-day pack trips take no more than eight people and are booked as part of a week's ranch stay.

FOR FAMILIES. The Routt National Forest through which you travel encompasses 1.4 million acres of wilderness. Among its trails are those used by early wranglers to move stock between Colorado and Wyoming. One, known as the Outlaw Trail, allowed Butch Cassidy and the Sundance Kid to elude law officers and get in and out of their hideout just north of the ranch, up along the Wyoming border. You move camp each day and have a chance to ride up and over the Continental Divide, if the weather holds. Back at the ranch, you can use the two hot tubs, hike, take trips into nearby Steamboat Springs, go mountain biking, or just relax in your cabin. This trip leaves the Sunday before Labor Day each year. Although many U.S. kids are already back in school, there have been an increasing number of European families, so you may have an international experience as well as a terrific pack trip.

 Vista Verde Ranch, Box 465, Steamboat Springs, CO 80477, tel. 303/879–3858 or 800/526–7433. Aug.–Sept.: 7 days, $1,395, including ranch stays 1 night before and 2 nights after the trip.

White Tail Ranch

6+

Jack and Karen Hooker own White Tail, a 1,400-acre packing and outfitting ranch in the Blackfoot Valley, about 65 miles east of Missoula, Montana. The heart of the operation is pack trips, both custom and scheduled, and riders can follow trails right from the ranch into two spectacular wilderness areas—the Bob Marshall and the Scapegoat.

FOR FAMILIES. You don't need any riding experience, and you can be practically any age: One returning guest is in his eighties, and the Hookers will consider kids younger than 6—but you must talk to them first. What they care most about is sharing with all kinds of people "a way of life worth preserving, a place of relaxation and meditation essential to American stability." If any place can have that kind of abiding effect, it's the Bob Marshall Wilderness, with a vista of incomparable beauty around every switchback. Still, some places stand out, like the world-famous Chinese Wall, a rock formation 22 miles long and 1,000 feet high in places. Scapegoat doesn't have the Chinese Wall, but it shares other attributes with the Bob Marshall: cool streams with deep holes hiding trout, flowering meadows, and emerald lakes.

State-of-the-art tents, excellent food, and a latrine with a real toilet seat secluded in its own tepee define the luxury campsites White Tail provides (these are progressive trips with new campsites most nights). There are wildflower and bird guides to study on your trip, if you wish, but much is learned—and laughed about—around the campfire each night, too.

 White Tail Ranch, Ovando, MT 59854, tel. 406/793–5666. June–Aug.: 2–10 days, $178–$189 per person per day; 10% discount for children under 12; families of 4 or more get an additional 5% discount.

Resources

Organizations

There is no national association of horse packing outfitters; however, most states have guide and/or outfitting associations and licensing agencies. You can locate these through state tourism offices. Because many guest ranches run horse packing trips, you might also want to contact the **Dude Ranchers' Association** (Box 471, LaPorte, CO 80535, tel. 970/223–8440). The association represents more than 100 ranches in states throughout the West and has information on many ranch activities, including pack trips.

Also See

If multiday riding treks and ranch work appeal to you, and if you want to ride a little faster, take a look at the Cattle Drives chapter. Families with children too young for a pack trip may find the chapter on Ranches helpful. At some ranches, a parent and older child may have the opportunity to join a short pack trip while the rest of the family stays at the ranch.

HOUSEBOATING

When you step behind the wheel or in front of the tiller of a house-boat, your destiny is your own. You and your family can explore the coves you want to, camp out on a deserted beach, or hike up from the water's edge when the mood strikes you. You sail as much or as little as you choose in a day, hug the shoreline to watch for wildlife, or seek the deep places where the best sport fish are found. Much of the heart and history of the nation lies along the shores of waterways that have made exploration and economic growth possible, and you can discover that, too, if you wish. On the other hand, with your houseboat as a movable feast and private lodge, your family might choose not to leave it at all (except, perhaps, by water slide when you want to cool off). Floating, relaxing, watching the scenery drift by—these are also options. The bottom line is this: When you are your own captain and crew, the choices are all yours. Such is the adventure, and romance, of houseboating.

Houseboating is a remarkably safe and roomy way to travel. Top speed is only about 6 to 9 miles per hour, so whether you like it or not, you take it easy. And because activities, such as swimming, biking, hiking, and fishing, are built into a houseboat vacation, it has appeal for families with children of all ages. Babies can watch the landscape go by and feel the breezes. They can ride in backpacks or bike seats, and they sleep soundly to the rhythmic rocking. Preschoolers and school-age children love the variety of daily activities and the constantly changing scenery. Teens love the cassette players that come with some boats, waterskiing, and freedom to explore some areas on their own. Everyone loves the water slides, on which the young, and young at heart, can zip and splash into the water.

Check to see if your boat has a running logbook. Children like to read, and add to, these journals in which previous renters have jotted down the secrets and wonderful discoveries they made on their journey—the best coves and beaches, the best restaurants, the small trail that wasn't mentioned in the area brochure. Who knows, your family might even be inspired to keep a journal of its own as your trip goes on—something you can all look back on in years to come.

Questions to Ask

Do I need any previous boating experience to captain a houseboat? Most companies do not require boating expertise, but some do.

What other requirements are there? Most companies ask that the renter and those who will be steering the boat be above a certain age and hold a valid driver's license.

Do you have life jackets that fit my child, or will I have to bring my own?
Some companies have vests for infants; others do not. Be prepared to give your
child's weight and chest measurement so you will know for sure if there is a coast
guard–approved safety vest that will fit. Boating and sporting goods stores sell life
jackets if you need to buy one.

What security deposit and/or insurance is required? All companies ask that
you send a sizable deposit well in advance of your sailing date. That deposit is usually
not counted toward your rental fee, and it will not be given back until you return
the boat in the same condition in which you took it out. Check to see how many
days prior to your trip you can cancel without forfeiting all or most of your deposit.
In addition to a deposit, some companies require you to purchase damage insurance; others offer it as an option. Some have their own insurance, with deductibles
that range from $250 to $1,500. Renters may be able to lower the deductible by
adding a few dollars a day to the rental fee. Because you are generally responsible
for paying the deductible in the event of damage to the boat, or for the damage
itself if there is no accident insurance, you'll have to decide whether purchasing
optional insurance is worth the extra money up front.

How early can I arrive for my rental? Some companies let you sleep on the
boat the night before you depart; others have a very specific timetable for your
arrival. If you need to be on Lake Powell, for example, at 9 AM, you will have to
arrive the previous night and make arrangements for camping or staying in a lodge.

What are the cabin arrangements? Houseboats differ, and depending on the
makeup of your family or group, one boat may be better for you than another.
Some boats come with double beds; others have a mix of queen beds, doubles, and
bunk beds. Some are more luxurious but sleep fewer people. Some beds offer
more privacy than others. Asking for brochures that show the boat layouts will help
you avoid disappointment with your accommodations.

What extras do you offer? Water slides, small power boats you can tow and use
for waterskiing, dinghies, fishing gear, tubes, and other water toys are available
through some rental companies, especially those operating in the western United
States. These will add expense, but they can make your experience even more fun.

**Do you offer maps, information about regional sights and attractions, and
suggestions for where to stop?** If you are unfamiliar with the part of the country
through which you'll be traveling, this is important. Almost all rental agents have nav-
igational charts and maps on board, but you also want information and directions
for the sights you shouldn't miss. There are many places to walk or bike along the
popular houseboating rivers and canals, and many lakes have excellent hiking trails
near their shores. Check out a guidebook and buy regional maps if you need to, but
remember that part of the joy of this type of travel is that you can be completely
spontaneous. You don't have to be locked into a rigid itinerary.

What are the rules regarding the use of life vests when the boat is in motion? Some companies require that all children under a certain age wear a life vest whenever you're moving. Whether or not this is mandatory, it's a good idea. Talk to your children ahead of time about the importance of wearing a life vest. If necessary, borrow one so that your child can wear it around a while and get used to it. You don't want your children to spend the vacation complaining. If you prepare them well ahead of time, it shouldn't be an issue.

What's the cost of fuel and docking charges? Most, but not all, houseboat rental companies work like car rental companies. They give you the boat with a full tank and you must return it with a full tank or pay to have it filled upon your return. Marine fuel prices are about 30% higher than car fuel prices. Docking charges vary greatly depending on whether you opt for a private marina or a state park. Charges for private marinas are generally by the foot and can range from 65¢ to $2 per foot per night. State parks typically charge $10–$12 per boat per night. Of course, the great thing about houseboats is that in most places you don't need to tie up at established docks, so these charges will often be minimal.

Is there someplace to shop for food when we arrive? If you're arriving by car, buy your food supplies at a regular grocery store before boarding. Stores in resort towns and at marinas tend to be very expensive. If you're arriving by plane, you'll probably have to shop at the marina, but you'll save some money by bringing what you can with you and purchasing only perishables at the last minute.

What is my rental fee and what's included? Rental rates are affected by many things, including the size of the boat, the season, and the number of days you wish to rent. Many houseboating companies operate for three or even four seasons, and rates change dramatically during the year. Moreover, some of the extras you pay for in the summer may be part of the package in off-seasons. Amenities may also affect price or at least alter how much you get for your money. Some boats come with linens; some don't. Some have grills for cooking out on deck, but others have only galley stoves. Microwaves, generators, stereo cassette players, TVs and VCRs all may be included, or they may be extra. There's a huge variation in what you pay and what you get, so ask lots of questions. All boats in this chapter have sleeping accommodations, a galley to cook in, a refrigerator, a bathroom, safety equipment, life vests for adults and older children, plates and pots and pans, and drinking water. Also included in the cost is parking for your car while you're houseboating. The range of rates shown goes from the least expensive boat in low season to the most expensive boat in high season.

Instruction

All houseboat rental companies give a short course—generally one to three hours—before you can take the boat out. Houseboats are so easy to steer that most, though not all, rental companies do not require previous boating experience.

In addition, all rental units have extensive information and instructions posted on board for reference. Although houseboating is not difficult, it's still important to pay attention to the initial lesson, and to take notes as you go through the information with the company. Docking, for example, can be tricky, especially in the more congested waterways. Make certain older children listen, too, because some discussion will relate to safety and to the use of equipment. If you're traveling with very young children, arrange in advance for a spouse or an older child to take charge of little ones so that you can concentrate on crucial information during the pretrip session.

Finding the Fun

Northeast: Collar City Charters, Mid-Lakes Navigation Company, Remar Rentals. **South:** Forever Resorts, Mid-Lakes Navigation Company. **Midwest:** Forever Resorts, Seeser's Mississippi Rent-a-Cruise. **Southwest:** Forever Resorts, Lake Powell Resorts & Marinas. **Canada:** Remar Rentals, Waterway Houseboat Vacations. **Mexico:** Forever Resorts.

Favorite Houseboat Companies

Collar City Charters

 ALL

Once a thoroughfare of commerce, the 363-mile-long Erie Canal opened in 1825. Linking Albany to Buffalo, and thus the Atlantic Ocean (via the Hudson River) to the Great Lakes, the Erie was the longest, grandest, most ambitious canal in New York State. It was, in fact, one of the great engineering feats of its time. Today the Erie has been rediscovered and revitalized, and you can trace the history of the state and several of its canals as you travel through the picturesque New York State Canal System. There is more to see and do than a family could cover in a one-week cruise. The Canalway Trail, for example, currently encompasses 150 miles of trail segments adjoining the canal on which families can hike, bike, and view wildlife. There are literally hundreds of towns to tie up at on the canal system, and you can shape your

adventure as you go. You don't have to stick to the Erie, either. From Troy, where Collar City Charters is based, boaters can travel north on the Champlain Canal all the way to Whitehall and the southernmost entry to Lake Champlain. Those who motor south on the Hudson will find natural wetlands and woods, graceful herons, villages, and sandy beaches.

FOR FAMILIES. Boats sleep up to six people, and there are two private staterooms, as well as a fold-out double in the saloon. All linens are included, and there are two bathrooms (heads, in nautical terms), a hot-water shower, a cabin heater for cool nights, and a marine band radio. The galley has a double sink, gas stove and oven, refrigerator with freezer, and lots of room. Collar City Charters also offers a family-friendly attitude. A call requesting information on life jackets for infants elicited this response: "If we don't have the right-size life jacket for your child, we'll find one." This is also one of the few rental companies that allows pets; the additional charge is $50 per pet.

What your kids will care about most, though, are locks, locks, and more locks. There are 57 of them throughout the New

York State Canal System, and they never fail to amaze. At the Lockport Locks north of Buffalo, your boat will be raised a whopping 49½ feet as you pass from one side to the other. That's cool enough to intrigue kids of all ages, including your normally blasé teenager.

If you're traveling on the Erie, stop in Chittenango, just east of Syracuse, to visit the birthplace of L. Frank Baum, beloved author of *The Wonderful Wizard of Oz*. There's a yellow-brick road in town. Whether it will get you to the Emerald City is uncertain, but if you visit the area in May, you won't want to leave anyway—that's the time of the annual Ozfest, with parades, games, and activities for modern-day Munchkins.

🏠 *Collar City Charters, Troy Town Dock and Marina, 427 River St., Troy, NY 12180, tel. 518/272–5341 or 800/830–5341. May–Sept.: 6 days, $1,500–$1,700.*

Forever Resorts

👫 ALL

With Forever Resorts, families have a choice of houseboat rentals on five lakes in four areas of the country. Lake Mead, spanning the Arizona-Nevada border, and Lake Mohave, just below Hoover Dam and south of Lake Mead, offer the starkly beautiful, dramatic landscapes unique to those places where water and desert meet. The Lake Mead National Recreation Area comprises more than 3,000 square miles of desert terrain, as well as lakes Mead and Mohave, which were both formed by the damming of the Colorado River. Hiking, rock climbing, fishing, windsurfing, and sailing bring millions of visitors to the area each year.

Lake Cumberland in Kentucky and Missouri's Lake of the Ozarks are lusher and greener. Both are in more populated areas than the desert lakes. Lake Cumberland, southeast of Louisville and northeast of Nashville, was created when Wolf Creek Dam stopped the flow of the Cumberland River, backing it up more than 100 miles. Sheer cliffs and green hills line the lake, in which fishing, swimming, and even scuba diving are popular. With more than 1,300 miles of shoreline, Lake of the Ozarks is huge—and more developed than the other lakes. But there are coves and wooded areas in which you can find complete privacy, if you wish. The Lake of the Ozarks Marina, where you pick up your houseboat, is near Camdenton, about 1½ hours north of Springfield, Missouri.

If you want to travel to foreign shores, try Lake Amistad (the Spanish word for "friendship") in the Amistad National Recreation Area bordering Texas and Mexico, about 150 miles west of San Antonio. Lake Amistad, a joint project for the two countries, was created by the damming of the Rio Grande just below its confluence with Devils River. The recreation area has more than 400 archaeological sites, including caves and mounds you can view along the lake. There are also Native American pictographs dating back more than 10,000 years that can be seen by boat at Panther Cave in beautiful Seminole Canyon. The lake is clear and blue; southwestern scuba enthusiasts call it paradise.

FOR FAMILIES. All boats sleep 10 people. Standard features include linens, two refrigerators, a microwave, 1½ baths, central air and heat, and a gas grill. There's excellent fishing on these lakes, and licenses are available at the marinas at all locations. The company has life jackets for all ages.

What will the kids like best? *Every* boat has the all-important—and monumentally fun—water slide. And children and teens are always delighted to learn that each boat comes with a cassette player and a TV with VCR. Parents may be less enthusiastic about that.

🏠 *Forever Resorts, Box 62410, Boulder City, NV 89006, tel. 800/255–5561. Year-round (all lakes not open all months): 3–7 days, $795–$2,895.*

Lake Powell Resorts & Marinas

👫 ALL

Nearly 2,000 miles of shoreline defined by massive red sandstone formations and piercing blue skies make Lake Powell on the Arizona-Utah border a magnificent place to play. The lake is 186 miles from end to end, but you can take forever to cruise the length of it if you choose. There are 96 major canyons to explore, ancient pictographs and Anasazi ruins to ponder, hiking trails, fishing coves, and beaches of shifting sands on which no footprints will be found. Nonne-Zoshi, or "Rainbow Turned to Stone," is the Navajo name for Rainbow Bridge, the tallest natural stone arch in the world. You can easily hike to it from the shore. The busiest season on Lake Powell is summer, so if you're looking for days of solitude, book in spring or fall when the weather is still fine and the rates are lower. You get your houseboat from one of the four marinas Lake Powell Resorts & Marinas operates on the lake.

FOR FAMILIES. You can choose among five lengths and four classes of vessels. Boats sleep 6 to 12 people, and amenities vary with the different classes, but all include life jackets for infants through adults. Depending on the boat, you might have a queen or double bed, and some boats have bunk beds for the kids. Linens are included in the deluxe and luxury categories. Separate small power boats are free in the spring and available for an extra charge the rest of the year. Tow one behind your houseboat and use it to explore small inlets, or to go onshore for an overnight camp-out. Waterskiing equipment and tubes can also be rented. Water slides are included in executive, deluxe, and luxury categories. Carp, a mixed-review fish for most adults, are a kid-favorite because they're so easy to catch throughout the lake. Fishing licenses can be purchased at the marinas, but bring your own poles. Carry a camera: This is one of the great houseboating lakes in North America.

🏨 *Lake Powell Resorts & Marinas, Box 56909, Phoenix, AZ 85079, tel. 602/331–5200 or 800/528–6154. Year-round: 2–7 days, $270–$3,495.*

Mid-Lakes Navigation Company

👫 ALL

For the uninitiated who think New York State begins and ends in New York City, a canal cruise will be an eye-opener. Upstate New York is a land of rolling hills, farms, and historic villages. Cayuga, New York, 35 miles west of Syracuse, is one spot to begin a cruise of the famous Erie Canal. You might choose to travel the Cayuga-Seneca Canal to Seneca Falls, or you can head east as far as Oneida Lake and north on the Oswego Canal. Your family can access state parks, including the eastern border of the 6-million-acre Adirondack Park (the largest American park outside Alaska), Finger Lakes National Forest, and two wildlife refuges from the canal system.

If you can't get the family together for the summer, Mid-Lakes Navigation Company also offers winter houseboating, December to April, through Florida's Okeechobee Waterway. Alligators, river otters, and manatees call these waters home. Bald eagles fly above and the elusive Florida panther has been spotted by a houseboater or two along the shores. You pick up your boat in Moore Haven, Florida, where the Caloosahatchee River joins the Rim Canal at Lake Okeechobee. Cruise east along the huge lake onto the St. Lucie Canal toward Stuart, 80 to 90 miles away on the Atlantic side, or west on the Caloosahatchee about 75 miles to Fort Myers and the Gulf of Mexico. Florida is much more of a land of adventure than Walt Disney ever imagined. Rich in wildlife and ecologically diverse, the state offers miles of open wilderness areas as well as Native American sites.

FOR FAMILIES. The houseboats sleep four, six, or eight passengers. All boats come with a gas range and gas grill, bedding, and a VHF radio. Nonskid surfaces are perfect for families with younger children or grandparents, and all windows have safety glass. There's a built-in swim ladder on every boat; you'll find a bicycle, too. You can also bring along your own bikes and strap them on the roof. Ride your bike on the Mohawk-Hudson Bikeway (between Cohoes and Fort Hunter in New York) or in small towns on the Okeechobee Waterway in Florida.

If you boat on the Erie as far as North Tonawanda, near Buffalo, stop at the Allan Herschell Carousel Factory Museum (Herschell is the best-known American carousel maker). In Seneca Falls you'll find the Women's Rights National Historical Park and National Women's Hall of Fame. The biggest adventure of all in New York are the locks that raise and lower boats almost 50 feet in some places.

 Mid-Lakes Navigation Company, Box 61, 11 Jordan St., Skaneateles, NY, tel. 315/685–8500 or 800/545–4318. New York, May–Oct.: 7 days, $1,300–$2,000. Florida, Dec.–Apr.: 7 days, $1,500–$1,800.

Remar Rentals

👫 ALL

Long before there were people or boundaries, long before time even existed, petals of flowers fell from the heavens onto the St. Lawrence River, creating the Thousand Islands. The native people who told this legend called the islands Manitouana, "Garden of the Great Spirit," and even today the name fits. A rich and remarkable diversity of plant and animal life thrives on these islands strung along a 50-mile stretch of the mighty St. Lawrence between New York State and Ontario, Canada. There are more than 1,800 of them—plenty to keep a houseboating family exploring for days. Some islands belong to the United States; some are Canadian. Twenty-one are part of the

St. Lawrence Islands National Park, Canada's smallest national park but no less impressive because of its size.

Clayton, New York, juts out into the river, giving Remar Rentals the perfect starting point for cruising the Thousand Islands, the St. Lawrence Seaway, and Canada's Rideau Canal System. Remar's steel-frame boats are similar to those used on Great Britain's canals. This is one of the few rental companies that require previous boating experience, due to the rocky shoals around the islands and the large seagoing vessels that travel parts of the river.

FOR FAMILIES. There are 39- to 55-foot boats sleeping 6 to 10 people. Guides to the islands and waterways are provided on board so you can plan the route that best meets your family's interests. Remar supplies linens, and a TV is standard equipment, too. A small dinghy comes with every houseboat, making island exploration fun and fishing in small coves a must.

 Remar Rentals, 510 Theresa St., Box 159, Clayton, NY 13624, tel. 315/686–3579. June–Sept.: 2–7 days, $525–$1,600.

Seeser's Mississippi Rent-a-Cruise

👫 ALL

Few rivers offer the history and romance that the great Mississippi does. Mark Twain, Lewis and Clark—these adventurous men traveled the Mississippi and made their names in part because of it. You can travel it, too, and although the wild and woolly early days of the river are long gone, there's plenty of adventure to be had, and much in the way of American history to be discovered, along its shores. Most houseboaters travel north from Clinton, where the river divides Iowa and Illinois. Less than 100 miles away is Dubuque and the Wisconsin border. You can see all three states simultaneously from Dubuque, which also has several museums including the National Rivers Hall of Fame. There are plenty of towns to stop in as you travel (historic Galena, Illinois, for example, is where you can see Ulysses S. Grant's home), and beaches to relax on by day and anchor off by night. Travel midweek to avoid summer weekend crowds.

FOR FAMILIES. Seeser's boats are 38 feet or 40 feet and sleep six or eight people. All linens, a gas grill, deck chairs, and all the boating charts you'll need are on board, and there's air-conditioning, too. Although rentals begin at 11 AM, you're welcome to arrive between 8 and 10 the evening before your trip to spend a relaxing night on the houseboat. Probably the most exciting part of the trip for kids will be the locks that are found every 20 miles or so on the river. If the stoplight is red, it means a boat is in there and you have to wait your turn. Once in, you rise or fall to meet the river, depending on which way you're traveling. Children never seem to tire of the ingenuity and novelty of the lock system.

⚓ *Seeser's Mississippi Rent-a-Cruise, 3610 S. 54th St., Clinton, IA 52732, tel. 319/243-1111. May–Oct.: 2–7 days, $220–$1,550.*

Waterway Houseboat Vacations

👫 ALL

Green forests, blue water, sandy beaches, quiet coves, and hundreds of miles of undeveloped wilderness: That's Shuswap Lake in southeastern British Columbia, one of Canada's best houseboating lakes. From it you can hike, dive, and climb rocks. You can also jet ski and fish, and you can golf nearby. There are plenty of secluded spots for picnicking, barbecuing, and overnight camping as well.

FOR FAMILIES. Waterway's boats sleep 10 or 12. They're equipped with a toaster,

maps, and child-resistant railings. These houseboats come with water slides and AM/FM cassette stereos. Voyager II and Mirage boats have compact disc players, and all Voyager and Mirage houseboats have hot tubs on board. (If kids ever get out of them, parents can enjoy the hot tubs, too.)

⚓ *Waterway Houseboat Vacations, Box 69, Sicamous VOE 2VO, British Columbia, Canada, tel. 604/836–2505 or 800/663–4022. Apr.–early Sept.: 3–7 days, $434–$3,078.*

Resources

Periodicals

Every spring *Houseboat Magazine* (520 Park Ave., Idaho Falls, ID 83402, tel. 800/638-0135) publishes a special vacation guide with extensive rental and destination information, including specifics about the marinas you'll be renting from (such as whether they have a motel or RV campground), places to leave your car or RV while you're houseboating, advice about local fishing, and more.

Books

The Amazing Impossible Erie Canal (Simon & Schuster) by Cheryl Harness, a critically acclaimed picture book for ages 5 to 10, gives the history of the building of the Erie Canal from start to finish.

Also See

For more boating adventures, turn to Sailing; Snorkeling and Diving; and Wildlife Encounters. You'll find a mix of small and large boats, slow and fast boats, and waters around the world to explore.

KAYAKING

Families have taken to kayaking like, well, ducks to water. That's not surprising. Kayaks can take you anywhere from the ocean waters where whales leap to the pristine wilderness lakes and rivers of America's heartland. You can glide through still waters or challenge yourself on rapids in almost every corner of the continent. In a kayak there's an unmistakable feeling of being not just on the water but of it, which gives an added thrill to the already fantastic opportunities to experience wildlife and nature close up.

Older children, in particular, have embraced the sport in record numbers. One reason is probably that kayaking allows a measure of independence that other types of boating don't. As manufacturers begin to design kayaks especially for a child's size, weight, and strength, more and more kids can paddle their own. These kid-size kayaks are easier to learn on and to handle, creating a great sense of accomplishment in young paddlers.

Kayaking promotes family togetherness, too. Two- and three-person kayaks make it possible for parents to take even young or inexperienced children with them on flatwater trips. Some kayaks are made with an extra-large cockpit opening that can accommodate up to two adults and a child. This sport also has special appeal for families with teenagers, who rarely think that family outings are cool. Kayaking is definitely cool, and it's a vacation idea that most preteens and teens will greet with an enthusiastic thumbs-up. Although kayaking is not the best sport for families with infants, toddlers, or preschoolers, almost anyone else can find a boat, class, or trip that's right for them.

Questions to Ask

Do you work regularly with children the age(s) of mine? Kayaking requires special skills in terms of both paddling technique and safety. It's important that instructors convey this information in an age-appropriate manner. Although instructors in children's classes probably have the requisite experience, the fact is that many kayak schools say they welcome older children in adult classes. That doesn't mean, however, that the teacher will know how to work with this age group. Adults and children learn differently. Even preteens and teens often learn best through games. Before you put your 12-year-old in an adult class with you, make certain he or she will be taught appropriately and be welcomed.

Are child-size life vests and clothing provided? Any time you're in a boat you need a coast guard–approved life jacket in the correct size. If the company you choose doesn't have the right-size vests, purchase them ahead of time from a marine or sporting goods store.

Are wet suits needed, and do you have them in my child's size? Some kay
ing courses and trips take place in cold water. A child—or an adult, for that m
ter—who's cold will have a miserable time. Ask the company if it provides or re
suits in the sizes you need. If not, either borrow them from someone you know,
check with local dive or other marine supply stores about buying or renting suits.

Do we need helmets? On a lake or pond you probably won't need a white-wate
helmet, but on any river water, even slow moving, a helmet is a good idea. Ask
about a helmet for yourself and for your children.

**Is the guide/instructor trained in child CPR, lifesaving, and first aid? What
type of emergency equipment do you carry with you?** Child CPR requires different steps than CPR for adults. If you'll be a long way from a hospital or medical
help, someone should be completely familiar with the procedures for reviving and
rescuing children. Many parents take these courses themselves—a good idea even if
the outfitter is trained. Also find out whether an outfitter is equipped with a radio
for emergency contact with a home base or local medical personnel, and whether.
there is emergency equipment on hand appropriate for children and adults.

**Are instructors certified by a reputable organization, such as the Ameri-
can Canoe Association or the British Canoe Union?** Certification means that
instructors are up on techniques and safety procedures, and it's one way to compare schools and instructors.

What kind of kayaks are provided? Sea (also known as touring) kayaks tend to
be more stable than their white-water counterparts, and easier for inexperienced
boaters to handle. They're used not just in the ocean and open water but on lakes,
ponds, rivers, and streams. There are double kayaks with two cockpits, which are
perfect for one parent and one child, or even triples with three cockpits. Ask about
the pros and cons of each type with regard to the ages and abilities of your kids.
Many outfitters also offer sit-on-tops—kayaks without the traditional cockpit. These
are wonderful for the slightly claustrophobic, and they're extremely easy to steer
and keep stable. Kids and beginners usually love them, though they're more for fun
than for serious learning.

Are child-size kayaks available? This isn't a requirement by any means, but it can
make a difference between accomplishment and frustration, for young children
especially.

How strenuous is the course or trip? All of the courses and trips listed are for
beginner or intermediate paddlers unless otherwise noted. This means you don't
need a lot of paddling experience; however, you should be in good physical condition. Ask how long your family will be paddling each day, and what the conditions
are likely to be. Will you be paddling against wind or tides, for example, either of
which can be exhausting.

Are there other activities on the trip? Courses may have you out from 9 to 4, with a break for lunch, so your free time is in the evenings. On extended trips, however, about six hours of paddling a day is typical before pulling into camp. With this schedule, there should be time for hiking, exploring, maybe beachcombing. These activities are often as important to children as the paddling, so find out what guides are likely to offer before you book.

What's included in the cost of the course or trip? Courses that take place at a school or an area near the school, whether they are one- or two-day classes, generally provide equipment, instruction, transportation from the school to a local river (if necessary) and lunch. Lodging is usually not part of the package, but schools can often help arrange it. Multiday trips include tents and most meals—plenty of hearty, excellent food—in addition to what courses cover. The vast majority of kayaking trips are camping trips. Prices for all courses and trips include what is listed above unless otherwise noted.

Instruction

Aside from paddling technique, Eskimo rolls (where you roll your kayak completely over in the water, so that you go from right side up to upside down and back without getting out of the cockpit), and other technical aspects of kayaking, you'll receive instruction on basic safety, water rescue and survival, and wilderness emergency information. This is especially important for parents taking children out into the wilderness and around water.

If your child is too young for regular courses or for the special kid's courses, be sure to ask about private instruction. These sessions often accommodate younger children, and they allow families to learn and play together.

Finding the Fun

Northeast: Adventure Quest, Maine Island Kayak Company, Outdoor Centre of New England, Outward Bound, Zoar Outdoor. **South:** Nantahala Outdoor Center, Outward Bound, Wilderness Southeast. **Midwest:** Kayak & Canoe Institute, Trek & Trail, Wilderness Inquiry. **Southwest:** Kayak & Canoe Institute. **Rockies:** Boulder Outdoor Center, Dvorak's Kayak & Rafting Expeditions. **West Coast:** California Canoe and Kayak School, Cutting Edge Adventures, REI Adventures. **Alaska.** REI Adventures. **Canada:** Kayak & Canoe Institute, Wilderness Inquiry. **Mexico:** Cutting Edge Adventures, Maine Island Kayak Company, Nantahala Outdoor Center, Zoar Outdoor. **Fiji:** Nantahala Outdoor Center.

Favorite Schools and Outfitters

Adventure Quest

 7+

Adventure Quest, one of the few paddling schools to specialize in teaching children and teens, holds classes in and around its 40-acre wooded preserve in south central Vermont. Peter Kennedy, the school's founder, is among the foremost outdoor educators in the country. His work with children is built on his belief that "young people need challenges in early life to help them better cope with obstacles in their future." Like most top outdoor instructors, Peter feels that the skills learned on a river or a rock are not just sports techniques—they are life skills that will serve children, or adults, wherever they go.

FOR FAMILIES. Adventure Quest runs Family Workshops in a variety of sports, including kayaking. These courses, which take place on various rivers in the Woodstock area, can be booked for one day or for several days. In the spring and fall families can probably stay at Adventure Quest's campground, but in summer it's reserved for student campers. There are also plenty of inns and campgrounds in the Woodstock area, as well as restaurants; ask Adventure Quest for suggestions. When you're off the river, you might enjoy a walking tour of Woodstock with its many historical houses and buildings, or you might just take a stroll over one of the area's covered bridges.

Another option is Adventure Quest's summer camp program for kids, River Quest, which includes an intensive kayaking course or samplers of several outdoor sports. Sign your children up for that while you take a course aimed at adults, then get together in the evenings to talk about paddling adventures. Because Adventure Quest is nonprofit, scholarships are available for qualifying students in the kids' summer program.

🏠 *Adventure Quest, Box 184, Woodstock, VT 05091, tel. 802/484–3939. Apr.–Oct.: 1 day, $200 for up to 4 people, $50 per day per additional family member. River Quest, June–Aug.: 7 days, $525.*

Boulder Outdoor Center

🏃 **10+**

More than 15 years ago the center opened as the Boulder Kayak School. Today, as the Boulder Outdoor Center (BOC), it continues to focus on kayaking, with classes not only for every level but in every season. If winter doldrums get you down, you can head to Colorado and learn how to paddle and roll in one of Boulder's warm indoor pools. When you've had enough of the water, you can ski on some of the best terrain in the Rocky Mountains, only a couple of hours away. In the summer months, Boulder and the Rockies offer hiking, rock climbing, friendly people, and good restaurants.

FOR FAMILIES. Ages 10 and up are welcome in all classes and clinics (parents must take the same class with children under 17). There are one-day courses, but the Novice Three-Day Clinic is an excellent choice for families. It combines a day of lake learning in Boulder with two days on a nearby river. For kayak instruction and a vacation high in the Rockies, consider the resort package. You'll kayak on a different part of the Colorado River each day for five days and spend six nights in an inn 8,000 feet up in the majestic mountains. The Boulder Outdoor Center proves its commitment to children by offering a 50% discount on classes (except the resort package) to all kayakers under 18. The reason? The center firmly believes that kayaking at an early age builds self-confidence and helps children mature.

🏠 *Boulder Outdoor Center, 2510 N. 47th St., Boulder, CO 80301, tel. 303/444–8420 or 800/364–9376. May–Sept.: 1–5 days, $69–$754.*

California Canoe and Kayak School

 10+

Keith Miller and Tamara Borichevsky are committed to helping students learn about nature and themselves through the art of paddling. They're also interested in passing along their teaching expertise: They hosted the first American Canoe Association Coastal Kayaking Instructor Workshop in the country. From their Oakland base, Keith and Tamara make good use of San Francisco Bay, the northern California coast, and the surrounding wetlands, sloughs, and estuaries to teach adventurous families about kayaking and share with them the beauty of the region's waterways.

FOR FAMILIES. There are sea and white-water kayaking courses for all levels, as well as surf and open bay classes. Families can also join river and coast trips in California and the Pacific Northwest. The school is happy to accept children as young as 10 or 11, but size is an important factor—a very petite 10-year-old, for example, will probably not be able to use the school's equipment. Families can participate in the appropriate level class or opt for private instruction.

Among the best trips: Families looking for a sea experience might choose the five-day San Juan Islands tour in June, especially if they enjoy seeing wildlife. Eagles and orcas reside in and around these magnificent islands off Washington State's coast. For those with some paddling experience under their belts and the ability to do a river roll, there are trips on Oregon's Rogue River, with forested canyons and Class II and III rapids, and on California's Klamath River, which has warm water, wildlife, and plenty of thrills.

If you want advanced instruction but still prefer to travel with your children, sign them up for special kids' classes during the summer. You can each take appropriate courses, then meet at the end of the day to compare notes. There are many lodging options near the school.

📮 *California Canoe and Kayak School, 409 Water St., Jack London Sq., Oakland, CA 94607, tel. 510/893-7833 or 800/366-9804. Year-round: 1–5 days, $65–$495.*

Cutting Edge Adventures

 7+

Co-owner Stefanie Abrishamian's contagious humor, enthusiasm, and easy way with kids are just some of the reasons she and her company are an excellent choice for a family kayak course or river trip. Another is her skill and professionalism—she and partner Leif Hansen have been guiding, teaching, and managing river outfitters for more than 14 years. Stefanie has taught kids as young as 7 to do Eskimo rolls. Cutting Edge is in northern California, in the shadow of the perpetually snow-covered Mt. Shasta and within easy reach of some of the nation's best rivers and lakes for family kayaking.

FOR FAMILIES. Cutting Edge offers a five-day Kayak School that begins with a day on Lake Siskiyou near Mt. Shasta, then continues with four days down the Klamath River. You can hone your skills while watching for eagles, ospreys, blue and green herons, and other wildlife. There are also one-day Kayak Roll Clinics on Lake Siskiyou, and private instruction in both hard-shell and inflatable kayaks is available on many of the rivers in the Mt. Shasta area.

Families with teens can travel to the Sea of Cortez (as the Gulf of California is sometimes known in Mexico) for an eight-day trip. Even novice kayakers can experience the wild beauty of Baja California and view the sea lions, dolphins, whales, and thousands of birds that live there. Hiking, snorkeling, and learning about local geology and plant life make this a trip best suited for ages 15 and up.

📮 *Cutting Edge Adventures, Box 1334, Mt. Shasta, CA 96067, tel. 916/926-4647. July–*

Aug.: 1–5 days, $50–$750. Baja, Oct.–Nov.: 8 days, $1,098 (airfare extra but can be booked through Cutting Edge).

Dvorak's Kayak & Rafting Expeditions

👫 12+

Well known for its rafting trips, especially those welcoming families, this Colorado outfitter also runs an excellent white-water paddling school and river trips on which families can play and learn together. Nathrop, almost exactly in the center of the state, is just a scenic three-hour drive from Denver and its great family museums. It's also an easy drive from Grand Junction—home of Dinamation International Society's Dino Camp and the not-to-be-missed Devil's Canyon Science and Learning Center—and from the most popular mountain towns, including Crested Butte, Durango, Telluride, Vail, and Aspen.

FOR FAMILIES. Your family can sign up for courses ranging from a half-day lake session to a 12-day river trip. Dvorak's recommends a three- to five-day tour on the Arkansas River as the best learning trip for novices. The Arkansas slices through canyons of granite and into valleys below the snow-capped Sangre de Cristo Mountains, presenting exhilarating challenges but nothing an enthusiastic family can't handle. Dvorak's guides will be there through every riffle and rapid, instructing, encouraging, and providing the kind of quality, personalized experience you would expect from an outfit that has been in business for more than a quarter of a century. Hard-shell and inflatable kayaks can be used.

🏠 *Dvorak's Kayak & Rafting Expeditions, 17921–B U.S. 285, Nathrop, CO 81236, tel. 719/539–6851 or 800/824–3795. May–Sept.: ½–12 days, $60–$1,720.*

Kayak & Canoe Institute

👫 7+

Part of the University of Minnesota at Duluth's Outdoor Program, the institute aims to "create an environment where participants can develop skills, learn about themselves, relax, enjoy, and share their gifts with others." Duluth, tucked into the western tip of Lake Superior and surrounded by protecting bluffs, is an ideal location for inner harbor expeditions. It's also near one of the country's great kayaking destinations, Wisconsin's Apostle Islands.

FOR FAMILIES. Families with children ages 7 and up can participate in the four-hour instructional course or in private classes; ages 15 and up are welcome to join all courses and multiday trips. White-water and sea kayaking fundamentals classes and tours range in length from four hours to a weekend. Intermediates who choose an overnight to the Apostle Islands, Lake Superior's magnificent archipelago, will see sea caves, sandy beaches, rocky inlets, lighthouses, and sunken ships. Farther afield, the institute also offers multiday summer kayaking and hiking trips for all skill levels in Isle Royale National Park, Michigan, where moose sightings provide plenty of excitement, and in Pacific Rim National Park in British Columbia, with its dense forests, sea caves, and bountiful kelp beds.

Summer is also when ages 13 to 18 can sign up for five-day summer camps. There are kayaking courses and classes combining kayaking and rock climbing. These activities take place during the day, so the family can get together again in the evenings to share their experiences. If a warm-weather getaway in February or March is more appealing, there's a hiking and sea kayaking (the name refers to the kind of kayak) trip to Lake Powell, which stretches 186 miles across Utah and Arizona.

Adult wet suits are available from the institute, and some would fit ages 12 and up.

🚣 *Kayak & Canoe Institute, University of Minnesota at Duluth, Outdoor Program, 121 Sports and Health Center, 10 University Dr., Duluth, MN 55812, tel. 218/726–6533. May–Aug.: ½–12 days, $35–$855. Lake Powell, Feb.–Mar.: 8 days, $695. Price does not include lunch for single-day classes.*

Maine Island Kayak Company

(👫 8+)

Maine Island Kayak Company (MIKC) is oriented as much to environmental concerns and the wilderness as it is to kayaking. What the staff likes best is to take people on multiday tours in and around Maine's wild islands. Kids must be at least 8 years old to paddle in a double kayak with a parent; 10-year-olds who can swim and who have some athletic ability and enough muscle strength can paddle their own kayak. The company is based about 20 minutes by ferry from Portland, Maine.

FOR FAMILIES. MIKC will design courses and expeditions for family groups, or you can sign up for a scheduled class. All boats are sea kayaks—primarily singles, but some doubles are available. Regular course offerings include the two-day sea kayaking and American Canoe Association (ACA) fundamentals course, which focuses on paddling techniques; equipment and kayak design; safety and rescue; and how to read wind, waves, tides, currents, and weather. Half-day and one-day instruction is also provided.

Among MIKC's tours are two- to six-day adventures in and around Casco Bay, Jewell Island, and Penobscot Bay. One of the most popular trips goes from Stonington to Acadia National Park's Isle au Haut, with its rugged cliffs and rocky ledges. On easy trips you can expect to paddle about 5 miles per day; on moderate trips, 10 miles. For those with children ages 12 and up, there are also winter kayaking tours. The Baja California journey from La Paz to the magical island of Espíritu Santo, with its sea caves and abundant wildlife, is a particularly good choice.

Call the company to discuss the ages and abilities of your family—they'll find or design a trip for you. Wet suits are available; a small will probably fit a good-sized 10-year-old.
🚣 *Maine Island Kayak Company, 70 Luther St., Peaks Island, ME 04108, tel. 207/766–2373 or 800/796–2373 (summer); 303/443–9100 (winter). May–Aug.: ½–6 days, $45–$745. Jan.–Feb.: 7 days, $1,200.*

Nantahala Outdoor Center

(👫 10+)

Nantahala, in the majestic Great Smoky Mountains of western North Carolina, is one of the premier paddling schools in the country. The company is employee-owned, which probably helps account for the enthusiasm and high quality of its instructors. Courses begin on flatwater (a lake) and move on to one to four rivers, depending on the class you choose. Plan to stay in the area either before or after your trip; Nantahala, only about 30 minutes from the southern entrance to Great Smoky Mountains National Park and 1½ hours from Asheville, rich in history and opportunities for family sightseeing.

FOR FAMILIES. Two- to seven-day standard courses, for ages 16 and up, include beginner, intermediate, and advanced levels, as well as special rolling classes. Private instruction is a more flexible alternative for families, and children ages 10 and up can attend with parents (discuss your child's weight, size, athletic ability, and interest with the school before signing up).

Sampler courses, for ages 13 and up, are one-day minicourses designed to give beginners an introduction to the sport. There's a Kayak Sampler (white-water instruction on local rivers) and a Kayak Touring Sampler in which you take sea kayaks onto nearby lakes and learn the basics while exploring exquisite inland waterways.

In addition to regular courses, there are also special kids' courses at all skill levels throughout the summer. Divided by age (10–12 or 13–15), these emphasize learning in a high-energy, fun atmosphere. Parents can take adult-oriented classes at the same time.

Base facilities at Nantahala include a bunkhouse, and some lodging is available in a motel, too; accommodations are limited, so book early. Limited day-care is available for small children while parents and older kids are kayaking. Wet suits can be rented.

Nantahala's adventure travel department schedules 7- to 12-day tours in North Carolina, Georgia, the Everglades, Baja California, and Fiji; age restrictions vary. A parent who's a strong paddler might be able to bring a preteen on a trip, using a double kayak. Call and discuss your skills and the ages of your children before signing up.
🏠 *Nantahala Outdoor Center, 13077 U.S. 19 W, Bryson City, NC 28713, tel. 704/488–6737 (courses) or 704/488–2175, ext. 333 (tours). Year-round (instructional courses Mar.–Oct.): 1–12 days, $70–$1,975.*

Outdoor Centre of New England

👫 12+

Because this north central Massachusetts school is very technically oriented, it's best for families with older children. The center is within an easy drive of Boston and most of Connecticut and Rhode Island.

FOR FAMILIES. Regularly scheduled courses accept kids 15 and up, but their adult orientation makes them right only for more mature teens and their parents. The school highly recommends private instruction for families with kayakers ages 12 and up (10- or 11-year-olds with some experience and a real interest will be considered). To get the most out of the Outdoor Centre's excellent instruction, a minimum two-day course is suggested. Learning takes

place on a flatwater lake in the mornings and on a nearby white-water river in the afternoons. For a modest extra chrage, you can stay in the lodge (separate men's and women's facilities) or in the guest house (private rooms); a large breakfast is included.
🏠 *Outdoor Centre of New England, 10 Pleasant St., Millers Falls, MA 01349, tel. 413/659–3926. Apr.–early Oct.: 1–7 days, $90–$359; 2 days, $185–$220 per person for private instruction, depending on number of family members in group.*

Outward Bound

👫 16+

Adventure travel has become extremely popular in the past decade, but Outward Bound was way ahead of its time. After more than 50 years in the adventure education business, it is still a leader in the field. Outward Bound has courses all over the country and the world in a variety of sports and activities. For kayaking courses, adventurers have a choice of Maine and Florida.

FOR FAMILIES. Outward Bound schedules two kayaking courses for families with teens aged 16 and up. Sea kayaking takes place in Maine's Penobscot Bay, where thousands of islands provide inlets and rocky shores to explore. The itinerary depends somewhat on the weather, but Hurricane Island, one of Outward Bound's largest base camps, is generally one of the stops. For those looking for warmer climates, there's kayaking and sailing along the Canaveral National Seashore of Florida. Participants in this course travel the Intracoastal Waterway and Indian River, and have a chance to visit the renowned Merritt Island National Wildlife Refuge.

As with most Outward Bound courses, which are designed to challenge you and test your limits, your family will also spend time rock climbing, rappelling, being challenged on ropes courses, and learning camping skills. The focus with this group is not just to learn kayaking and sailing but to enhance teamwork, problem-solving, and leadership skills.

🏠 *Outward Bound, Rte. 9D, Rte. 2, Box 280, Garrison, NY 10524, tel. 914/424–4000 or 800/243–8520. Maine, June–Sept.: 14–22 days, $1,595–$1,895. Florida, Jan.–Apr., Oct.–Dec.: 8 days, $895.*

REI Adventures

👫 15+

REI, the nationwide outdoor store from which many adventurers buy their gear and apparel, doubles as an excellent outfitter, with courses in a number of sports, including kayaking. The best for families are around the islands off the state of Washington and in the dramatic waters and scenery of Alaska's Glacier Bay. Neither requires previous kayaking experience.

FOR FAMILIES. The moderate sea kayaking trip called Marine Mammals and Birds of the San Juans is led by naturalists, with departures from June through September. As the name suggests, learning centers more on the environment than on kayaking itself. The San Juan Islands, off the coast of Washington, are home to orcas, harbor seals, river otters, and bald eagles; kayaking in and around the island coves and coast is an excellent way to see wildlife up close.

On an eight-day adventure to Granite Fjord in July or August, you travel among Alaska's glacier-blue icebergs and through tidal areas rich in marine and bird life. Hiking, birding, and relaxing are all part of the itinerary.

🏠 *REI Adventures, Box 1938, Sumner, WA 98390, tel. 206/395–8111 or 800/622–2236. June–Sept.: 6–8 days, $845–$1,495. Price does not include $15 REI membership per family.*

Trek & Trail

👫 10+

Trek & Trail, based in Bayfield, Wisconsin, on a peninsula at the western end of Lake Superior, has been running outdoor learning adventures in the Apostle Islands National Lakeshore and on Lake Superior for more than 17 years. The company has a strong commitment to bringing families and women into the wilderness and is 100% enthusiastic about working with children.

FOR FAMILIES. Sand Island Base Camp for Families is a three-day course that combines kayaking, hiking, and camping. You paddle to sea caves and shipwrecks and pass by awesome geologic formations. The trip runs on request in the summer months. The Mothers and Daughters Odyssey in July celebrates the special bond between moms and their daughters as you kayak and sail through the Apostle Islands archipelago. Evenings are spent on board the 40-foot *Madeline Brady*, with storytelling and stargazing as favored activities.

Families and children (usually ages 10 and up, but check with the company) are welcome on all other Trek & Trail trips, too. There's everything from a 3½-hour basic sea kayaking and safety course on Lake Superior to multiday trips for all skill levels. Most courses run between Memorial Day and Labor Day. Wet suits are often needed in chilly Lake Superior, and Trek & Trail has adult and child sizes for rent.

🏠 *Trek & Trail, Box 906, Bayfield, WI 54814, tel. 715/779–3320 or 800/354–8735. May–Sept.: ½–3 days, $40–$489; Sand Island Base Camp, 3 days, $689 for family of 3, $75 each additional family member. Basic courses generally offer a 50% discount for children under 12.*

Wilderness Inquiry

 5+

A leader in the wilderness adventure market for 18 years, this company places a special emphasis on making trips available both to people who have disabilities and to those who do not. On these trips children have the opportunity to learn new skills and respect for nature, along with respect for the differences among people. The company is based in Minneapolis but leads trips around the United States and in Canada.

FOR FAMILIES. Because all trips are in triple kayaks, children as young as 5 can go on most of them, although shorter trips may be best if you have younger kids. There are three- and five-day Apostle Island tours in northern Wisconsin, for example, and an eight-day Isle Royale tour in Michigan. A longer and more expensive choice is a 12-day trip in the Queen Charlotte Islands in British Columbia, recommended for families with kids who are at least 14. Known as the Galápagos Islands of the North because of their abundant wildlife and ecological diversity, the Queen Charlottes offer paddling in protected bays and guaranteed wildlife sightings. For longer trips such as this, some experience and good physical condition are important. Wet suits may be required on some trips, and Wilderness Inquiry provides both adult and child sizes at no cost.

A *Wilderness Inquiry, 1313 5th St. SE, Box 84, Minneapolis, MN 55414-1546, tel. 612/379–3858 or 800/728–0719. June–Sept.: 3–12 days, $295–$1,495.*

Wilderness Southeast

 16+

Wilderness Southeast, a nonprofit educational organization, focuses more on exploring nature than on teaching sports skills. The staff will advise kayakers about technique, but their real strength is their knowledge of the natural and cultural history of the desti-

nations. Among the staff members are an anthropologist, entomologist, biologist, environmental manager, and an environmental educator.

FOR FAMILIES. Coastal Georgia Sea Kayak, a four-day tour along the northern end of Georgia's wild coastline in May, October, and November, explores unspoiled beaches, marshes, and magnificent barrier islands. Atlantic bottle-nosed dolphins often tag along for fun. The seven-day Everglades 10,000 Islands course runs in December and January. Hiking the sawgrass prairies and wading in search of wild orchids and signs of the endangered Florida panther are intriguing highlights.

A *Wilderness Southeast, 711 Sandtown Rd., Savannah, GA 31410, tel. 912/897–5108. May, Oct.–Jan.: 4–7 days, $390–$840. Price includes pickup and drop off at airports near destination.*

Zoar Outdoor

 12+

Zoar has an 80-acre campus in the Deerfield River valley in northwestern Massachusetts. In one convenient location it combines everything a family needs to try out the sport of kayaking: a campground, kitchen, bathhouse with hot showers, outfitters store, volleyball court, and more. Zoar Outdoor has been teaching paddling and other outdoor sports for six years, and it continues to grow and get better each year.

FOR FAMILIES. Families with kids ages 12 and up can take part in any of the clinics scheduled from April through October. There are beginner, intermediate, and advanced instructional clinics that run two or three days, as well as special one-day rolling clinics. Families may also opt for custom classes, designed to meet the needs and goals of your group. Another choice is to sign up children (ages 10 to 15) for Kids Kayak Craze, a one-day course offered during July or August, while you take a course of your own.

As for trips, families with kids aged 12 and up can join the five-day Maine rivers exploration (based at an outdoor center with a lodge) or the three-day Maine islands voyage. Two-day expeditions include kayaking along the north shore of Massachusetts and Plum Island (participants make their own lodging arrangements for Saturday night); visiting and camping on Thatcher Island, off Cape Ann in Massachusetts; and exploring the Connecticut River where it flows into Long Island Sound. Also for families with good kayakers ages 12 and up, there's a seven-day Baja California sea kayaking journey in February and March.

🏠 *Zoar Outdoor, Box 254, Charlemont, MA 01339, tel. 800/532–7483. Apr.–Oct.: 1–7 days, $60–$625. Baja, Feb.–Mar.: 7 days, $950. Price does not include lodging for some clinics.*

Resources

Organizations

America Outdoors (Box 1348, Knoxville, TN 37901, tel. 615/524–4814), a trade organization for water-based outfitters, has a magazine listing outfitters and guides, though the group cannot recommend one member over another. The **American Canoe Association** (8550 Cinderbed Rd., Box 1190, Newington, VA 22122, tel. 703/451–0140) publishes a newsletter and certifies guides and instructors. The **Trade Association of Sea Kayakers** (TASK, Box 84144, Seattle, WA 98124, tel. 206/621–1018) can give you information about outfitters and clubs, as well as other aspects of kayaking.

Periodicals

Canoe & Kayak Magazine (Box 3146, Kirkland, WA 98083, tel. 800/692–2663) has many family-oriented articles, and most issues offer an extensive resource listing of outfitters, schools, and guides.

Kayaking Kids, published by Perception (Box 8002, Easley, SC 29641, tel. 803/859–7518; *see* information on the company's kayaks, *below*), is a free quarterly newsletter for young kayakers or those interested in getting into the sport. It has information on kayaking, on kids who are doing it, and on environmental issues.

Products

The following companies make kayaks especially for children: **Aquaterra by Perception** (tel. 803/859–7518 or 800/529–2596); **Daggar** (tel. 615/882–0404); **E.P.I** (216/564–5565); and **Wilderness Systems** (tel. 910/883–7410). Call to locate a dealer near you and ask about Demo Days. During Demo Days you can usually try out different brands of equipment in the water to find the kayak that's right for your child's size, strength, and ability.

Also See

Families who love to be on the water should also check out Canoeing, Sailing, Rafting, Snorkeling and Diving, and Wildlife Encounters. Whether you want calm or white water, domestic or exotic destinations, there's a world for your family to explore by boat.

NATIVE AMERICAN EXPERIENCES

Today families have wonderful opportunities to learn about the Native American peoples who are so integral to our country's cultural fabric. The importance of these firsthand encounters became clear to me on a visit to the Cherokee Heritage Center in Tahlequah, Oklahoma, not long ago. My 4-year-old kept peering intently at the Cherokee people working there. He seemed confused. Finally he asked, "But where do they keep their horses?" His sole experience of Native Americans, I'm embarrassed to say, was obtained from reruns of the spectacularly awful television show *F Troop,* but he left the center with a different perspective.

Fortunately there are many ways for any child to be exposed to the richness of native life rather than the old stereotypes, and these trips are one of them. Although native people were once reluctant to share their culture with outsiders, that is no longer the case. In recent years, tribal elders have agreed to meet with visitors to share their wisdom and knowledge, and native guides have begun to offer tours of their lands that focus as much on tribal history and cultural life as on the land itself. Native people across North America have devoted time and resources to preserving, or reestablishing if necessary, traditional languages, fine and performing arts, lore, spiritual practices, agricultural and hunting traditions, and crafts. The primary benefit of a renewal in traditional ways is a stronger native culture; a secondary one is that people outside the culture have exciting learning opportunities. And who better to learn from than native people themselves?

Questions to Ask

How do I know this program is legitimate? If your family has a desire to experience authentic Native American culture, the last thing you want is a hokey, "canned" experience. By talking at length to the people running the trips, you can usually tell if there's a real interest in native culture and if they have worked closely with Native Americans to organize the trips. You can also check with the tourism departments of the states you're going to visit, and you might want to ask for references from people who have traveled with the group.

What is the focus of this particular trip? Is it native culture? History? Tribal lands? Crafts and artwork are featured on some trips; on others the point is to experience the present-day lifestyle of a tribe. Some experiences with native guides focus on an activity—fishing or horse packing—and native culture is secondary. Many trips combine several elements.

Can we participate in tribal activities, such as crafts or other traditional pastimes? In many cases, yes. If this appeals to your family, talk to outfitters ahead of time to be sure native hosts and leaders at the villages know you want to try some activities. And let them know your children will be interested, too, if that's the case.

Will there be opportunities for one-on-one discussions? If this is important to you, choose a trip that's a more custom or personalized experience rather than a group one.

Will there be recreational activities in addition to cultural learning? You may be able to go horseback riding or fishing or hiking as part of some trips. Others focus almost entirely on the cultural or learning aspect. Young children have a more limited capacity for lectures and grown-up talk, so make sure there's enough action and diversity to keep your children's interest.

If someone in the family has a particular interest, can you make arrangements beyond what is described in the itinerary? Outfitters and tour operators who handle custom trips are the most likely to be able to arrange special activities. If you can't find what you want on a set itinerary, call some of the custom specialists in this chapter. Quite possibly you'll be able to design your own trip and still stay within your budget.

Will my children have native children their age with whom to interact? Trip leaders don't always give thought to this, so try to arrange it in advance. Children learn a great deal from each other through play and other activities.

What kind of lodging is there? Some outfitters arrange stays with Native American host families; others give you the opportunity to stay in a traditional tepee on a reservation or other land. In some cases you stay in motels, visiting tribal areas during the day. There are combinations of all of the above, too. Choose the trip that best meets your family's expectations for immersion in Native American culture.

What kind of food will we eat? Native foods are often part of the experience, and some may be strange to you or your children. You'll want to try everything, but do bring snack foods that your children like.

What's included in the cost? For the trips in this chapter, and in most other cases as well, lodging, some meals, and local transportation are included. Sightseeing, activities at reservations and villages, and participation in powwows, dances, and meetings with tribal members are also part of the package. It's up to you to get to and from the trip's starting and ending points.

Instruction

All of these trips involve learning; many include instruction in native crafts, dances, and music, or in traditional activities such as fishing or tracking wildlife. Sometimes you can learn to prepare foods or make medicines. In every case, tribal elders or experts will guide and teach you. Native encounters offer a rare opportunity for multicultural learning in its purest sense.

Finding the Fun

Northeast: Journeys into American Indian Territory. **Midwest:** Journeys into American Indian Territory. **Southwest:** Crow Canyon Archaeological Center, Grandtravel, Off the Beaten Path. **Rockies:** Anvil Butte Ranch, Grandtravel, Off the Beaten Path. **Alaska:** Athabasca Cultural Journeys. **Canada:** Arctic Odysseys, Off the Beaten Path. **Mexico:** Crow Canyon Archaeological Center.

Favorite Experiences

Anvil Butte Ranch

👫 5+

Anvil Butte Ranch, in south central Montana, is the place to combine a Native American experience and a western ranch stay. It offers culturally and historically oriented tours in addition to standard family guest ranch vacations. You always spend at least one night at the ranch, where guests sleep either in the main house or in a tepee village in a secluded area of the 3,000-acre property; breakfasts and showers are in the main house. Because there are no more than five guests at a time, a family can customize its experience to a large extent, with the help of owners Claudia and Leif Bakken.

FOR FAMILIES. Guests on the two Indian Culture family packages each summer attend the Northern Cheyenne Pow Wow in late June or the Crow Fair (the largest native powwow) in early August. These colorful, festive celebrations of native culture and life include dancing and parades, traditional foods, music, and art. During the powwows you stay in local motels as well as at the ranch. The trip price covers all your meals, unless you choose to go off on your own. The powwows are primarily spectator events, but back at the ranch your family will spend an evening around a campfire with local tribal members, talking and listening to ancient native stories. Other highlights are visits to nearby Plains Indians museums and the Little Bighorn Battlefield National Monument, which is just a few miles south of the Crow Indian Reservation.

🏠 *Anvil Butte Ranch, HC 71, Box 7335, Wibaux, MT 59353, tel. 406/795–2341. June–Aug.: 6–7 days, $2,502–$3,878 per family or group of 2–5 people.*

Arctic Odysseys

👫 12+

As its name implies, Arctic Odysseys specializes in introducing people of all ages and backgrounds to an area once accessible only to the most daring of explorers. This trip takes place in northern Canada with the Inuit. It still requires a special kind of family to venture into this wild and remote land, but those who do find that the rewards far outweigh the hardship or expense that Arctic travel involves.

FOR FAMILIES. The Summer Wildlife and Cultural Odyssey combines wildlife viewing and exposure to the traditional Inuit lifestyle. This is a totally customized experience, so you and your Inuit guide can modify the itinerary to suit your interests. For that reason, younger children can often be accommodated, but talk to owner Robin Duberow first.

You spend some time in established communities, such as Cape Dorset and Iqaluit (still shown as Frobisher Bay on some maps), on Baffin Island. During most of the trip, however, your family is traveling by 22-foot cargo canoe. You pick your way through the icebergs and stop at Inuit summer camps to visit with friends and relatives of your guide or to watch Inuit artists at work. Caribou, seals, walrus, and snow geese can usually be seen. If you have a license, you can learn to fish for Arctic char. The Inuit are permitted to hunt in their homeland, and, if you wish, your guide will demonstrate his people's hunting and tracking skills. If this is not of interest, the guide will teach you how to stalk animals for viewing and photography. A stop at the West Baffin Co-op in Cape Dorset, world-renowned galleries with carvings and other work by Inuit artists, is a special experience. Lodging at summer camps is typically in double-wall tents. The trip begins and ends in Ottawa, and includes flights between Ottawa, Iqaluit, and Cape Dorset. Temperatures range between 30°F and 60°F, so pay attention to clothing lists.

🏠 *Arctic Odysseys, 2000 McGilvra Blvd. E, Seattle, WA 98112, tel. 206/325–1977. July–Aug.: 5 days, $2,975; 9 days, $3,475.*

Athabasca Cultural Journeys

👫 8+

The Athabascan people did not want their ancestral home in north central Alaska destroyed by mining or logging, so they embarked on a commercial tourism enterprise to help sustain their tribe. The goal was to allow visitors to meet real families and see everyday Athabascan life while learning about the tribe's unique history and culture. Athabasca Cultural Journeys is owned and operated by the Athabascan people of Huslia, Alaska, who describe the tours as "a wilderness and cultural adventure" in which guests "experience Alaska through the eyes of native peoples."

FOR FAMILIES. Huslia is remote—a 90-minute bush-plane flight northwest from Fairbanks. You pass over native villages, the Yukon River, the Trans-Alaska Pipeline, and numerous historical and working gold mines. The Athabascan host families have traditionally been volunteer tribal elders, but if guests request host families with children, the company will try to accommodate that request. From Huslia, most guests travel with their hosts by riverboat deep into the Koyokuk National Wildlife Refuge to a native wilderness camp. Only six people at a time are allowed, both to maintain the quality of the experience and to lessen impact on the wilderness area.

The wildlife refuge, home to thousands of nesting migratory birds and birds of prey, as well as to moose, caribou, bears, wolves, otters, and beavers, presents many opportunities to see and photograph wildlife. Guests can also fish, hike, and visit archaeological sites. For the trip's cultural component, tribal members teach native history, traditions, and animal lore, and share traditional myths and legends. Families can try crafts and explore the use of barks and roots for eating and healing. At the primitive campsite, visitors stay in cabins or wall tents, and there is no running water. Food, however, is plentiful and includes native recipes using moose, caribou, bear, beaver, and fish.

Summer in Alaska means almost constant daylight, so there's plenty of time for all your activities. In fact, each itinerary is customized. You can spend more time in Huslia or opt for a traditional fishing camp—where you'd participate in drying and smoking salmon—instead of the wilderness camp. Flights between Fairbanks and Huslia are included in the cost.

🏠 *Athabasca Cultural Journeys, Box 10, Huslia, AK 99746, tel. 907/829–2261 or 800/423–0094. June–Aug.: 4 days, $1,650.*

Crow Canyon Archaeological Center

👫 16+

This prestigious archaeological center, whose main work is preserving, protecting, and uncovering ruins in southwestern Colorado (see Archaeology Adventures), also offers cultural explorations of ancient and present-day native societies in various parts of the American Southwest and Mexico. Trips change from season to season; the ones described here are representative of what Crow Canyon is likely to offer.

FOR FAMILIES. One Hopi exploration focuses on the history of the tribe's migration. Eric Polingyouma, a member of the Bluebird clan, leads visits to ancient ruins as well as to villages continuously occupied for many hundreds of years. While traveling some of the ancient migratory routes, you will come to understand the determination and quiet strength still characteristic of the Hopi. Participants also attend a traditional dance ceremony as the guests of Eric and his wife, Nancy. Travel takes place among the starkly beautiful mesas of northern Arizona that are home to today's Hopi people.

If the center has scheduled a trip to Mexico's Copper Canyon and the other canyons of the Sierra Tarahumara, where the Tarahumara people have lived for centuries, consider joining it. You can hike in the canyons—the deepest of which is more than ¼ mile deeper than the Grand Canyon—and meet natives who will talk about their homeland and the changes taking place in it as the outside world has discovered this region of astonishing beauty and ecological importance. The trip includes a ride on the famous Chihuahua al Pacífico railroad.

🏠 *Crow Canyon Archaeological Center, 23390 County Rd. K, Cortez, CC 81321, tel. 303/565–8975 or 800/422–8975. Sept.–Dec.: 7–9 days, $1,550–$2,995. Basic membership, a requirement, is $15–$40 per person, depending on age.*

Grandtravel

👫 7 – 17

A pioneer in intergenerational travel, Grandtravel makes available a wide variety of journeys, some of which include adventure. The concept of adventure here means a journey in which participants—in this case grandchildren and grandparents—explore new and exciting places and, perhaps more importantly, stimulating new ideas.

FOR FAMILIES. On the American Indian Culture trip, family members gain firsthand knowledge and understanding of Native American tribes throughout the Southwest. The trip is run twice each summer: once for adults with grandchildren aged 7 to 11, once for those with grandkids 12 to 17. The itinerary includes hotel lodging, and the majority of travel is by motor coach and train. However, there's a Navajo-guided Jeep tour of Arizona's Canyon de Chelly, a trail ride near Durango, Colorado, and a dramatic flight over the Grand Canyon to keep the adventurous at heart happy.

In Albuquerque the group visits the Indian Pueblo Cultural Center, which provides historical and cultural information about the Pueblo Indians of the Rio Grande Valley. In Santa Fe, grandchildren and grandparents attend a Pueblo Ceremonial Feast Day. Taos, New Mexico's 800-year-old pueblo, is an important stop, as is the Jicarilla Apache Reservation. In Canyon de Chelly, the ancestral home of the Navajo, or Dine, people, there's a Navajo ranger campfire program in addition to the Jeep tour. A visit to the Hopi Reservation in Arizona gives insight into how trade affected Native Americans in the 1880s; explorations of a variety of Anasazi ruins add further historical perspective. The trip starts in Albuquerque and ends in Phoenix.

🏠 *Grandtravel, 6900 Wisconsin Ave., Suite 706, Chevy Chase, MD 20815, tel. 301/986–0790 or 800/247–7651. June–Aug.: 10 days, $2,815–$2,995.*

Journeys into American Indian Territory

👫👤 6+

For the past nine years, anthropologist Robert Vetter and a staff of Native Americans have been giving nonnatives a chance to experience the diversity of native cultures through one-on-one contact with Native Americans around the United States. In that process of discovery, Vetter believes, people learn more about themselves as well. An educational consultant when not running Journeys, he is wholly enthusiastic about introducing children to native cultures.

FOR FAMILIES. The best trip for families with younger children is the three-day New England Experience, which takes place during June and August in the Berkshires of Massachusetts. Vetter will consider children younger than 6 on an individual basis. At this gathering of native people from west and east, there are separate activities for children and adults, but close interaction with native people is at the heart of everyone's experience. Unlike most powwows, where nonnatives are spectators, this trip is about participating; you learn traditional dances, play drums, and sing traditional songs. Expect storytelling, lectures, and a chance to learn about native foods and crafts.

Older children—12 or 13 and up—who have a real interest in Native American cultures can join the company's other journeys. Although none has activities especially designed for children, all offer firsthand learning opportunities. Two Oklahoma trips focus on native spirituality and include meetings with an Apache family or priest, stops at native spiritual centers, and a visit to the home of a Comanche master painter and flute player. Another journey to that state brings the past and the present into perspective with a look at Native American museums and archival collections, as well as meetings with tribal elders and families. Powwows, dances, and traditional games are also part of the experience. Still another Oklahoma trip centers around native crafts, with a chance not only to meet craftspeople but also to work on your own projects.

In Arizona, present-day native communities are understood in part through their past. Tribal elders lead explorations of ancient ruins, and museums devoted to native history provide information and insight. There's an optional horseback ride through the rugged landscape outside Scottsdale, and guests can try their hand at traditional basketry under the tutelage of a tribal craftsperson.

At Waswagoning, a re-creation of a traditional Ojibwa village in northern Wisconsin, visitors participate in a revival of the old tribal lifeways. This journey is co-led by Nick Hockings, a member of the Lac du Flambeau Band of Lake Superior Ojibwa, who has been featured in several films on the tribe. The area's natural beauty adds another dimension to an experience that includes a canoe trip, through which guests learn about traditional Ojibwa fishing techniques; a powwow; and introductions to Ojibwa language, legends, and crafts. At a visit to modern tribal headquarters, the group meets with community leaders.

On all these trips the group camps out in traditional native structures, mostly tepees but also wigwams, hogans, and wickiups, depending on the location. The price of the New England Experience covers all meals; other journeys include two meals a day. To allow for one-on-one contact and discussion, most trips are limited to a maximum of 20 participants.

🏠 *Journeys into American Indian Territory, Box 929, Westhampton Beach, NY 11978; tel. 516/878–8655 or 800/458–2632. Feb., June–Sept., Nov.: 3–8 days, $150–$795.*

Off the Beaten Path

👫👤 5+

Off the Beaten Path (OBP) excels in customized western adventures for people of all ages. Usually the company handles the arrangements but contracts with outfitters and guides to lead the trips. In some cases, such as one Native American encounter listed here, OBP runs its own trip. That's because owner Bill Bryan has a long personal and professional history with Native American people. He's also a published authority on the tribes of Montana (see Resources, below), where OBP is based.

FOR FAMILIES. Totally customized encounters range from a day spent with tribal members at reservations in various parts of the West to multiday stays with native guides. You might book several nights in the hogan home of a Navajo outfitter who will guide your family around Canyon de Chelly, the Navajo homeland in northern Arizona. You can stay with natives who have ranches or fishing lodges, or travel with native guides who run horse packing and fishing trips. OBP works with Blackfeet and Flathead tribe members in Montana; Blood and Piegan natives in Alberta, Canada; and numerous tribes throughout the Southwest. Your customized trip can concentrate on spirituality, family life, history, or any aspect of native culture that you want to explore.

OBP also runs its own eight-day tour, generally once or twice each summer, for families with children ages 12 and up. The trip, limited to about a dozen participants, focuses on the history and present-day culture of tribes in Montana and Alberta, Canada. The group spends time with tribal council members and reservation school principals, visits hospitals, and sees important historic sites. Meals are with tribal members. Participants usually learn how to raise a tepee; they have the option of staying overnight in one as well.

🏠 *Off the Beaten Path, 109 E. Main St., Bozeman, MT 59714, tel. 406/586–1311 or 800/445–2995. Year-round (all trips not available at all times): 1–8 days, $200 per family–$1,900 per person.*

Resources

Organizations

For a list of reservations that allow camping or for Native American events you can attend, write to the **Bureau of Indian Affairs** (U.S. Department of the Interior, Washington, D.C. 20245); tell them which states you want to visit.

Books

Kids Explore the Heritage of Western Native Americans (John Muir Publications), by the Westridge Writers Workshop, was written by students, many of whom live on reservations. Profiles of six families show what it means to be Native American today. Marlene Smith-Baranzini and Howard Egger-Bovet's *The Brown Paper School USKids History: Book of American Indians* (Little, Brown) mixes historical anecdotes with stories, drawings, and projects. This book covers tribes from the Southeast to the Pacific Northwest. Bryan and Cherry Alexander's *What Do We Know about the Inuit?* (Peter Bedrick Books) has information about the ancestors of the Inuit and the Inuit people today.

For adults, Michael Durham's *Guide to Ancient Native American Sites* (Globe Pequot Press) gives descriptive overviews and operating hours and fees for 144 sites in 29 states. Anyone booking a trip with Off the Beaten Path should see William L. Bryan's *Montana Indians: Yesterday and Today* (American Geographic Publishing).

Also See

Families interested in present-day Native American peoples may find the study of ancient civilizations appealing. Archaeology Adventures lists digs that focus on native cultures.

PANNING FOR GOLD

Gold has fascinated men, women, and children for centuries. In cultures and countries throughout the world, it has been used for money, jewelry, ornaments, utensils, containers, and religious artifacts. Hammered into furniture, applied to buildings, woven into fabrics, and mixed with paints, gold has also been celebrated in poetry and art, in legends and folktales.

The precious metal has figured prominently in the exploration and history of the United States. It symbolizes, as perhaps nothing else does, the possibilities inherent in the American dream. Although few ever struck it rich, the chance existed that any poor soul with a pick or pan and maybe a mule could find the mother lode.

Today gold panning survives because it's fun to revisit an exciting period in our history, and in part because Americans still love possibilities. Even though you probably won't add much to your bank account by gold panning, you can definitely add to the stories and lore your family collects as it travels. Those are the nuggets to treasure and pass on to children and grandchildren. And if you happen to find a bit of real gold while you're at it, well, pass that on, too, and keep the dream alive.

Gold-panning operations vary in terms of their focus. Some concentrate on the history of gold mining and panning in this country; others have a geological orientation. Most are short adventures lasting from a couple of hours to a day. There are some multiday experiences, and some gold panning takes place on one day as part of a longer trip.

Questions to Ask

What's the focus of the expedition? Some folks are serious about gold, and consequently there are some very technically oriented trips. If you have a rock lover, you may want an emphasis on geology, but not a course aimed at university students.

Do you find gold very often? It's unlikely that you will come across much gold, but a few flakes will thrill a child and make the adventure worth the price and the time. Most outfitters cannot guarantee finding gold, but they should be able to assure you that the area they take you to has at least a few possibilities and that you won't just spend several hours looking at mud.

Does the trip include some history of gold in this area? Gold panning is a perfect vehicle for giving children information about history, geology, sociology, and human nature. The quest for gold is filled with adventure, murder, double-dealing, good guys, bad guys, financial disaster, and huge, huge fortunes. Encourage your guide to pass along this kind of information, and do some research yourselves so you can make history come alive after a day of gold panning.

Is there a book or pamphlet on the history of gold in this area? Because many gold-panning outfitters are part of the local historical society or chamber of commerce or tourism department, they may be able to recommend something for you and your family to read. They may even have something themselves. A good story about an area can make all the difference in the world when it comes to a child's attention span on an outing.

Are there often families on the trip? You want someone who knows how to talk to kids. A geology professor on summer break may be able to tell you a great deal about the land formations in which gold is usually found, but if he or she can't make it interesting to your 9-year-old, you won't enjoy the experience.

How many people will be panning for gold in the same place? Some outfitters take only one family at a time; at other sites there may be a whole crowd. That can be fun, or it can be a vacation nightmare if you're the kind of family that likes to do things alone. Check so you won't be disappointed.

Is there a store at the meeting place or the site? Some gold-panning operations run out of mineral and rock shops, others out of re-created historical sites. Many families like to know in advance if there's going to be shopping to tempt their children, so they can talk with the kids about it in advance or be prepared to lay out some money if it turns out there are things your family really wants to buy. If this matters to you, ask.

What kind of clothes and shoes should be worn? Gold panning is usually dirty—and often wet—work. Mountain areas have unpredictable weather as well, so you want to be prepared even it's just "a three-hour tour." Remember what happened to Gilligan. Some people wear jeans; others might have fishing boots; others prefer shorts and Teva sandals. Ask the outfitter what's appropriate for the weather and the panning site.

What's included in the price of the activity? The answer will be different depending on whether you're talking about multiday adventures or one-day experiences. All the outfitters here include equipment and instruction; most supply local transportation if necessary for one-day adventures; and most give guests vials to put their gold in. Lunch is usually included only on multiday panning, though there are exceptions even in this group. It's always wise to check.

Instruction

Most gold-panning expeditions provide instruction on how to use the equipment, as well as explanations of the various techniques that prospectors have tried over the years. This information is about history as much as gold-panning, so take advantage of it.

Finding the Fun

Midwest: Ken's Minerals. **Rockies:** Telluride Outside. **West Coast:** Gold Prospecting Expeditions. **Alaska:** Grandtravel. **Canada:** Western Expeditions Company.

Favorite Expeditions

Gold Prospecting Expeditions

👫 9+

As you travel along California's Route 49 into Jamestown, a little more than an hour west of Yosemite National Park, you're following the richest gold vein in the world—the Mother Lode. It was here in the summer of 1848 that Reverend James Woods from Philadelphia found a 75-pound nugget near the bridge on Route 49. Later in the year, while searching for his lost jackass, a miner picked up 1,000 ounces of gold in just 100 square feet. Today you might discover gold in Jackass Gulch—or in dozens of other places in Tuolumne County—if you know how to look. Gold Prospecting Expeditions, one of the most extensive commercial gold-panning outfitters around, offers a wide range of experiences in the Jamestown area, from a visit to Jimtown, the re-created 1849 gold-mining tent camp, to multiday excursions into the Sierra Nevada.

FOR FAMILIES. Special one- and two-day family trips are aimed primarily at ages 9 and up, though many younger children have participated and enjoyed these excursions. You'll pan from about 10 to 3 each day, learning to use the basic placer prospecting tools, plus a sluice box; bring your own lunch. You can also choose to spend a day or two in Jimtown 1849, on Woods Creek, where historical interpreters in period clothing will tell you about life in a forty-niners' camp and demonstrate the tools of the

real gold-rush prospectors. Don't be surprised if "claim jumpers" show up with "guns" and stories about the dangers prospectors faced. Your family might chance upon Mark Twain telling some of the gold-rush camp stories that made him famous ("The Celebrated Jumping Frog of Calaveras County" was inspired by a local mining camp visit). Kids can also pan for gold in the special trough in front of the livery stables.

More adventurous families can join a variety of outings, including helicopter trips that focus on finding gold in California's backcountry river canyons, dredging trips, modern electronic prospecting, seven-day mining treks, or a three-day prospecting course that is an intensive introduction to everything you need to know about the science of searching for gold. If gold fever strikes your family, you can even buy or rent a real gold-mining claim.

🏠 *Gold Prospecting Expeditions, 18170 Main St., Box 1040, Jamestown, CA 95327, tel. 209/984–4653. Year-round: 2 hrs–7 days, $75–$950 (up to 3 children under 12 free with 2 adults on many excursions).*

Grandtravel

👫 7 – 17

Grandtravel is an organization dedicated to bringing grandparents and grandchildren together for experiences that will give them a chance to get to know one another in ways that day-to-day living does not. All of Grandtravel's programs have an inherently educational component, and itineraries are designed to promote learning through travel as well as fun between generations. The Alaskan Wilderness Adventure, which includes gold panning in Juneau, is no exception.

FOR FAMILIES. There are two trips each summer to Alaska—one for grandparents with grandchildren ages 7–11, and one for those with grandchildren ages 12–17. The two-week itinerary starts in Juneau and ends in Anchorage. Along the way you'll take a float trip through the Mendenhall River valley, visit a glacier, cruise a 75-mile canal from Juneau to Skagway, ride on a train to Frasier in British Columbia, explore the Yukon and Denali National Park, and go salmon fishing on the famed Kenai River. Gold, of course, is integral to Alaska's history, and this trip offers several opportunities to learn about it. You'll try your luck panning in Gold Creek near Juneau in the early part of the trip. Toward the end, in Nome—the gold rush capital of the Arctic—you'll visit historic gold dredges and see the black sand beaches from which prospectors ultimately took $3 million in gold. This is a trip of a lifetime, not only for what you gain from the places you explore but for what you gain by being together—and no amount of gold can buy that.

 Grandtravel, 6900 Wisconsin Ave., Suite 706, Chevy Chase, MD 20815, tel. 301/986–0790 or 800/247–7651. July–Aug.: 14 days, $5,090–$5,460 adults, $4,620–$5,040 children under 12. Price includes hotels, most meals, flights within Alaska during the trip, and travel by air-conditioned motor coach.

Ken's Minerals

👪 6+

Until 1874, the Black Hills were sacred Sioux land and off-limits to settlers. But when General George Custer and his men discovered gold in French Creek, near the present-day city of Custer, South Dakota, promises to the Sioux were quickly forgotten. Prospectors moved into the area, setting off a craze that turned into the Black Hills Gold Rush of 1876. Custer and his men eventually met an untimely end, but gold is still found today in French Creek. Ken Spring of Ken's Minerals has been teaching folks about minerals, rocks, and local geology for decades.

FOR FAMILIES. Ken's father, Gottfried, went into the rock business in 1936 after a grasshopper invasion destroyed most of the crops in the area. Grasshoppers, he reasoned, couldn't eat rocks. In 1955, Ken and Martha Spring set up their mineral shop on the eastern edge of Custer. His gold-panning trips are extremely popular. Taking just one family at a time to the section of French Creek (pronounced "crick") on his ranch, Ken will help you find gold; he'll also spin stories about the area to keep everyone entertained for a good hour-and-a-half or so. After panning for gold, you can head back to the shop, now run by Ken, Jr., and his wife, Karen, to pick up some rocks of your own. There's a good selection of rose quartz, the South Dakota state mineral mined about 6 miles away; on view is the Spring family private collection of gems, minerals, and rocks that come from all over the world.

 Ken's Minerals, HC83, Box 157, Custer, SD 57730, tel. 605/673–4935. Mid-June–late Sept.: 1½ hrs, $2.50–$20.

Telluride Outside

👪 7+

It was tellurium ore, not gold, that put the old mining town of Telluride on the map and gave it its name. However, there were—and are—flakes of gold to be discovered by those who know where to look. Before or after your panning expedition you can visit Bridal Veil Falls, Colorado's highest, and arguably most beautiful, waterfall. Or you can mosey on downtown and watch for the celebrities who have recently made this most beautiful of the state's mountain towns their home. Telluride Outside takes families on a variety of adventures in the area.

FOR FAMILIES. Telluride Outside is always happy to take children along on trips. Even

young ones can help parents pan; however, the guides feel it's those 7 and up who will get the most from the experience. These trips for up to 15 people last about 2½ hours and take place on the San Miguel River a short distance from town. Guides, who are almost always successful in helping families find gold flakes, tell stories of Telluride's colorful past while teaching gold-panning techniques. They'll also discuss the geological events that put gold in the area and drive your family to an old mine dump site to search for pyrite crystals (fool's gold). Special-focus excursions concentrate on regional geology, so ask about these if you have a budding geologist in the family.
🏠 *Telluride Outside, Box 685, Telluride, CO 81435, tel. 970/728–3895. Late May–Sept.: 2½ hrs, $20–$50 (children under 6 free).*

Western Expeditions Company

👫 12+

Family prospectors can try their luck in Canada's Manning Provincial Park, about three hours east of Vancouver, in the Coast Mountains. Although the park is now known for good camping, hiking, and birding (more than 160 species of birds have been sighted within its boundaries), this is also where gold was first found in 1853, setting off a gold rush that brought prospectors into British Columbia for many years. Among the earliest was John Allison, whose family stayed to ranch in what is now the town of Princeton, and whose name is given to one of the highest passes in the area. Among the more interesting characters, however, was Johnny Chance, who was so lazy he was

given the job of cook at the prospecting camp. The story goes that instead of hunting for food one day, he sat down on the banks of the Similkameen River to rest. Dipping his feet in the cool water, he looked down and discovered enough gold nuggets to make him and everyone in his camp rich. Western Expeditions, a family-oriented outfitter that also has great hiking trips, will share more local history and help you try your luck.

FOR FAMILIES. There may not be many nuggets left in the Similkameen, but there are plenty of flakes and someone in your family may find one. Children aged 12 and up do best on this full-day trip that starts and ends at the main lodge in Manning Provincial Park. Your guide will tell you some of the history of panning in the area and teach you how to locate gold in any likely river. If you find a flake, he'll give you a vial to take it home in. A traditional prospector's lunch of baked beans and sourdough bread is included (there are hot dogs for the kids if beans aren't among their favorite foods).
🏠 *Western Expeditions Company, 35704 Sunridge Pl., Abbotsford V3G 1E5, British Columbia, Canada, tel. 604/855–0840. May–Oct.: 1 day, $28–$43 (children under 10 free with a paying adult).*

Resources

Also See

Your family can learn more about the history of the American West on trips listed in Covered Wagon Adventures and Cattle Drives.

RAFTING

My love of rafting began when I first ran the McKenzie and Rogue rivers in the early '70s as a student at the University of Oregon. My older daughter, Kira, was luckier. She had the fun of experiencing her first river—the New, in West Virginia—when she was just 8. Molly, her sister, explored Jackson Lake and the Snake River, down through Moose, Wyoming, at the age of 4.

Rafting is simply a great family vacation. You don't need any experience or skills, and you can choose a trip on which you paddle or one on which you sit back and watch the scenery drift by as guides wield the oars. However and wherever you do it, the combination of floating downriver under blue skies and camping at night under millions of stars is unbeatable. The roomy rafts also make it possible to carry an amount and variety of food unheard of on many wilderness trips. When Molly and I rafted with OARS in the Tetons, we had French toast in the mornings, choices of cold cuts and sandwiches for lunch, and fresh salads and steak or homemade lasagna at night. Did we see spectacular wilderness areas and view wildlife up close? You bet. Did we rough it? Hardly.

Rafting outfitters have done more to entice children and parents onto North American rivers than any other water-sport group. Family-only raft trips seem to increase in number every season, with ever-better amenities for river-running kids. Storytellers, child-oriented naturalists, and off-river activities counselors accompany some trips; excursions to historical sites are part of others. Guides on family trips are chosen as much for their ability to work effectively with children as for their rafting skills.

On the other hand, most trips that welcome families do not send you through the intense white water that sets your heart pounding and adrenaline rushing. Family trips tend to tackle Class I to III rapids only, which means easy to moderate white water appropriate for kids 12 or 13 and younger. What you trade in excitement on a family river trip with younger kids, however, you make up in wildlife viewing, side hikes, and the joy of introducing your children to rivers and wilderness areas. If you are among the river-loving families with teens, you have a whole world of thrilling, chilling, and exquisitely beautiful rivers to choose from.

Dozens of rivers throughout North America are perfect for family raft trips. A number of outfitters listed here work the same rivers, but that doesn't mean you'd have the same experience with each of them. Finding the right river is important; choosing the right outfitter is crucial. Each has a distinct personality and creates a particular atmosphere on the river and in camp. Make lots of calls before you make a decision.

Questions to Ask

Are coast guard–approved life vests available for a child the size and age of mine? Most vests are sized according to height and weight, not age, so give outfitters your child's measurements to be sure they have one that will fit. If the right size isn't available, you'll have to borrow a life vest or buy one at an outdoor or marine supply store.

Are the guides trained in wilderness and water safety, first aid, and CPR? Always ask. Wilderness rivers take you a long, long way from medical care or help. If an accident occurs, you want guides who know the right emergency procedures.

How strenuous are trips and what do the classifications of rapids mean? The most common white-water classification system used in this country rates rapids from Class I to Class VI; Class I is barely more than a riffle, and Class VI is virtually unrunnable. Most family trips fall into Class III or below, though children 8 and up are sometimes allowed on rivers with a Class IV rapid or two. Outfitters take several things into consideration: the time of year, how fast the water is moving, and how high the water is. A second classification system, more common among the Grand Canyon outfitters than others, has Class I to Class X ratings. If you're uncertain which system an outfitter is using, ask.

How many hours will we raft each day? Five to six hours a day is average, though water level, weather, and the ability of guests and guides doing the paddling or rowing affect rafting time. Still, the pace allows for unhurried breakfasts and early enough arrivals at camp each afternoon to hike, fish, or relax. There are daily stops along the way on all river journeys. Trips designated especially for families often have more frequent stops and shorter days on the river.

Are there scheduled activities other than rafting? Hiking and fishing are the two most common river camp activities, and you must usually bring your own fishing gear and arrange for licenses for teens and adults ahead of time. Family trips almost always have camp activities, such as storytelling, crafts, games, nature walks, or berry-picking hikes.

What kinds of rafts are used on the trip? On most but not all of the trips listed, you'll be in oar-powered rafts that the guides are primarily responsible for maneuvering and rowing. Guests almost always have the option of a paddle raft if they request it, and a couple of trips use paddle rafts only. In these, all the passengers stroke according to the guide's directions. Very few of the outfitters in this chapter use motorized rafts. Typically, the rafts hold 6 to 12 people. Almost all outfitters will also bring along inflatable kayaks for additional fun.

Are the rafts self-bailing? This is by no means a requirement, but families seeking more comfort and less work may prefer self-bailers, which release water on their own. They stay drier on the bottom, so that your feet and gear will be drier, too. And no one will ask you to help bail if it rains or after you go through the big splashes. A self-bailer is also more stable and easier to maneuver than a raft with water sloshing around the bottom, and when it comes to kids on the river, stable is always preferable.

Are there dry bags? Most outfitters provide a dry bag for storing clothing and camping gear each day, but you generally can't get to your stuff until you camp. On-raft containers hold cameras and other items you want on board. A small dry bag or waterproof day pack of your own is a good idea, because shared containers don't usually have room for rain gear and warm layers for the kids.

Are snacks provided on the river? Children need to eat far more often than adults, so this is important. If the guides won't have easily accessible snacks in the rafts, bring your own on board in a day pack.

What's the average group size? Most outfitters listed here go out with 10 to 20 participants, plus 2 to 4 guides. Some trips may take only 6 to 8 people, however, and a few outfitters run trips with as many as 25.

What's included in the cost? All meals, guides, and local transportation to the put-in (launch site) and from the take-out (where the river trip ends) are included, as are life vests for all passengers, unless otherwise noted. Most rafting outfitters will bring along inflatable kayaks for a change of pace for adults and older kids, but some charge extra for this. In most cases you must bring your own tent, pad, and sleeping bag, or rent from the outfitter for a small additional cost. A few outfitters provide this equipment as part of the basic cost. Outfitters almost always arrange a safe place for you to leave your car during the trip; it might be their own parking lot or the lot of a local motel.

Instruction

Guides begin every trip with safety instructions for rafting and camping. These help both adults and children understand the importance of being careful around water. If guests are going to paddle, you will learn how to do that. You'll probably be taught a bit of river lingo, too, so you can follow the guide's paddling instructions. Beyond that, all you need to do is have fun.

Finding the Fun

Northeast: Unicorn Expeditions. **Mid-Atlantic:** Class VI River Runners. **Mid-west:** Kayak & Canoe Institute. **Southwest:** American River Touring Association, Canyonlands Field Institute, Denver Museum of Natural History, Dvorak's Kayak & Rafting Expeditions, Expeditions, Inc., Far Flung Adventures, Grand Canyon Dories/OARS Dories, Holiday River & Bike Expeditions, Sheri Griffith Expeditions. **Rockies:** American Wilderness Experience, American River Touring Association, Canyonlands Field Institute, Denver Museum of Natural History, Dvorak's Kayak & Rafting Expeditions, Echo, Glacier Wilderness Guides/Montana Raft Company,

Grand Canyon Dories/OARS Dories, Holiday River & Bike Expeditions, Hughes River Expeditions, Idaho Afloat, Kayak & Canoe Institute, OARS, Outdoor Adventures, Ouzel Outfitters, River Odysseys West, Wilderness River Outfitters. **West Coast:** American River Touring Association, Cutting Edge Adventures, Echo, Hughes River Expeditions, OARS, Outdoor Adventures, Ouzel Outfitters. **Alaska:** Canadian River Expeditions, Kayak & Canoe Institute, Wilderness River Outfitters. **Canada:** Canadian River Expeditions, Wilderness River Outfitters. **Mexico:** Cutting Edge Adventures, Far Flung Adventures. **Africa:** Cutting Edge Adventures.

Favorite Rafting Companies

American River Touring Association

 6+

The American River Touring Association—well-known as ARTA—donates a portion of its revenues to conservation organizations each year. This nonprofit corporation's philosophy is based on the belief that exposure to the wilderness benefits both individuals and the environment. Yes, ARTA *is* earnest about nature, safety, and environmental concerns—but it's just as serious about people having fun on its trips throughout the West.

FOR FAMILIES. Trips run spring through fall, but in summer ARTA schedules numerous family departures on five rivers. You can choose from among the South Fork of the American in California, Oregon's Rogue River, two portions of the Green in Utah, and either the Salmon or the Middle Fork of the Salmon in Idaho. Each river gives rafters something special in terms of scenery and focus. The American is a great two-day escape that uses only paddle rafts; the Rogue offers excellent wildlife-viewing possibilities; the geology and history of the Green are fascinating; and the Salmon abounds in great beaches, hot springs, and swimming opportunities. To encourage families to explore these rivers together, there's

a special discount for kids on family departures. Guides on all family trips genuinely enjoy working with kids, and the many side activities range from hiking and storytelling to pondering nature's mysteries.

American River Touring Association, 24000 Casa Loma Rd., Groveland, CA 95321, tel. 209/962–7873 or 800/323–2782. Apr.–Sept.: 2–7 days, $150–$1,070; 15% discount off children's rates on family departures for children under 18 accompanying an adult.

American Wilderness Experience

6+

The extensive list of rafting vacations in American Wilderness Experience's catalog shows just how much the business has grown. This trip broker represents many of the rafting outfitters in this chapter. Some standouts among its trips are a couple of vacations in Montana and Colorado that combine activities. If your family is debating which adventure to pursue, one of these may be the answer.

FOR FAMILIES. If you can't choose between a ranch stay and a raft trip, Glacier Raft Company and Bear Creek Ranch in Montana have put together three days at the ranch and two days of rafting. Kids aged 6 and up can handle this one. At the ranch, near the border of Glacier National Park and Great Bear Wilderness, guests can opt for exceptional riding, hiking, or fishing in a land of blue-white glaciers and high peaks. The 30-mile rafting trip down the Middle Fork of the Flathead runs through parts of Glacier Park and the Lewis and Clark National Forest. If horse packing into the wilderness appeals more than a stay at the ranch, try the five-day ride-and-raft trip, best for ages 8 and up. This adventure takes you into Flathead National Forest and ends with a raft trip on the Middle Fork of the Flathead.

Families with kids 8 and up can combine horse packing with rafting in south central Colorado on a trip from Adventure Specialists. The first three days are spent packing and camping in the Sangre de Cristo range. The group then heads down to a rustic inn for showers and a hot tub before two days on the Arkansas River, including a wild run through Royal Gorge.
🏠 *American Wilderness Experience, Box 1486, Boulder, CO 80306, tel. 303/444–2622 or 800/444–0099. June–Aug.: 5 days, $500–$855.*

Canadian River Expeditions

👫 8+

The icy Tatshenshini River flows through the Yukon and British Columbia, empties into the Alsek, and finally spills into the sea at the Gulf of Alaska. On the way it carves a silty swath through a vast wilderness landscape that humbles and awes its viewers. Canadian River Expeditions has been guiding on the Tat and the Alsek for almost 20 years. The guides know and love the Tat, and they willingly share the river with families who dare to come. The Tat is a personal favorite, but the company's trips through other parts of British Columbia are phenomenal, too.

FOR FAMILIES. Days on the Tat are long, often windy, and alternately warm and downright chilly. The fishing is not great, and you can't swim in the cold water. None of this matters, however, when you're walking on glaciers or observing wildlife such as black bears, moose, wolves, and even griz-

zlies. One spectacular hike with an ascent of about 3,800 feet is probably too much for anyone under age 12 or 13 (although children as young as 8 are welcome on this trip), and if you have a child who wearies of just observing nature's wonders, this 12-day expedition may not be for you. On the other hand, if your family wants to look out for hundreds of miles without finding one sign of human civilization, this trip will provide memories to last a lifetime.

Company co-owner Johnny Mikes, Jr., recommends the 11-day Best of B.C. trip as ideal for families with younger children. From Vancouver, the group travels by boat into the Discovery Islands and the coastal region's fjords, then by seaplane over the glaciers of the Coast Mountains and on to 40-mile-long Chilko Lake. After you fish and hike among the ancient firs for two days, the rafting begins. You journey on three rivers—the Chilko, Chilcotin, and Fraser—passing from the mountains down through wide-open grasslands and into the arid sandstone and cactus canyons of the Fraser. With its huge volume of water, the Fraser has plenty of the big roller-coaster rapids that all rafters love. A four-hour train ride takes you back to the coast through Whistler.
🏠 *Canadian River Expeditions, Box 1023, Whistler V0N 1B0, British Columbia, Canada, tel. 604/938–6651 or 800/898–7238. June–Aug.: 6–12 days, $1,475–$2,350; 20% discount for children under 18.*

Canyonlands Field Institute

👫 8+

Canyonlands focuses primarily on its youth program, in which students from Utah, Colorado, and beyond learn about the wonders of the Colorado Plateau—geology, wildlife, night skies, waterways, and more. Naturalists and other outdoor educators make up the institute's staff. Although family courses are limited, they are exceptional. Few river trips have an educational component as extensive as these.

FOR FAMILIES. Working with Elderhostel, the nonprofit organization well known for its study programs for older adults, Canyonlands sponsors an intergenerational trip that brings grandparents and grandchildren together for six days of discovery as they raft the San Juan River. Naturalists lead hands-on nature activities and games, teach participants low-impact camping and river-running skills, and delve into botany, geology, and a study of prehistoric rock art—all while having fun on the river. The group camps for four nights; the first night is spent at a lodge in Bluff, Utah, where the trip begins.

Similar in format to the intergenerational trip are the Family Camps. There are typically two each summer, both centered around rafting the mighty Colorado River. The minimum age for the three-day July trip is 6; for the Westwater Canyon adventure in August, which runs four days, it's 12. On these camping trips, much of the learning takes place in the afternoons and evenings at camp, with both family and separate kids' activities.

With three months' notice, the institute will set up custom river trips for groups of at least eight. Families with kids 12 and up can run the Colorado River from Colorado to Utah, floating through Ruby and Horsethief canyons and on to the rapids of Westwater Canyon. Colorado's portion of the Dolores River through Ponderosa Gorge is another option. A naturalist leads and outfits each trip, providing the same learning opportunities found on scheduled trips.

You don't have to be a CFI member to join any of the adventures, but members do get a discount of 10%, up to $15, on trips.
🏠 *Canyonlands Field Institute, Box 68, Moab, UT 84532, tel. 801/259–7750 or 800/860–5262. May–Aug.: 3–6 days, $265–$440 (scheduled trips), $275–$484 (custom trips). Family membership (optional) is $35.*

Class VI River Runners

 6+

If you think all the best white water is out West, you haven't run the New or Gauley rivers in the Appalachians of south central West Virginia. The New—which in spite of its name may be second only to the Nile in geologic age—cuts a deep and impressive gorge, with walls 1,000 feet high in places. As for the Gauley, each fall white-water enthusiasts arrive from all over the world to test their skills against a river that drops 650 feet in 27 miles and churns up more than 100 major rapids along the way. Class VI caters equally to 6-year-olds rafting for the first time and 16-year-olds looking for the ultimate adrenaline high. Parents will find in Dave Arnold and his co-owners the intelligence and spirit that characterize the very best river outfitters.

FOR FAMILIES. The upper New treats families with kids over 5 to Class I to II rapids, with a Class III thrill toward the end of this one-to three-day trip. Great swimming and rock jumping along the way, plus wildlife and historic points of interest, make this a memorable experience. For a one-day adventure, parents and teens can raft the more difficult portions of the river while family members under 12 have their own guided adventure on the upper New. You get together again in the late afternoon at Class VI's headquarters; check out the excellent barbecue at Smokey's, the outfitter's restaurant, while you're there.

The lower New River Gorge is for kids 12 and up from July to Labor Day; the minimum age is 14 the rest of the season. Prepare yourself for Class III to V rapids, along with the spectacular scenery of the deeply forested Appalachians. In spite of the rapids, swimming is good here, too. Special theme trips on the lower New include Sleuths; New River Up Close, led by a river ecologist; and Time Traveling on the New, a history-oriented trip. Age limits vary, depending on the section of the river.

The Gauley is for kids at least 15, with the exception of one fall run on the lower Gauley that accepts 14-year-olds. The faint of heart, out of shape, or sit-back-and-relax types should look for another river. The Gauley is work—and worth every bit of it, with a payback of world-class white-water and thrills. You can choose between one- and two-day trips.

For lodging before and after trips, there's an excellent campground minutes from Class VI and a variety of motels and bed-and-breakfasts. The elegant Greenbrier resort, with its own outstanding children's program, is about 1½ hours away. Class VI can help arrange these accommodations, as well as airfare.

 Class VI River Runners, Box 78, Lansing, WV 25862, tel. 304/574–0704 or 800/252–7784. Mar.–Nov.: 1–5 days, $39–$460.

Cutting Edge Adventures

👫 3+

Stephanie Abrishamian, co-owner of Cutting Edge, is enough of a kid at heart that children immediately relate to her, and so do parents. When you raft with Cutting Edge, you laugh—and learn—a lot on some of northern California's greatest rivers. Amazingly, one of them, the Klamath, has sections gentle enough for preschoolers but still delivers the thrills that rafting families want.

FOR FAMILIES. The Klamath is renowned for salmon and steelhead fishing and for Hell's Corner, one of the top 10 stretches of white water in the United States. Families, however, acclaim it as an accommodating river. Beaches make terrific campsites, and Class II and III rapids provide the requisite rush. The middle and lower Klamath have exceptional wildlife viewing opportunities; the river is on the Pacific flyway, a major migratory route for a variety of birds. Blue and green herons, bald and golden eagles,

falcons, ospreys, and cormorants all travel the Klamath. In the hills above it, mountain lions and bears still roam. One of California's great river side hikes follows a trail just ¾ mile long up Ukonom Creek, ending at Twin Falls. There's a choice of one- to five-day trips that cover about 12 miles a day. Storytellers come along to entertain rafters on all middle and lower Klamath trips.

Families with children 10 and up can try the upper Sacramento River, where Class III to IV rapids propel rafters through canyons and beautiful forested stretches. This two-day trip covers about 18 miles; you can choose camping or a lodge stay.

For the most adventurous, and for those at least 17 years old, Cutting Edge schedules a trip to Mexico that begins on the free-flowing Río Jatate in the Chiapas region of southern Mexico. The Jat runs through lush jungle and remote canyons, with waterfalls, chutes, and slides—Class III to V—to contend with. There's a chance to visit the Mayan ruins of Tonina. From the Jat the trip moves on to Río Agua Azul Park, a waterfall paradise with its own Mayan ruins. The last river is the Río Shumulja, a turquoise beauty with Class III and IV white water.

Families interested in overseas adventures should also ask about the Out of Africa trip, with river running on the Zambezi; the minimum age for this one is also 17.

 Cutting Edge Adventures, Box 1334, Mt. Shasta, CA 96067, tel. 916/926–4647. Apr.–Jan. (all trips not all months): 1–10 days, $50–$1,200.

Denver Museum of Natural History

👫 5+

Put kids, rafting, and dinosaurs together and you have a perfect family adventure package. Among its many outdoor study programs, the museum generally schedules a family rafting trip in Utah each summer that touches on paleontology, geology, river ecology, and anthropology, in addition to plain old river-rafting fun.

FOR FAMILIES. The Jurassic Journey/Green River Raft Trip begins at Dinosaur National Monument, east of Vernal, Utah, where huge dinosaur fossils are currently being excavated. The group rafts through the 2,000-foot-deep Lodore Canyon on the Green River; off the water, hikes to native rock art sites and historic outlaw cabins, wildlife watching, and in-camp games highlight the natural environment. Scientists from various disciplines lead the trip, and all kids aged 5 to 11 receive a Dinosaur Discovery Kit with fun activities and games.
🏛 *Denver Museum of Natural History, 2001 Colorado Blvd., Denver, CO 80205, tel. 303/370–6304. July: 4 days, $470–$590. Museum membership, a requirement, is $50 per family.*

Dvorak's Kayak & Rafting Expeditions

👪 5+

Years ago Dvorak's was one of only a handful of outfitters promoting river running for families. They have a lot more competition these days, but their long experience has shown them what rafting can do for families. With the right leaders, the Dvoraks say, rafting helps improve communication between family members by putting children and adults on an equal playing field. Guides, rather than parents, do the leading, allowing both children and adults to try new activities and learn together.

FOR FAMILIES. The outfitter runs family trips on five rivers throughout the West that have varying minimum ages; in addition, Dvorak's has two different family discount programs. Kids Go Free is available on the Green River in Utah and Colorado's Dolores; the minimum age on these rivers is 5 and 10, respectively. On family departure dates, each paying adult can bring a child

under 13 for free. The Family Discount Program applies on the Colorado River in Colorado, the Rio Chama in New Mexico, and the North Platte, which runs in both Colorado and Wyoming. On special dates, families of from three to six people receive a greatly discounted group rate. Choose a river based on the ages of your children. Kids 5 and up can handle portions of the Colorado and Rio Chama; those 10 and up are welcome on the North Platte. All family trips emphasize camp activities that families can participate in together, as well as a terrific rafting experience.

Kids can join other trips, too, so check out the catalog's extensive offerings. Teens and their parents can choose among plenty of wild rivers, but these aren't in the Family Discount Program.
🏛 *Dvorak's Kayak and Rafting Expeditions, 17921–B U.S. 285, Nathrop, CO 81236, tel. 719/539–6851 or 800/824–3795. May–Aug.: 2–6 days, $620–$1,645.*

Echo

👪 7+

In running rivers for a quarter of a century, the people at Echo have learned that people sign up for rafting trips for many different reasons. The company caters to all ages and interests, and not just in the variety of its trips—from classic white-water thrillers to special-focus music and yoga trips—but in the scope of each adventure. On its River Trips for Kids, in particular, the outfitter creates family voyages equally appealing to 7-year-olds and teens.

FOR FAMILIES. Family trips take place on the Salmon in Idaho, Oregon's Rogue River, and on the South Fork of the American in northern California. On each expedition, a Fun Director organizes educational activities and other neat stuff—whether it's looking for crawdads, skipping stones, or checking out animal tracks. Teens are encouraged to help the guides (all of whom can definitely be described as "cool"), or they can hang out with adults if they wish. A Kids' Raft gives children the choice of riding with new friends or with parents; some shore activities are just for the kids, too, so adults will have some time to themselves. These trips generally combine oar and paddle rafts and the option of inflatable kayaks. If you can't make one of the specially designated family trips, don't worry: There are always families on Echo's regular trips.

🛖 *Echo, 6529 Telegraph Ave., Oakland, CA 94609, tel. 510/652–1600 or 800/652–3246. July–Aug.: 2–5 days, $220–$915.*

Expeditions, Inc.

👫 8+

Former educators Dick and Susie McCallum own and operate a small, personalized company that specializes in one thing—running the Grand Canyon. Actually, they're still educating people, but their classroom is now a bit larger. Considered by many to be *the* quintessential river trip, the Grand Canyon has it all: heart-stopping rapids, vistas that attract top photographers, and side hikes into places of immense beauty. The McCallums try to accompany as many of the trips as possible and genuinely like sharing this magnificent country with everyone—the young and the young at heart.

FOR FAMILIES. Top-of-the-line trips of from 12 to 14 days run the entire 226-mile stretch of the Colorado River as it rushes from Lees Ferry to Peach Springs, Arizona. Although not family-only trips, these were designed to meet the interests of various ages; the combination of rafting thrills, fun, history, and great scenery draws lots of families. Expeditions, Inc., uses no motors. These are oar-powered rafts or, if enough people in the group are willing to make the commitment, paddle rafts. For a shorter trip, you can join the first part of the trip. A five- or six-day adventure (depending on the time of year) covers 87 miles of river, at the end of which you hike 9 miles up to the

South Rim by either the Bright Angel or Kaibab trail. If hiking 7 miles down into the canyon is intriguing, consider joining the second leg of the trip, an eight- or nine-day journey on 139 miles of the river.

On any of these trips, you can count on the experience of a lifetime and the ultimate in food and provisions—Expeditions, Inc., even supplies sleeping bags and pads. Although the McCallums don't have a hard-and-fast rule about age minimums, talk to them before signing up. They have a tremendous amount of experience with families on this river.

🛖 *Expeditions, Inc., R.R. 4, Box 755, Flagstaff, AZ 86001, tel. 520/779–3769. May–Oct.: 5–14 days, $950–$2,100.*

Far Flung Adventures

👫 7+

For almost 20 years, this company has introduced rafters to the geologically diverse regions and rivers of the Southwest and Mexico. Although Far Flung Adventures doesn't market itself as a family outfitter, many parents and children sign up for these river trips—and have a great time.

FOR FAMILIES. Far Flung guides on seven major rivers. One of the very best for families, the Rio Chama, flows from the Colorado–New Mexico border down toward the Rio Grande. Most of the 24-mile journey on this two-day trip is at 6,000 feet, with terrain that ranges from wide-open spaces to forests of fir and pine. It's Class II and III all the way. For an all-around great river and an excellent introduction to rafting, the Rio Grande and a series of canyons in and near Big Bend National Park in Texas provide a range of river experiences, from wide and tranquil to steep, narrow, and fast. The 85-mile run in the lower canyons, just east of the park, takes rafters through a maze of limestone cliffs and a stark landscape. Both the Rio Chama and the Rio Grande are good swimming rivers, too.

Families with older kids can also join trips on Arizona's Salt River and on the Gunnison and Dolores in Colorado. Minimum ages for these trips vary.

The most adventurous families with time in the fall or winter should consider Mexico's Río Antigua and Río Usumacinta. Lots of Class IV rapids on the Antigua, in Veracruz, keep everyone on edge, and native freshwater lobsters and tropical fruits satisfy the most demanding palate. The Usumacinta, close to the Guatemalan border, runs through North America's largest remaining tropical rain forest, home to tree frogs, howler monkeys, and parrots. On this expedition the group visits the ruins of huge Mayan ceremonial centers. Both Mexican trips are for ages 10 and up, but children should be interested in archaeology and foreign cultures as well as willing to spend 10 days on a river.

iA *Far Flung Adventures, Box 377, Terlingua, TX 79852, tel. 915/371–2489. Year-round (all rivers not all months): 1–10 days, $75–$1,650; 10% discount for children under 13.*

Glacier Wilderness Guides/Montana Raft Company

ii 6+

Using a few of the million acres of mountains, lakes, and streams in Montana's Glacier National Park, this company guides on both land and water, which makes its combination trips first class. The owners have hiked, camped, rafted, fished, and explored the Glacier area for most of their lives. They love it, and they know the secret places others will love, too.

FOR FAMILIES. Rafting adventures take place on the Middle and North forks of the Flathead. Families can join two- and three-day rafting-only adventures, but the gems in the trip list are hike-and-raft and ride-and-raft combinations in and near Glacier. You can structure the hike-and-raft several ways:

½ day of each activity, 2½ days of each, or four or six days of hiking and two days of rafting (with a motel stay in between). Groups are small, usually just four to six guests. For the ride-and-raft, choose a one-day or four-day combination with equal time for horseback riding and rafting. Glacier Wilderness Guides works with a horse pack outfitter for that portion of the trip.

iA *Glacier Wilderness Guides/Montana Raft Company, Box 535, West Glacier, MT 59936, tel. 406/888–5466 or 800/521–7238. May–Sept.: 1–8 days, $33–$830. On the ride-and-raft trips there are children's rates, but only on the rafting portion.*

Grand Canyon Dories/ OARS Dories

ii 7+

If you've never thought about running a river, let alone rafting for 19 days, call and ask for the illustrated Dories brochure. In this small work of art, the men and women of this company speak eloquently about rivers and the beautiful dory boats in which they run them. Dories, four-passenger wood boats maneuvered by oars, have a long and celebrated heritage. They provide an experience totally unlike riding in today's big synthetic rafts: You *feel* the river differently in a dory. If this appeals to you, and if you can take the time to immerse yourself in the natural world, this is the company for you.

FOR FAMILIES. Most families with children over 12 can handle the longest river journey, the full length of the Colorado from Lees Ferry to Lake Mead. For 19 days you explore the Grand Canyon's rock layers—half a billion years' worth of geologic history in shades of rose, gold, and violet. The dories shoot through mile-high walls and raging rapids. Camping experience might help, but you'll soon be old hands. Good hikers who are able to handle the near-vertical mile of the 9-mile-long trail between Phantom Ranch and the South

Rim can join the group for either the 8- or 13-day partial trip, depending on whether you leave or join up at Phantom Ranch. Whether you're going up or down, it's a strenuous hike. Those who choose to leave or join up at Whitmore Wash raft for 5 or 16 days and fly in and out by helicopter. If you travel all 19 days, you start and end in Flagstaff.

Less grand, perhaps, but equally satisfying are trips on the Salmon and Snake rivers in Idaho. These rivers are great for families with younger kids and perfect for dories; the Northwest was the birthplace of the river-style dory. The free-flowing Salmon is the largest undammed river in the American West. You can raft the upper portion of the Main Salmon or the lower gorge, or combine the two in a 12-day adventure. Along the way, there are fine hikes and long, clean beaches perfect for swimming. The 400-mile-long Salmon empties into the Snake at Hells Canyon, the deepest gorge in North America. Guides share the legends of the Nez Percé who lived here, including some tales about mythic gods who shaped the rugged landscape and the Snake's roaring rapids. For all its wildness, the Snake also shows rafters a gentler side. In a dory, you'll feel the rock and rhythm of the currents as you cannot in a raft.

🏔 *Grand Canyon Dories/OARS Dories, Box 1119, Angels Camp, CA 95222, tel. 209/736–0811 or 800/877–3679. Apr.–Oct.: 3–19 days, $517–$2,990.*

Holiday River & Bike Expeditions

(👫👤 6+)

Holiday has more than 30 years' experience taking all kinds of people rafting on the great rivers of Utah, Colorado, and Idaho. Dee Holladay, the company's founder, has a passion for rivers and river history. He believes that rafting is more than the sum of its parts—scenery, wilderness, solitude, and incredible white water. It's the time of your life. The company has also discovered that when rafting is combined with mountain biking, the thrills get even better.

FOR FAMILIES. Trips on the easiest rivers, the San Juan and the Desolation Canyon section of the Green in Utah, take kids 6 and up. Families with kids at least 8 can try such intermediate rivers as the Colorado (which is also expert-only at certain times of year), the Lodore Canyon section of the Green, and the Yampa, all of which run along the Colorado-Utah border. Idaho's great waterways, the Snake and the Salmon, are other possibilities for those 8 and up. The most adventurous families with teens at least 16 can go for an adrenaline rush on the Lochsa in Idaho and on the Colorado and lower Salmon in high-water season.

Four rafting and mountain biking tours give families the best of two adventures. On the White Rim Trail of Canyonlands National Park in Utah, you bike 65 miles in three days on a white sandstone bench that winds past spectacular formations. At the end, the group piles into rafts for a four-day run through the Colorado River's legendary Cataract Canyon. The Colorado is matched with another bike trip near the world's mountain bike mecca—Moab, Utah. Two days of quintessential wilderness biking through 25 miles of ponderosa pine country and red rock desert is capped with two days on the Westwater section of the Colorado. Other trips pair two days of biking on 46 miles of remote dirt road with either five days of rafting the Yampa or four days on the Lodore Canyon run of the Green. All these combination trips are for ages 12 and up (except the White Rim/Cataract trips in spring, which have a minimum age of 16) and those in good physical condition. Can you and your teen keep up with each other? Find out and forge a bond you may never have thought possible.

🏔 *Holiday River & Bike Expeditions, 544 E. 3900 S, Salt Lake City, UT 84107, tel. 801/266–2087 or 800/624–6323. May–Sept.: 2–12 days (rafting only), $299–$2,131; 4–7 days (raft and bike), $615–$1,069.*

Hughes River Expeditions

👫 6+

Jerry Hughes and Carole Finley, who run this company, have more than 50 years of guiding experience between them. That alone would make them a good choice for almost any rafter. They've also explored rivers with their own three children, ranging in age from preschool to preteen, so they are knowledgeable about introducing kids to the pleasures of rafting. Jerry and Carole grew up in Idaho and specialize in the state's white water. No outfitter knows more than these two about rafting the Salmon and the Snake—which is probably why they were chosen to lead trips for the National Geographic Society.

FOR FAMILIES. The huge beaches and warm, clear water of the Salmon River Canyon make it one of the best trips for young rafters, who can build sand castles and play safely in the many shallow back eddies out of the main current. Along with untouched river wilderness, the Salmon has roller-coaster rapids that are exciting and safe, whether you stay in the rafts or use the inflatable kayaks. Sites right on the sandbar make camping easy, too—no carrying gear over boulders and steep terrain.

The Snake River/Hells Canyon trip, with its pioneer and Native American sites, is another great choice for families, as is the Middle Fork of the Salmon. Families with younger kids who want to try the Middle Fork should pick a date after mid-June, when the water is calmer. This river runs through the 2.36-million-acre River of No Return Wilderness, the largest wilderness area in the continental United States. If early season suits your group, join a Wallowa/Grande Ronde adventure in Oregon, preferably in June. Beautiful grassy flats slope right down to the banks for exceptional camping; older kids can try an inflatable kayak on this trip.

Hughes has no special family departure dates, but you're likely to find kids on any summer trip. If you have a child under 6 who's comfortable around water and likes camping, give Jerry or Carole a call; they sometimes make exceptions on the age limit. 🏠 *Hughes River Expeditions, Box 217, Cambridge, ID 83610, tel. 208/257–3477. June–Sept.: 3–6 days, $650–$,1305; 10% discount for kids college age and under who are fully supported by their parents.*

Idaho Afloat

👫 6+

Idaho Afloat is one of a number of outfitters specializing in Idaho's great family rivers, the Salmon and the Snake. On every trip, owners Bruce and Jeanne Howard prove that rafting and pampering can coexist in a pristine wilderness area. They enjoy having families along and take more of them out each year. Bruce especially loves to help kids catch their first fish, so be sure to bring the fishing gear. Because the Howards don't have trip minimums, they won't cancel a trip. If just your group shows up, they'll make certain you have a vacation your whole family will remember forever.

FOR FAMILIES. Choose any trip on the Salmon or the Snake, and the campsite you arrive at each night has lawn chairs and a tablecloth on the dinner table; the guides will be ready with hors d'oeuvres and wine. The Howards supply all camping equipment, including sleeping bags and tents. Because your tent is set up for you, the whole family has plenty of time for guided hikes. There are petroglyphs, pit house ruins, and burial sites to explore, as well as historic homesteads built by pioneers who found Idaho too beautiful to leave. When the guides aren't cooking feasts, leading hikes, or negotiating rapids, they share their love of storytelling with everyone. The rivers, of course, provide the lion's share of the entertainment, and all the natural beauty a family could ask for. 🏠 *Idaho Afloat, Box 542, Grangeville, ID 83530, tel. 208/983–2414 or 800/700–*

2414. May–Sept.: 3–5 days, $635–$990;
10% discount for children under 16.

Kayak & Canoe Institute

👫 15+

The Kayak & Canoe Institute is part of the
University of Minnesota at Duluth's Outdoor Program. The institute always schedules one rafting expedition each year, and
rafting is now on the course list as well. If
you have an interest in learning how to run
your own trip, this is the place.

FOR FAMILIES. Raft Trip Leadership Training was designed for people who'd like to
guide professionally, but it's also ideal for
parents and teens who want to become
informed enough to rent rafts and run rivers
safely at their own pace. The three-day
course takes place on the St. Louis River,
about 20 miles from Duluth.

Each year the rafting expedition changes,
but Alaska and Idaho are the primary destinations. In Alaska, the Tana River at the base
of the Tana Glacier has Class II to IV rapids
before it empties into the Class II Chitina.
The group meets in Anchorage for this 116-
mile trip. In Idaho the institute opts for the
Main Salmon and Lochsa rivers. On this
one, you get to know your fellow rafters
long before you're on the river; the van ride
from Duluth to Idaho takes 28 hours.
🏠 *Kayak & Canoe Institute, University of
Minnesota at Duluth, Outdoor Program, 121
Sports and Health Center, 10 University Dr.,
Duluth, MN 55812, tel. 218/726–6533.
May–June: 3–11 days, $239–$775.*

OARS

👫 4+

The acronym stands for Outdoor Adventure River Specialists, but everyone knows
this outfitter as OARS. With more than 25
years of guiding experience and probably
more specially designated family trips on

more rivers than any other outfitter, OARS
is a natural choice for families. I traveled with
OARS on Jackson Lake and the Snake River
in Wyoming. Although the trip has changed
somewhat since Molly and I did it (you
travel in kayaks instead of rafts on the lake
now), the high quality of the guides remains
the same.

Working with a big company such as OARS
has advantages and disadvantages, though.
You don't talk to or meet the owners as you
can with small companies; there's also much
less customizing with OARS. On the other
hand, you can take advantage of the large
staff of travel specialists who will book not
only your rafting experience but also your
flight, lodging, and rental car.

FOR FAMILIES. There are family trips on
the Salmon and Snake in Idaho, the lower
Klamath in California, the San Juan in Colorado, the Rogue River in Oregon, and on
the Wyoming stretch of the Snake River and
Jackson Lake. With so many family departures, you can pick the river and terrain you
want and still be guaranteed playmates for
your kids. Age limits range from 4 on the
lower Klamath and Jackson Lake and the
Wyoming portion of the Snake to 7 on the
others. On the kayaking/rafting combination
on Jackson Lake and the Snake, 4-year-olds
will probably ride in motorized skiffs with
one parent rather than in the sea kayaks. A
nice feature of this trip, though, is that
there's plenty of exploring right around the
base camp on Grassy Island.

OARS guides are well attuned to children's
needs and really help parents out if kids get
restless. One guide per family trip serves as
the Fun Director and keeps the kids entertained. Each child also gets a "fun bag" with
games and toys for whiling away river time.
🏠 *OARS, Box 67, Angels Camp, CA 95222,
tel. 209/736–4677 or 800/346–6277.
Mar.–Sept.: 2–7 days, $145–$1,331.*

Outdoor Adventures

👪 7+

Outdoor Adventures may not have as many family-only trips as some of the larger companies, but they've thought of every detail and are genuinely committed to making family river trips both fun and affordable. The Salmon in Idaho and the Kern in California are their favorite rivers for families.

FOR FAMILIES. A special kids' activities coordinator joins the company's Salmon River family expedition, one of the best-ever trips for families. The 4½-day adventure runs three times each summer—and fills fast—so you need to book early. The river has everything a rafting family could want, from warm, lazy eddies to rolling rapids. Off-water activities have plenty of kid appeal, too: bug collecting, making musical instruments out of natural objects, panning for gold, carving sticks, weaving, hiking, or fishing (bring your own gear). River camping is exceptional, and you spend the final night at the Mackay Bar Ranch. Besides using the showers and hot tub at the ranch, you can sign up for a trail ride for an extra fee. The trip price covers the ranch stay and the flight back to Boise. Ask about Kids Float Free trips: They're a great deal, although kids (under 17) still pay off-river expenses, such as the flight to Boise. Children are welcomed on other Salmon trip dates, but only three have these special activities and a trip coordinator.

Guides trained to work and play with kids lead the lower Kern family trips that start in June. Special family rates apply on the Kern, the closest rafting river to Los Angeles—just three hours away. These rates, good on Monday and Wednesday only, vary with the size of your family: the bigger your family, the larger the discount. The Kern flows through Sequoia National Forest and is a river of surprising beauty and terrific white water.
🏠 *Outdoor Adventures, Box 1149, Point Reyes Station, CA 94956, tel. 415/663–8300 or 800/323–4234. Apr.–Sept.: 2–6 days,* $195–$1,095; ask about Kids Float Free and Kern family discounts.

Ouzel Outfitters

👪 6+

After a conversation with Kent or Beth Wickham, you'll understand why 80% of Ouzel's clients have rafted with the company before or have been referred by someone who went on an Ouzel trip. The Wickhams operate a small, very personalized business and speak to every customer themselves. Families are a big part of their business, but the company's literature doesn't direct kids and families to a particular expedition or river. Instead, the Wickhams take your family's requirements into consideration before they suggest a trip. Best of all, Ouzel runs several great family rivers in Oregon and Idaho, so you have choices as well as plenty of individual attention.

FOR FAMILIES. The Wild and Scenic River Act protects an 84-mile stretch of Oregon's Rogue River. Three-, four-, and five-day trips run through the 34-mile Wild section (roadless wilderness), as well as a few miles of the Recreational section (limited road access). The Siskiyou Range, through which the Rogue runs, has deep forests and clear creeks. Wildlife is abundant: otters, eagles, ospreys, herons, deer, and bears. The cool nights make for excellent sleeping, but days are dependably hot and dry. The Rogue has the thrills rafters seek in rapids such as Blossom Bar and Rainie Falls; sandy beaches to camp and play on and good places to swim add to its appeal. If you want a touch of culture on your adventure trip, the Oregon Shakespearean Festival in Ashland is nearby and well worth a visit.

Other rivers have a variety of attractions for families. The Deschutes, in the high desert of the Oregon's eastern Cascades, combines miles of lazy drifting with treacherous white water that demands your attention.

Desert canyons and excellent fishing are additional highlights on these one- to three-day trips. Families can also join Ouzel for one or two days on the McKenzie, a river whose exhilaratingly cool waters spill out of the western slope of the Cascade Range, less than an hour from the city of Eugene, Oregon. It's practically all Class II and III, but hold on to your raft when you reach Martin's Rapid. If you want more choices, Ouzel schedules trips on the Salmon in Idaho, too.

 Ouzel Outfitters, Box 827, Bend, OR 97709, tel. 503/385–5947 or 800/788–7238. Apr.–Oct.: 1–5 days, $65–$665.

River Odysseys West

 5+

The Salmon River in Idaho has become the river of choice for many outfitters with family trips, including River Odysseys West (ROW, to rafting enthusiasts everywhere). This outfitter, based in Coeur d'Alene, aims to run all its trips "with uncommon professionalism, unsurpassed personal service, and a commitment to protect and preserve the environment." If none of the family departures fit into your schedule, ROW has many other trips—and rivers—on which families raft. The office can tell you which expeditions other families have already signed up for.

FOR FAMILIES. ROW has five-day family adventures on the Salmon for both younger kids and teens. Family Focus trips are geared to parents or grandparents traveling with children aged 5 to 12. Typically, three to five families join each of four specially designated expeditions during the summer. Led by guides with degrees in environmental education, these trips give children a chance to learn about geography, geology, native and pioneer history, and nature through hikes, games, and just floating through the Idaho wilderness. Teen trips are for parents or grandparents and kids 13 to 18; there's usually one in July and one in August.

ROW takes both paddle rafts and inflatable kayaks on all family trips. These are great for kids who can handle independence and who want to challenge themselves physically. On family trips guides stop a bit more frequently, and there's swimming in calm portions of the river (with life jackets on). ROW's menu, always excellent, adds more kids' foods; children have an early dinner at about six, before the adults eat.

 River Odysseys West, Box 579, Coeur d'Alene, ID 83816, tel. 208/765–0841 or 800/451–6034. July–Aug.: 5 days, $795–$924.

Sheri Griffith Expeditions

 5+

Sheri Griffith Expeditions runs only protected rivers in national parks and national landmarks or proposed Wild and Scenic rivers. Sheri prefers these because regulations so severely limit the number of people permitted in the water that there's never a problem with wilderness gridlock. Sheri and company, whose slogan is "with a touch of class," have been in business for 25 years.

FOR FAMILIES. The Family Goes to Camp—Expedition Style is a five-day trip scheduled three times each summer through Desolation and Gray canyons on Utah's Green River. In spite of its name, Desolation is remarkably beautiful. Here, Butch Cassidy and his Wild Bunch hid from the law among the red sandstone formations. You explore the ranch of the McPhersons, who homesteaded the grassy river bottomland and often provided assistance to outlaws, including Butch. Before the cowboys arrived, ancient native tribes carved their stories into the rocks and then disappeared forever. Today the Green runs through the Uinta and Ouray Indian Reservation; the tribes farm and ranch in these canyons. Guides point out the 300 million years of rock exposed on the canyon walls, and you're almost guaranteed to see wildlife. The trip starts at the Canyonlands Airport in Moab, Utah, where participants take a charter flight to a mesa high above the river. The return to Moab is by van from the take-out site. Both shuttles are included in the trip price.

For those with less time, a two-day version of family camp takes place in Utah on a gentle section of the Colorado River, about 45 minutes from Moab. The company owns land in this remote area and will set up a semi-permanent camp each season. The group eats a real western-style dinner on long tables—something not usually available on raft trips—at an old ranch house on the property.

At family camp, assistants lead interpretive field trips and organize games for everyone. Parents and kids have time with each other and with their peers. If you're hoping to find activities that will get your family working and playing together, look no farther. These paddle raft trips require team effort and spirit. If someone really doesn't want to paddle, there's always room in the oar-powered supply boats.

 Sheri Griffith Expeditions, Box 1324, Moab, UT 84532, tel. 801/259–8229 or 800/332–2439. July–Aug.: 2–5 days, $150–$783.

Unicorn Expeditions

👫 6+

Unicorn's wilderness base camps in north central Maine—Lake Parlin Resort, near The Forks, and Big Moose Inn & Campground, close to Baxter State Park—serve as headquarters for its river trips and starting points for adventures on land as well. Maine's rough-and-tumble white-water rivers have a high minimum age, often 12 or 14, making them especially good for families with teens. Unicorn has a couple of trips for younger kids, too.

FOR FAMILIES. Families with river lovers aged 12 and up can tackle Alleyway and Magic Falls on the upper Kennebec; ages 14

and up test their strength and skills against Elephant Rock and Poplar Falls on the Dead. For parents with kids 6 and up, there's a gentler one-day ride on the lower Kennebec. Nonrafting kids aged 3 to 12 can play at Unicorn's base camps in the care of sitters (extra charge) who will take them swimming and canoeing, help make crafts, or arrange treasure hunts. At the end of the day, your family either cooks dinner in your cabin or tent, or, for an extra charge, eats at the restaurants at Lake Parlin or Big Moose.

If you and your kids 10 and up want to go for an overnight, the two-day camping and rafting trip on the Kennebec River uses motorized rafts. A noontime steak barbecue and a Maine lobster dinner are part of the cost.

Families can also book a three- or five-day family adventure package at Lake Parlin Resort, with activities including rafting, canoeing, mountain biking, hiking, sailing, and just hanging out in the hot tub or pool.

On any stay with this outfitter, one of the most popular family pastimes is the evening Moose Hunt in the woods around camp. Unicorn owner Jay Schurman says they find a moose to watch about 90% of the time.

 Unicorn Expeditions, Box T, Brunswick, ME 04011, tel. 207/725–2255 or 800/864–2676. Apr.–Oct.: 1–2 days (rafting), $39–$199; 3–5 days (adventure package), $642–$912 for family of 4.

Wilderness River Outfitters

👫 8+

Joe and Fran Tonsmeire started running rivers while in college during the '60s. They worked together on the Colorado River and eventually founded Wilderness River Outfitters in Salmon, Idaho. Although the company continues to evolve (see Biking), rafting remains its central activity. On the Tonsmeires' innovative trip list these days are some intriguing multi-activity adventures, especially those that combine hiking or hiking with packhorses and rafting.

FOR FAMILIES. The eight-day Salmon River rafting/hiking combination trip takes families with kids aged 12 and up into remote backcountry for four days of trekking the high ridges that divide the Sawtooth and Salmon River mountains from the Bitterroots. The adventure starts at almost 9,000 feet in the heart of the River of No Return Wilderness, but the pace is easy—hikes average 4 to 8 miles a day. There's plenty of time to fish in the alpine lakes (bring your own gear) and relax. You can do it all with nothing more than a day pack because horses carry the camping equipment and other heavy stuff. The last 4-mile hike down a steep trail leads to the river's edge, where the group loads the rafts for a four-day journey on the Salmon. This trip begins in Salmon and ends in Boise; everything, including tents and sleeping bags, is provided. On an eight-day hike and raft in Montana, you trek through the awesome Bob Marshall Wilderness over Holland Pass and down to the South Fork of the Flathead. This adventure starts and ends in Kalispell, Montana. Both trips are available without horse support if you want a complete backpack experience.

You can depend on Wilderness River for excellent rafting-only trips, too. The best for families are five-day adventures on the Salmon in Idaho (minimum age 8) and the Middle Fork of the Flathead in Montana (minimum age 11). The company also runs one of the great rivers of the north, the Tatshenshini, which flows down from the Yukon through British Columbia and Alaska. Rafters on this 11-day journey should be at least 12 years old.

Wilderness River Outfitters, Box 871, Salmon, ID 83467, tel. 208/756–3959 or 800/252–6581. June–Aug.: 5–11 days, $900–$1,980 (rafting only); 8 days, $1,350–$1,900 (raft/hike trips). Families choose 1 discount option: 30% discount for children under 13, or 5% discount for families of 5 or more.

Resources

Organizations

America Outdoors (Box 1348, Knoxville, TN 37901, tel. 615/524–4814) is the national association for river guides. Ask for the organization's magazine listing outfitters and guides; America Outdoors cannot, however, recommend one outfitter over another. The **National Association of Canoe Liveries and Outfitters** (Box 248, Butler, KY 41006, tel. 606/472–2202) will send consumers information on guides and outfitters. It also has a list of books and periodicals of interest to families about to embark on a river adventure.

Periodicals

Canoes and Kayak Magazine (Box 3146, Kirkland, WA 98033, tel. 800/692–2663) is devoted primarily to canoeing and kayaking but has many articles on equipment, technique, and environmental issues that will also be of interest to rafters. The resource section list many rafting opportunities from schools and adventure outfitters.

Products

The following companies make good riverwear or river accessories for children and adults: **Nike, Patagonia, REI outdoor stores,** and **Crazy Creek Chairs.** Nike has rive sandals and aqua socks, and Patagonia is a good source for warm, quick-drying fleece and quick-drying pants. REI has retail outlets and a catalog with reasonably priced fleeced and other warm, fast-drying apparel; it also sells life vests for children and adults. For more information about these companies, see Resources in Hiking and Backpacking.

RANCHES

A spirit of rugged adventure and the romance of the American West, past and present, are alive and well in guest ranches across the country. At a ranch your family can indulge its Wild West fantasies—and you can all learn a lot about riding, ranching, '90s-style cowhands, and caring for livestock as well. Fun is almost guaranteed—for everyone.

Ranch stays make perfect family vacations because they can accommodate many ages, abilities, and interests. I know this from my own family's experience. My lifelong love of riding made me a natural for a ranch guest, but my husband, Bill, was uneasy around horses. On our first visit to Paradise Guest Ranch in Wyoming, Kira was 11, Molly was 4, and Hutch was one. Of the kids, only Kira had ever even been on a horse, and Molly and Hutch were too young for the ranch's regular riding program. Nonetheless, Paradise was a resounding success for all of us. Bill lost his fear of riding and learned to lope, as did Kira. Molly thrived in the children's program, and Hutch made both human and animal friends. We took advantage of the riding program and the naturalist-lead hikes; Bill carried Hutch in a backpack on these while I indulged in advanced rides in the afternoon. Sometimes we just retreated from the action and took time to enjoy each other.

There are ranches for every budget and taste, from very simple to spectacular. Riding is definitely the central ingredient of a ranch vacation, but some ranches have so many additional activities that their guest lists frequently include nonriders. Many ranches have an organized children's activity program, and a few provide infant care. Others simply include children in all ranch activities. You can find a place with rustic accommodations and hearty, basic fare, or one that has elegant, well-appointed cabins and serves meals accompanied by fine wines. Guest capacity ranges from six people to well over a hundred, and seasons vary from one- to four-season operations. There are real working ranches that take guests, but most are primarily guest operations with ranch work that must be done.

While each ranch creates its own unique atmosphere, all help bring families closer together. Sing-alongs and bonfires, hayrides, and other events give you a chance to see each other in new and wonderful ways. At the end of a family ranch stay, you may well take home, as we did, not only the requisite western bandannas and hatbands but also a renewed appreciation for each other and what you've accomplished individually and together. Who could ask for more than that from any vacation?

It's important to note, though, that while every ranch listed in this chapter is terrific, not every ranch is right for every family. And unlike most of the other adventures in this book, a ranch vacation is not a single-activity vacation, so there

are more things to consider when making a choice. For families, the most important criteria in choosing a ranch are its size; whether or not there is a children's
program and, if so, for what ages; the riding program; and the activities besides
riding, both for families and for adults. Because these factors are important to
finding a good match, each ranch listing has a general introduction and sections
on the children's program, riding program, and activities besides riding.

Questions to Ask

Are there one-week stays only, or are shorter stays available? Almost all
ranches require a minimum one-week stay during the summer high season (or winter high season for those ranches in the Southwest), but some allow briefer vacations in off-seasons. A few ranches have shorter, or even no, minimum stays. Keep in
mind, though, that in off-seasons, there may be shorter stays but there may not be
counselors or a children's program.

Are families welcome all the time? Many ranches have adult-only periods—
sometimes just a week, sometimes a month or more—during times children are in
school, such as September or October. Spring is always an off-season for ranches
(except those in the Southwest), so although families may be welcome, there may
be no children's activity program and probably only a few children present. Most
formal children's programs run in the summer months only, or summers and holidays for year-round ranches, when college students are available to be counselors.

What is the riding program? These programs vary widely. Some ranches have
walk-only rides; others offer slow, medium, and fast rides each day. Some have only
hour-long outings; other ranches have short rides, all-day rides, and even overnight
rides. Children may or may not be permitted on adult rides, although parents can
sometimes join the kids' rides. Some ranches provide more formal instruction than
others; ask about this if it's important to your family. Rides may have as few as 4 participants and as many as 25. Typically, there are morning and afternoon rides each
day, along with special rides—brunch, lunch, all-day, or evening cookouts—throughout the week. For safety reasons, however, guests cannot go out on trails alone but
are led by the ranches' wranglers.

**Do we each get the same horse for the whole week? What if we don't like
the horse?** Most ranches with minimum weeklong stays assign each guest a horse.
That way, rider and horse get used to each other and become comfortable as a
team, which can make a difference even to a seasoned rider. On the other hand,
sometimes this doesn't work out. A ranch should be flexible enough, and have
enough horses, to make a change for your family.

**Are guests required to have riding boots, and if so, are loaner boots avail-
able?** Most ranches prefer but do not require riding boots; they do require sturdy
shoes or other boots with heels. Riding boots can be an expensive proposition if
you need to get them for the whole family. Some ranches have a trunk of boots

that are lent to guests, although there may be no way to guarantee your size or your child's size. If you decide to buy boots, break them in before your vacation.

At what age are children permitted to ride in the regular riding program and to go out on the trail? Six or 7 is often the age given, and it is usually dictated by insurance. However, some ranches won't allow kids out on the trail until they're 8, 9, or even 10. A few permit parents to put younger children in the saddle with them, which can be risky even for accomplished riders. If your children are too young for the trail, you'll probably want a ranch that has options such as a supervised children's program. Parents can also take turns staying at the ranch with younger children and taking part in other ranch activities.

Is there an organized children's program? If you have young children, especially children too young to ride with you, this will be important. While you are out riding, your kids can participate in age-appropriate activities, such as nature hikes, wildlife tracking, swimming, fishing, or learning Native American lore. Some ranches have corral riding sessions for children not able to go on the trail; at others, the staff may lead small children on ponies. You can usually use the programs in a variety of ways: just in the mornings or just in the afternoons, or all day. You can sign the kids in one day and not another. The bottom line is this: A good children's program is a place that kids *want* to be, a place where they can meet children from other parts of the country and the world and hang out with cool counselors. More good news is that children's programs, when available, are almost always part of the ranch package; care for infants and toddlers, however, sometimes costs extra.

If there isn't a supervised children's program or if there is but my child is too young for it, is baby-sitting available on an individual basis? Families with a baby or toddler will want to go to a ranch that provides something for this age group for at least part of the day, so that parents and older children can spend time together riding or taking advantage of other activities. Another option is to choose a ranch that allows you to bring along your own baby-sitter for free or for a nominal charge. Parents can also split up during the day, one spending time with the youngest child, the other having one-on-one time with an older child.

Where do we stay on the ranch? Most ranches have cabins of various sizes; some ranches also have rooms in a main lodge, although not many of these accommodate families. Cabins often have kitchens, which are handy for families with babies and with young children who get hungry between the ranch's set mealtimes. Western decor is prevalent, as are porches, fireplaces, and grand views. You probably won't spend a lot of time in your cabin, but it's nice to know that most are roomy, cheerful places.

What kind of food is served, and where do we eat? Hearty, delicious, and plentiful best describe ranch food; three meals a day are usually part of the package. Breakfast and lunch are often buffet affairs—except when guests eat lunch out on the trail, which is common throughout the week. Ranchers like to go all out for dinner; some even provide candles, wine, and gourmet fare. Many ranches serve meals family style; guests sit at long tables, making it easy for families to get to know different people during the week. In general ranches are not places to cut calories; barbecued meats and homemade pies and cobblers are often a big part of a week's menu, which also includes salads and fruit. If you do have a restrictive diet of any kind, however, the vast majority of ranch chefs will accommodate you.

Do parents and children eat meals together? At some ranches with supervised children's programs, kids eat lunch with counselors, either at a different time or apart from parents. At others, families usually eat together after the morning ride. If there is an all-day or lunch ride scheduled for adults or kids, however, families won't see each other again until late afternoon. Many family ranches also schedule an adults-only dinner at least once a week, during which counselors take their groups for a special kids' cookout or other activity. At a few ranches, children eat most or even all meals with counselors, usually at an earlier time, allowing parents to relax and meet other guests. Ask questions and know your family preferences before you choose a ranch.

If an adult doesn't ride, is there a reduced rate? What other activities are available? Some ranches do have a nonrider's rate; if an adult in your group doesn't want to ride at all, look for a ranch with this kind of discount. Keep in mind that ranches these days have a variety of activities besides riding. Almost all have fishing. Depending on the ranch, you can also take guided nature hikes, swim, play tennis, mountain bike, picnic, go boating or rafting, or even play golf. Some ranches have hot tubs and saunas; massages are available at a few. A number of ranches are near towns with places of historical interest, museums, or fun shopping.

Are there laundry facilities in the cabins or at a communal spot on the ranch? Dress at a ranch is almost always informal; jeans are standard throughout the day and often in the evenings, so you won't need to pack many different kinds of clothes. However, everyone's clothing will get plenty dirty. Many ranches have machines either in cabins or in a central location.

What's included in the cost? Ranch vacations are primarily all-inclusive. Lodging, meals, riding, the children's program, and other activities are included in the cost, unless otherwise noted. Baby-sitting for infants and toddlers is usually extra. Off-property activities, such as rafting, guided fishing trips, and visits to museums and local rodeos, are often—but not always—an extra charge. Alcohol is generally extra, if it's available. Most ranches will provide airport transportation for an extra charge. Prices given here are for high season, except as noted; sometimes rates are reduced for large families. Considering all that a family gets, ranch vacations can be very reasonably priced. However, if you want to save, plan a trip early or late in the season when rates are almost always lower. Not all facilities and activities are available in the off-season, though.

Instruction

Just about every ranch has instruction in horsemanship, although some ranches are more formal about it than others. Wranglers check all guests' abilities the first day, and progressive instruction helps riders move from walk-only rides to those that include trotting or even loping or cantering. Even if your family arrives with different skill levels, it's likely you will be able to ride together at some point. (Advanced riders, of course, can always choose to ride with less advanced riders at any time during the week.) While riding is a skill that can take years to develop to its highest level, it's also a sport in which you can improve quickly with practice and good instruction.

In addition to horsemanship, some ranches teach you about caring for horses, roping, and other skills. There are fishing classes for children and adults at many ranches, as well as instruction in skeet or trap shooting. A few ranches have courses in other types of activities, including photography, environmental issues, rock climbing, and wildflower or bird identification. In winter, cross-country ski instruction may be available. Some of these classes may be part of the regular program; others are an extra charge.

Finding the Fun

Northeast: Pinegrove Resort Ranch, The Timberlock. **Southwest:** Mayan Dude Ranch, White Stallion Ranch, Y.O. Ranch. **Rockies:** Anvil Butte Ranch, Aspen Canyon Ranch, Breteche Creek, Cherokee Park Ranch, Colorado Trails Ranch, Drowsy Water Ranch, Elk Mountain Ranch, Hidden Creek Ranch, Lake Mancos Ranch, Lone Mountain Ranch, North Fork Guest Ranch, Paradise Guest Ranch, Rainbow Trout Ranch, Red Rock Ranch, Seven D Ranch, Sky Corral, Skyline Guest Ranch. **West Coast:** Coffee Creek Ranch, Rankin Ranch, Rock Springs.

Favorite Ranches

Northeast

Pinegrove Resort Ranch

A five-minute talk with Dave Ohalloran, general manager and a member of the Tarantino family that owns and operates Pinegrove, will convince you that this is a place to bring your family. Although Pine-

grove is in New York's ancient Catskill Mountains, everything has been done to provide not only a family atmosphere but a genuinely western one as well. There are roping and blacksmithing demonstrations, cattle drives, and nightly "cattle calls," during which guests call the cattle in from the pasture to feed them. Lodging is in modern rooms with TVs and telephones, but you'll probably be too busy to make use of them. Although Pinegrove is a big place that can accommodate more than 300 guests, it's also small enough that families feel safe giving children freedom to explore on their own. From 1992 to 1994, the ranch completed extensive renovations of its buildings and spruced up the guest rooms.

CHILDREN'S PROGRAM. The nursery, for ages 6 weeks to 3 years, has one staff person for every child. Activities include walks, time at the playground, visits to the baby animal farm, and indoor fun such as arts and crafts. In day camp, for ages 3 to 10, campers do not ride with counselors; they go swimming, play miniature golf, spend time at the playground, and have tennis lessons, nature hikes, pony rides, and hayrides. There's also an extensive crafts program, and parents are invited to join their kids for this. In the teen program, run by older teens on the staff, the group chooses seven or eight activities each day. At Pinegrove, a staff "night patrol" looks in on kids in their rooms every 15 to 20 minutes while parents attend evening entertainment. Private baby-sitting at night is also available for an extra charge.

RIDING PROGRAM. Daily rides meet the needs of beginner to advanced riders; groups are large, typically 15 to 20 people. Trail riding is generally for those aged 7 and up, although younger children will be permitted if they can control a horse. Children can ride with parents but don't have to; they can join any ride that suits their skill level and interest. Instructional rides at a special facility out on the trail help guests progress from one ability level to the next. From Memorial Day to Columbus Day, Pinegrove also runs half-day cattle drives (extra charge) for advanced riders. Pinegrove also has lots of winter riding.

BEYOND RIDING. On the property, guests choose among fishing, boating, hiking, tennis, swimming indoors and out, miniature golf, bocci ball, archery, and riflery. At a nearby 18-hole golf course, ranch visitors can play one round of 18 holes at no charge. In winter there's downhill skiing geared for beginners and intermediates, as well as ice skating at the ranch, with equipment and lessons for guests.

 Pinegrove Resort Ranch, Box 209, Kerhonkson, NY 12446, tel. 914/626–7345 or 800/346–4626. Year-round: 7 days, $275–$550; children under 4 free. Ask about the 6-day summer special for a family of 3.

The Timberlock

👫 ALL

Part family camp, part ranch, part resort, Timberlock is a rustic, informal retreat in the Adirondack Mountains of northern New York. Only the main kitchen has electricity; guests' cabins are lit with gas lamps. Propane provides hot water, and heat comes from wood stoves. You pay separately for riding here, and there's no structured program, no activities anyone has to engage in—nothing, in fact, that anyone *has* to do. Owner Dick Catlin just wants to give families an opportunity to spend time together in a way they can't back home. Timberlock succeeds admirably, which is why guests return year after year. Because the ranch accommodates only about 65, it's a good idea to book as early as possible.

CHILDREN'S PROGRAM. Timberlock has a supervised area for children under 6 or 7, so that parents can pursue some activities their young children can't. This service is an extra charge, and parents should set up the times they want to use it when they book their stay. For the most part, though, families eat, play, and relax together.

RIDING PROGRAM. Adults and kids aged 6 and up can ride out on the trail, English or western style. There are three trail rides each morning, beginner to advanced, and guests can also take lessons in the riding ring. Timberlock has hard hats for children.

BEYOND RIDING. Guests can take advantage of 15-mile-long Indian Lake, along which Timberlock sits, for canoeing, sailing, fishing, and swimming. Tennis and archery are other options, or you can choose nature walks and birding. The Catlins' son, Bruce, and daughter-in-law, Holly, are both naturalists, and naturalist-led hikes and canoe trips are an important part of any weekly stay. Don't miss the wood shop, in which you can make your own canoe paddle, birdhouse, or something else you fancy.

🏠 *The Timberlock, Indian Lake, Sabael, NY, 12864, tel. 518/648–5494 (in season); R.R. 1, Box 630, Woodstock, VT 05091, tel. 802/457–1621 (rest of year). Late June–Oct.: 7 days, $294–$623; children under 2 free. Riding costs $20–$40 per ride, depending on length and destination; multiday trail ride packages are available.*

Southwest

Mayan Dude Ranch

(👫 **ALL**)

Bandera, 47 miles northwest of San Antonio, in the heart of Texas Hill Country, is home to this bighearted, hospitable ranch. Judy and Don Hicks, and all 12 of their children, are here to make guests—up to 167 of them—feel welcome. Accommodations are in stone cottages furnished with many handmade objects. Some have fireplaces; all are air-conditioned. There are also two-story lodges with motel-like rooms. Mayan is big, but it's down-home friendly and an ideal choice for families who really want to relax, perhaps by floating in a tube on the meandering Medina River as it flows through the ranch.

CHILDREN'S PROGRAM. Kids aged 3 to 6 and 7 to 12 are placed in separate groups; the program runs primarily in summer, although there are children's activities during holiday periods, too. The groups meet in the morning from 10 to noon and again from 1 to 3. The younger kids don't ride on the trail but keep busy with arts and crafts, treasure hunts, games, and outings. The older group joins parents on trail rides. They also swim, try roping lessons and archery, play baseball, and make leather crafts. The program is fairly flexible, and activities can change to suit the interests of the group. Kids eat dinner with their group and counselors twice a week.

RIDING PROGRAM. In the morning and afternoon each day, there are hour-long walking rides into one of the most beautiful areas of Texas. Typically, 25 guests go out on each ride. Kids aged 7 and up can join parents on the trail.

BEYOND RIDING. Guests can swim, tube, and fish (some poles available) in the cool Medina River or use the pool and two tennis courts. For an extra charge, you have access to a nearby fitness center and an 18-hole golf course. Those who wish to explore Hill Country can visit the Frontier Times Museum in Bandera, which has artifacts from pioneer days, and the late President Johnson's boyhood home, about 60 miles away in Johnson City. Sea World of Texas and Fiesta Texas, a family-oriented theme park, are in San Antonio.

🏠 *Mayan Dude Ranch, Box 577, Bandera, TX 78003, tel. 210/796–3312. Year-round: 1 day, $40–$98 (2-day minimum stay); children under 2 free.*

White Stallion Ranch

(👫 **ALL**)

The True family, which owns and runs White Stallion, believes guests get the best of two worlds on their 3,000-acre ranch. Although mountains and rugged, picturesque high desert surround the property, it is only 10 minutes around the mountain from Tucson. Longhorns graze the ranch, where up to 75 guests stay in Spanish-style adobe bungalows that have views of the cactus garden and the Tucson Mountains. Aside from the natural beauty of the area, White Stallion has much to offer families, not the least of which is plenty of time together.

CHILDREN'S PROGRAM. There's no formal program; parents and children of all ages are welcome to participate in activities on the ranch. With enough notice, however, baby-sitting can usually be arranged (extra charge) during the day or at night.

RIDING PROGRAM. One unique aspect of the program is that many rides take guests into nearby Saguaro National Monument to see the 50-foot cacti and abundant wildlife. Children under 5 ride in the saddle with parents or grandparents; those 5 and up ride the trail with their parents on their own horse. At about age 8, children can be tested to see if they meet the requirements for loping and cantering rides. There are at least two fast and two slow rides a day; during the week, all-day and breakfast rides are offered, as well as a haywagon ride to a lunch cookout. Both children and adults can help groom and saddle their horses if they want to.

BEYOND RIDING. Guests swim in the pool, take nature hikes, use the two tennis courts, play lawn games, or relax in a hot tub. Golf is available for an extra charge. The evening programs are very creative: During the busiest season, when many families are in attendance, a wildlife rehabilitator stops by with rescued animals, and a local astronomer brings telescopes to the ranch once a week so guests can take a close look at the stars shining over the desert. Tucson is well worth exploring for an afternoon or even a full day. The Arizona-Sonora Desert Museum, a microcosm of a desert environment, has exhibits and programs that will appeal to families with children of all ages.

🏨 *White Stallion Ranch, 9251 W. Twin Peaks Rd., Tucson, AZ 85743, tel. 602/297–0252 or 800/782–5546. Oct.–Apr.: 7 days, $539–$1,071; children under 3 free. Ask about daily rates.*

Y.O. Ranch

👫 ALL

One of the biggest working ranches in Texas, the Y.O. is also the largest exotic wildlife ranch in North America. Most guests come to view the more than 12,000 animals that live here, including giraffes, wildebeests, oryx, antelope, and zebra. The ranch is also famous for its herd of well over 1,000 Texas longhorns. The Y.O. can accommodate 30 to 35 guests in century-old renovated log cabins or in rooms in a larger house on the property; the chef is a master of southwestern fare.

CHILDREN'S PROGRAM. The ranch welcomes families with children of all ages, but it has no children's program and no baby-sitting services. However, during the summer there are one- to three-week sessions of Ranch Adventure Camp, for ages 9 to 14, so a family could book a Y.O. vacation and camp experience at the same time. The camp emphasizes environmental learning, with minicourses in ornithology, herpetology, ecology, firearm safety, rapelling, canoeing, swimming, and riding.

RIDING PROGRAM. There's a separate fee for the limited horseback riding, and you must reserve times before your arrival. Rides go out for a minimum of an hour. Good riders can participate in longhorn cattle drives each spring (extra charge).

BEYOND RIDING. Safari-style vehicles take guests out to observe the animals each day, and there are wildlife photographic safaris as well. These tours cost extra but are well worth the money. Although the safaris are the only scheduled programs, the Y.O. also has a swimming pool and 40,000 acres of land to hike and explore. Families have plenty of time to relax and to savor the delicious meals, too.

🏨 *Y.O. Ranch, Mountain Home, TX 78058, tel. 210/640–3222. Year-round: 1 day, $50–$85; no minimum stay required. Adventure Camp, June–Aug.: 7–21 days, $545–$1295. Riding is $16 per hour.*

Rockies

Anvil Butte Ranch

👫 ALL

Anvil Butte is unusual because owners Claudia and Leif Bakken run both a guest ranch and adventure tours. Your family can experience all that this third-generation, 3,300-acre ranch in eastern Montana offers, or you can use the ranch as a base for a Native American, dinosaur, or western history adventure (see Native American Experiences). There are only five guests at a time, so a family can pretty much create an individualized schedule, with activities on and off the ranch. Guests stay in the ranch house or about 2½ miles away in tepees; if you pick the tepees, you'll shower and eat in the house. Anvil Butte is a western ranch experience that's as laid-back or active as you want it to be.

CHILDREN'S PROGRAM. The ranch offers no formal activities, but the Bakkens welcome kids of all ages. They have grandchildren of their own and know just how to help kids enjoy the wide-open spaces of Anvil Butte. If your children are too young to ride, Claudia will entertain them back at the ranch.

RIDING PROGRAM. With only five guests at the ranch, the program is what you make it. Guests ride every day if they want to; small children can be led on horses near the ranch house. Experienced riders may be able to put a younger child on the horse with them while they ride slowly on ranch property. Kids about 6 and older can go out on the trail and ride around the ranch to help with chores. Anvil Butte is a working ranch, with cattle to move, fences to mend, and animals to water, feed, or maybe even brand.

BEYOND RIDING. After talking with your family, Claudia will put together a flexible itinerary. Many of the optional day tours focus on the history and cultural life of Montana. About 30 miles from the ranch is Medora, a town Teddy Roosevelt helped build. You can see his log cabin and museums dedicated to his contributions to the area, or take in the show at the music hall, complete with a dog act, juggling, and old-fashioned cowboy entertainment typical of the 1880s. Closer to the ranch is Wibaux, with its own museums and historical sites as well as a town pool and park. You can also visit neighboring ranches to see different types of cattle and learn how beefalo and buffalo are raised. Another place to explore is Ft. Abraham Lincoln, Custer's last post.

At Anvil Butte, you can hike, search for arrowheads, and explore a fossil bed right on ranch property. In the evenings there are campfires, cowboy poetry and sing-alongs, and western barbecues with the Bakkens' neighbors—or your family might just sit outside your tepee listening to the eerie howl of coyotes.

🏠 *Anvil Butte Ranch, HC 71, Box 7335, Wibaux, MT 59353, tel. 406/795–2341. June–Sept.: 7 days, $2,181–$3,318 per family, depending on week and family size (3–5 people in all).*

Aspen Canyon Ranch

 ALL

Just 90 miles west of Denver in the Williams Fork River valley, Aspen Canyon Ranch is easy to reach even though it's tucked away at 8,400 feet among the aspen and lodgepole pines. The ranch borders Arapaho National Forest and is a short drive from Rocky Mountain National Park. Thirty to 35 guests stay in cozy log cabins with fireplaces, private baths, refrigerators, and coffeemakers. Aspen Canyon is a relatively small ranch with a wide range of activities as part of its regular program. The staff is enthusiastic about providing a western experience during which guests will both relax and learn.

CHILDREN'S PROGRAM. The ranch has day care for children from infants to age 5; the activity program divides kids 5–18 into two groups by age. Five-year-olds ride on lead lines in the corral; kids 6 and up can go out on the trail with their group. There's also hiking, fishing, games, and leatherwork. Children eat with their own families except for the kids' weekly cookout. Ages 7 and up have an overnight adventure in which they sleep out not too far from the ranch.

RIDING PROGRAM. The rides, on ranch property and through Arapaho National Forest, take small groups of similar ability. Outings range from easy trips in the morning and afternoon to a challenging all-day ride. Children aged 6 and up can ride with their kids' group or on adult rides with their parents. You can choose personal instruction, and the wranglers will teach you not only how to ride but how to saddle up or rope like an old pro. For an extra charge, the whole family can opt for an overnight pack trip; very young children will ride with counselors so everyone can go.

BEYOND RIDING. Each family gets a gold pan at the beginning of the week so that everyone can try panning in the river that runs through the ranch. Lots of gold has been mined in the area through the years—maybe your family will get lucky. Fishing, guided or unguided hikes, and wildlife viewing are also popular at Aspen Canyon. You can always take on a job around the ranch, including haying and rounding up cattle. For an extra charge, families can sign up for a raft trip on the upper Colorado River; the ranch will also make arrangements for backpacking, mountain biking, overnight guided fishing trips with instruction (adults only), or local hot-air ballooning.

Aspen Canyon Ranch, 13206 County Rd. 3, Star Rte., Parshall, CO 80468, tel. 303/725–3518. May–Oct., mid-Dec.–Mar.: 7 days, $200–$995.

Breteche Creek

ALL

Part guest ranch, part wilderness learning center, Breteche Creek is a nonprofit educational institution in northwestern Wyoming that combines riding and other typical ranch vacation experiences with workshops on geology, ornithology, botany, ecology, nature writing, photography, astronomy, and Native American mythology. Each weeklong session includes just 8 to 20 participants, who stay in "tent cabins" scattered around the property. These have wood floors and walls with canvas tops; bathrooms and showers are in the main building. The founders of Breteche Creek believe that immersion in the natural environment helps us learn about our world.

CHILDREN'S PROGRAM. There's no formal program; children and adults learn together as they participate in workshops and seminars and investigate the wilderness surroundings. All ages are welcome, and workshop leaders will be glad to gear information to the children in attendance. On the other hand, parents should decide if children are too young to be engaged by these activities. Parents may want to take turns attending workshops and exploring the incredible natural setting with very young children—a path to learning in itself.

RIDING PROGRAM. There are horsemanship lessons and guided rides for various abilities. For an additional charge, guests can take private lessons with Breteche Creek's co-director, noted horse breeder and trainer Bob Curtis. Because the center is surrounded by a 7,000-acre cattle and horse-breeding ranch, there is also an opportunity to participate in wrangling and herding cattle. Guests of all ages can join in any riding activity, if they have the necessary skills.

BEYOND RIDING. Each day guests can choose among workshops, some of which might take place on horseback, or they can decide to kick back and explore on their own. There's also fishing, hiking, and excellent wildlife viewing—at last count more than 200 elk and 300–400 deer were living on ranch property. All seven-day sessions include a naturalist-guided tour of Yellowstone National Park. For an additional cost, you can receive instruction in fly-fishing, rock climbing, and windsurfing. Visits to local museums and the nightly rodeo in Cody can be arranged for an extra charge, too.

Breteche Creek, Box 596, Cody, WY

82414, tel. 307/587–3844 or 307/587–5067. Mid-June–Sept.: 7 days, $675–$975; daily rates are available (3-day minimum stay).

Cherokee Park Ranch

 ALL

One of the oldest guest ranches in Colorado, Cherokee Park was a stagecoach stop between Fort Collins and Laramie before it became a dude ranch back in 1886. Its authentic Old West character shows in furnishings and historical memorabilia from the early days, but among the many modern amenities are a heated pool and spa. Up to 35 guests stay in the main lodge or in cabins that have from two to four bedrooms. Owners B and Eli Elfland are renowned for their warm hospitality; their attitude carries over to the staff, too. Attentive care and enthusiasm are especially evident in the children's program.

CHILDREN'S PROGRAM. Kids aged 3 to 5 and 6 to 12 are in separate groups. The younger ones take pony rides around the ranch; the older kids have their own horses and a daily ride out on the trail. There's also hiking, fishing, nature studies, crafts, riflery, and an overnight in the ranch's tepee. Those too young for the overnight (usually the 3- and 4-year-olds) will be cared for in your cabin so you can join an adult overnight. The ranch schedules special hikes for teens, too, when enough of this age group are visiting. Kids eat with their parents unless adults are on the trail; an exception is a weekly adults-only candlelight dinner, during which the kids have a pizza party. The ranch can arrange baby-sitting for children younger than 3, or you can bring your own sitter for $200, which covers meals.

RIDING PROGRAM. Personal instruction is available every day in the riding ring, and trail rides for different levels range from an hour long to all day. The terrain includes open prairie as well as mountain trails. You can join one of the popular lunch rides, and

no one should miss the opportunity to join an overnight pack trip (extra charge).

BEYOND RIDING. Besides swimming in the pool, from mid-May through mid-August guests can take to the water for a day of rafting (extra charge). Ages 8 and up can paddle; younger children sit in the middle of the raft. There are free fly-casting classes for novice anglers of all ages—the ranch provides equipment—and half-day and full-day guided trips for experienced anglers with their own equipment (extra charge; accessories available at the ranch). Guided hikes are free, and there's trap shooting and black powder shooting with old flintlock rifles, too.

You can take a complimentary sightseeing trip to nearby Rocky Mountain National Park or, for an extra charge, visit Laramie's Wyoming Territorial Park, where the kids get to reenact a prison break. Don't miss the evening when a "mountain man" visits the ranch to talk about trapping and western life in the mid-1800s.

 Cherokee Park Ranch, Box 97, Livermore, CO 80536, tel. 303/493–6522 or 800/628–0949. May–Oct.: 7 days, $200–$1,100.

Colorado Trails Ranch

5+

The majestic San Juan Mountains in southwestern Colorado are a dramatic backdrop for Colorado Trails, which has one of the best riding programs of any ranch in the country. Owner Dick Elder's goal is to "see that every guest, child or adult, has the best vacation they ever had." Dick and his wife, Ginny, have been working toward that goal for 35 years, and they've given particular thought to activities for children. Up to 75 guests choose from three styles of cabins; some of the children's rooms have two bunk beds to accommodate large families. Also on the property are an opera house that is used for evening shows and entertainment, an old-fashioned soda fountain, and an antiques-filled turn-of-the-century parlor.

The Elders don't feel alcohol and children mix, so ranch policy is BYOB for use in your own cabin only.

CHILDREN'S PROGRAM. The extensive program usually has three age groups, ages 5–9, 9–13, and 13–18; there are no facilities at the ranch for younger children. The flexible program deemphasizes competition but gives kids a chance to participate in all ranch activities, including archery, riflery, swimming, and tennis. The kids 9–13 and the teens each have a campout, too. Those aged 5 and up take trail rides daily; the counselors who accompany the groups are adept at teaching kids as they ride.

RIDING PROGRAM. Colorado Trails offers both English and western riding and superb instruction; even advanced riders can learn something new here. A special strength of the program is the instructors' ability to make those who have never even been near a horse feel comfortable and in control. A variety of rides—walk, trot, cantering, and instructional—go out each day, so groups tend to be small. Many of the forest trails are groomed. Although children can't go on the adult rides, parents can join kids' rides. The owners suggest you ask your children first; most of them love being out on their own with cool wranglers and kids their own age.

BEYOND RIDING. On the ranch are two tennis courts, a heated pool, and a spa. Guests who want to learn to shoot can take instruction in archery, riflery, and trap shooting; there's an extra charge for the ammo and clay pigeons. You can also fish in several lakes and streams nearby. Hiking, nature walks, and photography are popular as well. For those who want a change of scene, Vallecito Lake is 12 miles away; the ranch provides a boat, driver, floating dock, and equipment for water skiers. For an extra charge, the ranch will arrange specially priced tickets to the professional rodeo in Durango, a town that has great shopping and a theater offering turn-of-the-century melodramas. You can also pay a fee for guided trips to

Mesa Verde National Park with its thousand-year-old Anasazi cliff dwellings.

Colorado Trails Ranch, 12161 County Rd. 240, Durango, CO 81301-6306, tel. 303/247–5055 or 800/323–3833. Mid-June–Aug.; 7 days, $2,285–$4,290 for a family of 3 and 4 respectively, depending on size of cabin; add $850 for each additional child.

Drowsy Water Ranch

"We treat your children as we do our own—with understanding, patience, love, and respect," owners Ken and Randy Sue Fosha say, and they mean it. This ranch just south of Rocky Mountain National Park in Colorado happily caters to families with children from age 1 to teens. It has one of the few programs for kids under 5 that has activities rather than baby-sitting. Most families will stay in the rustic but bright and cheerful log cabins that sleep one to nine people; there are lodge rooms, too. Cabins overlook Drowsy Water Creek or the ranch ponds. There's a good old-fashioned feel here and plenty of warm, western hospitality for about 60 guests.

CHILDREN'S PROGRAM. One- to 5-year-olds are kept busy while adults participate in scheduled ranch activities for part or all of the day. They have rides on lead lines, crafts, nature hikes, and games—lots of outdoor fun. Kids aged 6 to 13, called Range Riders, get their own horse for the week and ride together on the ranch and out on the trail. Counselors also lead games and crafts and take the group for picnics and hikes. These kids can try archery or the obstacle course, too.

RIDING PROGRAM. Slow, moderate, and fast rides go out daily, and guests can get in extra riding on all-day and cookout rides during the week. Instruction is always available. Many of the trails above the ranch have views of the Continental Divide and the Gore Range. Although the Range Riders can't ride with adults on the trail, parents can choose to ride with the kids. For an extra charge, parents and children 6 and up can take an overnight pack trip.

BEYOND RIDING. There's fishing on the property; the ranch provides equipment for beginners. Kids of all ages also love the ranch's playground. Your stay includes a rugged Jeep trip up into the mountains. You can arrange rafting, golf, and tennis nearby for an extra charge, or pay to attend the weekly rodeo in Granby. For romantics, there's an adults-only hayride at the end of the week while children have their own hayride and dinner.
 Drowsy Water Ranch, Box 147, Granby, CO 80446, tel. 970/725–3456 or 800/845–2292. June–mid-Sept.: 7 days, $435–$945.

Elk Mountain Ranch

👫 4+

At 9,535 feet, Elk Mountain is the highest guest ranch in Colorado, with a spectacular setting in the San Isabel National Forest. There are deer, elk, and wildflowers in abundance, and thousands of acres of unspoiled wilderness. Log cottages or a suite in the main lodge are ideal for families; the guest capacity is limited to 30. You'll always find fresh flowers and fruit in your room. Although the ranch has a full children's program, families spend a lot of time together here.

CHILDREN'S PROGRAM. Kids aged 4 to 7 have an extensive program. Aside from riding twice a day in the ring, they go on scavenger hunts, create crafts, and fish, among other pastimes. Children 8 and up are welcomed in all the ranch's activities, including riding. It's especially nice that even those younger than 8 can take part in brunch rides; vehicles bring them up to meet riders so that the whole family can enjoy the meal and the views. Guests can arrange evening baby-sitting for younger children when they book their stay (extra charge).

RIDING PROGRAM. Riding is exceptional at Elk Mountain. Each day there are rides on and off the trails, as well as excellent instruction in riding, tack, and the care and feeding of horses. You ride in very small groups through rock canyons, across high plateaus, and on trails far above the timberline. Children 8 and up can go out with parents on the adult rides. Don't miss the weekly brunch ride or the overnight camping trip; the overnight is included in July and August rates (additional charge in June and September).

BEYOND RIDING. Elk Mountain has free guided hikes to nearby Native American sites, old mines and ghost towns, and high meadows filled with wildflowers. There's also archery, riflery, and trap shooting. Bring your own fishing gear and the ranch will cook up your catch. You can also join complimentary van trips to Breckenridge or Aspen. For an extra charge, parents and kids 8 and up can spend a day rafting the Arkansas River with a local outfitter.
 Elk Mountain Ranch, Box 910, Buena Vista, CO 81211, tel. 719/539–4430. June–Sept.: 7 days, $535–$955.

Hidden Creek Ranch

👫 ALL

Adventure and ecological awareness go hand in hand at this ranch in the mountainous lake country of Idaho's panhandle. Iris Behr and John Muir, who opened Hidden Creek in 1993, envisioned a place where people could reconnect with nature as well as ride horses. All products used at the ranch are natural, biodegradable, and packaged in recycled containers; none has been tested on animals. There are cabins (built of dead standing timber) and lodge accommodations for 40, but guests shouldn't think spartan just because the philosphy is harmony with nature. Food is exceptional, the children's program is extensive, and the "Chocolate Fairy" turns down your bed each night.

CHILDREN'S PROGRAM. There's a full program for kids aged 3 and up during summer months, although it's entirely optional; families can spend as much of their day together as they wish. The youngest guests ride at the ranch under the supervision of counselors; kids 6 and up can join the regular trail rides. Other activities are hiking, fishing, crafts and nature studies, and picnics. Kids have their own campfire with storytelling and an overnight in a teepee. Care for children under the age of 3 (extra charge) must be arranged in advance.

RIDING PROGRAM. "If you want to see what men have made, you can ride in a car. If you want to see what God has made, you have to ride on a horse." That's the philosophy of the Hidden Creek riding program, which takes you into forests, grassy meadows, and magnificent mountain settings. There are daily rides for all abilities; groups are small. No one's left out of the weekly specials, either; these include everything from a sunset walk-only ride to the Daring Dude Ride for advanced riders. Families with kids 6 and up can ride together if they wish.

BEYOND RIDING. Among the hikes is an all-day trek to a nearby gold mine. Trap shooting, target riflery (extra charge for targets and ammunition), and archery are popular; the ranch also has a a stocked pond and fishing poles. Guides, equipment, and instruction are available for mountain biking. If your family wants to participate in Dirty Dudes Day, you can work around the property. Hot tubs are an option for the muscle sore or bone weary at any time, day or night.

 Hidden Creek Ranch, 7600 E. Blue Lake Rd., Harrison, ID 83833, tel. 208/689–3209. May–Nov.: 7 days, $500–$1,250.

Lake Mancos Ranch

ⁿ̈ⁿ ALL

The Sehnerts believe that a lot of American families still want an old-fashioned vacation without video games, pinball, or bars. At Lake Mancos Ranch, you can ride and relax in the heart of southwestern Colorado's authentic cowboy country. Up to 55 guests stay in cabins of various sizes; all have porches, two baths, and refrigerators. You can bring your own liquor for use in your cabin. This ranch is a good choice if at least one person in your family doesn't ride, since riding is not part of the basic cost.

CHILDREN'S PROGRAM. Lil'l Ropers is for ages 4 and 5; Cowpokes is the 5 to 9 group; Buckaroos are 9 to 12; and teens are the Mavericks. Lil'l Ropers have the opportunity to learn about horses while on the lead line; there's no extra charge for this. All other age groups spend time riding with their counselors if they opt to be in the riding program. There's also hiking, fishing, scavenger hunts, lawn games, hayrides, cookouts, camp-outs, and more. Teens have plenty of action of their own, including various sports and a Jeep trip.

RIDING PROGRAM. Adults and kids (usually age 5 and up) who choose to participate in the program go out on the trails in supervised groups. Parents and children generally ride separately, but there are family rides three times a week. In this rugged terrain the majority of the rides are walk/trot only, but you won't be bored; each day you explore a different area, from the ranch lands to the adjacent San Juan National Forest. Instruction takes place primarily at the beginning of your stay, but wranglers give pointers throughout the week.

BEYOND RIDING. Some favorite activities are guided hikes, swimming in the pool, and guided four-wheel-drive trips up into the San Juans. Guests of all ages can fish; there's equipment for kids. For an additional charge, your family can leave the ranch to take a ride on the Durango and Silverton Narrow Gauge Railroad (ask the ranch to make advance reservations for you) or to visit the famed ruins at Mesa Verde National Park, just 17 miles from the ranch. Rafting is another option for families with kids aged about six and up (extra charge).

 Lake Mancos Ranch 42688 Country Rd. N, Mancos, CO 81328, tel. 303/533–7900 or 800/325–9462. June–Oct.: 7 days, $726–$1,050. Riding is $16 per hour or $130 for the week.

Lone Mountain Ranch

👫 ALL

The Schaap family, who own Lone Mountain, believe that the enjoyment of nature is good for both the body and the mind. The ranch's location, high in the mountains at the northern end of the Greater Yellowstone ecosystem in Montana, provides abundant opportunity for nature discovery and learning for all ages. Guests have a choice of many activities and programs. Up to 70 people stay in cabins with fireplaces; ranch amenities include a massage therapist who, for an extra charge, is ready to soothe sore muscles during your stay.

CHILDREN'S PROGRAM. Kids aged 4 to 12 and teens participate in a variety of activities; there's no program for those under 4, but the ranch has information on quality day care in Big Sky. The 4- and 5-year-olds are given pony rides by counselors; ages 6 and up go on their own wrangler-led rides. Nature discovery hikes, animal tracking, panning for gold, orienteering, mountain biking, climbing wall challenges, camp-outs, and caring for the barnyard animals are all options, depending on the age group. Parents can join their children for any or all of these activities. Teens also take adventure hikes and have their own yurt, which serves as a game room and social center.

RIDING PROGRAM. Adults and children aged 6 and up are assigned their own horse. Children can ride in the regular adult program rather than on kids' rides if they prefer. Half-day, all-day, and instructional rides are available for every ability. First-time riders learn in the ring, building up skills and confidence before going out on the trail.

BEYOND RIDING. Lone Mountain has many programs for nonriders, including hiking and skiing (see Hiking and Backpacking and Cross-Country Skiing). There's some fishing equipment and instruction for kids, and plenty for adults; birding is popular, too. The ranch's friendly llamas will carry a picnic lunch while you and the kids lead them on a day hike; you can also choose to relax in the hot tub. Guided tours of Yellowstone, best for families with kids 6 and up, are part of any weeklong stay. Extra-charge activities include naturalist-led canoe trips and, in nearby Big Sky, golf, tennis, gondola rides, rafting, and rock climbing.

 Lone Mountain Ranch, Box 160069, Big Sky, MT 59716, tel. 406/995–4644. Year-round: 7 days, $300–$1,450; children under 2 free.

North Fork Guest Ranch

👫 ALL

A mere 50 miles from Denver and yet surrounded by the Mt. Evans Wilderness Area, North Fork is a ranch that encourages families to spend time together and to try a variety of activities as part of its regular program. Lodging is in log cabins, an impressive stone building, or the main lodge; full capacity is about 30 guests. The north fork of the South Platte River runs through the property.

CHILDREN'S PROGRAM. Counselors care for infants and kids up to about age 6; depending on age, children can try riding, hiking, fishing, swimming, crafts, and nature studies. The program's main purpose is to provide fun for children too young to accompany parents on rides or on the river rafting. The ranch has no supervised evening program or baby-sitting; nighttime activities are geared to the entire family.

RIDING PROGRAM. Wranglers give instruction throughout the week for those who want or need it, and each guest is assigned a horse for the entire stay. Rides for small groups go through high alpine meadows or stands of aspen and ponderosa pine. Children aged 6 and up can accompany parents on rides.

BEYOND RIDING. North Fork is unusual because river rafting and an overnight pack trip are included in the regular weekly rate, so almost all guests participate. Parents with children too young to raft can bring them along; counselors will take the kids on a land-based excursion on their own while parents are on the river. The eight-hour ride up to the overnight is best for ages 12 and up, but younger kids and other nonriders can travel to the campsite by vehicle and join their families. There's a weekly Orvis fly-fishing class (good for ages 10 and up), as well as hiking and trap shooting. The ranch has a heated pool and spa.

 North Fork Guest Ranch, Box B, Shawnee, CO 80475, tel. 303/838–9873. May–Sept.: 7 days, $300–$1,195.

Paradise Guest Ranch

 ALL

The ranch brand, FUN, is the first thing you'll see when you drive into Paradise. It's a promise owners Jim and Leah Anderson attempt to fulfill for all ages over the course of the weeklong stay. Beautifully renovated but authentically rustic log cabins provide families of all sizes with comfortable lodging and views of the picturesque valley in Wyoming's Big Horn Mountains in which the ranch sits. In July and August there are often 80 guests, many of them returnees who greet each other like long-lost friends. And then there's Buford, the ranch bloodhound, who greets everybody, period.

CHILDREN'S PROGRAM. Kids aged 3 to 7 and those 8 and up are grouped separately, and there are programs with hiking, fishing, crafts, and nature studies to occupy those under 7 and any older kids who don't want to join the adult rides. A ranch nanny will watch children under the age of 3 in the mornings only; private baby-sitting can be arranged for an extra charge. Kids have an overnight on the hill just above the ranch, and the teens have their own overnight pack trip.

RIDING PROGRAM. Kids 7 and up join their parents out on the trail. There are long, short, slow, and fast rides. Exceptional are the Learn to Lope rides high on the mesa. Paradise wranglers seem to be able to get almost everybody loping like pros before week's end. Jim will sometimes arrange for guests to move cattle on another piece of property he owns not far from the ranch.

BEYOND RIDING. Guided and self-guided hikes, fishing instruction for the kids (equipment provided), catch-and-release fishing for adults, swimming, and a once-weekly town trip into Buffalo provide a change from riding. So does the hot tub, although it's often too filled with kids to have room for adults. Paradise breeds and raises mules, and learning about these intelligent, hard-working animals is surprisingly interesting. Parents have a weekly adult-only candlelight dinner while the kids are on their overnight, and no one should miss Jim's evening of authentic cowboy poetry. For an extra charge, adults can arrange a pack fishing trip before or after a ranch stay.

 Paradise Guest Ranch, Box 790, Buffalo, WY 82834, tel. 307/684–7876. May–Oct.: 7 days, $500–$1,375.

Rainbow Trout Ranch

ALL

Located in southwest Colorado in the rugged and remote Conejos River valley, Rainbow Trout is 185 miles from Colorado Springs and just 80 miles from Taos, New Mexico. The centerpiece of the ranch is the 18,000-square-foot main lodge, built in the 1920s without, it is said, a single nail. Cabins are a short distance from the lodge and have a variety of floorplans, though all have porches. This ranch is a family haven where 60 guests of all ages are warmly welcomed and cared for.

CHILDREN'S PROGRAM. There are three groups: ages 3 to 5, 6 to 11, and teens. Children 6 and up have a full riding program that has more instruction both in the arena and on the trail than the adult program—but this doesn't mean it's not fun. Even instruction includes lots of games on horseback. Ages 3 to 5 are led by counselors in the arena. When not on horses, kids here are hiking, fishing, swimming, and exploring the natural surroundings. The teen program is very flexible and changes depending on the particular group, but hikes, picnics, volleyball, and fishing are all likely activities in addition to riding.

RIDING PROGRAM. Small groups, divided by ability, go on a variety of rides: slow, fast, long, short, leisurely, and scenic. Adults can join games and lessons in the arena if they wish, and they can always get pointers from wranglers out on the trail. If parents and children want to ride together, the ranch will arrange that.

BEYOND RIDING. Once a private fishing retreat for wealthy businessmen, Rainbow Trout has, as its name suggests, exceptional fishing. There are some supplies and a few fly rods for lessons, but you should get your license (mandatory for ages 15 and up) and most supplies before arriving. The ranch also has a heated pool and hot tub. You can take guided hikes or use trail maps to plan your own. Once a week a raft trip on the Rio Grande is scheduled (extra charge), combined with a tour of Taos (about an hour-and-a-half away); it's for ages 6 or so and up. One of the thrills for most families is a chance to ride The Cumbres & Toltec Scenic Railroad (extra charge), "America's longest and highest narrow gauge." Let the ranch know that you want to go when you book your stay, and they'll make the reservations for you.

Rainbow Trout Ranch, Box 458, Antonito, CO 81120, tel. 719/376–5659 or 800/633–3397. Late May–mid-Sept.: 7 days, $150–$1,050; ask about a baby-sitter's fee and 2-day stays in May and Sept.

Red Rock Ranch

👫 6+

Here's a small, working cattle and horse ranch in Wyoming that loves families. "Children are an important part of Red Rock . . . it wouldn't be the same without them" states the brochure, and the programs and facilities for children are indeed extensive. Set in a high valley of Jackson Hole's mountain country, the ranch gets its name from the imposing red rock formations in the area. Lodging is in authentic log cabins that accommodate no more than 30 guests on any week.

CHILDREN'S PROGRAM. There are no activities or baby-sitting services for children younger than 6. Kids 6 and up go on daily rides with wranglers. Along the way they might look for fossils, stop to wade in a crystal clear mountain creek, or search for cattle. There's also a weekly overnight. Parents can ride with their children on kids' rides, but only ages 16 and up join adult rides. Children eat dinner with their wranglers three times a week.

RIDING PROGRAM. There are morning and afternoon rides for all abilities, as well as all-day lunch rides on which you might see antelope, moose, coyotes, and other native wildlife. Because this is a working ranch, guests have opportunities to participate in authentic ranch chores, including checking cattle on the range or bringing out salt. A favorite activity of younger guests is slopping the pigs when these animals are in residence.

BEYOND RIDING. Fishing, hiking, swimming in the heated pool, or relaxing in the hot tub are ranch favorites. For an extra charge, you can arrange a raft trip down the Snake River or a guided fishing trip; almost everyone likes to visit Jackson for shopping or for the local rodeo and "shoot-out." The National Elk Refuge just north of town is well worth the visit, as is the Wildlife of the American West Art Museum.

 Rock Ranch. Box 38, Kelly, WY 83011, tel. 307/733–6287. June–Oct.: 7 days, $1,193; children under 6 half price.

Seven D Ranch

 ALL

Fifty miles northwest of Cody, Wyoming, lies the Sunlight Basin, surrounded by the Absaroka Mountains and the Shoshone National Forest. Taking only 28 guests at a time, the Seven D has log cabins set in a tranquil aspen grove with a crystal-clear creek meandering nearby. Few places are as peaceful as this, and few offer more for families. There are conveniences for parents with infants—cribs, diaper-changing areas, free laundry facilities, and microwaves—and a superb children's program that focuses on environmental education and western history as well as riding.

CHILDREN'S PROGRAM. For infants and children up to age 6, there's baby-sitting at no charge during the adult rides. Younger children will have a chance to experience lead-line rides in the corral. Ages 6 to 12 participate in an extensive program that includes environmental education, hiking, woodsmanship, and cave exploration. This group also learns about western culture, ranch life, and the natural history of the area. There are opportunities for riding and riding instruction every day.

RIDING PROGRAM. Each guest aged 6 and up is assigned a horse; children ride with counselors. Instruction is available for all ages and all levels. There are morning, afternoon, and all-day rides on trails with names as lovely as the Little Sunlight Trail or as evocative as the "Oh My God" Trail (named

by a guest). Multiday pack trips for good riders are possible with advance notice; there's an extra charge for these.

BEYOND RIDING. Guests can try world-class fly-fishing on Sunlight Creek (clinics provided), hiking, backpacking, and trap shooting at the ranch. Some off-property excursions (extra charge) are to the Cody Rodeo and the Buffalo Bill Historical Center in Cody, which includes the Whitney Gallery of Western Art, the Plains Indian Museum, and the Cody Firearms Museum. Most guests choose to spend all of their time in the relaxing atmosphere at the ranch, but day trips to Yellowstone are also possible for a separate fee.

 Seven D Ranch, Box 100, Cody, WY 82414, tel. 307/587–9885 (winter) or 307/587–3997 (summer). June–Aug.: 7 days, $1,003–$1,150; children 1–12 receive a 15% discount, children under 1 are free.

Sky Corral

ALL

Sky Corral is for parents and children who want to spend time together; the emphasis is on family activities and a flexible, low-key schedule. The ranch, which accommodates 38 guests, is 23 miles from Fort Collins, Colorado, in the Roosevelt National Forest, and a short drive from Rocky Mountain National Park. The main lodge has several rooms; families can also choose rustic cabins, some of which have wood stoves or fireplaces.

CHILDREN'S PROGRAM. Counselors will watch children under age 6 in the summer while parents are out on rides, including the all-day rides, but this is not a full-time program. Individual baby-sitting is available for an extra charge. Small children enjoy games, crafts, and storytime; occasionally there are lead-line rides in the corral. Children 6 and over ride out on the trail on children-only rides and with parents, too. There's a petting farm with lots of baby animals and a children's play area with swings. The teepee cookout is for all ages, and the under-6 set can have a sleep-out there if the group is is interested. The program is flexible enough to change with the interests of each week's guests.

RIDING PROGRAM. Families ride together and separately, and each guest aged 6 and up is assigned a horse for the week. Riders 6 and up have an overnight, but there's no care for nonriding kids during this. Cattle drives can be arranged for all riders, depending on ability rather than age.

BEYOND RIDING. The ranch has hiking, fishing, archery, and tennis in the summer, and cross-country skiing in winter. There's a heated pool, sauna, and hot tub. A raft trip is available June–August for everyone aged 7 and up.

Sky Corral, 8233 Old Flowers Rd., Bellvue, CO 80512, tel. 970/484–1362. Year-round: 7 days, $620–$970; children under 2 free. Daily rates are available Sept.–Apr.

Skyline Guest Ranch

 ALL

Skyline, in the increasingly popular vacation town of Telluride, in southwestern Colorado, has a unique feature: It makes the Telluride Montessori child care program, five minutes away, available to guests ages 3 and up at no extra charge. The ranch itself is extraordinarily beautiful, with views of 14,000-foot snowcapped peaks. Owners Dave and Sherry Farny formerly ran the Telluride Mountaineering School, so it's not surprising that Skyline has all kinds of outdoor activities, including guided climbing and mountain biking. Guests stay in lodge rooms or cabins; beds are outfitted with down comforters and sheepskin mattress pads. Only 35 guests visit at a time, so there's both an intimacy and a wonderful sense of comfort at Skyline.

CHILDREN'S PROGRAM. Many activities at the ranch are designed for children and

parents together. When parents are on hikes or rides more strenuous than their children can handle, kids join easier ones. Ages 6 and up learn not only riding but horse care, tack, horse anatomy, and other aspects of general horsemanship. While the ranch welcomes all ages, most activities are best for those 6 and older. However, at the Montessori child-care program in Telluride, children 3 and up can participate in hiking, swimming, picnics, and lots of outdoor fun. At the ranch, baby-sitting is available for children under 3 (extra charge), but this should be arranged well in advance.

RIDING PROGRAM. Adults, too, can learn about tack and safety, and all guests can take as much instruction as they wish. There are half-day or all-day rides every day. In the late afternoon children under 6, or those not strong enough to join the regular rides, can get on a horse at the ranch under the supervision of the wranglers. An overnight pack trip is part of a week's stay, and all ages can participate.

BEYOND RIDING. There's a midweek trip to Mesa Verde National Park, about a 1½-hour drive from the ranch. Guests can also take guided and self-guided hikes to a mining town, wildflower fields, and a hot springs, among other areas. You can climb a San Juan peak with an experienced guide—including the 14,017-foot Wilson Peak—but most climbs are for adults and older kids who have some hiking experience. There's fishing instruction and guided trips; equipment is available. Mountain bikes are also available at the ranch and guided bike rides are possible. For an extra charge, experienced riders can join spring and fall pack trips. In winter there's cross-country skiing at the ranch (equipment for those wearing a size five shoe or larger) and transportation to the Telluride ski area, 5 miles away, for downhillers. There's also skating, but no riding.

Skyline Guest Ranch, Box 67, Telluride, CO 81435, tel. 303/728–3757. June–mid-Oct., mid-Dec.–Apr.: 7 days, $1,100; children under 2 free. Ask about daily rates in winter.

West Coast

Coffee Creek Ranch

 ALL

Coffee Creek is a river-canyon ranch on the edge of the Trinity Alps Wilderness area in California. This is the perfect ranch for families with nonriders, since you only pay for the amount of riding you really want to do. Wildflowers and wildlife abound, and all cabins have porches and woodburning or potbelly stoves. The ranch accommodates up to 50 guests.

CHILDREN'S PROGRAM. Cowboys and Cowgirls are kids aged 3 to 7; Junior Wranglers are 8 to 12; and Bronc Busters are 13 to 17. Although counselors don't take kids riding, there's plenty to do. Depending on their age, children have pony rides, care for baby animals, pan for gold, and fish. Each child takes home at least two finished projects from the excellent creative arts program. There are also skits, lawn games, swimming, archery, and riflery. The youngest guests go in the wading pool; the older kids swim, slide, and jump in Coffee Creek. During trail ride hours, care is provided for children under age 3 in the Kiddie Korral.

RIDING PROGRAM. Rides are grouped by ability, not age. Those as young as 5 can go on certain, but not all, trails, and there are all-day, breakfast, and picnic rides. Coffee Creek has a separate daily or weekly fee for rides; an overnight pack trip is included in the weekly riding fee. Private lessons are also available for an extra charge. The ranch is particularly interesting because of the international staff, part of a cultural exchange program. Wranglers from Australia and New Zealand, for example, give guests a feel for cowboy life in another hemisphere. For an extra charge, families can arrange multiday wilderness pack trips.

BEYOND RIDING. There's a health club, swimming in the heated pool or in the creek, canoeing on the pond, guided hikes, fishing (equipment for kids only), panning for gold, lawn games, archery, riflery, and trap shooting. In the winter guests can try cross-country skiing, tubing, snowshoeing, sleigh rides, ice fishing, and dogsledding.

Coffee Creek Ranch, HC 2, Box 4940, Trinity Center, CA 96091, tel. 916/266–3343 or 800/624–4480. Year-round: 7 days, $555– $695. Riding is $27.50 for a regular ride, $55 for an all-day outing, or $250 for the week.

Rankin Ranch

 ALL

The Rankin family has been ranching in California since 1863, and their 31,000-acre spread in the Tehachapi Mountains, northeast of Bakersfield, has an old-fashioned, down-home atmosphere, from the cozy duplex cabins to the baby calves the kids love to feed. The ranch is casual and western, but there are elegant touches for the 25 to 35 guests: linen tablecloths, candles, and fresh flowers on the dining room tables.

CHILDREN'S PROGRAM. The program is for kids 4 and up, but baby-sitting for younger children can be arranged in advance for an extra charge. Ages 4 to 11 ride with counselors. Four- and 5-year-olds ride in the corral, and those aged 6 and up can go out on the trail, depending on how well they can handle a horse. There are also swim meets, picnics, games, and guided nature hikes, as well as a terrific crafts program. Children eat breakfast and lunch with their families; at dinner children sit at a special table with their counselors.

RIDING PROGRAM. Guests can sign up for one-hour morning and afternoon rides, which are mostly walking because of the terrain. A few wide-open meadows provide opportunities for advanced riders to canter and gallop. Because this is a working ranch, guests can sometimes help wranglers with chores, such as moving cattle. Children under 12 do not go on adult rides, but parents are welcome to sign up for the kids' rides. There are special teen rides when enough of that age group are present.

BEYOND RIDING. Guests use their own equipment for fishing and tennis, and there's archery and hiking. If you bring your own bikes, you'll find plenty of dirt roads to ride on and some exquisite scenery. One of the most popular activities is simply relaxing around the pool. Families also love the petting farm with its baby calves, sheep, pigs, and chickens.

 Rankin Ranch, Box 36, Caliente, CA 93518, tel. 805/867–2511. Wk before Easter Sun.–Oct.: $30–$125 per day; no minimum stay.

Rock Springs

ALL

Rock Springs sits just outside Bend, Oregon, in the foothills of the Cascade Range. About 50 guests visit at a time, staying in cabins with knotty-pine interiors and sun decks. "Family tradition is revered at Rock Springs," the owners say, and there's no question that families are important here. Every detail has been thought of, down to the cookies, fresh fruit, and beverages that are always in the lodge so guests of all ages can help themselves between meals.

CHILDREN'S PROGRAM. Divided into groups for ages 3 to 5 and 6 to 12, kids stay with counselors from 9 to 1 and again from 5:30 to 9 in the evening. In between these two shifts, one counselor is on duty, so parents can take an afternoon ride or participate in another activity. In this very child-directed program, the kids decide together what activities they would like throughout the week. Choices include riding, outdoor games, nature walks, swimming, sports, arts and crafts, an overnight, folklore, and storytelling. There's also a playground area and playhouse. Families eat breakfast together, but kids eat lunch and dinner in their own dining room adjacent to the adult dining area.

RIDING PROGRAM. Twice-daily rides go out with no more than eight people, grouped by age, ability, and interests. Children aged 6 and up can join trail rides with parents or go in groups with their counselors; younger kids are helped on a lead line around the barn area. There's an all-day lunch ride and bareback riding in the pasture on Friday afternoon. Instruction is available if staffing permits.

BEYOND RIDING. The ranch has a heated swimming pool and a boot-shaped hot tub. There are two lighted tennis courts; you can ask about special tennis weeks with free clinics by well-known coaches. A fly-fishing guide visits the ranch once a week, and guides can be hired for trips off ranch property. For an extra charge, families with kids aged 6 and up can try white-water rafting on the Deschutes River, 15 miles from the ranch. There are also plenty of opportunities for day trips to nearby museums, including the High Desert Museum and Warm Springs Native People's Museum. The caves at Lava Lands State Park are another popular area attraction.

 Rock Springs, 64201 Tyler Rd., Bend, OR 97701, tel. 503/382–1957 or 800/225–DUDE. Memorial Day, late June–Labor Day, Thanksgiving, Christmas: 7 days, $775–$1,275; ask about special rates for infants and nannies.

Resources

Organizations

The following organizations have information about guest ranches in their particular areas. The **Dude Ranchers' Association** (Box 471, LaPorte, CO 80535, tel. 970/223–8440) has more than 100 members in western states. An excellent magazine with all kinds of information about ranches and ranch stays is available from this group. The **Colorado Dude and Guest Ranch Association** (Box 300, Tabernash,

CO 80478, tel. 970/887–3128) and the **Wyoming Dude Rancher's Association** (Box 618, Dubois, WY 82513, tel. 307/455–2584) send out material about ranches.

Some tour operators or specialty travel advisers can make reservations for you at ranches as well as provide information that will help you choose a ranch. **American Wilderness Experience** (2820A Wilderness Pl., Boulder, CO 80301, tel. 303/444–2622 or 800/444–3833) books vacations at ranches throughout the West and Southwest. **Off the Beaten Path** (109 E. Main St., Bozeman, MT 59715, tel. 406/586–1311 or 800/445–2995) specializes in custom western adventures and works with dozens of ranches. **Rascals in Paradise** (650 5th St., #505, San Francisco, CA 94107, tel. 415/978–9800 or 800/U–RASCAL) has organized a couple of different family weeks at ranches and has a stellar reputation as a family travel resource. **Pat Dickerman's**

Adventure Guides (7550 E. McDonald Dr., Scottsdale, AZ 85250, tel. 602/596–0226 or 800/252–7899) can help you match your family to the right ranch.

Books

Gene Kilgore's *Ranch Vacations* (John Muir Publications; revised 1994) is an outstanding resource that covers almost every ranch in the United States and Canada. Although there is only minimal information about children's programs, the guide states clearly which ranches have children's programs and whether or not families are welcomed at those that don't have formal programs.

Also See

If visiting a ranch in winter interests your family, see Cross-Country Skiing, which lists a number of ranches that have opportunities for skiing.

ROCK CLIMBING

A few years ago the words *rock climbing* were not part of the vocabulary of most Americans, and certainly not related to anything families might do together over vacation. That's all changed. Today, 5-, 6-, and 7-year-olds scramble up indoor climbing walls from Connecticut to California and every place in between. My own 5-year-old, Hutch, visits the Boulder Rock Club weekly. Concentrating intently on his next move, closer to the ceiling than the floor, he pauses to beam down at me as his instructor calls up, "Good job!" I am earthbound; he is ready to scale greater heights. Now parents are stepping into harnesses, too, joining their children in a sport that is challenging, exhilarating, and a self-esteem builder of the first order.

Rock climbing has become a relatively safe sport as equipment and technique have improved over the years. Generally you climb, in a harness attached to safety ropes, from the ground up a rock face, finding hand- and footholds as you go. After reaching the top—or however far you choose to climb—you descend, using your feet against the rocks to help you down. Those passionate about the sport think of it as a kind of natural puzzle, one that stimulates the mind as well as the body. There seems to be no single profile that fits the average rock climber. Although good physical condition is a must, you and your children of all ages might be surprised to find that working your way up a hunk of granite out in beautiful country does more for your soul than you believed possible. Happily, there are a variety of opportunities to discover the rock climber in you.

Many indoor climbing schools offer weekend or even weeklong courses in addition to their daily classes. Several of the top outdoor schools in the country have integrated rock climbing into their programs. Both are excellent choices for families just beginning the sport, as well as for those who really want to have fun with it as a recreational pastime. America's premier alpine climbing schools, on the other hand, are for people who want to be serious climbers. Guide-training and intensive mountaineering courses are at the core of what these schools offer. If you and your family want to work toward self-guided trips in backcountry, a dedicated mountaineering and climbing school would be the best choice.

Courses vary in terms of how long you spend on the ground and on the rocks; four to six hours of actual climbing is typical on the first day, with six or seven possible on days two and three. Fifty-foot climbs are typical of beginner routes. You will probably be paired with a partner, and the two of you will take turns climbing and belaying (handling the safety ropes of the other climber) throughout the course. Children 12 and over can usually learn to belay, too. Climbers younger than that are too small and not technically skilled enough to handle belaying.

Questions to Ask

Is there child-size equipment, including helmets and harnesses that can be adjusted to fit a child properly? For safety, it's imperative that helmets and harnesses fit correctly. Although climbing shoes aren't mandatory in some courses, they do provide better traction than tennis shoes and will certainly make a difference at the intermediate level. Some instructors believe they make a difference for beginners, too. If rock shoes are not supplied, ask about a rental source near the school or even consider buying.

What is your teaching accreditation or certification, and how many years experience do you have? American Mountain Guides Association (AMGA; see Resources, *below*) is the organization in this country that accredits schools and guide services and certifies individual guides. In Europe, Canada, and a number of other countries, the organization that provides the same service is an international union of mountain guides (UIAGM; see Resources, *below*). If a school is accredited, it means certain standards have been met and approved teaching methods are used. Instructors must keep up on the latest technology and safety issues and participate in a peer review process. Look for schools that are accredited by AMGA, not just members of it; an organization can pay to be a member but does not have to meet standards or be subjected to peer review. Individual guides certified by either AMGA or UIAGM have passed rigorous exams and technical tests. These are critical guidelines, but they are not necessarily an indicator of who is a good teacher as well as a good climber. Always ask how long a guide or instructor has been climbing, then ask specifically about his or her experience with family teaching. Even on the phone you can get a feel for whether or not a school or guide will be accepting and welcoming.

What is the ratio of students to instructors? Three students for one teacher is an excellent ratio, though in some beginner classes a slightly higher ratio is acceptable because only one or two students will climb at a time.

What kind of emergency training do you and your staff have? You need someone trained in basic first aid and rock rescue, at a minimum. Although rock climbing has become a safer sport, it's best to be climbing with someone who is trained to help on the spot. Moreover, if someone in your group gets halfway up the rock face and can't make it down, you want a teacher who can help that person down.

What happens if I or my children panic halfway up a rock? The truth is, both children and adults may be certain they can make a climb until they actually get up there. You don't want an instructor who uses teasing or belittling ("My 5-year-old niece can do this climb" or "Crying is what babies do") to get frightened climbers to continue. Compassion, encouragement, and positive reinforcement are the skills good teachers use, and no student should be made to feel bad for making it only halfway up. There's always a next time.

If my children are too young for regular courses, is private instruction an option? Regular rock climbing courses, like those for kayaking and some other sports, are often designated for teens and older. Most schools, however, do give private instructional trips for families with children as young as 6.

At what age can my child climb in a course without me? You may be a more advanced climber, or you may feel that your child learns better with peers or even that your child will have more success with instruction if you aren't there. That's okay. Some schools have courses just for kids, or they'll take children in courses without parents as long as parents give permission and can be reached if necessary. You can take your own class and be with your children after your climbs. If this kind of setup seems best for your family, find a school that will accommodate you.

If lodging isn't provided, do you have a list of options or will you help with booking? Many multiday courses are in wonderful camping areas, and the prices for these sessions generally, but not always, include camping. Other courses take place near inns or motels; a number of areas even have special climbers' inns, with dorm-style lodging and lots of climbing camaraderie. Some climbing outfitters will help with lodging and book rooms for you; others may just give you a list and let you make reservations.

What is included in the course? The prices for courses include guides, instruction, and technical climbing gear, such as harnesses and ropes, unless otherwise noted. Some outfitters supply helmets as part of the gear; others require that you rent them. Rock climbing shoes are available for rent from outfitters or from a local store recommended by the outfitter; a few outfitters, as noted, include shoes in the course price. Many but not all schools and guides provide local transportation to climbing sites. Most will also give clients information on local lodging, but lodging is not included, except as noted. Lunch is sometimes supplied but more often you must bring your own, even if you are camping. With such a wide range of possibilities, it's a good idea to ask about specifics, even if you think everything is spelled out in the brochure.

Instruction

Rock climbing is not a sport you can teach yourself; instruction is an absolute must. All the courses and trips are instructional, whether they take place on the grounds of the school or on some of the most famous rock faces in the country.

A Note about Ages

The minimum age listed first is for regular scheduled outdoor courses. When two ages are given, the second is for private or indoor classes, depending on the school. Younger children are often accepted for private instruction, but few schools are willing to pinpoint a specific age. Read the complete listings for details. Most schools make the decision on a case-by-case basis, taking into consideration a child's previous climbing experience, athletic ability, familiarity with the wilderness, enthusiasm for the sport, and the parents' own attitudes and abilities.

Finding the Fun

Northeast: Adirondack Rock & River Guide Service, Adventure Quest, Appalachian Mountain Club, Eastern Mountain Sports Climbing School, Zoar Outdoor. **Mid-Atlantic:** Appalachian Mountain Club. **South:** Nantahala Outdoor Center, Outward Bound. **Midwest:** Sylvan Rocks; Vertical Pursuits, Outdoor Program. **Southwest:** Eastern Mountain Sports Climbing School, Fantasy Ridge Mountain Guides, National Outdoor Leadership School. **Rockies:** Adventures to the Edge, Boulder Rock School, Colorado Mountain School, Eastern Mountain Sports Climbing School, Exum Mountain Guides, Fantasy Ridge Mountain Guides, National Outdoor Leadership School. **West Coast:** Alpine Skills International, American Alpine Institute, Eastern Mountain Sports Climbing School, Outward Bound, Timberline Mountain Guides, Wilderness Connection. **Canada:** American Alpine Institute, Yamnuska, Inc.

Favorite Schools and Outfitters

Adirondack Rock & River Guide Service

14+, 6+

Rock & River, whose core curriculum is climbing, has an unsurpassed setting—the 6-million-acre Adirondack Park, birthplace of the mighty Hudson River and depository of some of the oldest rocks known to humankind. The park, which encompasses nearly two-thirds of upstate New York, is a geologist's and rock climber's dreamscape.

FOR FAMILIES. People aged 14 and up can take two-day courses in beginning and novice rock climbing. The student/teacher ratio is four to one in the beginner course, two to one in the novice. Low-key and no pressure are the operative descriptions of these courses. There's a 30-foot indoor wall at the school's facility, so courses run rain or shine; the introductory courses begin here. After these courses families move up to intermediate and advanced levels. You can also combine excellent adventures in remote regions

of Adirondack State Park with private guiding and instruction, which is available for one to five days. Children 6 and up can be accommodated in private classes, and the school highly recommends these for families.

Backcountry Skills Seminars for Teens, begun in 1995, are five-day courses that teach route finding, shelter building, and minimum-impact camping, as well as rappelling and rock climbing. Families can choose to split up during the days, letting the teens go with their peers while parents climb together.

This school has its own reasonably priced lodging, ranging from a streamside lean-to to lodge rooms with private baths. Lunch is included in courses.

🏠 *Adirondack Rock & River Guide Service, Box 219, Keene, NY 12942, tel. 518/576–2041. Apr.–Oct.: 1–5 days, $145–$640, special parent/child rates for private guiding.*

Adventure Quest

7+

The central Vermont town of Woodstock, on the Ottauquechee River, is most noted for its historic houses and classic New England town square. Many vacationers think of Vermont as a ski destination, but summer recreation in the wooded, rolling hills and in the Green Mountains has become increasingly popular. Adventure Quest, one of the country's foremost outdoor schools, is committed to helping families learn and play together in challenging workshops.

FOR FAMILIES. Family workshops on rock climbing last one or several days. Eight participants is the maximum, and they can range in age from 7 to, well, who knows? Adventure Quest considers rock climbing a lifetime sport, one you can enjoy until you just don't want to do it anymore. In most cases families will start on the school's climbing wall and progress to local rock faces on which everyone in the group will feel comfortable learning. The student/teacher ratio is three to one, and courses include lunch and local transportation.

In spring and fall you can probably book space in Adventure Quest's campground; in summer it's used for kids (ages 7 to 17) in the school's Mountain Quest and River Quest camp programs. Mountain Quest includes rock climbing. Families with widely differing abilities might consider signing the kids up for camp while parents take a course of their own during the day. There are many inns and lodges in the area if you prefer to sleep indoors.

🏠 *Adventure Quest, Box 184, Woodstock, VT 05091, tel. 802/484–3939. Apr.–Oct.: 1–7 days, $200 per day for up to 4 people; $50 each additional family member.*

Adventures to the Edge

(👫 **7+**)

Jean Pavillard of Colorado's Adventures to the Edge is exactly the sort of person you want to have with your family on a climb: competent, steady, calm, and compassionate. He has been certified by the international union of mountain guides (UIAGM) for more than 18 years. He absolutely loves what he does, and his attitudes have been passed on to his staff, too. Adventures to the Edge excels in custom trips for all ages and abilities, and the outfitter will put together a climb for your family that will allow each of you to discover and conquer your own "edge."

The company is headquartered in Crested Butte, Colorado, a mountain town known for laid-back skiing in winter and mountain biking in summer. Much of the town's Victorian architecture has been preserved, yet Crested Butte is neither chi-chi nor cute. It's friendly but still rough around the edges—and a terrific place for vacationing families to relax between adventures.

FOR FAMILIES. Families with kids aged 7 and up can climb in the forested backcountry outside Crested Butte. Climbs often take place in Taylor Canyon, about 20 miles from town by way of Jack's Cabin Cutoff, a dirt road that from late October to late April is restricted to use by local wildlife such as elk and bighorn sheep. Come summer, humans are allowed, and the road leads to an area that's perfect for beginners. Guides—generally in a ratio of two instructors to five students when children are present—teach throughout any adventure, whether you're climbing or not.

Pavillard and his staff will assist with all aspects of your trip, including airline reservations and lodging. The campgrounds in the area are primitive but lovely; accommodations in town range from condos to hotel rooms. If you want fine food and wine as your standard rations, they'll arrange that, too, just as they'll create a budget climbing vacation. Because Pavillard is Swiss, Adventures to the Edge also runs summer climbing camps in Europe, as well as guided European tours that offer a native's inside knowledge as well as a thorough understanding of American family adventurers. For multiday trips, Adventures to the Edge provides all gear except sleeping bags.

🏠 *Adventures to the Edge, Box 91, Crested Butte, CO 81224, tel. 303/349–5219 or*

800/349–5219. Apr.–Oct.: 1–7 days, $280 per day for a group of 3, plus guides' expenses; $50 per day for each additional group member; $600 for weeklong European climbing camps, plus airfare, lodging, and meals.

Alpine Skills International

👫 10+

Based high in the California Sierras, surrounded by Tahoe National Forest, Alpine Skills International (ASI) has been teaching mountaineering and other backcountry skills for nearly 20 years. With a lodge at Donner Pass that serves both as a headquarters and the focal point for camaraderie among its students, ASI offers excellent climbing and a cozy bed to return to each night. Visitors may also want to see the nearby Donner Memorial State Park, which commemorates the infamous Donner Party stranded there in 1846 by early blizzards; those who survived resorted to cannibalism to do so.

FOR FAMILIES. ASI will take families with children aged 10 and up and teach them to climb. Talk with the directors about your children first, however, and let them help you choose the right course and time. There's Rock Climbing…the Beginning, two days of learning skills and practicing on routes that present a variety of challenges. Once you are confident about basic belaying, rappelling (a method of descending), and movement, try The Next Move, the intermediate course. If you want an intensive five-day experience, the Rockskills Seminar blends the two courses described above into one great learning experience. The student/teacher ratio is four to one for these classes.

At night, climbers of all ages, nationalities, and backgrounds hang out in the lodge. Some meals and lodging are included in ASI's course prices; bring your own sleeping bags, though.

🏠 *Alpine Skills International, Box 8, Norden, CA 95724, tel. 916/426–9108. June–Sept.: 2–5 days, $138–$498.*

American Alpine Institute

👫 17+

The American Alpine Institute in northern Washington has access to excellent climbing sites in both the United States and Canada. This very technical school is for people who have a serious interest in climbing, especially those who are learning rock climbing as a foundation for other alpine skills, such as ice climbing, climbing with crampons, and ascending world-class peaks. That doesn't mean it's not for some beginners, though. "If a skill is learned the correct and safe way the first time, it needs to be learned only once," notes the institute's brochure, and the school aims to help students do exactly that.

FOR FAMILIES. Regular courses are for people aged 17 and up. You can take the two-day Introduction to Rock or more advanced courses at a choice of locations in the Cascades or in Canada. Camping and lodging are available in most areas; the school will give you suggestions.

The Cascades are best known for their volcanoes (Mount St. Helens is probably the most famous), but these mountains are geographically and ecologically diverse. Two favorite areas for Intro to Rock are Leavenworth, on the warm and sunny east side of the Cascades, and Index, cooler and shadier because of its west side location; both have fine-grained granite and a range of climbs. Because the region has excellent crags for both beginners and experts, this makes a particularly good destination for families whose members have varying experience and skills.

Forty miles north of Vancouver, British Columbia, and 90 miles above Bellingham, Washington, Howe Sound cuts into the Canadian coast to create a fjord almost 30 miles long. At the head of the fjord is the logging town of Squamish and its striking white granite walls. Mountain bikers, sailboarders, and rock climbers come here, but it's still far from any crowds. Whether you're a beginner or an expert you'll find a pitch and a climb here. Beginners can spend days on the Smoke Bluffs perfecting the one-pitch climb. Climbers who are ready for multipitch (rock faces with a variety of angles) and steep ascents can tackle the Apron, with more than 50 separate routes, or perhaps the Chief, a 2,000-foot wall of near-vertical granite.

Beginner courses have a four to one student/teacher ratio, intermediates a three to one, and guided climbs have one instructor to two students. If parents and children choose private guiding, the institute will take climbers under 17. Talk with the staff about your child's skills, physical ability, and experience.

🏠 *American Alpine Institute, 1515 12th St., Bellingham, WA 98225, tel. 206/671–1570. Mid-Apr.–Oct.: 1–4 days, $145–$580.*

Appalachian Mountain Club

👫 10+

The Appalachian Mountain Club has climbing courses at its outdoor centers in New Hampshire's White Mountains and in the Delaware Water Gap National Recreation Area on the New Jersey–Pennsylvania border. White Mountains workshops take place in some 700,000 acres of national forest, with the Presidential Range as a backdrop. Families choosing workshops in the 70,000-acre Delaware Water Gap in the Pocono Mountains use the Mohican Outdoor Center as a base. If you want something to do in addition to rock climbing, both areas have many recreational activities for all ages.

FOR FAMILIES. In May, June, August, and September families can join Introduction to Rock Climbing in the White Mountains, famous for Cathedral Ledge and White Horse cliffs. This two-day course is designed for beginners or those with little previous experience. You'll learn the technical aspects of climbing and bouldering (moving without a

harness on rocks), including rappelling, tying harness and rope knots, and belaying. The price of the class covers two nights' lodging and meals. The club's lodge at Pinkham Notch Visitor Center accommodates more than 100 overnight guests in two-, three-, or four-bunk rooms. Pillows, linens, and towels are provided; you share bathrooms and hot shower facilities. The hearty meals are served family-style, and you can buy trail lunches to take to your class.

A Weekend on Rock is scheduled in June, August, and September at the Delaware Water Gap center. The course focuses on basic skills, such as equipment inspection, climbing techniques, belaying, and rappelling. Lodging in rustic cabins and a stick-to-your-ribs dinner on Saturday night are included in the price. Cabins have bunk rooms that sleep 4 to 10 people. Pillows are provided but you have to bring other bedding and towels.

Although there is no minimum age for these courses, the club suggests that ages 10 and up will probably benefit most from the technical information. You should notify them in advance that children will be taking the course, so the instructor will be prepared.

🏠 *Appalachian Mountain Club, Box 298, Gorham, NH 03581, tel. 603/466–2727 (general information, course catalog, or to register for White Mountain courses), 908/362–5670 (to register for Delaware Water Gap course). June–Sept.: 2 days, $260–$340.*

Boulder Rock School

👫 7+, 5+

Expert rock climbers from all over the world come to Colorado's Flat Irons and Eldorado and Boulder canyons, but beginners can play and learn here, too. Boulder Rock School's instructors know the region and the best routes; they also have a wealth of experience working with young children. At the end of a long day of climbing, you can explore Boulder's Pearl Street Mall, stopping along the way for a great meal or an ice-cream cone or to watch the street performers.

FOR FAMILIES. There are one- and two-day courses for ages 12 and up on Wind Tower, Bastille, or other great formations in the area. All classes meet at the Boulder Rock Club in town, where the school is located; if the weather is inclement, you can still climb at the club's extensive indoor facility. The student/teacher ratio is three to one.

Private instruction and guiding is a good choice for families with children under 12. Talk with the school about your kids and the goals of your family. When younger children are in the group, you will not get as much technical information and may not spend quite as much time climbing.

The school has several other options that might suit your family. It runs five-day summer camp sessions for teens 13 to 16; sessions meet weekdays from 8 to 4. This allows parents to sign up for climbing in more difficult areas or to take an advanced course while their teens are involved in their own program. The student/teacher ratio is four to one in the camp sessions. There are also 1½-hour classes at the Boulder Rock Club throughout the year for adults and children aged 5 and up.

The Boulder area has numerous inns, family lodges, and motels, as well as mountain campgrounds. The school supplies rock shoes in all sizes at no charge.
🏠 *Boulder Rock School, 2829 Mapleton Ave., Boulder, CO 80302, tel. 303/447–2804 or 800/836–4008. Year-round: 1–2 days, $109–$309. Summer camp: 5 days, $375.*

Colorado Mountain School

🚹🚺 12+

The only guide service licensed to operate in Rocky Mountain National Park, Colorado Mountain School (CMS) has a personal, flexible approach to teaching. There's a wide choice of scheduled classes, from one-day to seven-day courses and climbs, and you can mix and match them for the combination that works best for your family, budget, and time frame.

Rocky Mountain National Park, with its high meadows and wildflowers set against Colorado's snowy peaks and deep blue skies, is an adventuring family's playground. Besides climbing here—where some of the world's great alpine climbers test themselves on such classics as Longs Peak—you can hike on more than 355 miles of trails, attend family ranger talks, ride, and fish. Camping is good, too; there are five public campgrounds in the park and numerous private ones just outside. Your family might also take a drive on Trail Ridge Road, which at 12,183 feet is the highest continuous paved road in the United States.

FOR FAMILIES. Children aged 12 and up can join regular classes. Your family can be your group, or you can ask to join another family with children of compatible ages (there are no guarantees, but the school will try). CMS takes a learn-by-doing approach, so plan on plenty of climbing even in beginner courses. The best bets for families are the three-day courses at all levels, which give you information and then let you practice and reinforce what you've learned. If you know rock climbing is for you, jump right into the five-day course. At the end of it you'll be climbing the rocks other people only dream about. CMS has its own travel agent to help you with lodging and other arrangements.
🏠 *Colorado Mountain School, Box 2106, Estes Park, CO, 80517, tel. 970/586–5758. May–Oct.: 1–7 days, $115–$1,032.*

Eastern Mountain Sports Climbing School

🚹🚺 7+

Affiliated with the outdoor stores of the same name, this school is serious about climbing and has classes in a variety of areas. It's headquartered in North Conway, New Hampshire, in the foothills of the White Mountains, where gently sloping granite cliffs—perfect for beginners and intermediates—abound.

Classes are also held in Connecticut in the Trapp Rock region about 20 minutes west of Hartford, and in New York's Shawangunks, near New Paltz. The "Gunks," as they are called, are climber-friendly even though they're steep, which means they have plenty of hand- and footholds. On weekends, however, they can get pretty crowded. If a climber in your family likes to shop, take a basic course from the school at Hammond Pond in the Chestnut Hill section of Brookline, Massachusetts. In this wooded park, you can climb 50-foot pudding stone cliffs (an unusual mix of sedimentary rocks), then check the shopping area across the street. In Colorado, you can take basic courses all along the Front Range, including Boulder and Eldorado canyons and Vedauwoo, near Fort Collins.

FOR FAMILIES. Standard basic and intermediate courses, for ages 13 and up, run from one to four days. These courses are given throughout the week in New Hampshire and on most days in Connecticut, New York, Massachusetts, and Colorado. The student/teacher ratio is three to one.

Families in which the adults have some climbing experience but the kids don't might consider Children's Introduction to Climbing in New Hampshire. This daylong course for 7- to 12-year-olds allows rock lovers to experience the fun and excitement of climbing while receiving technical information at a level and rate they can absorb. The student/teacher ratio is five to one. While the kids are learning, parents can sign up for one of Eastern Mountain Sports' more advanced courses.

Climbing Lessons for Adolescents, another one-day class in New Hampshire, is a slightly higher level course, but it's still for

those with little or no climbing experience. The course emphasizes the technical aspects of the sport and responsible climbing, and there's plenty of time for climbing as well. It's aimed primarily at ages 12 to 15, but children younger than 12 can also take the course with a parent. The student/teacher ratio is three to one.

If your family is ready for serious treks, the school also offers destination climbing in Acadia National Park in Maine; Red Rocks, Nevada; Joshua Tree National Park in California; Canyonlands in Utah; and in Ecuador. Good rocks, it seems, are everywhere. Rock shoes are supplied for domestic courses.

🏠 *Eastern Mountain Sports Climbing School, Main St., North Conway, NH 03860, tel. 603/ 356–5433 or 800/310–4504 (register for all courses at this address and phone number). Apr.–Oct.: 1–4 days, $100–$530.*

Exum Mountain Guides

 14+

One of the top schools in the country, Exum has been teaching and guiding since 1926. The school and the instructors have strong experience, and families serious about climbing will do well to learn from them. The Tetons, northwest Wyoming's spectacular, rugged peaks, provide a dramatic landscape on which to hone your skills. When you aren't climbing, your family will find plenty to keep them busy in Grand Teton National Park, in nearby Yellowstone, and in the town of Jackson. Don't miss the nightly "shoot-out" in Jackson or the weekly rodeo, both summertime activities. Families can combine rock climbing with a stay at some fine ranches in Wyoming (see Ranches).

FOR FAMILIES. Adults and kids 14 and up can join one-day climbing schools at basic to advanced levels. Moms and daughters may be interested in Women That Rock, a course just for women. There are also one- and two-day climbs in various parts of the

Tetons for ages 13 and up. The student/ teacher ratio can go as high as eight to one in beginner courses, but six to one is far more common. Families with younger children should book a private guide; call the school first to discuss your child's physical ability, size, and experience.

Many of Exum's students stay at the American Alpine Club Climbers' Ranch, 2 miles south of Jenny Lake, which offers bunks and the companionship of other climbers. The school will help you find other lodging if you wish.

🏠 *Exum Mountain Guides, Grand Teton National Park, Box 56, Moose, WY 83012, tel. 307/733–2297. May–Sept.: 1–2 days, $65–$430.*

Fantasy Ridge Mountain Guides

👫 ALL

"Fantasy Ridge is about having fun…learning about climbing on rock, snow, and ice; achieving an understanding of mountains, nature…It's about calculated risk, adventure, travel, friends, and…life." That quote from the Fantasy Ridge brochure sums up what's great about rock climbing in general, and Fantasy Ridge in particular. The positive attitude of the school and its instructors ultimately translates to students' confidence that they can do the climbs. Fantasy Ridge is based in Telluride, a town tucked into the mighty San Juans in southwestern Colorado and originally made famous by such desperadoes as Butch Cassidy, who robbed his first bank here in 1889. Today celebrities have put Telluride on the map, but that doesn't change the area's enduring beauty or its historical importance.

FOR FAMILIES. There is no minimum age, but there is a requirement for joining these courses: The kids must want to do it. Director Michael Covington loves to teach children, but he won't accept any whose parents seem to be pressuring them into

climbing. Best bets are Stage One, a five-day seminar for novices, or Stage Two, also five days, but for intermediate and advanced climbers. The courses take place at Telluride's Ophir Wall, a 600-foot granite cliff; Elk Park, along the Animas River (you take the Durango–Silverton narrow-gauge railway to get there); or at Indian Creek, near Canyonlands National Park in Utah. Student/teacher ratios are four to one for Stage One, two to one for Stage Two. This company hosts many families, who can participate in regular courses and climbs as their own group, a less-expensive alternative than private instruction, which is also available.

All five-day courses are camping courses, for which you will need some of your own camping gear. The company will help you find lodging for other courses.

🏠 *Fantasy Ridge Mountain Guides, Box 1679, Telluride, CO 81434, tel. 970/728–3546. Apr.–Sept.: 1 hr–5 days, $25–$875.*

Nantahala Outdoor Center

👫 13+

If you're uncertain about investing in a multiday rock climbing course or trip, Nantahala, in Bryson City in the Great Smoky Mountains of western North Carolina, has just the answer. Climbing sites near the school have routes for all abilities. After you take your one-day sampler course, head south about 30 minutes to Cherokee, the southern gateway to magnificent Great Smoky Mountains National Park, where you can explore by foot, bike, horse, car, or RV. The ancient peaks and valleys of Appalachia's verdant mountains beckon with many opportunities for sightseeing and more adventures.

FOR FAMILIES. Adults and kids 13 and up can take a Rock Climbing Sampler throughout the summer. You'll start the day at a climbing wall. Students learn basic techniques for climbing and belaying in the morning, and by afternoon the group is rappelling down a nearby natural rock face. No experience is necessary. The center doesn't provide lodging for sampler courses but will help you find it.

🏠 *Nantahala Outdoor Center, 12077 U.S. 19 W, Bryson City, NC 28713, tel. 704/488–6737. June–Aug.: 1 day, $70.*

National Outdoor Leadership School

👫 17+

National Outdoor Leadership School (NOLS) is not an adventure tour operator, and the guides will not serve or pamper you. It is, however, a superb school that has been teaching people about wilderness skills, conservation, and leadership for more than 30 years. Physically and mentally demanding, a NOLS course aims not only to give students specific skills but to provide an understanding of the world and our place in it.

FOR FAMILIES. The 21-day course begins with a hike of several days into remote wilderness areas in Arizona or Wyoming. Your destination depends on the date you choose, but the class is the same. The Arizona course is given in April; the Wyoming/Rocky Mountain course is available June through August. On the hike students learn about low-impact camping, off-trail navigation, cooking, and other basic skills of wilderness exploration. Once base camp has been established, the emphasis is on climbing, with plenty of practice time on a variety of rock faces. At the end of this course you will have the ability to plan and complete your own backcountry climbing expedition safely and with a minimum of impact on the wilderness.

Some equipment is provided for these camping courses; check with the school to see what gear you need to supply. For college students, this course is worth five credit hours.

🏠 *National Outdoor Leadership School, 288 Main St., Lander, WY 82520, tel. 307/332–6973. July–Aug.: 21 days, $2,150, plus $150 equipment deposit.*

Outward Bound

 14+

Outward Bound's goal is to help students expand self-awareness individually and as a member of a working team, and to have students leave a course with the knowledge that they are capable of things they never dreamed possible. The organization's parent/child rock climbing course begins and ends in Asheville in North Carolina's Appalachian and Great Smoky mountains. Lush and green, this region has the highest peaks in the Appalachians, as well as trails, white-water rivers, and historic sites to explore before or after your course. Take time to see the famed 250-room Biltmore Estate in Asheville and to try a llama trek in the Pisgah National Forest (see Trekking with Llamas, Goats, and Burros).

FOR FAMILIES. The eight-day parent/child weeks combine rock climbing and backpacking, in addition to a ropes course, and are for ages 14 and up. You have your choice of spring or summer dates. Backcountry camping is scenic and you learn outdoor skills as you go. Ages 16 and up with some climbing experience can also accompany parents on the regular seven-day rock climbing courses scheduled in spring and fall at Joshua Tree National Monument in California; the course starts and ends in Palm Springs. These courses include camping, and Outward Bound supplies some equipment. The organization doesn't feel rock shoes are a necessity.

🏠 *Outward Bound, Rte. 9D, R2 Box 280, Garrison, NY 10524, tel. 800/243–8520. Parent/child course, Mar.–Aug.: 8 days, $745. Joshua Tree trip, Mar.–Apr., Sept.–Jan.: 7 days, $995.*

Sylvan Rocks

👫 5+

Rich in history and legend, the Black Hills of South Dakota have ghost towns, craggy peaks, lakes, and, of course, the Mt. Rushmore National Monument and Crazy Horse Memorial. The vast Black Hills National Forest spreads over more than 1 million acres. Legend says Paul Bunyan built the hills as a cairn for his huge blue ox, Babe, when Babe died after eating a red-hot stove and too many giant flapjacks. Geologists beg to differ, claiming that the Black Hills are the result of a massive geologic uplift that pushed a dome of ancient granite to the earth's surface. However the hills were formed, the area is a vacationer's and climber's delight. Here Sylvan Rocks provides its students with physical and mental challenges, safe climbing, fun, and teachers who have not only extensive climbing experience but the ability and attitude to teach all ages and all levels.

FOR FAMILIES. The two-day beginner package is for parents and children as young as 5 or 6. It focuses on building confidence on steep rock faces, safety, communication, proper use of equipment, tying knots, belaying, and rappelling. The second day takes you out on new faces to reinforce the previous day's instruction. The student/teacher ratio is three to one.

There are also three-day basic and novice classes. Those who have completed basic courses can join trips to Devil's Tower (the northeastern Wyoming formation made famous in *Close Encounters of the Third Kind*) and to Joshua Tree National Monument in California. Classes include rock shoes.
🏠 *Sylvan Rocks, Box 600, Hill City, SD 57745, tel. 605/574–2425. Year-round (Apr.–Oct. in Black Hills): 1–3 days, $125–$350. Call for prices on other trips.*

Timberline Mountain Guides

👫 8+

The Columbia River divides Oregon and Washington, creating one of the most impressive river gorges in the United States. On the Washington side of the river, not far from The Dalles Dam, is Horsethief Lake State Park. Timberline Mountain Guides owner Roy Holland believes this is some of the best teaching terrain in the country. These basalt faces of 20 to 50 feet have hundreds of climbs for all abilities.

When you're not climbing, the Columbia River Gorge has windsurfing, hiking, and, on the Oregon side, the historic Columbia Gorge Hotel. An hour-and-a-half from the park, in Oregon's Mt. Hood National Forest, is the Timberline Hotel and the outfitter's office. On the drive up to Timberline, think of Jack Nicholson: This is the long and winding road he took to his fateful employment in *The Shining*.

FOR FAMILIES. Children aged 8 or 9 and up can attend courses with parents, but all climbers must be in good physical condition and up for the challenge of learning. There are one-day courses for basic through advanced levels and two- to six-day Rock Camps for beginning, intermediate, and advanced climbers. The student/teacher ratio is four to one for basic courses, three to one in intermediate and advanced courses. Rock shoes are supplied for classes, and Timberline has information on convenient campgrounds and other lodging.
🏠 *Timberline Mountain Guides, Box 23214, Portland, OR 97281, tel. 503/636–7704. Mar.–Nov.: 1–6 days, $75–$450.*

Vertical Pursuits, Outdoor Program

👫 5+, 3+

Duluth sits on the western tip of Lake Superior in a region popular for many outdoor adventure activities, including rock climbing. With the Outdoor Program, part of the University of Minnesota at Duluth, you can try the area's two major types of climbs—sea cliffs and inland domes—as well as a couple of independent rock faces that aren't either. The sea cliffs along Lake Superior give climbers the thrill of inching their way up a rock face over raging waters. On beginner climbs at the sea cliffs, such as Shovel Point, you go from the top down instead of from the bottom up. The inland domes in forested state parks have a different atmosphere and provide easy access to the Superior Hiking Trail, which goes from Two Harbors, Minnesota, all the way to Canada.

FOR FAMILIES. Parents and kids 5 and up can take the weekly one-day introductory climbing course that lets beginners hone skills on rock faces in the Duluth area. Ely's Peak, about 15 minutes from town, is an excellent beginner's area because it has moderate routes with a range and variety, as well as scenery, often found only on more advanced climbs. Ages 3 and up can also practice and have instruction on an indoor climbing wall. One of the most popular courses, a weekend trip, combines an inland dome (Carlton Peak, about 1½ hours from Duluth) on day one with a sea-cliff climb (Shovel Point, in Tettegouche State Park) on day two. The student/teacher ratio is five to one. You can camp on multiday courses; the Outdoor Program can rent most of the necessary equipment.

The Outdoor Program's strongest point, however, is its customized courses for families and other groups, and for all ages. You and your instructors determine the course length (one-hour to multiday) as well as your family's goals and how they will be met.

The program also offers Adventure Camp for kids 13 to 18. This five-day course (days only) teaches teens about safety, leadership, and rock ecology, besides climbing skills. Some climbs take place on cliffs along the north shore of Lake Superior. For teens aged 13 to 16 who aren't sure which outdoor skill they most want to learn, a five-day Sampler includes climbing, kayaking, sailing, and canoeing, as well as instruction in leadership, teamwork, and the natural history of the region. If these options appeal to your family, parents can sign up for courses of their own and meet their children at the university at the end of each day.

🏔 *Vertical Pursuits, Outdoor Program, University of Minnesota at Duluth, 121 Sports and Health Center, 10 University Dr., Duluth, MN 55812, tel. 218/726–6533. Late May–Aug.: 1–5 days, $50–$265.*

Wilderness Connection

👫 13+, 4+

Wind, weather, and time have eroded the outcroppings of California's Joshua Tree National Monument into boulder gardens of arresting beauty. The rocks draw climbers and many other visitors, although the thousands of Joshua trees that gave the monument its name are striking in their own right. From mid-September to mid-June, Wilderness Connection will teach you in Joshua Tree. From mid-June to mid-September, lessons take place at Suicide and Tahquintz rocks, 7,000 feet up in the cool pine forests of the San Jacinto Mountains above Palm Springs. Both areas are less than 50 miles from Palm Springs and about three hours from San Diego and Los Angeles.

FOR FAMILIES. Ages 13 and up can participate in any of the regular courses. The basic 2-day rock seminar is most popular with beginners, but there are also three-, four-, and five-day seminars. Women's Rock Camp, a possible choice for mothers and daughters, is three to five days of climbing designed just for women. The student/teacher ratio is generally four to four.

Families with children as young as 4 or 5 can arrange private guiding and instruction, tailoring the course to your family's needs. For groups of six or more, there's also Rock Climbing Experience (ages 4 or 5 and up welcome), which gives you private instruction at a very family-friendly rate. Wilderness Connections supplies rock shoes for courses and will give students the names and numbers of motels and campgrounds near the climbing sites.

🏠 *Wilderness Connection, Box 29, Joshua Tree, CA 92252–0029, tel. 619/366–4745 or 800/890–4745. Year-round: 1–5 days, $45–$420.*

Yamnuska, Inc.

👫 **14+, 6+**

Canmore, on the boundary of Banff National Park in Alberta, was once a mining town supplying coal to the railroad. Now it serves as a base for many recreational activities in the nearby mountains. The majestic Canadian Rockies provide plenty of challenges to the new or experienced climber, and many rewards, too. From the international airport at Calgary, it's an easy drive to Canmore and also to the mighty interior ranges of British Columbia, where Yamnuska schedules some of its trips. If your family has never visited the Canadian Rockies, this is the way to do it.

FOR FAMILIES. Parents and kids aged 14 and up are welcomed on weekend courses. Basic Rock, Basic Rock Plus, and Advanced Rock are all two- to three-day courses. Complete Rock is five days of intensive instruction; talk to the school about your teen before signing up for this more adult-oriented course. Yamnuska also has extensive private instruction, which it highly recommends for families. If your children are at least 6, you can schedule private guiding and courses in and around Banff, Canmore, and Lake Louise, all areas that have much to offer visitors whether they're climbing or not. There's reasonably priced lodging in Banff and Canmore; in the mountains, Yamnuska often uses huts that are available to its clients at nominal rates. Rock shoes can be rented, but not in very small sizes.

🏠 *Yamnuska, Inc. Box 1920, 1316 Railway Ave., Canmore T0L 0M0, Alberta, Canada, tel. 403/678–4164. May–Sept.: 1–6 days, $85–$550.*

Zoar Outdoor

👫 **7+**

Cool, densely forested, and green, the Berkshire Mountains of Massachusetts have several excellent climbing locations and are one of the most popular vacation destinations in the eastern United States. Zoar's 80-acre complex in Charlemont, in the far northwest corner of the state, is just a short drive from Chapel and Rose ledges, two excellent places for families to learn together. Zoar's experience working with families and kids is extensive, and the school truly welcomes them in classes.

FOR FAMILIES. Rock climbing clinics come in one- or two-day sessions, aimed at ages 7 through adult. The beginner clinics, with a student/teacher ratio of six to one, teach the basic skills needed for climbing behind an experienced leader. Private instruction is also available. You can stay in Zoar's campground for a nominal fee (using your equipment or theirs), or they'll help you book lodging at a nearby motel, inn, or bed-and-breakfast.

🏠 *Zoar Outdoor, Box 254, Charlemont, MA 01339, tel. 617/339–4010 or 800/532–7483. May–Oct.: $90–$170.*

Resources

Organizations

The **American Mountain Guides Association** (AMGA; 710 10th St., Suite 101, Golden, CO 80401, tel. 303/271–0984) can send you a list of accredited schools and certified guides across the country.

The address of the international guides' association, **Union Internationalle Associa-**

tion **Guide Montagne** (UIAGM), changes with each president, but you can write to the Vaud chapter president, Rene Pavillard (brother of Jean Pavillard of Adventures to the Edge), at Box 26, 1854 Leysin, Vaud, Switzerland. He'll answer your questions or forward correspondence to the proper office.

Periodicals

Climbing (1101 Village Rd., Suite LL-1-B, Carbondale, CO 81623, tel. 970/963–9449) publishes eight issues a year and occasionally has articles on family climbing and introducing children to the sport.

RV ADVENTURES

When our children were 1, 5, and 11 years old, Bill and I piled them into a 27-foot motor home and traveled from Virginia to Florida and back, stopping at campgrounds each night. More recently, we tested a 29-foot recreational vehicle (familiarly known as an RV), covering eight heartland states in 16 days. My children rank these among their best vacations ever. Next time we'd like to explore several national parks, with plenty of hiking, rafting, and riding along the way. We might stay in organized campgrounds or we might park where there's not another soul around. RVs give you plenty of options.

Recreational vehicles are ideal for family vacations, including intergenerational trips with grandparents. Young families are the fastest-growing segment of the RV population, and with good reason: RVs get you into the outdoors and the wilderness safely and easily. Very young children who are unfamiliar with sleeping bags, latrines, and tents in the middle of the woods may feel more at ease in an RV than at a backcountry campsite. Similarly, although some grandparents are uncomfortable backpacking and tent camping, they are likely to appreciate the physical comfort of an RV adventure. Families with infants can take a two-week camping trip and still have a way to refrigerate and warm formula or baby food. For parents who worry that a toddler might wake up and wander away from a tent in the middle of the night, RVs have doors that lock.

Many campgrounds that welcome RVs offer spacious wilderness surroundings and privacy; some are veritable outdoor resorts, with a restaurant, hiking trails, fishing, boating, and swimming. Some have hookups that allow you to use the campground's water and electrical supplies; others are remote sites providing only a relatively level spot in a spectacular setting.

Because different kinds of places appeal to different people, this chapter describes a range of RV destinations: national parks, forests, and monuments; state parks; and private campgrounds. The selections are based on my family's experience and the opinions of other seasoned RV travelers. Keep in mind that there's no reason a family has to stay at the same type of campground every night. You can opt for a full-service RV resort one night; the next evening you might camp in a wilderness area with nature's own amenities—a sky full of stars and a peaceful, welcoming solitude.

Questions to Ask

Where can I rent or buy an RV? There are RV dealers across the country; many have both sales and rental departments. Look under "Recreation Vehicles—Renting and Leasing" in the yellow pages for the sources nearest you. For a complete listing of dealers, contact any of the RV organizations listed in Resources (see *below*), such as Go Camping America or the Recreation Vehicle Rental Association.

What kinds of RVs are best? There are many options. Some families prefer motor homes, all-in-one vehicles that range in length from 17 to 40 feet. In a motor home you can get snacks and use the bathroom without having to stop and search for a gas station or restaurant. (Children and adults should always be buckled into seat belts or car seats when the vehicle is in motion.) Alternatively, you might choose a pop-up, which you tow with your car by day and literally pop up into a spacious and well-equipped camper at night; beds, bathroom, and often a refrigerator and air conditioner are included. A pop-up gives you a bit more freedom to explore with your car, but you have to set up camp each night. Truck campers (those fitted onto the bed of a pickup truck) and full-size travel trailers (fully equipped trailer homes you tow) are also available. Prices vary greatly according to size of the vehicle and, if you're renting, the season. In general, pop-ups and truck campers are the least expensive to rent; full-size motor homes are the most expensive option.

How far in advance is it necessary to reserve? Summer is the most popular time for RV vacations; rental companies may well be out of the vehicle you want on a particular week unless you book several months in advance. Still, cancellations do occur, so it pays to keep calling.

Are RVs allowed in all campgrounds? No, but they are welcome in most. At some sites, especially publicly owned campgrounds, there may be a size limit for RVs. Listings in campground directories and government campground publications often mention the maximum length allowed; read the specifications carefully.

What kind of gas mileage do RVs get? If you're driving a motor home, 6 to 12 miles per gallon is possible; about 8 miles per gallon is typical. Pulling a car or boat behind your RV will decrease your mileage. Other factors affecting mileage are your vehicle's engine size and capabilities, the type of terrain, and the weight of the RV. Pulling a pop-up or trailer home with your car will affect your gas mileage, too.

What service is available in the case of a breakdown? Before your trip, find out whether or not your RV rental company has breakdown insurance or a roadside help policy that will cover you. You might also consider joining the Good Sam Club (see Resources, *below*), which offers road service for RVs.

How is sewage disposal handled? Dumping waste is easier than it sounds. When you pick up your rental RV, you'll learn how to attach a hose to a campground's sewer hookups and how to flush the waste by loosening and tightening valves. Keep a pair of gloves handy for handling the waste hose. If you stay at a campground without sewer hookups, eventually you will have to stop at a campground with a dump station and pay a fee of a few dollars to empty your waste tanks. A good campground directory (see Resources, *below*) will tell you where to find dump stations.

What is the electrical source in an RV, and can it be tapped only when the RV is parked? Most campgrounds have electrical hookups—outlets into which you plug the RV's heavy-duty electrical cord. If there are no hookups, you switch on the generator found in most RVs. With few exceptions, the only time you'll need your generator while you're driving is if you use the microwave or the water pump (either to make the sink faucet run or to flush the toilet), or if you're driving in a very hot or very cold area and need additional air-conditioning or heat. At night, in a campground without hookups, you'll use the generator for all of the above and for lights. Most campgrounds have a quiet time, usually starting at 10 PM, after which you cannot use generators because of their noise. In most modern RVs, the refrigerator and stove work on propane, so even when you're parked and the generator is off, your refrigerator will stay cool and you'll be able to cook a late-night meal. Most rental RVs come with full propane tanks; you can purchase more propane in many campgrounds.

If I'm renting a pop-up and towing it with my car, do I need a special hitch? Some companies can supply what you need; others require that you purchase a low-cost part. Ask before you rent.

What's included in the cost of a rental? This varies widely, so shop around. Generally speaking, you get the vehicle at a daily or weekly rate, plus a mileage allowance—typically 100 miles per day. Beyond these basics, there are many variations. Bedding packages, for example, are available from some suppliers; dishes, silverware, and pots and pans may or may not cost extra. Some suppliers have CD players, TVs, and VCRs, which give antsy kids something to watch when they can't see out the window at night. Before renting an RV, consider the options and your needs, then judge the prices accordingly.

What's included in the cost of a campground? Campgrounds charge per RV site. The base rate is generally for two adults and does not include hookups. Another $1 or $2 per night is added for water and electricity, and sewage hookups cost an additional $2–$3. A nominal fee is charged for children—typically $2–$4 per night. Most campgrounds let very young children stay for free, although the age cutoff varies widely. If you're camping in a national park, a national monument, or a state park, you will also be required to pay an entrance fee, separate from the campground fee. If your family plans to visit a number of national parks and monuments, consider buying a Golden Eagle Passport, which costs only $25 and covers the entrance fees to as many parks as you visit during a year. These passes are available by mail from some regional park service offices, or you can buy one at any park with an entrance fee. Golden Age ($10, for visitors who are at least 62) and Golden Access (free for people with disabilities) passes must be purchased in person. These have no expiration date.

Instruction

Most rental companies will show you how to work everything before you leave in your vehicle. RVs aren't hard to drive, but they take a little getting used to. If you've never driven an RV, ask for pointers on how to back up, how to hook up the electrical and water lines at campgrounds, and how to dump waste water. Make certain you also know how the generator works, and listen to safety instructions about which switches must be shut off when you stop for gas.

Finding the Fun

Northeast: Lake Placid/Whiteface Mountain KOA. **Mid-Atlantic:** Shenandoah National Park. **South:** Chattahoochee National Forest, Cherokee/Great Smokies KOA, Everglades National Park, Great Smoky Mountains National Park, Mammoth Cave National Park. **Midwest:** Porcupine Mountains Wilderness State Park, Rafter J Bar Ranch Campground. **Southwest:** Lake Powell Resorts & Marinas, Palo Duro Canyon State Park. **Rockies:** Colorado National Monument, Great Sand Dunes National Monument. **West Coast:** Big Bear Shores RV Resort & Yacht Club, Joshua Tree National Monument. **Alaska:** Denali National Park, Denali/McKinley KOA. **Canada:** Burnaby Cariboo RV Park.

Favorite RV Destinations

Northeast

Lake Placid/Whiteface Mountain KOA

 ALL

Kampgrounds of America, known far and wide as KOA, is a national chain of campgrounds. KOAs are privately owned but must meet standards set by the national headquarters, so certain features and facilities remain consistent. All are family-friendly, and prices are reasonable—even more so if you get a KOA Value Kard (see Resources, *below*). Showers and rest rooms are clean and well maintained; you can generally find a playground and a well-stocked store and/or a snack bar; and there are almost always outdoor activities for families. Pools, lakes, or streams are quite common, and KOAs generally welcome pets.

The Lake Placid/Whiteface Mt. KOA is an excellent choice for families visiting northern New York. Just 9 miles northeast of the town of Lake Placid, in the heart of Adirondack Park and the ancient Adirondack Mountains, this 85-acre campground gives you access to many outdoor adventures. Although the facility is not remote, its pine and white birch forest setting at the base of Whiteface Mountain is splendid.

FOR FAMILIES. In the summer you can hike or fish right at the campground along a half-mile stretch of the Ausable River, famous for its trout. Other campground activities are canoeing, tennis, miniature golf, swimming, hot tubbing, and, in winter, cross-country skiing. A choice of full and partial hookup and non-hookup sites (144 in all) gives families plenty of options.

Adirondack Park is an excellent place for hiking, rock climbing, and multiday canoe adventures; there's also great skiing on Whiteface Mountain. Lake Placid has hosted the Winter Games twice, and the Olympic facilities are well worth touring.

🏨 *Lake Placid/Whiteface Mt. KOA, Fox Farm Rd., Wilmington, NY 12997, tel. 518/946–*

7878 or 800/496–0238 (reservations only).
Year-round: $19–$33 per night.

Mid-Atlantic

Shenandoah National Park

 ALL

National parks are among the most popular
RV camping destinations. All are excellent
for families on adventures, but some parks
have special appeal for RVers. One of these
is Shenandoah, which lies along a breathtaking stretch of the Blue Ridge Mountains in
northwestern Virginia. Within the park, the
105-mile-long Skyline Drive follows the
crest of the mountains and is arguably one
of the most scenic roads in America, and a
must for RVs.

FOR FAMILIES. Big Meadows Campground, site of one of the park's two visitor
centers, is among the most popular campgrounds in the park; reservations are essential between May and October. There's a
restaurant at Big Meadows and access to
the Appalachian Trail. Three other campgrounds—Matthew's Arm, Lewis Mountain,
and Loft Mountain—have sites available on a
first-come, first-served basis. None of the
campgrounds has hookups.

Throughout the park there are excellent
opportunities for hiking, fishing, and bird-
watching. Ranger-led family campfire programs in the summer give children and parents insight into the natural world of
Shenandoah.
*Shenandoah National Park, Superinten-
dent, Rte. 4, Box 348, Luray, VA 22835, tel.
703/999–2266. Big Meadows Reservations,
Destinet, Box 85705, San Diego, CA 92138,
tel. 800/365–2267. Mar.–Oct.: $10–$14 per
night, plus park entrance fee.*

The South

Chattahoochee National Forest

 ALL

The many national forests scattered
throughout the United States are another
terrific camping option for RVing families.
Although most have true wilderness settings, it's not unusual for a national forest
campground to be close to a major city,
near well-maintained roads; such is the case
with Chattahoochee National Forest. This
wild land of deep gorges and rushing water
lies just over 100 miles north of Atlanta,
close to the Tennessee and North Carolina
borders. The Appalachian Mountains in
northern Georgia are untamed but remarkably accessible.

FOR FAMILIES. Lake Conasauga Campground is within Chattahoochee National
Forest, about 4 miles north of the town of
Chatsworth. An extensive network of hiking
trails readily accessible from local roads
makes this area ideal for RV adventures. The
70 campsites have no hookups, but the
campground has what most families love—a
lake. No motors are allowed on the water,
so you can fish, boat, and swim in peace.
This is a primitive campground with no
amenities—just gorgeous scenery to
explore and enjoy.
*Chattahoochee National Forest, Cohutta
Ranger District, 401 Old Ellijay Rd.,
Chatsworth, GA 30705, tel. 706/695–6736.
Apr.–Oct.: $5 per night.*

Cherokee/Great Smokies KOA

 ALL

This KOA is in Cherokee, North Carolina, at
the gateway to Great Smoky Mountains
National Park (see below). If you want to
take a break from exploring wilderness or

America's highways, you can spend a couple of days here taking advantage of all that's at your RV's doorstep. Between activities at the campground and excursions to the park and the town of Cherokee, your family will have plenty to do.

FOR FAMILIES. At the campground, three stocked trout ponds provide a perfect outlet for the youngest anglers; you can rent fishing poles at the KOA store. Among the other facilities are a playground, tennis courts, a pool and a river for swimming, and a hot tub. Most of the 430 sites have hookups. For those who want to leave their RVs parked and set up, the campground has shuttle service into the national park.

Besides outdoor recreation, families can experience the cultural aspect of the area, which has long been inhabited by the Cherokee. A short drive from the campground are many Native American institutions and sites, including the Cherokee Heritage Museum and Gallery, with an interpretive center that focuses on tribal culture and history; the Oconaluftee Indian Village, a replica of a native village of about 250 years ago; and the Museum of the Cherokee Indian. All give families valuable information about the Cherokee people's past, present, and future.
🏠 *Cherokee/Great Smokies KOA, Star Rte. 39, Cherokee, NC 28719, tel. 704/497–9711 or 800/825–8352 (reservations only). Year-round: $16.50–$28 per night.*

Everglades National Park

Not all national parks are summer destinations. In fact, although Everglades National Park in southern Florida is open year-round, the best time to visit it is in late fall or winter, when insects are not a problem and the heat and humidity are quite bearable. Renting an RV is also less expensive in winter, so if savings are important to your family, a win-

ter RV trip to Everglades National Park may be rewarding in many ways.

FOR FAMILIES. Encompassing 1.4 million acres of marsh, Everglades National Park is a fragile ecosystem supporting an astonishingly diverse population of plants and animals; children of all ages will find it intriguing. Though much of the park is accessible only by boat, land activities—such as hiking, birdwatching, and interpretive programs—are also highlights. Rangers give talks throughout the year, but these are far more frequent in the winter months.

Flamingo Campground in the park has no hookup facilities or hot showers, but it is at the southern entrance to the Everglades and is the site of one of the park's visitor centers. The 340 campsites are assigned on a first-come, first-served basis. Campers can explore adjacent hiking trails and rent canoes or skiffs for water-based exploration.
🏠 *Everglades National Park, Superintendent, 40001 State Rd. 9336, Homestead, FL 33034, tel. 305/242–7700; Flamingo Campground, tel. 305/247–6211. Year-round: $8 per night, plus park entrance fees.*

Great Smoky Mountains National Park

👫 ALL

Because the Smokies are a wonderful—and popular—family destination, it pays to know more than one camping option (see Cherokee/Great Smokies KOA, *above*). Families who want to concentrate on Great Smoky Mountains National Park, which straddles North Carolina and Tennessee, may find that staying inside the park is the best way to experience it fully.

FOR FAMILIES. The park's verdant deciduous forests shelter more than 1,500 types of flowering plants, as well as bears and other wildlife. If your children love flowers, and if they have even a remote interest in birds, this is the place to be. There are nature walks and interpretive programs for all ages. You can also ride horses on well-maintained trails. Although the park merits a visit on its own, your family can combine a stay with other adventures that take place nearby; the Canoeing, Kayaking, Rock Climbing, and Trekking with Llamas, Goats, and Burros chapters of this book all list outfitters in the vicinity.

Three of the park's 10 campgrounds—Elkmont, Cades Cove, and Smokemont—are on the Destinet (formerly MISTIX) system and can be reserved in advance. The rest take campers on a first-come, first-served basis. None of the park's campgrounds has hookups or showers; plan to fill your water tank before arriving so you can shower, cook, and use the bathroom in your RV.
🏕 *Great Smoky Mountains National Park, Superintendent, 107 Park Headquarters Rd., Gatlinburg, TN 37738, tel. 423/436–1200. Year-round: $6–$11 per night, plus park entrance fees.*

Mammoth Cave National Park

(👫 **ALL**)

Here's a national park with a single focus—the Mammoth Cave. The longest cave system in the world, Mammoth extends for more than 300 miles, and much of it remains unexplored. Most parents don't feel experienced enough to take their children caving on their own, but at Mammoth you can combine an RV trip with a highly informative guided caving adventure.

FOR FAMILIES. If the huge vertical shafts and eerie underground rivers don't impress your children, the strange inhabitants of the caves surely will; these include eyeless fish, white spiders, and blind beetles. Exploring the caves with park rangers is the main event here; cave walks of various lengths and varying degrees of difficulty make it possible for almost anyone to visit, and some tours are designed especially for children.

For those who prefer to stay above ground, the park has backcountry hiking trails, guided nature walks, summer interpretive programs, and boating.

None of the four park campgrounds has hookups, and three do not take reservations. If your family likes to plan ahead, you can make reservations for the Maple Springs Group Campground through the chief ranger's office.
🏕 *Mammoth Cave National Park, Mammoth Cave, KY 42259, tel. 502/758–2328. For cave tours ($5.50–$25), contact Destinet, Box 85705, San Diego, CA 92138, tel. 800/967–2283. Year-round (all stores and services not open every month): $6 per night; there's no entrance fee to the park.*

Midwest

Porcupine Mountains Wilderness State Park

(👫 **ALL**)

State parks are an excellent camping choice for families with RVs. Some are primarily back-to-nature experiences with little in the way of amenities, which suits those families looking for a great place to camp in the woods. Porcupine Mountains Wilderness State Park is just such a place—a 63,000-acre wilderness area on the northwest end of Michigan's Upper Peninsula, not far from the Wisconsin border.

FOR FAMILIES. Otters, bears, coyotes, grouse, deer, and bald eagles all make their home among the forests, streams, and mountains here. Humans, too, are in evidence, hiking the trails in spring, summer, and fall, and cross-country skiing in winter. Fishing, swimming, and picnicking are other prime activities in the park, or your family can spend time simply relishing the sight of deep gorges and awesome waterfalls. Union Bay Campground has 100 sites with electrical hookups; Presque Isle Campground has 90 sites and no hookups.

🏠 *Porcupine Mountains Wilderness State Park, 412 S. Boundary, Ontonagon, MI 49953, tel. 906/885–5275. Year-round: $6–$10 per night.*

Rafter J Bar Ranch Campground

(🧍🧍 **ALL**)

The Rafter J Bar is a Holiday Trav-L-Park campground, a national chain similar to Kampgrounds of America (see Resources, *below*). Like many private campgrounds, it's a destination in itself, a place traveling families can stay put for a couple of days—or longer—and enjoy a campground as they would a hotel or resort. There's plenty to bring families to this area, though: South Dakota's Black Hills, in which the J Bar Rafter is set, are filled with history, legends, and adventure opportunities (see Panning for Gold, Rock Climbing, *and* Covered Wagon Adventures). The ranch is an easy drive from Mt. Rushmore, Crazy Horse Monument, Wind Cave National Park, Mammoth Site of Hot Springs, and Custer State Park.

FOR FAMILIES. The Rafter J Bar sits at 5,200 feet among wooded, rolling hills. Large meadows separate five camping areas that are shaded by ponderosa pines; more than half of the 258 sites have full or partial hookups. For swimmers there's a pool and a hot tub, and four lakes are a short distance from the ranch. Guests can rent bikes; they can also ride horses on a trail in the Black Hills National Forest. Those too young for the trail have supervised pony rides at the campground and use the playground. A trout stream on the property entices anglers of all ages; bring your own poles. Rental cars are available for guests who want to explore while leaving their RV parked and hooked up.

🏠 *Rafter J Bar Ranch, Box 128, Hill City, SD 57745, tel. 605/574–2527. May–Oct.: $16–$26 per night.*

Southwest

Lake Powell Resorts & Marinas

(🧍🧍 **ALL**)

These campgrounds are less important for what they have than where they are—on the shores of Lake Powell. This 186-mile-long stretch of brilliant blue, banked by imposing red rock formations and sandy beaches, starts just below the Arizona border and extends well into Utah. Families come to Lake Powell from all over the country to try their hands at piloting a houseboat (see Houseboating) and to explore other parts of the Glen Canyon National Recreation Area, which covers more than a million acres. At almost all the campgrounds, families can combine RVing with boating and hiking adventures.

FOR FAMILIES. Lake Powell Resorts & Marinas operates several National Park Service campgrounds and its own private campgrounds in the same general locations: Wahweap, Bullfrog, and Hall's Crossing. The park service sites are primitive, with no hookups, and there are no reservations allowed, but the campgrounds do have interpretive programs by rangers throughout the summer. The private campgrounds accept reservations and have full services and full hookups.

At the southern end of the lake, near Page, Arizona, are the Wahweap campgrounds. The company runs a lodge here, as well as a marina that sells groceries and camping supplies. This is one place you can rent a houseboat and set out to explore the lake. The park service visitor center in this area has exhibits to intrigue all ages.

At Hall's Crossing and Bullfrog, both at the lake's midpoint but on opposite shores, there are marinas; Bullfrog has a visitor center. You can rent houseboats at these marinas, too. The ferry between the two takes RVs.

In addition to standard services at all the marinas, there are good-value RV packages that combine two nights at camp with boat tours or houseboat rentals. You can also make reservations for Colorado River rafting and float trips through this company.

 Lake Powell Resorts & Marinas, Box 56909, Phoenix, AZ 85079, tel. 602/278-8888 or 800/528–6154. Year-round: $15.10–$27.90 per night (RV spaces only); 2-night RV/3-night houseboat rental packages, $312–$1,084, depending on season and size of boat.

Palo Duro Canyon State Park

ALL

In the middle of the horizon-to-horizon desolation of the Texas panhandle, about 18 miles south of Amarillo, Palo Duro Canyon is an improbable paradise of all-encompassing beauty. At 110 miles long, the canyon is one of the largest in the country, and it will intrigue even those who thought they had no interest in geology. Its bottom layer of rock matches the top layer of the Grand Canyon; if you set Palo Duro on top of the Grand Canyon, every known geologic layer of the earth would be represented. There is more here than canyon walls of muted purple, red, and gold, though: Palo Duro State Park combines an extraordinary landscape with a multitude of services and amenities.

FOR FAMILIES. You can camp in a variety of places in the canyon's bottomland. Cottonwoods, grasslands, and the Prairie Dog Town Fork of the Red River create shady, pleasant spots from which to explore. Of the seven camping areas with about 100 sites for RVs and tents, some have electricity and water; others just have water. There are hiking and mountain biking trails, and you can rent bikes at the park's trading post. The Lighthouse Hiking Trail is several miles up and back, but very young children can walk

on the first part of it. Be alert for interesting creatures along the way—you might even see tarantulas in their native habitat.

For a moderate fee you can take a trail ride on horseback or—a favorite of young children—a ride on the Sad Monkey Railroad, a miniature steam train named for the rock formation it winds past. Ask the engineer to point out the remains of the oft-photographed juniper tree that was thought to be at least 500 years old when it died. If you have older children who can stay up late, don't miss the summer production of *Texas!* at the amphitheater. The canyon walls serve as a backdrop, and a brilliant fireworks display ends the show.

 Palo Duro Canyon State Park, Rte. 2, Box 285, Canyon, TX 79015, tel. 806/488–2227 or 512/389–8900 (reservations only). Year-round: $12 per night, plus entrance to park.

Rockies

Colorado National Monument

ALL

Administered by the park service, national monuments range from natural landmarks to man-made structures and sites of historical importance. The Colorado National Monument falls under the first category: Vast canyons, towering monoliths, and unusual rock formations create compelling vistas at this often overlooked site near Grand Junction. Hikers, bikers, and rock climbers find challenges in and near the monument. It's also a favorite among dinosaur lovers, who come to the area to participate in digging expeditions at nearby Mygatt-Moore Quarry and to visit the superb Devil's Canyon Science & Learning Center (see Digging for Dinosaur Bones and Other Fossils). Families with a variety of ages and interests will enjoy the monument for its own sake, however, and for its campground high above the canyon floor, on the scenic rim drive.

FOR FAMILIES. Peace and quiet abound at the 5,800-foot-high Saddlehorn Campground, a relatively primitive campground with just a few RV sites, no hookups, and no showers. The campground does not accept reservations. Hikers of all abilities will find plenty of trails leading down from the canyon rim; the hardy can hike from the canyon floor up. For families with very young children, an excellent, easy nature walk of about a half mile begins at the visitor center, just down the road from the campground on the rim drive. Another hike popular with families ends at Devil's Kitchen, a canyon formation that looks like a huge red-rock kitchen, complete with appliances. You can reach that trail from the lower road.

🏕 *Colorado National Monument, Superintendent, Fruita, CO 81521, tel. 303/858–3617. Year-round: $8 per night, plus entrance fee.*

Great Sand Dunes National Monument

(👫 **ALL**)

At the base of the jagged Sangre de Cristo Mountains in south central Colorado are the 700-foot-high dunes of the Great Sand Dunes National Monument. Because they rise from a base of 5,000 feet above sea level, these are the highest dunes in the world—and a unique playground for families. The campground of the monument provides a very different perspective from that at Colorado National Monument (see above), one from which you look up, not down, for the best views.

FOR FAMILIES. You can hike for miles, find places to be alone, and play in Medena Creek at the monument—but you probably won't be able to get your children to do anything but jump like crazy around the dunes. Although there are interpretive talks and nature activities throughout the summer, the ideal time to visit is in late spring and early summer, before the creek dries up. It's best to walk on the dunes in the

early morning and late afternoon—they're often too hot in the middle of the day. Snowshoeing and cross-country skiing are popular here in the winter.

Pinyon Flats Campground, the only one right in the monument, has about 44 RV sites, but not all the spaces can accommodate vehicles of every size. Although there are no hookups and no reservations, this is one place where you don't want to settle for a campground outside the monument. The fun is definitely right here. For more information on other activities, such as Jeep tours, check out the visitor center on U.S. 150.

🏕 *Great Sand Dunes National Monument, 11999 U.S. 150, Mosca, CO 81146, tel. 719/378–2312. Year-round: $8 per night, plus an entrance fee May–Oct.*

West Coast

Big Bear Shores RV Resort & Yacht Club

(👫 **ALL**)

This is an excellent example of a private campground right in the middle of a national forest. California's huge San Bernardino National Forest stretches from the city of San Bernardino to Palm Springs and encompasses several wilderness areas, ski areas, mountains, and lakes. The campground is in Big Bear Lake, a resort town that has become a year-round community with an emphasis on outdoor activities.

FOR FAMILIES. At Big Bear Shores RV Resort, guests can indulge in lake and pool swimming, hot tubbing, boating (rentals are available), and fishing. In winter, snowmobile trails and skiing bring families back, so you can use your RV year-round here. There are 170 sites with hookups.

🏕 *Big Bear Shores RV Resort & Yacht Club, 40751 North Shore Dr., Big Bear Lake, CA 92313, tel. 909/866–4151. Year-round: $39–$49 per night.*

Joshua Tree National Monument

 ALL

Joshua Tree National Monument in California is most appealing in what is off-season for many other areas: Because of extreme weather conditions (heat and wind), the best times to visit are February to April and October to December. The monument, about 140 miles east of Los Angeles, covers more than 970 square miles and preserves sections of two deserts—the Mojave and the Colorado. Rock climbers from all over the world test their skills on mountains that rise from the desert to heights of 1,000 to 6,000 feet (see Rock Climbing), and hikers are rewarded on a multitude of magnificent trails. Joshua Tree is a natural for an RV adventure: The only way to cover most of this vast area is by private vehicle, and there's no better means of transport for family exploration than an RV.

FOR FAMILIES. Six of the eight campgrounds are free and available on a first-come, first-served basis. There's a charge for Cottonwood Springs and Black Rock Canyon campgrounds, and only Black Rock takes reservations; if you're a plan-ahead type family, that's probably your best choice. All the campgrounds have access to the trees, trails, and rocks that make the monument unique. Campers must have their own water and firewood at all campgrounds, so fill your RV's water tank before arriving and check your propane tanks if you're planning on cooking inside instead of using firewood.

You can pick up trail maps and other information at the visitor center, just north of the Twentynine Palms entrance. Families with young children should check out the Hidden Valley Nature Trail, a mile-long loop enclosed by a wall of rocks; the trail starts near Hidden Valley Campground. Other easy trails begin near the White Tank, Cottonwood Springs, and Black Rock Canyon campgrounds. Fortynine Palms Canyon (not

far from the Twentynine Palms entrance) and Lost Palms Canyon (near Cottonwood Springs campground) are reached by way of mostly moderate trails, but allow several hours for these hikes. Look for desert tortoises along the trails. In spring and fall there are guided hikes and campfire programs.

🏠 *Joshua Tree National Monument, Superintendent, 74485 Monument Dr., Twentynine Palms, CA, 92277, tel. 619/367–7511. Year-round: $8–$10 per night, plus entrance fees.*

Alaska

Denali National Park

 ALL

For many travelers, Denali is synonymous with Alaska—huge, untamed, and full of adventure. Within the park's 6 million acres is 20,320-foot Mt. McKinley, or Denali, as the native people call it; yet the moose, grizzly bears, and caribou that roam closer to the earth—and to a child's vantage point—may seem even more impressive to young visitors. If your family is ready to brave the wildness that makes Denali so awesome, camp inside the park and let its spirit seep into your soul.

FOR FAMILIES. Wildlife viewing, hiking, interpretive walks and talks, cross-country skiing, and dogsledding are all possible in Denali, though these activities are appropriate for different ages. Camping in the park, however, is an experience for children and adults alike, as long as you're not looking for services and amenities. Riley Creek, Savage River, and Teklanika are the only three campgrounds accessible by vehicle. Riley Creek has the best facilities, including a store—but none of the campgrounds has hookups, and reservations are not taken.

🏠 *Denali National Park, Superintendent, Box 9, Denali Park, AK 99755, tel. 907/683–2294. Year-round (all facilities not open all year): $12 per night, plus entrance fee.*

Denali/McKinley KOA

(👫 ALL)

A trip to Alaska doesn't have to mean primitive backcountry camping, and there are many reasons to choose an organized campground with full facilities rather than a remote, primitive site in such a rugged area. Families traveling with very young children or grandparents, and those with little camping experience, may do better with the comfort and security of private campgrounds. Perhaps most important, you can make reservations at private campgrounds so that you'll never end up stranded. However, many families enjoy both wilderness campsites and organized, private campgrounds. There's a place for both—often on the same trip.

FOR FAMILIES. The Denali/McKinley KOA, about 10 miles north of the park entrance, is surrounded by all the beauty Denali has to offer. Guests spend most days in the park, then return in the evenings to hot showers, a store, flush toilets, firewood, and good company. You can play miniature golf or take in a nightly family movie, and there's a recreation room, too. Kids under 17 stay free at this popular campground, but reservations are highly recommended for the 90 sites.
🏕 *Denali/McKinley KOA, Mile 248.5, Box 340, Healy, AK 99743, tel. 907/683–2379 or 800/478–2562. May–Sept: $18.25–$26 per night.*

Canada

Burnaby Cariboo RV Park

(👫 ALL)

Urban campgrounds like this one are used by many adventure-oriented families as convenient meeting places for groups preparing to travel into wilderness areas. Vancouver is particularly appealing because it offers easy access to many Canadian adventures, as well as outdoor activities within the city limits.

The famous Capilano Suspension Bridge, for example, stretches 450 feet across and 230 feet above the Capilano River; walking across it is not for the faint of heart. Lynn Canyon Park, in North Vancouver, has miles of easy and rugged hiking trails as well as a suspension bridge of its own, hanging some 20 stories above Lynn Creek. Grouse Mountain, just 15 minutes from downtown, has hiking trails, a tram that hikers can ride to alpine meadows, rivers for gold panning, and, in winter, sleigh rides and skiing. Visitors can also learn about Native American influences in Lynn Canyon Park and Grouse Mountain. Vancouver Island, much of it unpopulated wilderness area, is popular for many outdoor activities and adventures and is easily accessible by ferry from the city of Vancouver.

FOR FAMILIES. Burnaby Cariboo RV Park, a private RV park with 217 sites, lies within Greater Vancouver and yet is surrounded by the 400-acre Burnaby Lake Regional Park, where bird-watching and walking are favorite family pastimes. This park has an equestrian center and a nature center with activities for families, too. A full-service, first-class facility, Burnaby Cariboo has a pool, hot tub, playground, and other amenities; it also has a tour service that will help you book guided fishing tours and other adventures.
🏕 *Burnaby Cariboo RV Park, 8765 Cariboo Pl., Burnaby V3N 4T2, British Columbia, Canada, tel. 604/420–1722. Year-round: $23–$30 per night.*

Resources

Organizations

National Park Service (Office of Public Inquiries, National Park Service, Department of the Interior, Room 1013, Washington, D.C. 20013–7127, tel. 202/208–4747) will send a general information kit on the parks and monuments. To make reservations at the campgrounds that accept them, call **Destinet** at 800/365–2267. The **U.S. Forest Service** (Office of Information, Box 96090, Washington, DC 20090, tel. 202/205–1760) can give you information about national forest campgrounds. To make reservations for these campgrounds, call 800/280–2267 at least 10 days in advance of the date you have in mind.

Go Camping America (Box 2669, Dept. 23, Reston, VA 22090, tel. 800/477–8669) will send you a free booklet with information on RV campgrounds, rentals, and trip planning. It also has a comprehensive listing of RV-related organizations and services.

The Good Sam Club (Box 6060, Camarillo, CA 93011, tel. 805/389–0300) offers a wide array of services for RVers, including a road service similar to what AAA offers car drivers, mail forwarding, insurance, travel information, and organized trips.

Recreation Vehicle Rental Association (3930 University Dr., Fairfax, VA 22030, tel. 703/591–7130 or 800/336–0355) has a directory with more than 250 listings of American and Canadian dealers who rent all types of RVs. It is available free when you order *Rental Ventures,* a guide to renting RVs. **Cruise America** (11 West Hampton Ave., Mesa, AZ 85210, tel. 602/262–9611 or 800/327–7799, for reservations only) and **Go Vacations Inc.** (777 W. 190th St., Gardena, CA 90248, tel. 310/329–8999) are two nationwide rental organizations. Both have fly-and-drive options that allow you to pick up your rental in the area where you'll be traveling. In Canada, **CanaDream** (510 1212-31 Avenue NE, Calgary T2E 7S8, Alberta, tel. 403/250–3209) puts together RV vacation packages through its rental division, Canada Campers.

There are three major campground chains, and all of them will send you a directory of their member campgrounds: **Best Holiday Trav-L-Park Association** (1310 Jarvis Ave., Elk Grove Village, IL 60007, tel. 800/323–8899), **Kampgrounds of America** (KOA) (Box 30558, Billings, MT 59114, tel.

406/248–7444; also ask about purchasing a KOA Value Kard, which gives you a 10% discount on all registration fees), and **Leisure Systems, Inc./Yogi Bear's Jellystone Park Camp-Resorts** (6201 Kellogg Ave., Cincinnati, OH 45230, tel. 513/232–6800 or 800/626–3720). In Canada, **Alberta Country Vacations** (Box 217, Trochu, Alberta T0M 2C0, tel. 403/442–2207) will send you a free brochure listing its member ranches and farms, some of which have RV sites.

Periodicals

Don't leave home without a pile of campground directories in your RV. Although the ones listed are generally comprehensive, each has strengths and weaknesses, so it's best to use several at once. *Trailer Life Campground & RV Services Directory* (3601 Calle Tecare, Camarillo, CA 93012, tel. 805/389–0300) comes from the Good Sam Club and includes discounts for club members. *Wheelers Recreational Vehicle Resort & Campground Guide* (1310 Jarvis Ave., Elk Grove Village, IL 60007, tel. 708/981–0100) rates the various campgrounds, giving them one to five stars, with three being standard. *Woodall's Campground Directories* (28167 North Keith Dr., Lake Forest, IL 60045, tel. 708/362–6700) publishes a North American edition and smaller eastern and western editions. Woodall's awards one to five diamonds for facilities and recreation at each campground.

Roads to Adventure (TL Enterprises, 2575 Vista del Mar, Ventura, CA 93001, tel. 805/667–4000 or 800/765–1912) is a magazine with articles aimed at families who combine RVing and adventure travel; it comes out once or twice a year.

Books

The helpful *Mobil Travel Guide* series consists of eight paperback books that cover regions of the United States and one guide to major cities. The listings of sights and attractions are almost as comprehensive as those in guidebooks devoted to a single state, but the eight books take up far less room in your RV than 50.

If you plan to travel extensively in the national parks, Fodor's *National Parks and Seashores of the East* and *National Parks of the West* have detailed information about the sights and services in and around favorite parks, including driving tours, campground specifics, tips about sports activities, and facts about flora and fauna.

Millbrook Press publishes two excellent books for school-age children: Michael Weber's *Our National Parks* and Eleanor Ayer's *Our National Monuments*. Both have color photographs and plenty of interesting facts.

Also See

Families who like the idea of an adventure that's a movable feast—and bed and bathroom—should look at the Houseboating and Sailing chapters. Keep in mind, too, that many of the trips in Archaeology Adventures, Digging for Dinosaur Bones and Other Fossils, Kayaking, and Rock Climbing require participants to arrange their own accommodations, often at nearby campgrounds; RVs are perfect for these.

SAILING

Sailing is about teamwork, whether you are learning the basics as a family or working together to crew. That's a skill that will benefit both parents and children long after they've left a sailing school or vacation behind. Sailing isn't all about work, though. These adventures by their very nature are the stuff of fantasy: uninhabited islands; intriguing wildlife and turquoise waters; coral reefs teeming with exotic fish; interesting cultures; you, your family, the wind, and the wide-open sea, with nothing but time on your hands. Depending on whether you choose a school or a sailing vacation, you will work more or less. Either way, you will join a long and honored heritage of seagoing families who have come to believe that there is no better way to strengthen ties and explore the world than by boat.

Questions to Ask

Is the trip safe—and fun—for children? Thousands of young children have spent time on boats, but not every boat is right for every child or family. Open railings and slippery decks, for example, are dangerous for young children left to play on their own; parents must ask themselves if they are prepared to be on constant watch. Some courses include the deliberate capsizing of a boat so that students can learn how to handle that situation. Will your child be overly frightened by this? If so, perhaps he or she is too young to take the course, regardless of whether the school will allow it. By asking questions about courses and about the layout of the boat, you'll be able to make a knowledgeable decision.

Do you have life jackets on board for children the sizes and ages of mine? This is crucial: If a school or ship does not have a life jacket to fit your child, you must get one. Go to a marine supply store or reputable outdoor store and pick a coast guard–approved life vest made for the type of water and area you will be in. Read the labels carefully. A life vest intended for use in calm, inland water will not protect your child in open seas.

How many years of experience does the captain have sailing in this area? When you go on a sailing vacation, ideally you want a skipper and crew who know the area well. This is both for safety's sake and because they should be able to give you interesting stories and facts about the history of the land and waters you're sailing near, about plant and animal life, and about the local people.

What does licensed captain mean? In the United States, boat captains—and other sailors carrying passengers for hire—must be licensed by the coast guard. Other countries have corresponding licensing agencies; before you charter a boat with a captain, make sure he or she is, in fact, licensed.

Are your instructors certified, and what are their qualifications? There are two organizations with certification criteria for instructors: the United States Sailing Association (US Sailing) and the American Sailing Association (ASA). These competing organizations have differing criteria, with the result that there is no universal standard for instructors in this country, particularly with regard to recreational sailing. Some very good instructors may not have joined or been tested by either organization. If you're looking for quality instruction, certification is just one measure. Experience is an equally valid measure, so ask how long instructors have been teaching (bad teachers don't last long with a school or company), and how long they've been sailing. This is a sport in which qualifications definitely improve with experience. If, however, you're taking bareboat cruising courses and other advanced courses for sailing boats with engines because your goal is to be able to captain and crew your own boat, your instructor should have a coast guard license. When you're taking day sailing courses, coast guard licensing is not an issue.

Will I be certified when I finish this course? There are no universally accepted criteria for certifying students. Some schools offer their own certificate; some offer their own and one from US Sailing or ASA. A school's certificate has limited importance. If you went to the Caribbean to charter your own boat, the company probably would not even ask you for certification. If, however, you could not prove sailing competence based on experience, it would require you to take a licensed captain with you at your own expense—but you could still charter the boat. On the other hand, a certificate proves that you've learned a certain number of things and sailed a certain number of hours, and it tells instructors that you are ready to move on to the next level. And it's nice to hang on your wall.

Can we help crew? If you're joining a sailing expedition or chartering a boat, and if learning is important to your family, choose a ship on which guests are allowed and encouraged to help out and learn the fundamentals of sailing. If your children are interested in learning, make certain the captain and crew want to teach children and have some experience doing so.

Do you carry snorkeling or other recreational gear for children? Snorkeling is an ideal activity for families on boats; so is fishing. Many charters carry snorkel and fishing equipment—but not always in children's sizes. Ask ahead of time, because you can't generally buy child-size gear in exotic locations.

Is any other recreational equipment available? Some boats carry kayaks or canoes; some have dinghies and inflatables. You may be able to windsurf or scuba dive from some boats. If there's a particular water sport you're interested in, make a request well in advance of your sailing date.

What's included in the cost? If you sign up with a sailing school, courses are usually instruction only, with no meals or accommodations included; that's the case with courses listed here. If you take a course during which you live on the boat, however, accommodations and meals on board are included, unless otherwise noted. There are also resort courses, which combine sailing school with lodging and the use of facilities at the resort where the school is located. When you charter a boat or join a scheduled trip on a sailing vessel, accommodations, meals, activities, sailing instruction, and sightseeing are included. Airport pickup may also be part of the trip fee. Alcohol is usually extra, as is dive equipment.

Instruction

Sailing schools, of course, are mostly instruction, though they often combine learning with playing in some of the world's most popular vacation spots. Charters and sailing adventures, on the other hand, generally give live-aboard guests the option of working alongside the crew or doing nothing at all. Although relaxing is great, why not use some of the time for hands-on learning from real sailors—people who have a unique experience and perspective to share. Learning to sail this way is just too good an opportunity to miss.

Finding the Fun

Northeast: North End Shipyard Schooners, Offshore Sailing School, Outward Bound. **Mid-Atlantic:** Annapolis Sailing School, Offshore Sailing School. **South:** Annapolis Sailing School, Ocean Voyages, Offshore Sailing School. **West Coast:** Ocean Voyages. **Alaska:** American Wilderness Experience, Rascals in Paradise. **Hawaii:** Ocean Voyages. **Canada:** EcoSummer Expeditions. **Caribbean:** Annapolis Sailing School, Ocean Voyages, Offshore Sailing School. **Central America, South America, Europe, Africa, Asia, Australia:** Ocean Voyages. **South Pacific:** Rascals in Paradise, Specialized Odysseys.

Favorite Schools and Charters

American Wilderness Experience

 ALL

Small boats traveling along the 1,000 miles of protected waterway in Alaska's Inside Passage can bring visitors closer to the real Alaska than large cruise ships could ever do. The passage is marked by deep fjords and magnificent snowy peaks, and there are hundreds of islands, small villages, and extensive forested areas that provide food and shelter for black and brown bears and bald eagles.

Along the coast are otters, seals, and sea lions; in the deeper waters, orcas and humpbacks leap and glide. Sound Sailing, the operator American Wilderness Experience contracts with for this adventure, has two 42-foot sloops and a wealth of experience to share with families in America's great northern frontier. You can embark in Ketchikan, Petersburg, Sitka, or Juneau.

FOR FAMILIES. Each boat has two double berths—one forward, one aft—to accommodate a family of four or five (three small children could share one double berth). You don't need any sailing experience, and all family members are welcome to help or to learn to crew under the guidance of a licensed captain. The pace and itinerary are flexible. You can take the dinghy ashore for beachcombing and inland hiking, or relax in a natural hot spring. You can learn about natural history as well as Tlingit history and culture from the captain, who has a particular interest in these subjects. There's first-rate fishing equipment on board, so plan on testing your skills against Pacific halibut or salmon. This experience combines comfort and personal attention with a wilderness setting that has few rivals in terms of its richness of wildlife and impressive land- and seascapes.

🏠 *American Wilderness Experience, Box 1486, Boulder, CO 80306, tel. 303/444–2622 or 800/444–0099. Apr.–Sept.: 7 days, $1,000–$1,500, depending on season.*

Annapolis Sailing School

👪 5+

Annapolis Sailing School is one of the oldest and largest sailing schools in the country. Its main campus is on Chesapeake Bay in Maryland, but it has branch schools in St. Petersburg and Marathon, Florida, and in St. Croix in the U.S. Virgin Islands. All Annapolis Sailing School courses are primarily hands-on. With the exception of about four hours of lecture time, classes take place in boats on the water.

FOR FAMILIES. Become a Sailing Family is the popular course in which parents and kids work together to master the sailing of 30-foot sloops. Offered only at the Annapolis campus, this is one of the few courses that includes lodging and meals. It combines the beginner weekend course with five days of cruising. Families spend three nights at motels in Annapolis, then four nights out on a boat in Chesapeake Bay. An instructor is on board at all times.

If you want to vacation together but learn separately, the school suggests you combine adult courses with Kid Ship, for ages 5 and up. Kid Ship, also scheduled only in Annapolis, coincides with the school's adult courses. While parents are learning on 24-foot

sloops, children are on 12-foot Holder Hawk sailboats, which most kids find manageable and unintimidating. These are not live-aboard courses; families are out on the water from about 9 to 4, then on their own in the evenings.

🏠 *Annapolis Sailing School, Box 3334, Annapolis, MD 21403, tel. 410/267–7205 or 800/638–9192. Mar.–Oct.: 2–5 days, $225–$475 adults, $180–$300 children (Kid Ship); 7 days, $1,700–$3,565 for 2 to 6 students in the family course.*

EcoSummer Expeditions

👪 3+

Wilderness, adventure, teamwork, good times, new friends—that's what EcoSummer believes families will experience on its trips. One of the best for families is a sailing voyage around Canada's Queen Charlotte Islands, a group of more than 150 islands off the coast of northern British Columbia. Many are uninhabited, and some are important cultural sites of the Haida people. All are biologically and ecologically rich; among the animals you can spot are sea lions, eagles, peregrine falcons, puffins, whales, and dolphins. For families who want wilderness and native culture in one place, the Queen Charlotte Islands are a dream destination, and there is no better way to see them than by boat.

FOR FAMILIES. The *Ocean Light* is a 76-foot, all-wood cutter that sleeps eight in an unusual layout—a relatively open plan with no walls or dividers separating the double and single berths. Owner and skipper Tom Ellison is a naturalist and experienced seaman who has led trips to the Charlottes since 1979. Daily sailings leave time for walks through spruce and cedar forests, beachcombing, and visits to huge seabird and sea lion colonies. Ancient Haida totem poles still stand guard over abandoned villages. Skung'gwai (Ninstints), a United Nations World Heritage Site, has the largest stand of totem poles in their original location in North America. There's an extensive library on board and, for those who like the tranquillity of paddling, a kayak and canoe. Although airfare between Vancouver and Sandspit, where the voyage begins, is not included in the trip cost, EcoSummer will book the flight for your family.

🏠 *EcoSummer Expeditions, 936 Peace Portal Dr., Box 8014–240, Blaine, WA 98230, tel. 604/669–7741; in U.S., 800/688–8605; in Canada, 800/465–8884. July–Aug.: 7 days, $1,645.*

North End Shipyard Schooners

👫👤 10+

North End Shipyard Schooners consists of three owner-operated vessels working cooperatively and sailing from North End Shipyard wharf in Rockland, Maine. The *Isaac H. Evans* and the *American Eagle* have both been designated National Historic Landmarks. The *Heritage* was built at the shipyard in 1983. There are no set itineraries; the ships go with the prevailing winds, anchoring in a different scenic harbor each night. There are hundreds of islands to sail around and explore along Maine's rocky mid-coast area.

FOR FAMILIES. Of the three boats, only the *Isaac H. Evans*, a 65-foot schooner for 20 passengers, has designated family departures; there are generally three each summer. Captain Ed Glaser specializes in family cruises because, he says, "Some of my best memories are of vacationing in Maine with my parents." Glaser knows how to teach and talk to young people. Families are encouraged to help around the ship, but they don't have to. Activities include whale-watching, stargazing, swimming, and exploring the small coves where the ship anchors. Captain and crew are adept at telling salty tales of the sea, and they may even play an instrument or two. The food is plentiful (much of it kid favorites, like spaghetti and pizza), and every cruise includes an old-fashioned Maine lobster bake.

Only two sailors can fit in a cabin, so a family of four needs two separate cabins. If there are just three of you, your child will probably bunk with another passenger of the same sex and age.

🏠 *North End Shipyard Schooners, Box 482, Rockland, ME 14841, tel. 800/648–4544. July–Aug.: 3 days, $345–$375.*

Ocean Voyages

👫👤 ALL

For 17 years Ocean Voyages has arranged small group sailings and maritime adventures for all kinds of sea lovers, including families. Founder Mary Crowley, an accomplished sailor, introduced her daughter Colleen to sailing as a toddler. Since then, they've sailed most of the world's oceans together. Whether your family is looking for a charter or a scheduled sailing, whether you want to sail in the Pacific, the Caribbean, or the Mediterranean, Ocean Voyages will find a boat and a crew to give you the oceangoing vacation of a lifetime.

FOR FAMILIES. When you call, ask for the Family Sailing information sheet. It lists 11 boats in 11 different parts of the world—all ships that Ocean Voyages knows welcome families. There's a 72-foot yacht crewed by a French couple and their son sailing off Costa Rica; it takes just four to six passengers. If Greece and Turkey appeal, there's an eight-passenger yacht sailing around the Greek islands and along Turkey's Turquoise Coast. A 10-passenger, 71-foot yacht and its family-of-four crew will take you on a nature-oriented trip around Scotland and Ireland. See the Hawaiian Islands —and snorkel, swim, whale-watch, and surf while you're doing it—via a six-passenger boat. The Scandinavian crew of *Jennifer*, a 50-foot yacht on its way around the world, invites you to join part of its voyage in Australia, Indonesia, Thailand, Africa, or beyond; *Jennifer* sleeps four to six guests.

There are also ships sailing off California, Florida and the Bahamas, the Pacific Northwest, the Galápagos Islands, the Grenadines, and just about any other place your family can imagine or want to go. Most charters are for one week; however, there are discounts for voyages of three weeks or longer. 🏨 *Ocean Voyages, 1709 Bridgeway, Sausalito, CA 94965, tel. 415/332–4681. Year-round (all ships not available all months): 7 days, $750–$2,100, depending on location and group size.*

Offshore Sailing School

(👫 8+)

Steve Colgate, America's Cup and Olympic sailor, has always believed that sailing is for everyone. Since he founded Offshore Sailing School in 1964, the school has taught more than 78,000 people of all ages and backgrounds. Offshore has schools in Jersey City, New Jersey, and in Greenwich, Connecticut, besides branches at five first-class resort areas: South Seas Plantation on Captiva Island, Florida; Treasure Isle Hotel, Tortola, British Virgin Islands; Marigot Bay Resort, Marigot Bay, St. Lucia; Admiral Farragut Inn, Newport, Rhode Island; and locations in St. Petersburg, Florida. For those who can't leave home, the school's famous Learn to Sail Tour travels to more than 20 cities between April and October.

FOR FAMILIES. Families with children 12 and up can join any of the school's courses. If there are at least four family members—enough to fill one boat—the school is flexible on the minimum age but feels that the instruction is most appropriate for kids 8 and older. A family of four participating in the same course also gets a discount. There are six basic courses, which you can take at the school sites or, in some cases, as part of a resort package.

Learn to Sail, with three-, four-, and eight-day versions, is for beginners and intermediate sailors; it's taught on 27-foot Olympic-class Solings or Laser 28s, with no more than four students to a boat. The extensive

list of topics covered includes nautical terminology, hull speed, mechanics of wind and sail, crew overboard recovery—even sailing backward. More experienced sailors can take Performance Sailing, Bareboat Cruising Preparation, Live-Aboard Cruising, and Introductory or Advanced Racing.

The South Seas Plantation branch on Captiva offers six-day summer family packages that combine sailing school and use of the resort's well-regarded supervised children's program. Accommodations at the resort are included in three packages. For families who want to learn together, there's Junior Captains for parents with children 8–11; Teens at the Helm is for families with kids 13–17. A third package is Dry-Docked Kids, for parents who want to learn to sail but have children ages 3–11 who don't; while parents are sailing, children stay in the resort's kids' program.

Finally, families might consider Fast Track to Cruising, which combines Learn to Sail and Live-Aboard Cruising in a 10- to 14-day course at several of the school's vacation destinations. At the end of this course, you'll crew your own boat—without instructors—on a 24-hour minicharter. 🏨 *Offshore Sailing School, 16731 McGregor Blvd., Fort Myers, FL 33908, tel. 813/454–1700 or 800/221–4326. Year-round (all locations not all months): 3–14 days, $375–$595, courses only, $695–$2,995, resort packages, depending on accommodations and season; 6 days, $475–$1,600 per person for Captiva family package.*

Outward Bound

(👫 14+)

For more than 30 years Outward Bound has challenged novice and experienced sailors alike to master the skills to navigate Maine's rugged coast and waters. The organization's philosophy is that during this weeklong course your family will develop not only strong sailing skills but bonds that will strengthen relationships on and off the water.

FOR FAMILIES. The course starts and ends in Rockland, Maine, and participants spend about six days sailing in Penobscot Bay and two days on land activities on a few of the 3,500 islands in the area. Usually, 10 to 12 people share one boat; to a large extent, the weather dictates your schedule. Using a 30-foot open ketch, your family must combine teamwork, leadership, and seamanship skills to succeed in meeting Outward Bound's goals. The entire group rotates responsibilities throughout the course, and among the skills you master are sail handling (including tacking and jibing); navigation (chart and compass use and course plotting), and boat handling, which means helmsmanship as well as fundamentals like anchoring and rowing. In addition to sailing, you try rock climbing, rappelling, and a ropes course.

At night you camp out on islands in platform tents for about half the course and sleep on the boat the rest of the time. The boat does not have berths or cover. In the Outward Bound tradition, you will learn how to construct a shelter over the boat if the weather demands it.

 Outward Bound, Rte. 9D, R2 Box 280, Garrison, NY 10524, tel. 914/424–4000 or 800/243–8520. June–Aug.: 8 days, $895 first person, $695 each additional family member.

Rascals in Paradise

 3+

Rascals represents several yachts around the world that are ideal for one family or for two families to charter together. Like all of the outfitters, hotels, and resorts Rascals contracts with, the charter owners and captains are chosen not only for their sailing expertise and knowledge of the areas in which they work but for their love of sharing their world with children and parents.

FOR FAMILIES. Typical of a Rascals charter is the *Discovery*, a 65-foot yacht owned and operated by Dean and Rose Rand and their four daughters, ages 3–12. The Rands try to match their kids with the ages of the children on each sailing: If older children are coming, they bring their older girls along; when families have young children, the Rands' younger daughters sail, too. The *Discovery*, which explores Alaska's Prince William Sound, has 6 cabins for 12 passengers; the Rands are happy to let families help out with ship chores if they wish.

Although the exact itinerary depends upon the weather, the group's interests, and the location of wildlife, the boat usually sails to Barry Arm and Harriman Fjord, past the expansive Columbia Glacier with its 300-foot-high walls of blue ice, and through Orca Bay. Families can see where the *Exxon Valdez* ran aground and watch sea lions and puffins. There's a hike to a waterfall and several opportunities to go ashore via inflatable Zodiac rafts. The food—fresh baked goods, seafood, steaks, salads, vegetables, and wine—will please kids and parents. At night the ship anchors in protective coves. On six- and eight-day voyages, you spend two nights at a family-friendly bed-and-breakfast in the Rands' small hometown of Cordova, on Prince William Sound. There you can meet local families and explore a glacier and other sights away from the coast.

If Alaska is not for your family, ask Rascals about charters in Fiji, Australia, Tonga, Tahiti, Papua New Guinea, Vanuatu, and the Solomon Islands.

 Rascals in Paradise, 650 5th St., 505, San Francisco, CA 94107, tel. 415/978–9800 or 800/872–7225. May–Sept.: 3–8 days, $975–$2,540; children 8–15, half-price; children under 8, $200–$400.

Specialized Odysseys

 ALL

Dense tropical rain forest and volcanic ridges and cones cover the 26-mile-long island of Taveuni, the third largest of the Fiji Islands.

The island is home base for *Seax of Legra*, a 42-foot charter yacht represented by Specialized Odysseys. Orchids, palms, ferns, and tagimoucia, Fiji's national flower, thrive on the island, as do many species of birds. It is truly an island paradise, with the requisite picture-postcard waterfalls and empty white sand beaches. Offshore, brilliant living corals, world-renowned reefs, and an astonishing variety of marine life make sailing seem more like a dream than reality.

FOR FAMILIES. *Seax of Legra*, owned and operated by Warwick and Dianne Bain, can accommodate up to a family of five. One cabin has a double and a single berth; the other has two singles. The Bains have made a point of creating a very flexible itinerary. If your family wants to be dropped off on a secluded isle for a day of beachcombing, swimming, and relaxing, fine. If you prefer to snorkel, you can do that, too; the boat carries gear for adults only, so bring equipment for the kids. There are also hikes and bird walks on Taveuni. You can help crew, or learn to crew, if you wish, but you can also do absolutely nothing. The Bains will help certified divers rent gear and schedule dives with local guides. If you want to be certified, they'll help arrange that; complete your dry-land work before arriving in Fiji so you can start right out in the water.

A land stay at the Bains' beachside home can be added to any yacht charter. Land rates include homecooked Fijian meals and the services of a nanny. You can arrange guided hikes and bird walks as well as meetings and meals with local Fijian families. Parents with infants or very young children might consider staying at the house each night and going out in the *Seax* by day. Parents and older children can sail, swim, and snorkel while a nanny cares for and entertains babies and young children on Taveuni. 🏨 *Specialized Odysseys, 3430 Evergreen Pt. Rd., Box 37, Medina, WA 98039, tel. 206/*

455–1960. Year round: 1–14 days, charter rates from $690 per day to $5,000 per wk. for a family of 4; day rates are $95 per person per day; land rates, $365 per family per night.

Resources

Organizations

The **American Sailing Association** (13922 Marquesas Way, Marina del Rey, CA 90292, tel. 310/822–7171) and **United States Sailing Association** (Box 1260, Portsmouth, RI 02871, tel. 401/683–0800) are the major sailing organizations in this country. Call ASA for a list of affiliate members or schools in your area that teach ASA courses. US Sailing has a "Where to Sail" pamphlet listing rentals, schools, and US Sailing programs across the country. Both organizations have books and other materials available for sale.

Periodicals

Cruising World (The Sailing Company, 5 John Clark Rd., Newport, RI 02840, tel. 401/847-1588) is a monthly magazine for sailors who cruise the world in their own sailboats; it's also interesting reading for novice sailors. Periodically there are articles that discuss family sailing and educating children about cruising. An annual special section on chartering that lists and rates companies is a must for anyone considering a charter vacation. The classified ads have opportunities for crewing, too.

Also See

If you can't decide between sailing and an animal-encounter vacation, see Wildlife Encounters; some of these adventures include both. If you want to be on and *under* the water, see Snorkeling and Diving.

SNORKELING AND DIVING

The ocean is like a circus—a place where brilliant colors, balletic grace, and heart-in-your-mouth thrills exist in a swirling world unto itself. Or perhaps it's more like a vast, watery classroom, filled with fascinating creatures that tell us about life under the sea and sometimes about ourselves. Children, of course, know about the underwater world from myths and fairy tales as well as from the science and nonfiction books they carry home from schools and libraries. Bringing kids and water together is a natural. What, after all, could be better than getting wet and seeing amazing creatures close at hand?

Many adults feel the same way, and families have several options for exploring underwater. Snorkelers float facedown in the water and look at the sea below. Almost any child who can swim and is comfortable in the water can snorkel, though some young children don't like wearing a mask over their face or breathing through a tube. Diving is more complicated. You must be certified (pass written and practical tests) or take a certification course on site before you can dive with a licensed dive operator. The minimum age for certification is 12.

Because snorkeling and diving are often particularly good around reef areas, many of the places listed here are ideal for both activities. Parents, however, should be aware that snorkelers and divers don't always go out together. A number of resorts with children's activity programs are included because these allow parents and older kids to dive while younger children snorkel or play and explore with peers and counselors.

This chapter presents a cross section of snorkeling and diving experiences. All of these entries, like those in the chapter on Wildlife Encounters, are away from the mainland United States. Most are in other countries—places where you are not likely to encounter crowds or cloudy waters, and where the sea life is unusual in some way. These resorts or operators are all known for their work with children and families as well as for their expertise around the water. The selections are truly adventure vacations, which is not to say that you can't don a mask and fins for half-day and day trips at many resorts in Florida, California, or even Michigan.

Of the more than 25 dive and snorkel trips here, some are based on ships, some are resort-based, and others are for adventurers who want to aid in scientific research while snorkeling or diving. The choices are for a variety of ages, abilities, and interests. Most are in places where families can learn the sports, or where already certified divers can share their passion with other members of their family. On all these adventures, the sea will both intrigue and educate.

Questions to Ask

What kind of equipment is used for snorkeling and diving? Snorkelers need a mask to see clearly in the water, fins on their feet for easier swimming, and a snorkel tube through which to breathe. Young children will require some time to get used to this equipment. Divers use the same equipment as snorkelers (some carry a snorkel so that if they surface far from the boat, they can swim back easily); this is often referred to as personal equipment. They also use dive gear. The most important pieces of gear are regulators and BCDs (buoyancy control devices), which you inflate and deflate depending on whether you want to go up or down. Serious divers usually own their own. Divers also need weight belts to help them dive down, as well as two gauges, one to measure depth and one to measure the air in the tanks. A tank or tanks, generally carried in a backpack, provide air. Some divers wear wet suits.

Is snorkeling equipment available for rent? What about diving equipment? If you don't have snorkeling equipment and don't want to borrow or buy it, make certain rentals are available on the boat or at the resort—and in the right sizes. You'll need properly fitting masks and fins and snorkels small enough for children the ages of yours. Also, if anyone in your family wears glasses, you may want to ask a dive shop about purchasing a prescription mask. Dive packages and dive operators generally supply the necessary diving equipment but not personal gear.

Do you have diving certification courses? Many resorts and resort areas have certification courses. The main certification organizations in this country are the National Association of Underwater Instructors (NAUI) and the Professional Association of Dive Instructors (PADI). Resorts and resort areas are likely to offer courses from these organizations. NAUI and PADI teach basically the same skills, although their instructional methods differ. Courses generally combine anywhere from 25 to 32 hours of instruction divided between classroom and pool work, plus checkout dives (a real dive in fairly shallow water on which your instructor tests your skills). Kids 12 to 15 can take the same course with parents and receive junior certification; the only difference is that they must be accompanied by an adult on dives. If you want to devote more of your vacation time to actual diving, you can take the classroom and pool portion near your home and finish up at a resort or with a dive operator in the location of your choice. If you do this, make sure the resort or operator accepts the type of certification you have started at home.

Do you have a resort course? If you don't want to commit to full certification, most resorts offer a less expensive resort course, with anywhere from 6 to 20 hours of instruction, pool work, and dive time over one to five days. Resort courses certify you to dive only at that resort and only during that stay. The minimum age is 12.

Do we have to be certified in advance to dive? At some resorts and on some boats, instruction is not an option; you must be certified and have your C-card (certification card) with you in order to dive. Be clear about this beforehand if you are not yet certified.

Can snorkelers go out with divers? Sometimes snorkelers and divers visit the same site together. Even operators who allow this, however, may change their minds if the weather or sea is rough or if the boat is full. If you have children who are not old enough to dive and who plan to snorkel, be aware that you may not be able to go out together.

Is there snorkeling right from shore? Resorts that have snorkeling from their shores, or boats that take snorkelers to the shores of cays and islands, make life easy for parents with young children. It's much less intimidating for kids to learn to snorkel in water they can stand in.

What happens with ear pressure? Diving creates the same kind of pressure that airplane trips and high altitudes can. If your preteen or teen is prone to ear pain in these situations, discuss ahead of time how to clear your ears by holding your nose and blowing out. Talk to your pediatrician, too.

What's included in the cost? Certification courses generally include class materials (such as a manual), instruction, gear to learn with, transportation to dive sites, and checkout dives. Equipment for checkout dives is often an extra charge. Dive packages at resorts typically give you one or two dives daily, transportation to dive sites, and lodging. Some cover meals; this is noted in individual listings. You often get dive equipment, such as tanks, weights, and belts, as part of the deal. Personal gear—snorkels, masks, fins—is usually not included. Dedicated dive boat vacations are pretty much all-inclusive: equipment, gear, dives, local transportation, accommodations, and meals. Snorkel equipment for adults, though not for kids, is often available. Diving instruction, however, is generally not provided on these boats. Any exceptions in the pricing for these various experiences are noted in the individual listings.

Instruction

Depending on the resort or boat you're diving from, you will already have had all your instruction—and a certification card to prove it—or you'll need to sign up for a resort or certification course before you can dive. Any good snorkel boat operator will give basic instruction on snorkeling if your family needs it, though practice is what will make you comfortable in the water.

Finding the Fun

Hawaii: Earthwatch. **Mexico:** Club Med, Rascals in Paradise. **Central America:** American Wilderness Experience, Earthwatch, Ocean Voyages, Rascals in Paradise. **Caribbean:** Club Med, Earthwatch, Hyatt Regency Grand Cayman, Rascals in Paradise. **Australia:** Earthwatch. **Around the Pacific:** Continental Micronesia, Earthwatch, Rascals in Paradise.

Favorite Places to Snorkel and Dive

American Wilderness Experience

 6+

Thirty-five miles off the coast of Honduras, in the Islas de la Bahía, is Roatán. On a palm-covered island near Roatán, the private bungalows of Anthony's Key Resort blend into a lush tropical hillside or overlook a quiet lagoon. Under the clear, warm Caribbean waters lies the longest barrier reef in the Americas—a diving and snorkeling site of astonishing beauty. Several times during the summer, American Wilderness Experience has special weeks for families at Anthony's Key, with some activities beyond the usual ones.

FOR FAMILIES. Divers or anyone coming here to learn to dive will not be disappointed. Three boats leave daily from the resort, and there is shore diving during the day and at night. Boats go out twice weekly for night dives, too. The area is also a snorkeling paradise, with waters just offshore that will keep snorkelers happy for hours at a time.

Anthony's Key Resort has a special relationship with the Institute for Marine Sciences, which is based in the area and runs the popular Dolphin Discovery programs. Participants in the program learn about, and interact with, the institute's dolphins. A special Dolphin Discovery Camp for ages 6–15 is set up to coincide with dive weeks for parents booking through American Wilderness Experience (see Wildlife Encounters), so that whether or not the whole family dives, everyone can experience the resort's abundant marine life and natural beauty. Certified divers don't miss out on close encounters either: Many wild dolphins live in these waters and frequently visit with divers.

Nondivers can ride horses on the beach, paddle in canoes, and explore nature trails. The resort organizes children's and family activities each week and arranges baby-sitting, too. The all-inclusive package means no surprises: Meals, diving, riding, and most other resort activities are included in the price.

🏨 *American Wilderness Experience, Box 1486, Boulder, CO 80306, tel. 303/444–2622 or 800/444–0099. Apr.–Sept.: 8 days, $910–$1,150. Late May–early Sept.: 8 days, Dolphin Discovery Camp, $500.*

Club Med

 4 mos.+

Club Med and adventure? Well, yes … and no. You won't camp out or find a backcountry experience, and you're not far from the amenities of modern civilization. Still, there are several reasons adventuring families should consider Club Med. For an extra charge, you can enroll in weeklong programs called "intensives" that immerse you in a sport for most of each day; scuba diving is one of these. Keep in mind, too, that some Club Meds are more rustic than others, and some are more nature oriented than sybaritic. A number of clubs, like Sonora Bay in Mexico, are in remote areas where development hasn't infringed on the natural beauty of the environment.

FOR FAMILIES. Club Med Sonora Bay, 260 miles south of the Arizona border, is cradled between the Bacochibampo Mountains and the piercing blue of the Gulf of California. Though a few guests may choose to sunbathe on the two sweeping beaches, most come for the sports: diving and horseback riding. Sonora Bay has a dedicated dive center with both resort and certification courses, and there are fish-filled sites for every level of diver. Boats head out twice daily to various areas, and there's one night dive each week. On Seal Island, divers have a chance to swim with the resident sea lions and explore the caves at the island's southern end. Visibility generally ranges from 20 to 80 feet; while that's limited compared to other popular dive spots, underwater boulders throughout the area provide shelter for an extensive variety of marine life, from sea horses and nurse sharks to scorpion fish and moray eels. Snorkelers can swim right off the resort's shore with the club's instructor; snorkel trips visit Seal Island twice each week (extra charge).

There's no formal children's activity program, but ages 6 and up are welcome. However, if both parents plan to be active in sports, this club is probably best for older children who are interested in spending most of their time diving or snorkeling. Sonora Bay also makes an ideal destination for families with both dedicated divers and riders. The riding program is excellent, including an intensive course in English-style jumping and dressage. Families who want to mix their diving or riding with other activities can try kayaking and desert mountain biking here (extra charge for guided tours).

You can also dive at five of Club Med's six family resorts—clubs that are dedicated specifically to families and offer supervised activities for children 2–12 (in Florida and Mexico, the programs accept kids as young as 4 and 12 months, respectively). These are Eleuthera, in the Bahamas; Punta Cana, Dominican Republic; St. Lucia, West Indies; Sandpiper, Florida; and Ixtapa, Mexico. A special program at these clubs is one-on-one scuba in the pool for ages 4 and up. This is a unique opportunity for divers who want their children to learn something about the sport; few dive operators or resorts have child-size equipment. Using tiny scuba gear and a great deal of patience, instructors take kids one at a time to the bottom of the pool, where they learn the correct hand signs for "okay" and "not okay" and get a feel for diving. At Club Med Eleuthera, ages 8 and up can also practice in the resort's natural protected lagoon.

St. Lucia is the only family club with an intensive dive course; families with children of dif-ferent ages can combine diving and kids' club activities here. Children must be at least 12 to participate in the intensive dive course.

 Club Med, 40 W. 57th St., New York, NY 10019, tel. 212/977–2100 or 800/258–2633. Sonora Bay, Mar.–Oct.: 8 days, $490–$700 without airfare, $770–$1,310 with airfare. Family resort prices vary widely by club and season; call and ask. Price does not include diving charge of $225 for intensive course, $125 for resort course, $125 for two-dive-a-day package for certified divers; dive packages are generally 6 days total of diving or diving and instruction combined.

Continental Micronesia

ALL

Continental Micronesia, the vacation package division of Continental Airlines, deals specifically with the countries of Micronesia. One of these, the Republic of Palau, is 700 miles east of the Philippines—a nine-hour flight from Hawaii. Palau comprises 343 islands spread over 100 miles and is one of the world's top dive sites. Jacques Cousteau named Palau's Ngemelis Wall the world's best wall dive, and CEDAM International, an organization dedicated to Conservation, Education, Diving, Archaeology, and Museums, nominated Palau as number one of the seven diving wonders of the world.

This is a destination for diving and snorkeling families who love to visit the hot new spots before most of the rest of the world even knows they exist. A first-rate hotel, Palau Pacific Resort, caters to families, even those with infants. With one call to Continental Micronesia you can book airfare, lodging, dive and snorkel packages, museum visits, rental cars, and sightseeing.

FOR FAMILIES. Palau Pacific Resort, a 20-minute drive from Koror, Palau's capital, has family resort amenities that are unusual in this part of the world. Snorkeling is excellent right from the beach—perfect for young children—and there's child-size equipment for rent. Creatures as fascinating as two-foot giant clams can be glimpsed along the reef close to shore. The resort also has a pool, a nature trail, and lots of water sports equipment for rent, including underwater cameras (there are classes in underwater photography). The recreation staff will customize any activity upon request. They can arrange a family snorkeling instructor, for example, or guided nature hikes, or kayaking lessons—all free of charge, except for equipment rental fees.

Independent tour operators have desks at the hotel for booking tours; in some cases you can even prebook through Continental Micronesia. One operator, Sam's Dive Tours, leads hiking tours to the spectacular Ngardmau Waterfall and to Palau's stone monoliths and other archaeological sites. You can also rent a car at the resort and drive to the Palau National Museum in Koror, where Palauan history, legends, and culture are interpreted through artifacts and traditional carved storyboards.

Palau's waters, however, with huge caverns, unspoiled reefs, and live coral formations, are what make it a world-class destination. No one should leave without taking a boat tour of the famous rock islands, which appear to float above the surface of the water. You can snorkel and dive from these boats, so families of divers and nondivers can stay together. Among the most compelling sightseeing attractions is Jellyfish Lake, filled with thousands of these eerily translucent creatures. Because the jellyfish here have no natural enemies, they don't sting. Snorkelers come from all over the world to float among them; others study the jellyfish from a raft. A new company, Adventure Kayaking, has 1- to 10-day kayaking tours for those who want to see Palau from the vantage point of a hard-shell, sit-on-top kayak—boats easy enough for children to master quickly. And of course, there's the diving. To dive with many operators you must be 16, certified, and have your certification card

with you. Splash, operating at Palau Pacific Resort, has both resort and certification courses.

Palauans are very family oriented, which makes the country a wonderful place to travel with kids. It also helps that the main language in Palau is English and the currency is the U.S. dollar. Everyone in the family does need a passport, though.

🏨 *Continental Micronesia, 300 N. Continental Blvd., Suite 600, El Segundo, CA 90245, tel. 310/322–8100 or 800/945–9955. Year-round: 7 days, Palau Pacific Resort, $411–$1,091 for lodging, depending on room and season; children under 18 free in room with parents, and those under 6 eat free at the breakfast and dinner buffet. Most tours are half-price for ages 6–12; those under 6 are usually free. Diving packages through Continental Micronesia run $45–$115 per day; airfare is $1,450–$1,550, with 33% discount for children 2–11.*

Earthwatch

With Earthwatch, a nonprofit organization, your family can combine a love of snorkeling or diving with a desire to contribute to scientific research. From the Caribbean to Australia's Great Barrier Reef, researchers on Earthwatch-supported projects are working to better understand marine life or to protect endangered species and threatened environments. Snorkelers and divers aid scientists by observing, photographing, and tagging fish and marine animals. If you have teenagers, pick a place or pick a species—the Earthwatch world is your oyster, so to speak.

FOR FAMILIES. You must be a certified diver to work at Earthwatch dive sites; plan on two dives a day, or two to four hours in the water. Snorkelers average three to five hours a day in the water. Participants also do much related work on land: cataloging, marking, sketching, and sometimes working with electronic equipment. Some sites are for divers or snorkelers only; at others, both groups work together. Volunteers on these projects stay in everything from campsites and field stations to houses and hotels. Lodging is generally included in the cost (though campers may need to bring their own camping equipment), and volunteers usually take turns with food preparation.

Not surprisingly, the Caribbean offers lots of opportunities. Bimini in the Bahamas is home to lemon sharks and to shark researcher Sam Gruber. Snorkelers assist him in studying how sharks live and reproduce, as well as their role as the top predators in their environment. Also in the Bahamas, a project on the island of San Salvador uses both snorkelers and divers to study reef damage. On St. John, in the U.S. Virgin Islands, volunteers in a program called Fish, Food, and Fate explore how ciguartera, the serious and sometimes fatal poisoning caused by eating any one of 400 species of normally edible fish, moves up the food chain. Scientists hope to discover why a toxin deadly enough to kill people eating the fish doesn't kill the fish themselves.

Reefs throughout the world attract marine researchers. Working in waters far to the west of the U.S. mainland, scientists hope to prevent permanent damage to Maui's reefs from human development and to find out how reefs in general recover from human and natural threats. On two daily dives, volunteers perform such functions as surveying coral species and measuring water quality. Snorkelers have an opportunity to explore reefs in Belize, and snorkelers and divers together are helping researchers study Australia's Great Barrier Reef and biodiversity in the reefs off China's southern coast. Earthwatch scuba divers are also monitoring butterfly fish in Fiji because they believe these common reef inhabitants are so closely linked to the ecology of the coral that they can serve as a barometer to measure a reef's overall health.

 Earthwatch, 680 Mt. Auburn St., Box 403BO, Watertown, MA 02272, tel. 617/926–8200 or 800/776–0188. Year-round (all sites not available at all times): 8–15 days, $995–$1,995.

Hyatt Regency Grand Cayman

3+

The Cayman Islands deserve their reputation as one of the world's top dive spots, and neither divers nor snorkelers will be disappointed in the clarity of the water or the abundance of sea life. The Caymans, however, are a popular destination, which means this adventure is in well-developed surroundings. Nevertheless, the Caymans—and particularly the Hyatt on Grand Cayman—are a good choice for families because few other places in the world offer the same quality of diving *and* a full-service, supervised activity program for very young children. Parents and older kids can venture into the deep while those too young to do so explore on land.

FOR FAMILIES. Red Sail Sports operates at the Hyatt and has both resort and full-certification courses for would-be divers. The resort course includes two hours of instruction followed by a test; pass the test and you can dive in the afternoon with an instructor. Boats leave twice daily for a number of spots around the islands. Hyatt dive and learn-to-dive packages include lodging, a sunset cruise, a round of golf, and a Red Sail T-shirt.

One of the all-time great snorkeling experiences for children (they should be comfortable with the sport in advance) and adults alike is the catamaran trip to Stingray City; the extra charge for this includes lunch. In an area of open water, some two dozen stingrays practice the graceful art of underwater flight. These rays are so used to human companions that you can touch them and swim among them with no fear. If you want to see the rays from a deeper perspective, dive boats stop here, too.

On land, kids can take nature walks, learn traditional Caymanian crafts and Caribbean dancing, and visit local museums with Camp Hyatt, the resort's supervised program for ages 3 to 12. The program runs daily year-round, except in September and October when it's on weekends only; the extra per-day charge for each child varies with the number of hours spent in camp. All campers take snorkel lessons in the pool. Families who want a land destination to explore together can look at turtles of all sizes and ages at the Turtle Farm in West Bay, one of the primary sightseeing stops on Grand Cayman.

🏨 *Hyatt Regency Grand Cayman, Box 1698, Grand Cayman, tel. 809/949–1234 or 800/553–1300. Year-round: 4–8 days, $545–$1,819 for dive and scuba school packages; a portion can be deducted for a nondiving adult in the same room. Children under 18 stay free in room with parents.*

Ocean Voyages

👨‍👧 10+

Off the coast of the tiny Central American country of Belize stretches the second longest barrier reef in the world. Although Belize welcomes visitors, it hasn't yet developed the kind of tourism that results in dive spots crowded with charters. Serenity, solitude, and first-class diving and snorkeling are the draws, and there's no better way to experience them than from the *Rembrandt van Rijn*. The 168-foot Dutch schooner, which can be booked through Ocean Voyages, attracts families and others who want to explore the country's bountiful reefs and isolated cays and islets. Sailing on this three-masted tall ship that uses both wind and motor power is an adventure in itself. The winter months are peak season, but because the ship is fully air-conditioned, you can travel comfortably even in the more humid summer months.

FOR FAMILIES. The *Rembrandt* sleeps just 32 guests in air-conditioned cabins that have double beds or upper and lower twins, as well as private bathrooms and showers. Two cabins accommodate a family of three. The ship carries gear for 24 divers, but you must be certified before your trip. Although there's also snorkeling equipment (adult sizes only) on board, you spend so much time snorkeling during the weeklong trip that the crew recommends bringing your own gear to assure proper fit. You can arrange to rent children's equipment ahead of time; gear will be on board when you arrive. The ship is equipped with two scuba compressors, an air bank, and 30 tanks, as well as Zodiac landing craft for expeditions to uninhabited islands and cays. You can snorkel from those shores or hike and bird-watch. The crew is knowledgeable about local marine and bird life, and they do give snorkel lessons.

Sailings start and end in Belize City, and Ocean Voyages will help arrange airfare, though it's not part of the charter price. Also ask about land stays before or after sailing. Blackbird Caye, an island resort for snorkelers, divers, and windsurfers, accommodates guests in thatched cottages on an atoll along the reef. Hidden Valley, in a jungle setting, has cottages, lots of wildlife, and natural pools and waterfalls; it's near Mayan ruins, too. The staff of an environmental institute at the resort leads nature walks and studies.

🏨 *Ocean Voyages, 1709 Bridgeway, Sausalito, CA 94965, tel. 415/332–4681. Year-round: 8 days, $879–$1,239; children 10–16 in cabin with a parent, $109.*

Rascals in Paradise

 ALL

Rascals is a tour company exclusively devoted to family vacations, whether you book custom trips or join scheduled family weeks. Rascals works with many high-end resorts around the world, but its trip list has bargains, too. On scheduled family departures, an escort arranges activities of all kinds for kids and families. Because Theresa Detchemendy and Debbie Baratta, the company's owners, believe that children should learn something about where they are traveling, a cultural component—such as visits with local families—is part of each trip. Although only a small portion of its family weeks qualify as adventure, this company has many trips, and few people in the travel business know as much about traveling families as the professionals at Rascals.

FOR FAMILIES. The Divers with Kids program lists 11 resorts that are great for both divers and younger children. Most of the hotels offer resort and certification courses. Some allow children to snorkel at the same sites at which parents are diving, though that's never guaranteed. Still, parents and children should have plenty of time to enjoy both the marine life and each other at all these resorts. Regardless of your destination, Rascals is a full-service agency that can book your air (not included in prices) and anything else you need. Most trips include at least two meals a day, sometimes three, and airport transfers are almost always part of the package. Diving is often, but not always, extra, depending on the resort.

In the Caribbean, you can choose from such family diving resorts as the Mariners Suites and Beach Cottages on Anguilla, where diving and lounging in hammocks among the sea grape trees are equally enticing, and Small Hope Bay Lodge in the Bahamas, 10 minutes away from the Andros Barrier Reef. Small Hope Bay has protected, clear waters and shallow beach areas for young children. Virgin Gorda's Bitter End Yacht Club offers sailing, motorboating, and hiking in addition to diving and snorkeling. Families who opt for the San Dollar Condominiums in Bonaire can explore caves and tidal pools or sail as an alternative to viewing the marine life in the reef just offshore.

Far to the west but still in the Caribbean are resorts in Mexico, Belize, and Honduras.

Mexico has one of the best and most affordable hotels for families with young snorkelers, the Club Akumal Caribe. Although Akumal is not far south of Cancún, it is everything that city is not: uncrowded, noncommercial, peaceful. You can snorkel right from the beach or take in Palancar Reef, across the water in Cozumel. There are brilliantly colored fish and exotic coral formations, along with sunken Spanish galleons. Don't miss a chance to visit nearby Tulum, the only Mayan ruin on the coast. In Belize, Victoria House on Ambergris Cay has family snorkel and picnic trips, as well as lots of water and land sports. Most important, you can explore the second largest barrier reef in the world and intriguing coral atolls. Rascals also has family week departures to Anthony's Key Resort off the island of Roatán in Honduras. Kids take advantage of some of the children's and family activities at the resort, but the Rascals escort sets up special experiences and programs for the group.

Beyond the Caribbean—way beyond in some cases—are more choices for the most adventurous families. Hotel Buena Vista on the Sea of Cortez in Baja California, Mexico, fronts miles of white, undeveloped beaches. The hotel was built over a natural hot springs, and mineral baths, massages, and facials are a big lure for some guests. The more active, though, can try mountain biking and horseback riding in addition to diving. Buena Vista is one of the least expensive of Rascals' family week hotels. Vatulele Island Resort on Fiji is a luxury hotel that gives equal importance to family time and romance. Guests dive and snorkel in shimmering aqua waters and hike through rain forests during the day. At night, parents can dine together in one of the world's most beautiful spots while children visit with peers. Also on Fiji, Plantation Island Resort is more casual and very family-oriented; it has its own year-round children's program, which the escorts from Rascals supplement. Every kind of water sport is available, and many of the kids' activities focus on Fijian culture. Finally, Rascals schedules a family week at Palau Pacific Resort in a Micronesian diving paradise, the Republic of Palau. 🏠 *Rascals in Paradise, 650 5th St., #505, San Francisco, CA 94107, tel. 415/978–9800 or 800/872–7225. Year-round: 8–9 days, $2,080–$7,181 for a family of 4.*

Resources

Organizations

Contact the following organizations for information about certification, for the locations of retail shops and resorts from which you can get instruction and gear, and for written material on great dive destinations around the world: **National Association of Underwater Instructors** (Box 14650, Montclair, CA 91763, tel. 909/621–5801) and **Professional Association of Dive Instructors** (1251 E. Dyer Road, #100, Santa Ana, CA 92705, tel. 714/540–7234 or 800/729–7234, ext. 565). Known as NAUI and PADI, respectively, these are *the* certification organizations in the United States. They can also tell you about snorkeling.

The **Handicapped Scuba Association International** (1104 El Prado, San Clemente, CA 92672, tel. 714/498–6128) is a certification agency for instructors who work with people with special needs. It also has a Dive Buddy program for family members of physically challenged individuals. If you have a special-needs teen, for example, you can learn what you need to know to dive with your child. Send $2 and a stamped, self-addressed envelope for more information.

Periodicals

Rodale's *Scuba Diving Magazine* (Box 7589, Red Oak, IA 51591, tel. 800/666–0016 for subscriptions or 912/351–0885 for back-issue information) covers all aspects of diving, such as travel, health, safety, and equipment. Family diving is part of the mix, too. *Skin Diver Magazine* (Box 52595, Boulder, CO 80322, tel. 800/800–3487 for subscriptions or 213/782–2960 for back-issue information) includes travel and destination articles. It plans to increase coverage of snorkeling and good snorkeling destinations.

Products

VSI (5927 Priestly Dr., Suite 200, Carlsbad, CA 92008, tel. 619/930–0700, ext. 3021 or 800/367–8648) makes snorkel gear for children under two labels: Voit and the higher-end Body Glove. Check your local dive shops or call for the nearest dealer.

TREKKING WITH LLAMAS, GOATS, AND BURROS

Children, especially young ones, require lots of gear. But as luck—or nature—would have it, they must depend on parents to haul it around. This system can be a problem in the world of long-distance and back-country hiking. Parents with packs can't also carry infants and toddlers in a back-pack-style child carrier, and adding another person's gear to an already heavy pack may be an impossibility. The end result is that many families feel they can't trek into remote areas or hike longer, more difficult trails until their children are old enough—about 11 or 12—to walk a good distance and carry their own gear.

Fortunately, there is another way: Trekking with animals is a nature-loving family's dream come true. The natural affinity between children and animals makes them ideal companions. Most children are happy to help lead and care for their four-footed hiking friends, which has the added bonus of occupying them on the trail and in camp. And even though they think they're just having fun, children who hike with animals are learning responsibility and patience as well.

Perhaps best of all, trekking with animals literally takes the load off parents, freeing them up to carry nonwalkers or preschoolers into some of the continent's most beautiful terrain. Animal trekking opens backcountry up to school-age children, too—6- to 8-year-olds who can walk (and run and leap and dawdle) over several miles of rugged trails each day, but not with a heavy pack.

Families have several choices of animal companions. Llamas are the most popular; these smart, agile South American natives have been domesticated beasts of burden for more than 5,000 years. Although they don't like a lot of petting, llamas are gentle, good-natured souls. They're among the most environmentally friendly of pack animals because of the leathery padding on their two-toed feet; they make about the same impact on the wilderness as a deer. Goats are another choice; despite their smaller size, these animals can carry 40 to 60 pounds. They are very friendly and affectionate, and their size makes them less intimidating than llamas. Goats do require a lot of water, which they must pack into the back-country, and that is probably the reason they aren't used as much as llamas. As for burros, they're gentle, strong, surefooted, and particularly well suited to the High Sierra in California, where they've been used as pack animals for years.

Pick a part of the land you want to explore, an animal your family wants to bond with, and head into the backcountry. Keep your camera handy: Trekking with animals and kids is a nonstop photo opportunity that will fill albums with friendly, furry faces you'll remember clearly long after the details of the trails and ridges you hiked have faded from memory.

Questions to Ask

Does each hiker get to lead an animal? On some treks this is the case; on others, two hikers share an animal. Sometimes the animals may be tied in a group, with the guide leading the whole gang. Depending on the age of your children, one style will probably suit you better than the others. Find out how things work so your kids won't be either disappointed or overwhelmed.

Can my children or I help care for the animals? This is a learning experience as well as fun, and it can make the difference between a good and a great trip for some families. If animal care interests you, pick an outfitter that encourages guests to join in.

How many miles do you walk each day? These treks average 4 to 6 miles in a day, though some cover as little as 1½ miles and others as many as 10. Make sure that your children can walk the distance or that you can carry them in a backpack, because riding the pack animals is never allowed.

What kind of terrain will we hike? As important as the number of miles is the difficulty of the trail. One mile through a level forested area may be doable for a 5-year-old, whereas a mile on a steep canyon trail is not. Most outfitters rate their trips easy, moderate, or strenuous, based on the difficulty of the terrain; check the classifications and ask specific questions.

Which trip is best for families? Even among the easy or moderate treks, some are better for families than others, and some are better for younger children. The outfitters here named their best family trips without hesitation because they've seen lots of families out in the wilderness. Listen to their advice. Even when llamas, burros, or goats are carrying the gear, kids still have to be able to negotiate the trails safely and in a reasonable amount of time.

How much personal gear can we bring? Many outfitters have a limit—frequently about 20 pounds per person—depending on whether the animals will be carrying gear for one person or two. This is a good opportunity to teach your children how to economize on equipment and gear, weigh things, and set priorities. Of course, if they choose a second stuffed animal over a warm jacket, you'll have to convince them to choose again.

What gear must we bring? Some outfitters supply sleeping bags; others do not. Read equipment lists carefully and ask if you are uncertain. Also, many treks are in mountainous areas, where the weather can change drastically in a matter of minutes and the temperature can fluctuate significantly from daytime to evening. Clothes that can be layered and that dry quickly are best for everyone.

Will there be other activities on the trip? A few treks include wildlife viewing, nature studies, fishing, geology lessons, and hikes without the animals as part of the itinerary. Depending on the ages and interests of your children, such activities might be almost as important to you as the main event. Look for the trip that meets your needs in every way.

Do you offer tours of your farm or ranch? Some llama outfitters, especially those specializing in day hikes, will give minitours so your family can see babies and other llamas not on your trip. These tours are usually, but not always, free. This can be a very special treat for kids, so don't be shy about asking. If you're staying at the outfitter's headquarters, a tour is probably part of the package.

What's included in the cost of the trip? Outfitters provide animals, guides, food, tents, and sleeping pads, unless noted otherwise. Gourmet meals are common—one outfitter even wakes you up with hot towels and coffee. Sleeping bags are not usually included, but there are some exceptions. Local transportation varies: You may meet at company headquarters and then be taken with your group to the trail-head; in other cases you must get to the trailhead on your own. Most outfitters will give you some help finding accommodations in the area before and after a trip, though they don't usually provide lodging themselves.

Instruction

Animal trekking involves minimal instruction, although before the trip you will be given information on how to lead an animal properly if you will be doing that, how to move around them safely (for the animals' protection and your family's), and what you can expect in terms of their personality and behavior. If caring for and feeding the animals is part of the trip, you will learn as you go. Your children must listen to these instructions, too.

A Note about Ages

The age in the listings is the outfitter's suggestion for children old enough to hike the trip on their own. When two ages or ranges are given, it means the outfitter will allow children on the trip who are young enough for parents to carry in a backpack. The younger range is generally 1–3; however, you know your children and your capacity for carrying them.

Finding the Fun

Northeast: Appalachian Mountain Club, Northern Vermont Llama Company; Telemark Inn. **Mid-Atlantic:** Virginia Highlands Llamas. **South:** Avalon Llama Treks. **Southwest:** American Wilderness Experience, Derringer Outfitters. **Rockies:** American Wilderness Experience, Off the Beaten Path, Red Rock 'n Llamas. **West Coast:** Hurricane Creek Llamas, Sierra Club, Wallowa Llamas. **Canada:** Strider Adventures.

Favorite Packers

American Wilderness Experience

👫 10+

Although American Wilderness Experience (AWE) is not an outfitter itself, it works with some of the country's best outfitters to bring adventure of all kinds to people who want to experience the solitude and beauty of life in the wilderness. AWE offers two llama trips in New Mexico and Colorado. Ten is the recommended minimum age for both these treks, but AWE may make exceptions for families with hiking and wilderness experience. Discuss this first before booking a trip.

FOR FAMILIES. The five-day Pecos Wilderness trek departs from Santa Fe for New Mexico's Pecos Wilderness, the southern terminus of the Rocky Mountains. This is classic alpine terrain, with wildflower meadows, blue lakes, towering peaks, forested valleys, and rushing streams. You camp in several different places, and there are also some layover days. A naturalist can answer all the questions kids and parents might have about the area's geology and plant and animal life. Bighorn sheep, elk, and wild turkeys are among the native residents. This trip, which typically has about 12 trekkers, includes sleeping bags, solar-heated showers, and delicious southwestern cuisine.

If Colorado is where you want to meet your llama, start your trip at the Lost Trail Ranch outside Alamosa, in the Rio Grande River valley (for an extra charge, airport pickup can be arranged). The next day you head into the San Juan Mountains and an area that was once the sacred land of the Ute people. This trek has an unhurried pace through alpine meadows, cool canyons, and dense forests. There's lots of time for photography, nature study, and fishing, and to relax in campsites beside glacial lakes. A pre-trip night at the ranch is part of the adventure; group size is about eight.

🏠 *American Wilderness Experience, Box 1486, Boulder, CO 80306, tel. 303/444–2622 or 800/444–0099. June–Sept.: 5–6 days, $620–$685.*

Appalachian Mountain Club

👫 13+

Join this venerable organization and you'll meet other families, guides, naturalists, and a host of people who love the wilderness and respect nature. Members get a discount on trips and courses. The Appalachian Mountain Club has llama trekking in New York at its Catskill Mountains center in the High Peaks region.

FOR FAMILIES. The focus of this weekend trip is really to teach novices all about llamas and give them a chance to spend time around the animals. Participants arrive Friday night and stay in the Valley View Lodge. Saturday morning, everyone learns a bit about their four-footed hiking companions before the group takes off for a 6- to 8-mile hike on mountain trails. Return to the lodge Saturday evening for dinner, videotapes, and discussions about caring for, showing, and breeding llamas. Sunday morning is spent at the lodge playing games with the llamas and finding out more about them.

🏠 *Appalachian Mountain Club, Pinkham Notch Visitors Center, Box 298, Gorham, NH 03581, tel. 603/466–2727 for general information and a full catalog, tel. 518/624–2056 for reservations at the Catskill Center. Sept.: 2 days, $175; discount for members.*

Avalon Llama Treks

👫 1 – 3, 4+

Mark and Laura Moser have been leading llama treks into the mountains of western North Carolina for six years. The fact that Mark is a gourmet chef with a degree in horticulture, while Laura has a degree in sociology and is a part-time nanny, is icing on the cake for families. Lovely surroundings, sensational food, and child-oriented sensibilities make Avalon hard to beat.

FOR FAMILIES. Avalon is small enough that Mark and Laura are able to tailor each trek to the group's needs with respect to length, difficulty, and food. All trips take place on the lush trails of Pisgah National Forest, an easy drive from Asheville. Infants and toddlers in backpacks are welcome, and ages 4 and up can hike many of the trails.

The two-day trek is the most popular with families; one night in the wilderness is often a good amount of time for very young children. Among the Mosers' favorite trails is the Mt. Mitchell Commissary Ridge Trail. The Mt. Mitchell summit—6,684 feet—is the highest point east of the Mississippi, but you don't have to climb to the top for spectacular views or cool temperatures. When the valley is in the 80s, the ridge trail temperature hovers around 60°F, providing a welcome respite.

Each hiker leads a llama on the overnights, and the Mosers prefer to limit overnight groups to six to eight people, though they do make exceptions. On day trips, which accommodate up to 12 participants, hikers share the llamas' gentle company. Best of all, Avalon makes it easy for families by supplying all camping gear, including sleeping bags.
 Avalon Llama Treks, 450 Old Buckeye Cove Rd., Swannanoa, NC 28778, tel. 704/299–7155. Apr.–Nov.: 1–3 days, $45–$300.

Derringer Outfitters

👫👤 10+

The Gila wilderness area of southwestern New Mexico is a land of high desert, mountains, abundant wildlife, ancient cliff dwellings, and deep peace and solitude. The Gila National Forest includes some 3 million acres of land, and the Derringers' ranch lies

in the northern part of it, 20 miles south of the small town of Quemado and 200 miles southwest of Albuquerque. Whether your family wants a ranch or wilderness experience, you can have it here. David Derringer has been outfitting and guiding for more than 12 years. He's an expert in canoeing, fishing, and horse packing, in addition to packing with goats, and he welcomes the chance to share his knowledge with families. Exceptions may be made on the minimum age, but talk to the Derringers first.

FOR FAMILIES. The ranch is home not only to David and his wife, Susan, but to numerous chickens, ducks, turkeys, a handful of goats (with more on the way), 9 cats, 4 dogs, and 18 horses. The ranch goats—good-size Nubians and La Manchas that stand 36–38 inches at the shoulder—are extremely friendly and loving. Goats are also easy on the environment, which makes them an ideal pack animal in wilderness areas. You can lead a goat if you'd like, but there isn't always a goat for each trekker.

The Derringers take only 5 to 10 guests at a time, so every visit is personalized. They recommend a five-day, all-inclusive stay (lodging, meals, adventures, and activities) during the summer as best for families, though fewer days with individually priced activities are also available. You can spend all your time packing with the goats, or you can take day treks. You might also choose to go goat packing for three days and spend two days on the ranch canoeing, hiking, riding, learning archery, and feeding and caring for the animals. On a family trek, guides will take you 4 to 5 miles a day through the Ponderosa pine and juniper trees, across the creeks, and even up to the area on the ranch where ancient Native American ruins and pottery shards can be found.

Ranch accommodations are in 16-by-16-foot tents with cots and dressers (toilets are outside), or in the newly built cabins. The ranch is at 8,000 feet, so be prepared: It might be 85° during the day and 45° at night. If you get up early to watch the elk wander down to one of the ranch's many streams, dress warmly.

 Derringer Outfitters, Box 157, Quemado, NM 87829, tel. 505/773–4860. Year-round: 5 days, $400–$600.

Hurricane Creek Llama Treks

6+

Twelve thousand years ago glaciers carved what is now the Eagle Cap Wilderness out of northeast Oregon's landscape. Today rugged granite and marble peaks rise from flower-filled alpine meadows and pine forests; clear streams and lakes teem with rainbow and brook trout. Elk, bighorn sheep, mountain goats, and mule deer are often seen on the ridges and in high valleys. People, however, are harder to find. Eagle Cap remains uncrowded and unspoiled, a terrific place to trek with children and llamas. You could not be in better hands than with Stanlynn Daugherty, owner of Hurricane Creek Llama Treks and the person who wrote the book on llama trekking—literally (see Resources, *below*).

FOR FAMILIES. Stanlynn recommends 3 of her 10 trips for families with younger children. Eagle Cap Wildflowers, a six-day trek in mid-July, takes hikers along the lower reaches of Hurricane Creek when the wildflowers are nearing their peak. You can fish along the way, too. Brownie Basin Base Camp in late July is ideal for 6- and 7-year-olds or those with limited hiking experience. You hike to several alpine lakes where the fishing is surpassed only by the scenery. The trip coincides with Chief Joseph Days rodeo weekend, so arrive in Joseph early to catch the action. For families with limited time, the Wilderness Weekend Getaway in early August offers a streamside camp in the shadow of Eagle Cap's highest peaks.

Parents with older children and hiking and wilderness experience might opt for the Hells Canyon Base Camp in the remote Hells Canyon National Recreation Area. On

this trip, you look across North America's deepest gorge to the mountains of Idaho and hike canyons and rims high over the Snake River.

All Hurricane Creek trips include a night at the Bed, Bread and Trail Inn in Joseph, Oregon, before and after the trip, as well as dinner and breakfast at the inn before the start of your adventure. The outfitter also supplies transportation between the inn and the trailhead.

 Hurricane Creek Llama Treks, 63366 Pine Tree Rd., Enterprise, OR 97828, tel. 505/ 432–4455 or 800/528–9609. July–Aug.: 3–5 days, $395–$650; 20% discount for children 6–18.

Northern Vermont Llama Company

1 – 3, 4+

Your family can trek with llamas through the Green Mountains of Vermont near the resort areas of Smugglers' Notch and Stowe. Although this company offers day trips only, Vermont and the Green Mountains are the setting for so many family adventures—kayaking, canoeing, and rock climbing, to name a few—you could easily spend a week here and not try the same activity twice.

FOR FAMILIES. The cross-country ski trails of Smugglers' Notch, a year-round family resort, make ideal llama trekking trails in spring, summer, and fall. All treks meet at Smugglers', but you don't have to be a guest there to join up with Lindsay and Geoff Chandler of Northern Vermont Llama Company. Half-day, full-day, and sunset treks are all good choices for families with babies and toddlers in backpacks or for parents with preschoolers. Walks are leisurely, with ample break time to meet the needs of the littlest explorers. On a typical full-day hike, you walk for 1¼ hours and then take a morning break, followed by an hour-long hike. After lunch and rest time of an hour or so, the hike back to Smugglers' is about 1½ hours. All treks include fresh fruit, Lindsay's baked goods, and Vermont's own Ben & Jerry's ice cream.

If you have time at the end of your hike, follow Lindsay 10 miles back to the farm in your car. Most of the 10 to 15 babies born each year at the 35-acre llama and Christmas tree farm arrive in summer, so there's a good chance you'll get to see a few.

 Northern Vermont Llama Company, R.R. 1, Box 544, Waterville, VT 05492, tel. 802/ 644–2257. May–Oct.: ½–1 day, $25–$50.

Off the Beaten Path

👪 1+

Off the Beaten Path (OBP) specializes in custom western vacations and works only with experienced outfitters who provide the highest quality service. Once you arrange a trip, OBP takes care of every detail. Although custom can mean expensive, OBP is also dedicated to helping families plan the trip of a lifetime—even when the budget is a consideration.

FOR FAMILIES. OBP works with llama packers in the Rockies. There are trips in the towering Tetons of Wyoming, in Colorado, and around West Yellowstone in southern Montana, among other spectacular places. When you ask about a family llama trek, OBP takes down extensive information about your family: ages, experience, budget, vacation needs and dreams, where you most want to go and what you most want to see, and how much time you have. OPB then makes suggestions about the outfitter and trip they believe will give you the best experience.

Off the Beaten Path, 109 E. Main St., Bozeman, MT 59715, tel. 406/586–1311 or 800/445–2995. June–Sept.: $125–$160 per day; some trips offer children's discounts.

Red Rock 'n Llamas

👪 10+

Headquartered almost midway between Bryce Canyon and Capitol Reef national parks, this company has been leading treks into the remote red-rock canyons of the Escalante River and Capitol Reef in southern Utah for six years. Its mission is twofold: to offer safe, comfortable, fun llama pack treks and to give informative tours that concentrate on the total ecology of the area, including geology, archaeology, anthropology, and flora and fauna. Both the landscape and the trip focus make these adventures best for families with older children.

FOR FAMILIES. The best family trip is the three- or four-day trek along the upper corridor of the Escalante River Canyon. The river is slow in this stretch, but the canyon walls are as impressively steep as they are anywhere along the 75-mile length of the canyon. One day is spent in the awesome narrows of Death Hollow, and natural plunge pools provide cool relief from the hot summer days.

Before or after your llama trek, consider a visit to nearby Capitol Reef National Park with its red sandstone cliffs capped by domes of white sandstone. Ranger programs are evening highlights; during the day there's a 25-mile drive through the park, some of it unpaved.

Red Rock 'n Llamas, Box 1304, Boulder, UT 86716, tel. 801/335–7325. July–Aug.: 3–4 days, $360–$450; children's discounts are available.

Sierra Club

👪 7+

Gentle, strong, friendly, and occasionally confounding, burros make ideal trekking companions for families hiking the High Sierra in California. The Sierra Club's burro-assisted hikes are extremely popular, so if you want to go along, sign up early. Leading and caring for the burros is somewhat demanding, so families should be prepared for a little work as well as a lot of fun. Good physical condition is a must.

FOR FAMILIES. Traditionally, two or three of the weeklong burro trips each summer are designated as family departures, each one accommodating about 12 people. The Cottonwood Lakes Basin trip takes families into the southern Sierra and Inyo National Forest. Numerous lakes, home of the rare golden trout, are wonderful settings for campsites; on several layover days there's time for relaxing and fishing. The Miter Basin and Sequoia National Park trip follows a moderate route across ridges and glaciated Sierra landscape. Fishing, day hikes, and just lounging around are all part of the agenda. Those who join the Mt. Langley trip will visit Inyo National Forest and Sequoia National Park, hike over Cottonwood Pass and onto the northern edge of the Kern Plateau, fish, and explore the High Sierra timberline.
🏠 *Sierra Club, 730 Polk St., San Francisco, CA 94109, tel. 415/923–5522. July–Aug.: 7 days, $595 adults, $395–$400 children. All participants 12 and up must be Sierra Club members; application and fees can be sent in with the trip reservation form.*

Strider Adventures

If llama trekking with a small group in British Columbia's backcountry sounds like an adventure your family is ready for, contact the people at Strider. You can choose treks through the majestic Canadian Rockies, the Cariboo Mountains, or the alpine meadows and lakes of the high country. The company also has trips along the glaciers and rivers of the area's remote parks. If you're lucky, you'll see the magical northern lights in addition to vast star-filled skies, wildlife, waterfalls, and unforgettable panoramic views.

FOR FAMILIES. Families are welcomed on all Strider llama treks. There are two-,

three-, four-, and seven-day scheduled adventures, or you can opt for a custom trip of any length. The Caledonia Mountain trek includes a round-trip hike of 10 kilometers (a little more than 6 miles) and walks along alpine lakes and meadows. Fang Mountain is a 6-kilometer (almost 4-mile) hike though alpine bowls and along ridges and bluffs. Both Caledonia and Fang are destinations for two- and three-day treks. A remote lake in the rugged Dezaiko Range is a 35-kilometer (about 20-mile) hike for families on three- or four-day trips, and those who join the seven-day, 80-kilometer (50-mile) trek will hike into the Canadian Rockies and up a long, gentle grade over the Continental Divide.

You have to bring your own high-quality, warm sleeping bag, but Strider supplies binoculars and field guides in addition to transportation to and from Prince George and trekking and camping equipment.
🏠 *Strider Adventures, R.R. 1, Site 24, Comp. 7, Prince George V2N 2H8, British Columbia, Canada, tel. 604/963–9542 or 800/665–7752. June–Sept.: 2–7 days, $220–$660; 50% discount for children under 16, and additional 10% discount for family groups of 4 or more.*

Telemark Inn

This Maine inn at the base of Caribou Mountain, on the edge of White Mountain National Forest, was built in 1900 as a private wilderness retreat. Today Telemark Inn accommodates 12 to 14 people, who come for the serenity of the wilderness and to trek with llamas, among other activities (see Cross-Country Skiing). An appreciation for nature is at the heart of what Telemark offers, which is one reason it's very popular with families. Llama trekkers learn not only about the animals but about alpine ecology, local geology, and the area's wildlife. On these treks, all those who want to can lead their own llama.

FOR FAMILIES. One-, three-, and four-day llama treks take guests over the Maine border into New Hampshire, near Mt. Washington. These are Himalayan-style treks, meaning that guides go ahead and set everything up before your party arrives in camp each afternoon. You're awakened with hot towels and coffee brought to your roomy, domed tent. Yes, it's pampering, but this doesn't take away from the emphasis on nature—and it's fun. Throughout the trek there's time to swim, hike without the llamas, and relax. One popular option is a 2-mile nature hike to a moose pond—and the chances are good that you'll catch a moose grazing. Inn owner Steve Crone will take children as young as 3½ on any llama trek, but talk to him first about the trip and your child's personality and abilities.

If your family can't decide between a canoe adventure and a llama trek, ask about the six-day combo trip: three days each of llama trekking and Maine lakes canoeing.

Not all llama-trekking guests stay at the inn before or after a trip, but if you have the time, it's well worth a visit. Sit down on the huge old front porch and, just for a day or two, let time pass you by.
🏠 *Telemark Inn, R.F.D. 2, Box 800, Bethel, ME 04217, tel. 207/836–2703. June–mid-Sept.: 1–4 days, $75–$495 adults, $50–$375 children.*

Virginia Highlands Llamas

(👫 5+)

The ancient, rolling terrain of the Appalachians beckons hikers of all ages and abilities, and friendly llamas, too. This company in Virginia's southwestern corner has day hikes of varying difficulty, one of which is perfect for young hikers who need time to play as they go.

FOR FAMILIES. The journey doesn't sound like much—just 1½ miles—but when you add in time for lunch, wading in the creek, and inspecting a natural spring that pumps

out 350 gallons of water a minute, it's a full day of llama trekking and an excellent summer choice for children 5 and up. Virginia Highlands is somewhat flexible about age, but ask before bringing a younger child.

In the spring and fall, when it's a little cooler, you and your older kids—those 8 and up—might choose to climb Big Walker Mountain. This trek is a strenuous 3 miles out and 3 miles back on steep, rugged trails, so be prepared.
🏠 *Virginia Highlands Llamas, Rte. 1, Box 41, Bland, VA 24315, tel. 703/688–4464. Apr.–Nov. (all treks not available all months): 1 day, $60.*

Wallowa Llamas

(👫 1 – 3, 6+)

Although most people who have never been to Oregon think only of its fir forests and green valleys, the state also has cliff-lined coasts, high volcanic mountain ranges, red-rock desert, and areas where endless wheat fields sweep away to the horizon. Oregon's northeast corner is primarily high desert, mountains, and wilderness—the perfect setting for llama trekking.

Wallowa Llamas generally takes eight llamas for 10 trekkers, and they're put in two strings of four llamas each. Hikers don't usually lead their own llama; however, the guides might let you lead the string of four as you get accustomed to working with the animals during the trip. Guests are always welcome to help feed and water the llamas in camp, and to help bring them in when it's time to break camp.

FOR FAMILIES. Like Hurricane Creek Llama Treks (see *above*), Wallowa Llamas has easy treks for families into the Eagle Cap Wilderness in the Wallowa Mountains, not far from the Idaho border. Infants and toddlers have made this four-day trip in backpacks, and most 6-year-olds are capable of walking it.

For something a little unusual in the moderate range of difficulty, families with children aged 7 or 8 who have good hiking experience should consider Wallowa Llamas' three-day Hells Canyon Trip, which takes hikers to the Idaho side of the Snake River. How do you get there? You and the patient llamas are transported from Hells Canyon Dam across the Snake to the trailhead by jet boat. After a 10-mile hike and a couple of days in the canyon, your group—llamas and all—reboards the jet boats for the ride upriver to Oregon.

Teens and their parents ready for a seven-day mountain adventure can choose Across the Rugged Wallowas, the company's strenuous, 32-mile trek. U.S. Forest Service regulations allow only four guests and two guides on this trip, so sign up early if this one is for you. 🏕 *Wallowa Llamas, Rte. 1, Box 84, Halfway, OR 97834 tel. 503/742–2961 or 503/742–4930. Apr.–Oct.: 3–7 days, $285–$770.*

Resources

Organizations

Contact the **International Llama Association** (2755 S. Locust St., Suite 114, Denver,

CO 80222, tel. 303/756–9004 or 800/949–5262) for a catalog with a variety of material: information about llamas; a list of reference books, pamphlets, videos, and other educational materials; and a list of packers and breeders across the nation.

Books

Stanlynn Daugherty, owner of Hurricane Creek Llama Treks, is the author of the informative *Packing With Llamas* (Juniper Ridge Press). Order it from a bookstore or call 503/432–4455 or 800/528–9609.

Also See

If your family loves traveling the backcountry with four-footed friends, consider the trips in Horse Packing, Covered Wagon Adventures, and Cattle Drives. The chapter on Ranches also has vacations on which you can get to know horses and other animals. For up-close meetings with more exotic creatures, turn to Wildlife Encounters.

WILDLIFE ENCOUNTERS

Almost from birth, children show immense joy in the fact that we share this planet with finned, winged, and four-footed creatures. While the benefits of teaching children about animals and giving them a chance to meet the creatures of the world up close and personal are clear, there is another reason for seeking out this type of trip: Wildlife encounters are also good for adults. They bring out the child in us, take us back to a time when we saw the world as full of wonder. I have seen this transformation take place among adults on all the animal encounter trips I've taken. In the Galápagos, adults and children vied for the sea lions' attention and made faces at the somber-eyed iguanas. When the captain of our boat announced that a troop of dolphins was leaping off our bow, the adults were the first ones to the railing.

Whether you choose a vacation on which you actually hug a wild creature (as is possible in Baja California and on the ice floes in the Gulf of St. Lawrence) or one on which you observe them at close range, the rewards are immediate and long-lasting. Some animal encounters benefit the animals, too, because tourist dollars provide important funding or because tourists themselves provide research assistance.

It's worth noting that some outfitters and tour operators—not, of course, those described here—may be more interested in the bottom line than in protecting animals. By choosing a trip carefully, you're ensuring that future generations will be able to experience the magic of these encounters, too.

Unlike other family adventures, most of the wildlife encounters in this chapter take place outside the United States. Of course, on different adventures across the country you will also see wildlife, and the trip descriptions highlight that aspect. These encounters, however, were chosen because they are extraordinary ones that focus on the animals, many unique to their habitat. A family's contact with these creatures great and small can be the experience of a lifetime, with the power to change a child's perceptions not only of the world's animals but of our place in the universe.

Questions to Ask

How long will we be watching for animals each day, and is there an option to cut it short if my kids get fidgety? As much as children love animals, few enjoy the long trips and dragged-out waits that many animal encounters require. That's why trips planned just for families are designed to move quickly, without unnecessarily long waiting periods and delays. Still, even on non-family trips, outfitters do their best to accommodate everyone, so you may be able to make special arrangements in certain cases. Some trips, however, cannot be altered; when you're flying to ice floes by helicopter, for example, you're bound to a strict schedule. Study your itinerary carefully. If there are morning and afternoon encounters, you will probably have the option of going on just one. Ask about the possibility of child care while you're away from camp. Find a trip that's right for your child's age, temperament, and capacity for sitting.

Are shots or other health precautions necessary? Many animal encounter trips take place in foreign countries that require innoculations and other kinds of medication. Check far in advance and ask a pediatrician or the local health department about health precautions in foreign countries, especially as they relate to children. Always pack basic children's medication—acetaminophen, an antihistamine, cough syrup, motion sickness pills, and antidiarrhea pills; these are often hard to find in foreign countries. If your child is prone to ear infections or any other ailments, you may want to ask your pediatrician for an antibiotic that doesn't need to be refrigerated.

Is any special clothing required? On some trips, such as those to the Arctic, special cold-weather apparel is crucial. While outfitters often provide outerwear that will fit children, they may not have all that's necessary. Finding extreme-weather clothing for kids can be difficult in the United States, let alone in foreign destinations, so plan ahead.

What kind of luggage and gear should we pack? Almost all flights on small planes in the Arctic or Africa have limited capacity for luggage. Because many of these adventures have lodging in small quarters anyway—tents and ship cabins, for example—it's a good idea to pack lightly. Attire for adventure is always casual; keep in mind that you'll be getting dirty. Some African safari camps offer laundry service if you wish it.

What's the primary language spoken where we're going? If you're lucky enough to travel to a foreign land, take advantage of the opportunity to expose your children—and yourself—to a new language. Buy a phrase book before you leave so your family can learn to say basic phrases and the names of animals in the local lingo. There are also language audiotapes for both adults and children that can help you make language part of the travel experience.

Is there anyplace to purchase film during the trip? There's nothing worse than running out of film on your trip of a lifetime, and opportunities for purchasing film on most of these trips are extremely limited. In the Galápagos, for example, film is available only in one or two ports. At camp in Baja, it's not available at all. Carry plenty of film with you and also the batteries in your camera before you leave, even if you don't think you need them. Batteries are almost impossible to find at adventure destinations.

Should we tip our guides? Your guide or naturalist is your window onto a world that you've paid a great deal to see. A good guide can make the difference between a mediocre trip and an incredible one. When it comes to children, good guides work extra hard to bring the world alive to them, too—not always an easy task. Parents may show appreciation for guides' efforts in the form of tips. On trips of this sort, $10 per adult per day is appropriate; an extra few dollars for the children is a good way to encourage your guides to keep up the good work. In addition, I like to have my children give their favorite guides a note, a picture, a Polaroid shot, or any other small token of their appreciation.

What's included in the cost? Lodging, most meals, transportation throughout the expedition, entrance fees to sites included in the itinerary, all group equipment, and the services of qualified guides and naturalists are part of the package, unless otherwise noted. In some cases, as with those tour operators running African safaris, airfare to and from certain cities in the United States is also included. When air is not part of the trip cost, outfitters and operators can usually arrange it for you, often at a better rate than you could get on your own. Hotel stays may be required before and after trips because of flight schedules; these are generally an additional expense.

Instruction

Much of the instructional aspect of these trips is related to safety—both yours and the animals'—and to teaching **visitors** how to minimize human impact on the earth's fragile environments. In areas where the weather and conditions are extreme, you must follow instructions about proper clothing and emergency procedures. To make this process fun for kids rather than a chore, enlist their help. They can help check that your family follows all the guidelines.

Finding the Fun

West Coast: Sea Quest Expeditions. **Alaska:** Alaska Wildland Adventures, Natural Habitat Adventures. **Canada:** Arctic Odysseys, Natural Habitat Adventures. **Caribbean:** Natural Habitat Adventures. **Mexico:** Baja Discovery, Baja Expeditions. **Central America:** American Wilderness Experience, Overseas Adventure Travel, Temptress Voyages. **South America:** Galápagos Network, Overseas Adventure Travel. **Europe:** Natural Habitat Adventures. **Africa:** Big Five Tours & Expeditions, Natural Habitat Adventures, Overseas Adventure Travel, Rascals in Paradise.

Favorite Outfitters

Alaska Wildland Adventures

 6+

Alaska Wildland Adventures believes that Alaska should be experienced personally, "not passively viewed through the windows of a tour bus or via the endless buffet of a luxury cruise liner." The company, however, also understands the needs of both children and senior citizens; trips specifically for these groups explore the "real" Alaska at a comfortable, easy pace.

FOR FAMILIES. Every summer, a special Family Safari departure caters to parents with children aged 6 to 11. On this trip you might see moose, bald eagles, and spawning salmon in the Kenai Mountains; sea otters, puffins, seals, sea lions, and maybe even whales during a boat tour of Kenai Fjords National Park; and Dall sheep, caribou, Alaska brown bears, and more moose in Denali National Park. There are hikes, nature walks, drives, and a train ride back to Anchorage at the end of the eight-day adventure. Accommodations are in hotels and a backcountry lodge. Because this trip is modeled after the Senior Safari itinerary, it's also a perfect vacation for parents, children, and grandparents to share together.

If you'd rather stay put in one place for your whole vacation or even just a part of it, consider booking a few nights at Denali Backcountry Lodge, which is managed by Alaska Wildland Adventures. Because of the level of hikes typically offered at the lodge, as well as the long bus ride required to get there, this place is best for families with children aged 8 and up. The lodge lies deep within the park in Kantinsha, along the spectacular Denali Park Road as it winds through the Alaska Range, past aptly named Wonder Lake. Grizzlies, moose, caribou, wolves, fox, Dall sheep, and golden eagles are commonly seen on the park road and on adventures that depart from the lodge each day. Transportation to and from the park entrance is included in the cost of a lodge stay.

🏨 *Alaska Wildland Adventures, Box 389, Girdwood, AK 99587, tel. 907/783–2928 or 800/334–8730. June–Sept.: 1–8 days, $260–$2,550; discounts for groups of 3 or 4 sharing accommodations.*

American Wilderness Experience

👫 6+

Although some dolphin encounter programs have been accused of disregarding the dolphins' health and well-being, this does not mean that all these programs are problematic. When reputable marine scientists are able to care for the dolphins and to teach

humans about these remarkable animals, the programs have long-term beneficial effects for both groups. The experts at the Institute of Marine Sciences on the Bay Islands off the coast of Honduras have developed a program at nearby Anthony's Key Resort that practically guarantees a transcendent experience for all involved. American Wilderness Experience, a specialist in environmentally friendly vacations with outfitters and tour operators who are ecologically responsible, is the U.S. agent through which you can book such encounters.

FOR FAMILIES. Dolphin Discovery Camp, for children aged 6 to 15, centers on the world of the Atlantic bottlenosed dolphin. Under the supervision of the Institute of Marine Sciences staff, children have outdoor sessions on snorkeling, dolphin feeding and training, swimming, and marine experiments, as well as short classroom slide shows and discussions. When not working with the scientists, campers go horseback riding, take nature hikes, view the awesomely clear waters and coral reefs by glass-bottom boat, and otherwise play in what can only be described as paradise. Parents are welcome to join their children for some activities, and families take all meals together. The program is designed, however, to give parents (and older teens) time to do what most adults come here to do—scuba diving in water with visibility that ranges from 75 to 100 feet (see Snorkeling and Diving). Accommodations are in private bungalows set around the lush, tropical island.

🏨 *American Wilderness Experience, Box 1486, Boulder, CO 80306, tel. 303/444–2622 or 800/444–0099. May–Sept.: 8 days, $500; discount for more than one child in camp. Adult packages, $910–$1,150.*

Arctic Odysseys

👫 12+

Arctic Odysseys has been taking adventurers to the North Pole and the area around it for nearly 20 years. The polar bear odyssey may be the star in this outfitter's trip list, but families have other treks to choose from (see Native American Experiences), all of which provide unsurpassed access to the north country.

FOR FAMILIES. Wager Bay, some 30 miles south of the Arctic Circle, has one of the world's greatest concentrations of polar bears. Because the bay can be reached only by chartered aircraft, you view these white giants unhindered by crowds of other wildlife watchers. Boats take you amazingly close for a look at the paddling bears (if they don't paddle, they sink). While polar bears are the reason most people come here, they are by no means the only wildlife in the area. On the way to and from Winnipeg, Canada, where the trip begins and ends, and on hikes around Wager Bay, participants may see beluga whales, caribou, arctic wolves and hares, seals, gyrfalcons, peregrine falcons, and a host of other north-country birds. Accommodations at the bay are in an Inuit-owned and -operated lodge; Inuit guides lead the boat trips and hikes as well. Because of the extreme northern location of this trip, participants must be at least 12 years old—but owner Robin Duberow will consider slightly younger children on an individual basis.

The "Discover the Worlds of the High Arctic" itinerary gives families insight into the fascinating history of the Arctic and a glimpse into the native cultures of the region. Caribou, snow geese, beluga whales, narwhals, polar bears, and bowhead whales are all likely to be viewed from the low-flying planes that provide most of your travel. From boats off Cape Dorset, seals are a common sight, and if you choose to hike around the Eureka Weather Station on Ellesmere Island, you're likely to see arctic wolves and foxes.

Families considering either of these trips should keep two things in mind. First, the unpredictable arctic weather and tides often cause delays or force leaders to change itineraries altogether. If your family doesn't want to be flexible, look for a different adventure. Second, Arctic Odysseys uses native guides and stops at small, out-of-the-way towns and villages on these trips. There are wonderful opportunities to meet the native people and to learn about their unique culture.

🏠 *Arctic Odysseys, 2000 McGilvra Blvd., Seattle, WA 98112, tel. 206/325–1977. July–Aug.: 8–10 days, $4,450–$4,980; ask about family discounts.*

Baja Discovery

 5+

With red rock and gold sand set against deep blue seas, Mexico's Baja California is as incomparably beautiful as it is remote. Moreover, Baja is an extremely child-friendly place; local boatmen and crews on the Baja Discovery tours will make your children feel welcomed and loved. Both trips begin and end in San Diego.

FOR FAMILIES. Baja Discovery runs two trips specifically for families. The Gray Whale Discovery at San Ignacio Lagoon takes families to the only place on earth where whales regularly swim up to boats and seek human contact. Known as Friendlies, these whales stick their heads up next to skiffs half their size and look whale-watchers directly in the eye. Wild and under no obligation or enticement to stay (Mexican law forbids humans from chasing, feeding, or harassing the whales in any way), Friendlies love having their heads patted and their backs rubbed. They also have an incredible sense of humor; it's not unusual for one to push the skiff around and splash the humans on board for as much as an hour. Much of this trip is a waiting game—whale lovers may spend hours circling the waters in vain—so patience and the ability to sit for long periods of time are a must; the age minimum is 8. Three nights are at the company's tented campsite on a point overlooking the lagoon, and one night is spent at a hotel in the small village of San

Ignacio, about two hours inland. Families can choose a departure date from January through March, when the grays come to San Ignacio to mate and give birth to their young. The price includes everything except one breakfast from the time you leave San Diego until you return.

The La Unica and Sea of Cortez Islands trip is the best way to see the heart of Baja—wind-sculpted boulders, cactus "forests," wine-producing and agricultural regions, and the rich and varied flora and fauna of the central desert. Participants travel in a van for two days—stopping to look at things that will engage even very young travelers (minimum age is 5) and spending the night at hotels. On the way down to La Unica on the Sea of Cortez (also known as the Gulf of California) you visit a park, several towns, a museum, a turtle research station, and more. At the coast, participants board 28-foot *pangas* (Mexican fishing skiffs) that travel to La Unica Island. Days three through five are spent exploring the remote desert islands and emerald waters of the Sea of Cortez, home to whales, dolphins, sea lions, and countless marine birds. There's snorkeling, fishing, hiking, and relaxing by day; at night, families sleep in palm-thatched *palapas* (open-sided dwellings with thatched roofs), each with cots and personal bath and shower facilities. On day six there's time for a final swim, followed by a leisurely drive up through Baja to San Diego. This trip runs in May, June, and October and includes everything but meals at the two hotels during the van trip.

 Baja Discovery, Box 15257, San Diego, CA 92195, tel. 619/262–0700 or 800/829–2252. Jan.–June, Sept.–Oct.: 5–8 days, $970–$1,640; family discounts may be available on some trips.

Baja Expeditions

🚹🚹 5+

In business for 22 years, this company has been taking adventurers to Baja California

longer than any other. Baja Expeditions' trips are learning-oriented, with a special emphasis on the fragile and unique environment of the Baja land and seas; lectures and slide shows are daily events.

FOR FAMILIES. On the San Ignacio Lagoon gray whale adventure, the outfitter sends boats out several times daily in search of Friendlies. Participants sleep at a desert campsite on the lagoon, with roomy dome tents, comfortable cots, and fluffy sleeping bags that are practically luxurious. There's a shower tent with solar-heated water, and the food cooked by the Mexican staff is hearty and delicious.

Children are treated with extra love and care by the crew, but adults outnumber children by far on these trips; try to book a departure on which another family has signed up. Parents are responsible for their children at all times. When you sign up for the trip you will be asked whether or not your child can swim and is comfortable around water, and how you feel your child will function in a primarily adult environment. This trip includes van transfers between San Diego and Tijuana and charter flights between Tijuana and San Ignacio.

Baja Expeditions offers other whale-encounter trips, such as an eight-day voyage to see the blue whales, the largest creatures on earth. The trip takes place aboard an 80-foot motor vessel, and participants may spot dolphins and six other kinds of whales in addition to blues. About two-thirds of each day is spent cruising, but there's also time for hiking, snorkeling, and exploring—a combination that's ideal for children and teens. Families can also choose an 11-day adventure that brings you close to the whales, dolphins, mantas, and whale sharks of the Sea of Cortez, or a trip on Magdalena Bay—calmer than San Ignacio—to encounter Baja's magnificent gray whales. All of these trips start and end in the Baja city of La Paz.

🏠 *Baja Expeditions, 2625 Garnet Avenue, San Diego, CA 92100, tel. 619/581–3311* or 800/843–6967. Jan.–Nov.: 7–11 days, $1,425–$1,795; some family discounts available.

Big Five Tours & Expeditions

 ALL

Africa remains the ultimate destination for those seeking an exotic animal encounter and a cultural experience most people only dream of. The animals of this huge continent fill children's books, making them recognizable and, in some ways, surprisingly accessible to children. Not too long ago only hardcore adventurers traveled to Africa. Now, it attracts all kinds of people, including families. Big Five Tours & Expeditions is one of the tour operators that has made it possible for children, even very young ones, to discover this amazing land.

FOR FAMILIES. Big Five has special two-week family safaris to Kenya during the summer and over the December holidays. There is no minimum age, but children older than 4 are likely to appreciate and retain the experience in a way younger children cannot. Besides wildlife viewing, the rich itinerary includes visits to museums, a crafts and cultural center, and the home of the late Joy and George Adamson, of *Born Free* fame. As you travel, you'll see giraffes, zebras, elands, oryx, flamingos and eagles, and of course, lions, leopards, elephants, rhinos, and buffalos. There are stops at the famous Masai Mara Game Reserve, where much of *Out of Africa* was filmed (parents will also enjoy the tour of Karen Blixen's Nairobi home); the Kongoni Game Valley; and Lake Naivasha, in Kenya's northern frontier. Big Five makes a point of getting off the beaten path, even in this wild land, to spend time at private ranches and wildlife sanctuaries. The group also tours the headquarters of Provide International, a nonprofit organization created by Big Five to aid mothers and children in Nairobi; part of your safari payment helps fund the center. All children receive daily lessons in Swahili

and participate in sing-along sessions. An *ayah* (nanny) accompanies all family groups. Accommodations are at deluxe hotels; prices include airfare via Swissair between several East Coast cities and Nairobi.
🏨 *Big Five Tours & Expeditions, 819 S. Federal Hwy., Suite 103, Stuart, FL 34994, tel. 407/287–7995 or 800/244–3483. June–Aug. and Dec.: 15 days, $3,995–$4,995.*

Galápagos Network

 7+

Nature, history, and science come together on the Galápagos Islands as they do nowhere else on earth. Scattered across 17,000 square miles of the Pacific Ocean about 600 miles off the coast of Ecuador, this archipelago is home to the only marine iguanas in the world, as well as to sea lions, giant tortoises, penguins, and seals. The 13 major islands and 17 islets have more birds than most people see in a lifetime: bluefooted boobies, pink flamingos, hawks, doves, pelicans, warblers, mockingbirds, herons, ducks, cormorants, flycatchers, and, of course, Darwin's finches, the little birds that inspired Darwin's theory of evolution. A visit to the Galápagos, now a national park of Ecuador, will help families understand what a fragile world we live in.

FOR FAMILIES. Ages 7 and up are welcome on all five Galápagos Network ships. The 48-passenger, 195-foot *Corinthian* is a luxury expedition ship, and the largest, with a 1,000 square-foot observation lounge, Jacuzzi, and solarium. The *Letty, Eric,* and *Flamingo* are identical 20-passenger, 85-foot motor yachts. All accommodations are in outside cabins; most sleep only two, though there are several with room for three. Polished wood and superb service allow passengers to feel pampered; the most luxurious accommodations are on the *Sea Cloud,* an 85-foot deluxe motor sailer that sleeps 8 to 10 passengers. Rates vary by ship, cabin, and itinerary. Your choice of four- to eight-day excursions determines the number of islands you visit. Most trips give you a chance to snorkel with sea lions, and national park regulations require a stop at Darwin Station on the island of Santa Cruz (one of the only islands where you can purchase souvenirs, T-shirts, and some supplies).

All cruises have at least one naturalist/guide on board to lead hikes and provide information about the natural and cultural history of the archipelago. Guides work well with children, and lectures are interspersed with other activities so that even young children remain intrigued. Everyone can use the snorkeling gear on board and swim at expansive white-sand beaches on various islands.

A trip to the Galápagos Islands will not be a solitary wilderness experience; several groups often visit the same islands at once. Fortunately, permits to sail the islands are severely limited by national park administrators, and guides are good at leading groups on different paths. Not included in the price of the cruise is the national park tax of about $80 per adult ($40 per child), payable in U.S. dollars upon arrival in the Galápagos Islands.

🏛 *Galápagos Network, 7200 Corporate Center Dr., Suite 309, Miami, FL 33126, tel. 305/592–2294 or 800/633–7972. Year-round: 4–8 days, $475–$1,850; 50% discount for children 7–12 on the cruise and on Saeta Airlines, owned by the same parent company. Call 800/827–2382 to book your airfare.*

Natural Habitat Adventures

 6+

Getting close to animals in their natural habitat is what this outfitter is all about. Starting with a profound respect for nature and a belief that people don't have to sacrifice every comfort to take part in the world's greatest nature vacations, Natural Habitat Adventures has become one of the premier companies of its kind. Whether

participants are on a pure vacation or a trip on which they help researchers and scientists, the result is the same: an unforgettable encounter with some of the world's most intriguing inhabitants.

FOR FAMILIES. The top family trip is indisputably Seal Watch in Canada. Each March some 250,000 doe-eyed harp seals give birth to their fuzzy white offspring on the massive floating ice fields just west of the Magdalen Islands in the Gulf of St. Lawrence. Adorable and unafraid, some of the babies even allow visitors to pet them. These treks were begun as part of a plan to provide tourist dollars to the local community so that selling seal skins would no longer be the only way residents could make a living. As a result, participation in this trip may ultimately help save future seals from death. The trip begins and ends in Halifax Nova Scotia, and combines additional activities such as tubing and cross-country skiing. Accommodations are in a cozy hotel.

You may have seen beautifully photographed documentaries in which a few lucky people stood on wooden platforms watching the giant brown bears of Alaska fish for salmon at Brooks Falls in Katmai National Park. Though you can arrange this on your own, permits are limited and difficult to obtain. A better option is Natural Habitat's Alaska & Brown Bear Watch, which includes a stay in Denali National Park. On this trip you will see grizzlies and in all likelihood Dall sheep, moose, and caribou as well; take a boat ride in the Kenai Fjords, home to whales, porpoises, and sea lions; and visit Exit Glacier and Kenai Peninsula Wildlife Refuge. Much of your time at Brooks Lodge is spent on platforms that are only a few feet from the bears.

Natural Habitat Adventures will take children as young as 6 on both the seal and brown bear watches, but consider carefully whether or not your child can handle the elements, the proximity of the animals, and the great amount of travel.

Natural Habitat Adventures runs dozens of additional trips; families can see animals from the mountain gorillas of East Africa to polar bears in Churchill, Manitoba. You can swim with wild Atlantic spotted dolphins in the Bahamas and Caribbean humpback whales off the coast of the Dominican Republic. If research appeals to your family, you can help scientists with a variety of marine projects on a research vessel in the Azores, some 950 miles west of Lisbon. Another research option is a Puffin Watch in Scotland at the Fair Isle Bird Observatory. Different trips are appropriate for different ages, so talk to the staff to determine the best trip for your family.

🏠 *Natural Habitat Adventures, 2945 Center Green Ct., Boulder, CO 80301, tel. 303/449–3711 or 800/543–8917. Year-round (all trips not available all months): 5–16 days, $1,695–$11,490.*

Overseas Adventure Travel

(👫 6 – 12)

Whether you're looking for a traditional African safari in Tanzania, a Costa Rican adventure, or a cruise in the Galápagos Islands, Overseas Adventure Travel (OAT) has family departures to suit your needs. OAT has been bringing families to remote and unusual places since 1988. It excels in giving travelers of all ages a chance to really know and understand people in other cultures.

FOR FAMILIES. The Serengeti Family Safari in December travels to all the exotic places you'd expect—the fabulous Ngorongoro Crater where practically every beast from *The Lion King* can be found, including lions, rhinos, wildebeests, zebras, and thousands of pink flamingos; the Olduvai gorge, in which Louis and Mary Leakey changed anthropology with their discovery of the Zinjanthropus skull; Tarangire National Park, Tanzania's third largest, home to a diverse selection of wildlife as well as to the oddly appealing baobab tree; and of course, the great Serengeti itself, vast and rich in wildlife. Traveling through the Masai homeland and through the tribal lands of the Mbulu people in northern Tanzania, the group visits a Tanzanian school or church, has a meal with a Tanzanian family, and interacts with the Masai and other people in traditional marketplaces and towns. The safari bus carries games and books, and the Tanzanian crew members are all family men who enjoy sharing their knowledge of wildlife and African culture with children. Accommodations are mostly in safari camps, along with a lodge and a couple of hotels.

On the Costa Rica Family Adventure, also in December, participants drive, hike, and ride horseback through this tiny country's rain forests, cloud forests, and volcanoes. Butterflies, hummingbirds, and the brilliantly plumed quetzal, sacred to the Mayan and Aztec peoples, are among the animals you might see, along with monkeys and iguanas. On a private farm at La Providencia Ecological Reserve, your children will join local children in planting trees to help with a reforestation project. You stay in small hotels and lodges.

You can choose an August or December departure for the family adventure in the Galápagos Islands, with overnights and sightseeing in Quito as well. There's also a visit to the famous Otavalo market in the Andean highlands, where the native people in their traditional dress are as striking as the crafts and goods they sell. The group flies from Quito to the Galápagos, where six nights are spent on board a small yacht (group size is limited to 12). Your family has time to explore numerous islands, to study a mind-boggling number of exotic and unafraid creatures, and to snorkel, swim, and hike. You can climb up the 350-foot cinder cone known as Pinnacle Rock, too.

🏠 *Overseas Adventure Travel, 349 Broadway, Cambridge, MA 02139, tel. 617/876–0533 or 800/221–0814. Aug. and Dec., 9–15 days, $1,790–$4,590. All family trips include airfare from designated U.S. cities.*

Rascals in Paradise

👫 7+

Rascals in Paradise, a tour company just for families, works with outfitters and hotels worldwide that are especially accommodating of children and parents. Trips with Rascals are cultural adventures on which all participants not only see new places but truly experience the people and heritage of the country. A special escort educates and entertains the children and provides support for parents. The learning on these trips happens through storytelling, engaging activities, and face-to-face contact with interesting people. Micato, the outfitter who handles this trip to Africa, wholeheartedly supports Rascal's approach.

FOR FAMILIES. The two-week Family Safari begins in Nairobi, Kenya, with visits to the Giraffe Centre, where you study these elegant animals from a treetop aerie, and the Langata Ostrich Farm. Leaving the city, you see lumbering rhinos at the Rhino Reserve and chimpanzees at the Jane Goodall Institute's sanctuary. Another stop lets families witness an exciting nighttime game run. At Island Tented Camp on Lake Baringo, in the land of the Njemps, you paddle canoes with members of the tribe and watch for hundreds of species of birds; there's also a visit to a local school in the bush. Lake Nakuru National Park is home to thousands of flamingos, and in this area you will participate in a tribal dance and learn Swahili songs. Returning to Nairobi, the group flies to the Masai Mara Reserve, passing over the dramatic Great Rift Valley and the Serengeti. Enormous herds of grazing animals, as well as lions, cheetahs, hyenas, and hippos, roam the reserve. On a final return to Nairobi, there's a visit to the Railway Museum to learn about the role of trains in the colonization of East Africa. The group dines with the Pinto family, owners of Micato, on the last night. All lodging and meals are included on this safari, and Micato has a no-tipping policy.

🏠 *Rascals in Paradise, 650 5th St., #505, San Francisco, CA 94107, tel. 415/978–9800 or 800/872–7225. Feb.–Dec.: 14 days, $1,895–$2,943 (Apr.–June), $2,195–$3,375 (other months).*

Sea Quest Expeditions

👫 5+

Kayaking is the mode of travel for Sea Quest's San Juan Archipelago adventure in Washington, but the trip's focus is whale-watching. These islands straddling the border with British Columbia provide plenty of opportunities for families to observe orcas up close, especially in summer. Besides orcas, visitors to the wildlife-rich San Juans can also spot minke whales, gray whales, Dall's porpoises and harbor porpoises (both whales), and a variety of other marine life, birds, and animals. There is no better way to approach these creatures than in a sea kayak. Travelers can skirt the islands and camp in areas inaccessible to land-based travelers.

FOR FAMILIES. Children older than age 5 are welcome on one-day trips, provided they travel in a three-person kayak with two adults. For the multiday adventures, children must be at least 8 years old and ready for a two-person kayak, although the ability to handle a kayak with just one adult has less to do with age than with physical considerations. A child must weigh at least 100 pounds and be in good health and condition to participate. Sea Quest's San Juan trips begin and end in Friday Harbor on San Juan Island (accessible via Seattle, Vancouver, or Victoria).

Families concerned about kayaking near orcas should be aware that these intelligent animals have never injured a human in the wild. Moreover, the orcas living within the San Juan Islands are used to boaters and are among the most studied and well-known whales in the world. Learning and adventure go hand in hand on these expeditions. A biologist accompanies all of Sea Quest's San Juan groups to answer your family's questions about the whales and other aspects of life in these islands. The trip involves kayaking about four to five hours daily, mostly with prevailing currents. No previous paddling experience is necessary, though participants must be in good physical condition. No Eskimo rolls—upside-down flips—are performed in the state-of-the-art sea kayaks; the boats are extremely stable. The group receives instruction in basic paddling techniques.

🏠 Sea Quest Expeditions, Box 2424, Friday Harbor, WA 98250, tel. 360/378–5767. May–Oct.: 1–5 days, $59–$449.

Temptress Voyages

👫 2+

In recent years Costa Rica has become a major family vacation destination, primarily because of its easy access to startlingly beautiful wildlife and vegetation. Politically stable and safe for tourists, Costa Rica has jungles, beaches, mountains, and, most importantly, incredible animals to observe. For families who want to see a lot of the country with a minimum of packing and unpacking, a cruise with Temptress Voyages is ideal.

FOR FAMILIES. Over the course of six nights and seven days the *Temptress Explorer* takes 99 passengers along Costa Rica's Pacific coastline (three-night, four-day cruises are also available). The ship sails at night; during the days, passengers hike through verdant rain forests, where kids keep track of numerous wildlife sightings. There are four kinds of monkeys to be discovered: howler, spider, whiteface, and squirrel. You'll also see toucans, macaws, and sloths, both two- and three-toed varieties. Iguanas and lizards abound, including the popularly named Jesus Christ lizard that walks on water. Butterflies are ubiquitous, and snakes are easy to find. You may spot a *fer-de-lance* snake, one of the deadliest in

Costa Rica. (You needn't worry about being bitten by snakes; they are shy, and the ship naturalists who always accompany you will watch for them.) And if you're really lucky, a poison dart frog may cross your path. Dolphins play offshore, and whales occasionally surface as well.

The company offers a supervised program for children aged 2 through 12. There's a youth director (a former teacher) on board, and more counselors are added if the number of families requires it. One of the three guided hikes at every stop is designed specifically for children, though adults are welcome too. Special nature briefings use language children will understand. Children also picnic on Costa Rica's stunning beaches (children's menus are available), and the ship carries enough water-sports paraphernalia to keep preteens and teens occupied when they aren't hiking. Waterskiing, snorkeling, and kayaking are all options. This flexible program generally runs from 9 AM to 9 PM; children can spend all or part of that time with the children's group, and parents can spend as much time as they wish with the children's groups.

In December 1995, the company began a similar cruise operation in Belize. Call and ask about the children's program on that ship.

🏠 Temptress Voyages, 1600 Northwest LaJeune Rd., Suite 301, Miami, FL 33126, tel. 305/871–2663 or 800/336–8423. Year-round cruises; children's program June–Sept.: 4–8 days, $495–$1,695.

Resources

Organizations

Many organizations protect animals and encourage membership and participation by families and children. These groups don't have trips, but they can help foster an interest in the world's wildlife. The **International Fund for Animal Welfare** (IFAW, 411 Main St., Yarmouth Port, MA 02675, tel.

508/362–6268 or 800/932–4329) has worked particularly hard to stop both Canadian seal hunts and whaling by Japanese and Norwegian hunters. They send out literature to school children and others, try to answer questions, and accept monetary support for their efforts. You can adopt an orca through **Save the Whales** (Box 2397, Venice, CA 90291, tel. 408/899–9957 or 800/942–5365), which also has an excellent educational program that goes to schools. If you'd rather adopt a finback whale, contact **Allied Whale** (College of the Atlantic, 105 Eden St., Bar Harbor, ME 04609, tel. 207/288–5644); the adoption program funds research. **Friends of the Sea Otter** (2150 Garden Rd., Suite B4, Monterey, CA 93940, tel. 408/373–2747) has information about otters, a map of where to spot them on the Monterey Peninsula, and a catalog of otter-related items you can buy. Ask for the Family Traveler Pack and/or the Educational Packet for Children; money goes to support educational programs and research. **Wolf Haven International** (3111 Offut Lake Rd., Tenino, WA 98589, tel. 360/264–4695 or 800/448–9653) is the organization through which you can adopt a wolf. Adoption and membership include a subscription to the organization's quarterly magazine, *WolfTracks*. You can visit the organization's facility near Olympia, Washington, and take a tour to see the wolves Wolf Haven has rescued.

Books

A Visit to Galápagos (Abrams), by Katie Lee, is an excellent picture book with paintings and drawings of many of the islands' most famous inhabitants, as well as informative text. *Swimming with Sea Lions and Other Adventures in the Galápagos Islands* (Scholastic), by Ann McGovern, describes a young traveler's 15-day boat trip around the islands. There are also numerous children's books about Darwin and his discoveries; many of the best are now out of print but still readily available in libraries. A recent one, Piero Ventura's 70-page *Darwin: Nature Reinterpreted* (Houghton Mifflin), tracks Darwin's entire *Beagle* voyage and takes a look at his theories and writings.

Patricia Arrigoni's *Harpo, The Baby Harp Seal* (Travel Publishers International, tel. 415/456–2697 or 800/942–7760) is a beautifully photographed story about a baby seal on the ice floes off the Magdalen Islands (where Natural Habitat Adventures' trip takes place). The book is aimed at ages 7–10 but has appeal for all ages.

Also See

There are lots of other ways and places to meet animals up close. Snorkeling and Diving lists adventures with amazing marine life encounters. Horse Packing, Cattle Drives, and Covered Wagon Adventures have trips that involve horses, and Ranches includes encounters with horses, mules, farm animals, and, in one case (the Y.O. Ranch in Texas), exotic wildlife.

APPENDIX: FINDING THE ADVENTURES

Here is a geographical list of activities, outfitters, and schools in this book. Descriptions of the outfitters and schools appear alphabetically in the chapter on each activity.

IN THE U.S.

ALASKA

Archaeology Adventures
Earthwatch

Biking
Backcountry

Dogsledding
American Wilderness Experience

National Outdoor Leadership School

Hiking and Backpacking
Alaska Wildland Adventures

All Adventure Travel

Camp Denali

REI Adventures

Horse Packing
American Wilderness Experience

Kayaking
REI Adventures

Native American Experiences
Athabasca Cultural Journeys

Panning for Gold
Grandtravel

Rafting
Kayak & Canoe Institute

Wilderness River Outfitters

RV Adventures
Denali National Park

Denali/McKinley KOA

Sailing
American Wilderness Experience

Rascals in Paradise

Wildlife Encounters
Alaska Wildland Adventures

Natural Habitat Adventures

ARIZONA

Archaeology Adventures
White Mountain Archaeological Center

Biking
Backcountry

Escape the City Streets

Canoeing
Laughing Heart Adventures

Cattle Drives
American Wilderness Experience

Digging for Dinosaur Bones
Dinamation International Society

Hiking and Backpacking
Hiking Holidays

Sierra Club

Horse Packing
American Wilderness Experience

Houseboating
Forever Resorts

Lake Powell Resorts & Marinas

Kayaking
Kayak & Canoe Institute

Native American Experiences
Crow Canyon Archaeological Center

Grandtravel

Journeys into American Indian Territory

Off the Beaten Path

Rafting
Expeditions, Inc.

Far Flung Adventures

Grand Canyon Dories/OARS Dories

Ranches
White Stallion Ranch

Rock Climbing
National Outdoor Leadership School

RV Adventures
Lake Powell Resorts & Marinas

CALIFORNIA

Biking
Backroads

Canoeing
Laughing Heart Adventures

Cattle Drives
Hunewill Circle H Guest Ranch

Cross-country Skiing
Backroads

Fishing
Fly-Fishing Outfitters Clinics

Trinity Canyon Lodge

Hiking and Backpacking
REI Adventures

Sierra Club

Horse Packing
Mammoth Lakes Pack Outfit

Kayaking
California Canoe and Kayak School

Cutting Edge Adventures

Panning for Gold
Gold Prospecting Expeditions

Rafting
American River Touring Association

Cutting Edge Adventures

Echo

OARS

Outdoor Adventures

Ranches
Coffee Creek Ranch

Rankin Ranch

Rock Climbing
Alpine Skills International

Eastern Mountain Sports Climbing School

Outward Bound

Sylvan Rocks

Wilderness Connection

RV Adventures
Big Bear Shores RV Resort & Yacht Club

Joshua Tree National Monument

Sailing
Ocean Voyages

Trekking with Llamas
Sierra Club

Wildlife Encounters
Baja Discovery

Baja Expeditions

COLORADO

Archaeology Adventures
Crow Canyon Archaeological Center

Canoeing
Boulder Outdoor Center

Cattle Drives
American Wilderness Experience

Broken Skull Cattle Company

Cross-country Skiing
Adventures to the Edge

C Lazy U

Digging for Dinosaur Bones
Dinamation International Society

Dogsledding
Telluride Outside

Fishing
Orvis Fly Fishing School

Telluride Outside

Hiking and Backpacking
REI Adventures

Horse Packing
Adventure Specialists

Fantasy Ranch

Vista Verde Ranch

Kayaking
Boulder Outdoor Center

Dvorak's Kayak & Rafting Expeditions

Native American Experiences
Grandtravel

Panning for Gold
Telluride Outside

Rafting
American Wilderness Experience

Canyonlands Field Institute

Dvorak's Kayak & Rafting Expeditions

Far Flung Adventures

Holiday River & Bike Expeditions

OARS

Ranches
Aspen Canyon Ranch

Cherokee Park Ranch

Colorado Trails Ranch

Drowsy Water Ranch

Elk Mountain Ranch

Lake Mancos Ranch

North Fork Guest Ranch

Rainbow Trout Ranch

Sky Corral

Skyline Guest Ranch

Rock Climbing
Adventures to the Edge

Boulder Rock School

Colorado Mountain School

Eastern Mountain Sports Climbing School

Fantasy Ridge Mountain Guides

RV Adventures
Colorado National Monument

Great Sand Dunes National Monument

Trekking with Llamas
American Wilderness Experience

Off the Beaten Path

CONNECTICUT
Rock Climbing
Eastern Mountain Sports Climbing School

Sailing
Offshore Sailing School

FLORIDA
Canoeing
Outward Bound

Wilderness Southeast

Houseboating
Mid-Lakes Navigation Company

Kayaking
Nantahala Outdoor Center

Outward Bound

Wilderness Southeast

RV Adventures
Everglades National Park

Sailing
Annapolis Sailing School

Ocean Voyages

Offshore Sailing School

Snorkeling and Diving
Club Med

GEORGIA

Canoeing
Nantahala Outdoor Center

Wilderness Southeast

Kayaking
Nantahala Outdoor Center

Wilderness Southeast

RV Adventures
Chattahoochee National
Forest

HAWAII

Biking
Backcountry

Hiking and Backpacking
All Adventure Travel

American Wilderness
Experience

Backroads

REI Adventures

Sierra Club

Sailing
Ocean Voyages

Snorkeling and Diving
Earthwatch

IDAHO

Biking
Backroads

Rafting
American River Touring
Association

Echo

Grand Canyon Dories/OARS
Dories

Holiday River & Bike
Expeditions

Hughes River Expeditions

Idaho Afloat

Kayak & Canoe Institute

OARS

Outdoor Adventures

Ouzel Outfitters

River Odysseys West

Wilderness River Outfitters

Ranches
Hidden Creek Ranch

Trekking with Llamas
Wallowa Llamas

ILLINOIS

Houseboating
Seeser's Mississippi Rent-a-
Cruise

IOWA

Houseboating
Seeser's Mississippi Rent-a-
Cruise

KENTUCKY

Houseboating
Forever Resorts

RV Adventures
Mammoth Cave National
Park

MAINE

Biking
Backroads

Northern Outdoors

Canoeing
L.L. Bean

Sunrise County Canoe
Expeditions

Cross-country Skiing
L.L. Bean

Telemark Inn

Fishing
L.L. Bean

Hiking and Backpacking
Hiking Holidays

Sierra Club

Kayaking
Maine Island Kayak Company

Outward Bound

Zoar Outdoor

Rafting
Unicorn Expeditions

Rock Climbing
Eastern Mountain Sports
Climbing School

Sailing
North End Shipyard
Schooners

Outward Bound

Trekking with Llamas
Telemark Inn

MARYLAND

Hiking and Backpacking
Sierra Club

Sailing
Annapolis Sailing School

MASSACHUSETTS

Biking
Brooks Country Cycling &
Hiking Tours

Fishing
Orvis Fly Fishing School

Hiking and Backpacking
Appalachian Mountain Club

Kayaking
Outdoor Centre of New
England

Zoar Outdoor

**Native American
Experiences**
Journeys into American
Indian Territory

Rock Climbing
Eastern Mountain Sports
Climbing School

Zoar Outdoor

MICHIGAN

Biking
Michigan Bicycle Touring

Sun, Sky, Wind

Kayaking
Kayak & Canoe Institute

Wilderness Inquiry

RV Adventures
Porcupine Mountains
Wilderness State Park

MINNESOTA

Canoeing
Boundary Country Trekking

Gunflint Northwoods
Outfitters/Gunflint Lodge

Kayak & Canoe Institute

Outward Bound

Wilderness Inquiry

Cross-country Skiing
Gunflint Northwoods
Outfitters/Gunflint Lodge

Dogsledding
Boundary Country Trekking

Gunflint Northwoods
Outfitters/Gunflint Lodge

Outward Bound

Wilderness Inquiry

Fishing
Gunflint Northwoods
Outfitters/Gunflint Lodge

Kayaking
Kayak & Canoe Institute

Rafting
Kayak & Canoe Institute

Rock Climbing
Vertical Pursuits, Outdoor
Program

MISSISSIPPI

Canoeing
Wolf River Canoes

MISSOURI

Houseboating
Forever Resorts

MONTANA

Biking
Backcountry

Wilderness River Outfitters

Cattle Drives
Cow Camp

Hargrave Cattle & Guest
Ranch

Laredo Enterprises

Montana High Country
Cattle Drive

Off the Beaten Path

**Covered Wagon
Adventures**
Carter County Wagon Train

Myers Ranch Wagon Trains

Cross-country Skiing
Izaak Walton Inn

Lone Mountain Ranch

Off the Beaten Path

**Digging for Dinosaur
Bones**
Earthwatch

Fishing
L.L. Bean

Montana River Outfitters

Horse Packing
Great Divide Guiding &
Outfitters

White Tail Ranch

**Native American
Experiences**
Anvil Butte Ranch

Off the Beaten Path

Rafting
American Wilderness
Experience

Glacier Wilderness
Guides/Montana Raft
Company

Wilderness River Outfitters

Ranches
Anvil Butte Ranch

Lone Mountain Ranch

Trekking with Llamas
Off the Beaten Path

NEBRASKA

**Covered Wagon
Adventures**
Oregon Trail Wagon Train

NEVADA

Biking
Escape the City Streets

Cattle Drives
Cottonwood Ranch

Hunewill Circle H Guest
Ranch

Horse Packing
Cottonwood Ranch

Houseboating
Forever Resorts

Rock Climbing
Eastern Mountain Sports
Climbing School

NEW HAMPSHIRE

Hiking and Backpacking
Appalachian Mountain Club

Rock Climbing
Appalachian Mountain Club

Eastern Mountain Sports
Climbing School

Trekking with Llamas
Telemark Inn

NEW JERSEY

Rock Climbing
Appalachian Mountain Club

Sailing
Offshore Sailing School

NEW MEXICO

Archaeology Adventures
Denver Museum of Natural
History

Fishing
Derringer Outfitters and
Guides

Hiking and Backpacking
Hiking Holidays

Horse Packing
American Wilderness
Experience

**Native American
Experiences**
Grandtravel

Rafting
Dvorak's Kayak & Rafting Expeditions

Far Flung Adventures

Trekking with Llamas
American Wilderness Experience

Derringer Outfitters

NEW YORK

Biking
Brooks Country Cycling & Hiking Tours

Canoeing
Bear Cub Adventure Tours

Cross-country Skiing
Appalachian Mountain Club

Hiking and Backpacking
Appalachian Mountain Club

Houseboating
Collar City Charters

Mid-Lakes Navigation Company

Remar Rentals

Ranches
Pinegrove Resort Ranch

The Timberlock

Rock Climbing
Adirondack Rock & River Guide Service

Eastern Mountain Sports Climbing School

RV Adventures
Lake Placid/Whiteface Mountain KOA

Trekking with Llamas
Appalachian Mountain Club

NORTH CAROLINA

Biking
Nantahala Outdoor Center

Canoeing
Nantahala Outdoor Center

Hiking and Backpacking
Hiking Holidays

Kayaking
Nantahala Outdoor Center

Rock Climbing
Nantahala Outdoor Center

Outward Bound

RV Adventures
Cherokee/Great Smokies KOA

Great Smoky Mountains National Park

Trekking with Llamas
Avalon Llama Treks

OKLAHOMA

Native American Experiences
Journeys into American Indian Territory

OREGON

Kayaking
California Canoe and Kayak School

Rafting
American River Touring Association

Echo

Hughes River Expeditions

OARS

Ouzel Outfitters

Ranches
Rock Springs

Rock Climbing
Timberline Mountain Guides

Trekking with Llamas
Hurricane Creek Llama Treks

Wallowa Llamas

PENNSYLVANIA

Biking
Brooks Country Cycling & Hiking Tours

Vermont Bicycle Touring

Hiking and Backpacking
Appalachian Mountain Club

Rock Climbing
Appalachian Mountain Club

RHODE ISLAND

Sailing
Offshore Sailing School

SOUTH CAROLINA

Canoeing
Nantahala Outdoor Center

SOUTH DAKOTA

Covered Wagon Adventures
Grandtravel

Digging for Dinosaur Bones
Earthwatch

Horse Packing
Dakota Badland Outfitters

Panning for Gold
Ken's Minerals

Rock Climbing
Sylvan Rocks

RV Adventures
Rafter J Bar Ranch Campground

TENNESSEE

Archaeology Adventures
Earthwatch

Canoeing
Nantahala Outdoor Center

RV Adventures
Great Smoky Mountains National Park

TEXAS

Canoeing
Outward Bound

Houseboating
Forever Resorts

Rafting
Far Flung Adventures

Ranches
Mayan Dude Ranch

Y.O. Ranch

RV Adventures
Palo Duro Canyon State
Park

UTAH

Biking
Backcountry

Escape the City Streets

Canoeing
Laughing Heart Adventures

Cattle Drives
Off the Beaten Path

Rockin' R Ranch

**Digging for Dinosaur
Bones**
Dinamation International
Society

Hiking and Backpacking
Sierra Club

Horse Packing
American Wilderness
Experience

Rockin' R Ranch

Houseboating
Lake Powell Resorts &
Marinas

Kayaking
Kayak & Canoe Institute

Rafting
American River Touring
Association

Canyonlands Field Institute

Denver Museum of Natural
History

Dvorak's Kayak & Rafting
Expeditions

Holiday River & Bike
Expeditions

Sheri Griffith Expeditions

Rock Climbing
Eastern Mountain Sports
Climbing School

Fantasy Ridge Mountain
Guides

RV Adventures
Lake Powell Resorts &
Marinas

Trekking with Llamas
Red Rock 'n Llamas

VERMONT

Biking
Backroads

Bike Vermont

Vermont Bicycle Touring

Canoeing
Adventure Quest

Cross-country Skiing
Backroads

Dogsledding
Adventure Guides of
Vermont/Konari Outfitters

Fishing
Orvis Fly Fishing School

Hiking and Backpacking
Hiking Holidays

Horse Packing
American Wilderness
Experience

Kayaking
Adventure Quest

Rock Climbing
Adventure Quest

Trekking with Llamas
Northern Vermont Llama
Company

VIRGINIA

Biking
Vermont Bicycle Touring

Hiking and Backpacking
Hiking Holidays

Sierra Club

RV Adventures
Shenandoah National Park

Trekking with Llamas
Virginia Highlands Llamas

WASHINGTON

Biking
Backcountry

Backroads

Hiking and Backpacking
All Adventure Travel

Backroads

REI Adventures

Sierra Club

Kayaking
California Canoe and Kayak
School

REI Adventures

Rock Climbing
American Alpine Institute

Timberline Mountain Guides

Wildlife Encounters
Sea Quest Expeditions

WEST VIRGINIA

Rafting
Canyonlands Field Institute

WISCONSIN

Dogsledding
Trek & Trail

Houseboating
Seeser's Mississippi Rent-a-
Cruise

Kayaking
Kayak & Canoe Institute

Trek & Trail

Wilderness Inquiry

**Native American
Experiences**
Journeys into American
Indian Territory

WYOMING

Biking
Backcountry

Cattle Drives
American Wilderness
Experience

Cheyenne River Ranch

Cow Camp

High Island Ranch and Cattle
Company

Off the Beaten Path

Covered Wagon Adventures
American Wilderness Experience

Grandtravel

Teton Country Wagon Train

Cross-country Skiing
Denver Museum of Natural History

Off the Beaten Path

Digging for Dinosaur Bones
Dinamation International Society

Horse Packing
American Wilderness Experience

Skinner Brothers

Rafting
Dvorak's Kayak & Rafting Expeditions

OARS

Breteche Creek

Ranches
Paradise Guest Ranch

Red Rock Ranch

Seven D Ranch

Rock Climbing
Exum Mountain Guides

National Outdoor Leadership School

Sylvan Rocks

Trekking with Llamas
Off the Beaten Path

OUTSIDE THE U.S.

AFRICA

Archaeology Adventures
Earthwatch

Hiking and Backpacking
Butterfield & Robinson

Sailing
Ocean Voyages

Wildlife Encounters
Big Five Tours & Expeditions

Natural Habitat Adventures

Overseas Adventure Travel

Rascals in Paradise

ASIA

Archaeology Adventures
Earthwatch

Sailing
Ocean Voyages

Snorkeling and Diving
Earthwatch

AUSTRALIA-NEW ZEALAND

Archaeology Adventures
Earthwatch

Biking
Backcountry

Digging for Dinosaur Bones
Earthwatch

Sailing
Ocean Voyages

Rascals in Paradise

Snorkeling and Diving
Earthwatch

CANADA

Archaeology Adventures
Earthwatch

Biking
Backcountry

Backroads

Canoeing
Kayak & Canoe Institute

Outward Bound

Sunrise County Canoe Expeditions

Wells Gray Park Backcountry Chalets

Cross-country Skiing
Wells Gray Park Backcountry Chalets

Dogsledding
Arctic Odysseys

Boundary Country Trekking

Kanata Wilderness Adventures/Wells Gray Ranch

Fishing
Babine Norlakes Lodge

Hiking and Backpacking
All Adventure Travel

American Wilderness Experience

Backroads

Canadian Mountain Holidays

Hiking Holidays

REI Adventures

Sila Sojourns

Wells Gray Park Backcountry Chalets

Western Expedition Company

Horse Packing
Spatsizi Wilderness Vacations

Houseboating
Remar Rentals

Waterway Houseboat Vacations

Kayaking
Kayak & Canoe Institute

Wilderness Inquiry

Native American Experiences
Arctic Odysseys

Off the Beaten Path

Panning for Gold
Western Expeditions Company

Rafting
Canadian River Expeditions

Wilderness River Outfitters

Rock Climbing
American Alpine Institute

Yamnuska, Inc.

RV Adventures
Burnaby Cariboo RV Park

Sailing
EcoSummer Expeditions

Trekking with Llamas
Strider Adventures

Wildlife Encounters
Arctic Odysseys

Natural Habitat Adventures

CARIBBEAN

Archaeology Adventures
Earthwatch

Sailing
Annapolis Sailing School

Ocean Voyages

Offshore Sailing School

Snorkeling and Diving
Club Med

Earthwatch

Hyatt Regency Grand
Cayman

Rascals in Paradise

Wildlife Encounters
Natural Habitat Adventures

CENTRAL AMERICA

Hiking and Backpacking
Butterfield & Robinson

Sailing
Ocean Voyages

Snorkeling and Diving
American Wilderness
Experience

Earthwatch

Ocean Voyages

Rascals in Paradise

Wildlife Encounters
American Wilderness
Experience

Overseas Adventure Travel

Temptress Voyages

EUROPE

Archaeology Adventures
Earthwatch

Biking
Backroads

Brooks Country Cycling &
Hiking Tours

Nantahala Outdoor Center

**Digging for Dinosaur
Bones**
Earthwatch

Hiking and Backpacking
Butterfield & Robinson

Hiking Holidays

Rock Climbing
Adventures to the Edge

Sailing
Ocean Voyages

Wildlife Encounters
Natural Habitat Adventures

MEXICO

**Digging for Dinosaur
Bones**
Dinamation International
Society

Horse Packing
Adventure Specialists

Houseboating
Forever Resorts

Kayaking
Cutting Edge Adventures

Maine Island Kayak Company

Nantahala Outdoor Center

Zoar Outdoor

**Native American
Experiences**
Crow Canyon
Archaeological Center

Rafting
Cutting Edge Adventures

Far Flung Adventures

Snorkeling and Diving
Club Med

Rascals in Paradise

Wildlife Encounters
Baja Discovery

Baja Expeditions

SOUTH AMERICA

**Digging for Dinosaur
Bones**
Earthwatch

Horse Packing
Adventure Specialists

Rock Climbing
Eastern Mountain Sports
Climbing School

Wildlife Encounters
Galápagos Network

Overseas Adventure Travel

SOUTH PACIFIC

**Digging for Dinosaur
Bones**
Earthwatch

Horse Packing
Adventure Specialists

Kayaking
Nantahala Outdoor Center

Sailing
Rascals in Paradise

Specialized Odysseys

Snorkeling and Diving
Continental Micronesia

Earthwatch

Rascals in Paradise